T0341639

Tools for Radical Democracy

Additional Titles from Chardon Press

THE CHARDON PRESS SERIES

Fundamental social change happens when people come together to organize, advocate, and create solutions to injustice. Chardon Press recognizes that communities working for social justice need tools to create and sustain healthy organizations. In an effort to support these organizations, Chardon Press produces materials on fundraising, community organizing, and organizational development. These resources are specifically designed to meet the needs of grassroots nonprofits—organizations that face the unique challenge of promoting change with limited staff, funding, and other resources. We at Chardon Press have adapted traditional techniques to the circumstances of grassroots nonprofits. Chardon Press and Jossey-Bass hope these works help people committed to social justice to build mission-driven organizations that are strong, financially secure, and effective.

Kim Klein, Series Editor

JB JOSSEY-BASS

Tools for Radical Democracy

HOW TO ORGANIZE FOR POWER IN YOUR COMMUNITY

Joan Minieri
Paul Getsos

foreword by
Peter Edelman

BICENTENNIAL
1807
WILEY
2007
BICENTENNIAL

John Wiley & Sons, Inc.

Published by Jossey-Bass
A Wiley Imprint
989 Market Street, San Francisco, CA 94103-1741   www.josseybass.com

Wiley Bicentennial logo: Richard J. Pacifico

Jossey-Bass books and products are available through most bookstores. To contact Jossey-Bass directly, call our Customer Care Department within the U.S. at 800-956-7739, outside the U.S. at 317-572-3986, or fax 317-572-4002.

Jossey-Bass also publishes its books in a variety of electronic formats. Some content that appears in print may not be available in electronic books.

Library of Congress Cataloging-in-Publication Data

Minieri, Joan, date.
  Tools for radical democracy: how to organize for power in your community/
Joan Minieri, Paul Getsos; foreword by Peter Edelman.
        p. cm.—(Chardon Press series)
  Includes index.
  ISBN 978-0-7879-7909-6 (pbk.)
1. Community organization. 2. Community power. I. Getsos, Paul, date.
II. Title.
  HM766.M56 2007
  322.4—dc22

                                                            2007019897

Printed in the United States of America
FIRST EDITION
PB Printing   10 9 8 7 6 5 4 3 2 1

CONTENTS

FOREWORD

As a law professor I tell my students that what good lawyers do is persuade someone or some group to do something they wouldn't have done otherwise. Of course, if you're licensed to practice law, you can do that by trying to persuade a judge or jury. But lawyers (and anyone else) can also try to persuade a legislative body or another public official or someone else to do something they wouldn't have done otherwise.

Here is where this important book comes in—and why it's not just for organizers. Because, whoever you are, if you want to be effective in persuading someone to do something they wouldn't have done otherwise, you probably need to do more than just have a talk with them.

A little over a decade ago, Joan Minieri, Paul Getsos, and Gail Aska, along with a nucleus of mainly low-income women who were outraged by Mayor Rudy Giuliani's policy choices in implementing the 1996 federal welfare law, started Community Voices Heard. This book, which as its title says is about how to organize for power in your community, draws heavily on their experiences in fighting back.

I always think of CVH as the little engine that could. CVH started with a pretty small group of people in East Harlem, and by the time it was at its peak strength during the welfare policy debate, dozens and dozens of public officials in New York City and Albany knew it well—in some cases much better than they wanted to. Like the little engine in the beloved children's book, they pulled the train of advocacy for better welfare policy up a pretty big hill, powered by the voices of thousands of people who had no individual connection to the corridors of power. CVH continues to be a force for economic justice.

Joan Minieri and Paul Getsos (the wonderful Gail Aska passed away not too long ago, and we all mourn her) march us through the steps of organizing, from getting started, through building a base, on to campaigns, to building a movement for change. Of course, it's not a recipe book. You're not assured of baking a fabulous cake even if you combine all the ingredients perfectly and bake them for exactly the right amount of time. But it's also true that if you don't have the money to buy the outcome you want, you'll find out here what you need to do. You'll win some and you'll lose some, but this is the way to go about it.

There are a couple of points I'd like to stress, both of which are made in this book. One is that the work Joan and Paul lay out is a 365-day-a-year job. It includes both issue advocacy and electoral politics. You have to comply with the tax laws if you have a tax-exempt organization but, that said, I've been shocked over the years by how many people who organize and advocate around issues don't see the inescapable connection to the ballot box. (I hasten to say I'm equally shocked by the election junkies who don't seem to lift a finger about issues during the time between elections.) We simply have to get more people elected who share our values and our aspirations. Of course, we have to keep them honest after they're in office, and we have to get people to act right who don't especially care about our agenda. That's the between-elections part, but connections among organizing, advocacy and elections, and the elections part itself are critical. It's seamless. It all fits together. People in electoral politics, lawyers, advocates, and students should all consider the tools Joan and Paul offer in this book.

The second point is that there are layers to any issue campaign. From the neighborhoods and communities, coming to the halls of power, are the people. That's the point of the organizing. But there is also the message level, strategies that necessitate involving people with different talents, to reach the media and bring to the broader public in simple, clear words the objective of the campaign. Then there is the policy level, the framing of the technical details of what is being demanded, and the interaction of the policy people with everyone else both in the framing of the requests and in the decisions about compromise that are inherent in nearly every effort to get changes in public policy. All of these strategies are evident in the story of Community Voices Heard.

So doing democracy well is complicated. Regular people have busy lives. Lower-income people struggle from day to day, sometimes for sheer survival. It's not at all easy to exercise people power. The power of money is much simpler to wield. It goes from A to B. People power involves going from A to Z.

But it has to be done, or we will not have the outcomes we want, no matter what happens at the ballot box. We all know, or should know, that winning the election is only the beginning. We have a radical problem in our democracy—too few people have acquired too much power, and the rest of us have far too little. The solutions offered in this book are the right ones. They simply involve the use of tools available to all of us. What Joan Minieri and Paul Getsos have given us here is a guide to help us do our best to get policies implemented that live up to the election results (and get better policies even when the election results are not as good as we wanted).

So read, and act!

Peter Edelman
professor of law, Georgetown University Law Center,
and former assistant secretary,
U.S. Department of Health and Human Services

For Gail Aska and for our families

PREFACE:
WHY WE BELIEVE IN ORGANIZING
AND BUILDING POWER

We both came of age during the rise of the conservative agenda in the United States. Yet during the last twenty-five years we have seen first-hand that organizing and building power for social justice is not only possible in this political climate—it works. We have seen community-based organizing campaigns win changes in social policy, improve the administration of programs that serve millions of people, preserve and protect our environment, and force companies to pay living wages, provide benefits to their workers, and pay for community benefits and improvements.

WHY WE WROTE THIS BOOK

We wrote this book to share the lessons and the tools that we developed while successfully organizing low-income people over the course of twelve years. We believe that others can apply these lessons to their organizations and issues and achieve similar results. We know that there are good books that cover community organizing from a variety of perspectives. However, while teaching about social change and training people in community organizing during the last few years, as well as talking with others who are doing the same, we have become aware of a need for a book that explains in depth how to involve community leaders in every aspect of an organization and how to run an effective campaign. We realized also that such a book needed to offer a set of tools that activists can apply directly to their work.

When we met and started organizing together in the mid-1990s, we brought a range of experiences to cofounding, along with our colleague Gail Aska, an organization to build the power of low-income people.

Joan's early experience was in helping to lay the groundwork for an organizing project based in the churches of a low-income neighborhood in New York City, where she learned how to understand and connect the self-interest of a diverse range of pastors and lay leaders and to help people believe in the potential for organizing despite their previous failed attempts. Organizing homeless people and conducting mass mobilizations for housing justice, she experienced both the thrill of taking to the streets and the power of a silent vigil. In this work, she also saw the importance of providing real leadership development, not just prompting people without skills or training to take the spotlight.

Working on electoral campaigns, Paul learned the importance of involving large numbers of people and the importance of accountability, as well as how to work in a multiracial and multiclass organization. Doing environmental work, he learned the importance of one-on-one conversations and of helping people move to action on their immediate concerns. Demonstrating with ACT-UP and the antiwar movement, Paul deepened his understanding of how disruption, direct action, and mass-movement organizing could deliver wins to a community under attack. Paul started organizing when President Ronald Reagan's budget cuts affected his Social Security benefits.

When we met one another, we each wanted to take our work to a deeper level. We saw an opportunity where our intervention could make a difference and a connection with a constituency that wanted to build power. We saw a need to organize. *Tools for Radical Democracy* is another way for each of us to expand our work for justice, helping other people to organize more effectively, build their power, and make their communities and the world better.

ACKNOWLEDGMENTS

We first acknowledge that many of the ideas, concepts, and tools we share in this book come from a long history of organizing. Organizers from a variety of schools and disciplines have developed and adapted them over the years.

We thank the members, leaders, board members, supporters, and current and former staff at Community Voices Heard, who made possible the learning on which we base this book. Many of them helped to test and develop the tools that we outline. We also acknowledge that throughout our years of organizing and training organizers and leaders, we have appreciated using the Midwest Academy's text, *Organizing for Social Change*.

We especially acknowledge and thank Frank Haberle and Dirk Slater for being supportive partners in the process of writing this book and in their many years of supporting our work at Community Voices Heard. We thank Frank for his willingness to prioritize the writing and for helping to keep the project focused, always with the deepest personal commitment to its goals. We are grateful to Dirk for his nineteen years of patience, support, and helpful discussion about much of the work that this book is based on. A very special thanks goes to Joan's children, Alin, Mariel, and Eirnan Shane, for their understanding.

We also thank all the wonderful and visionary people associated with the Ford Foundation's Leadership for a Changing World Program—staff and awardees—who provided us with the opportunity to begin to explore these ideas more deeply and who supported our efforts to begin the writing process.

Together and individually, we would also like to thank the following people: A very special thanks goes to Henry Serrano both for ongoing feedback and commentary on specific pieces of the book and for his general support. We thank David Cohen for providing feedback on the entire first draft of the manuscript and Megan Hester for reading and commenting on a full section at an important point in the process. Other friends and colleagues who have been helpful in this project include Zoila Almonte, Laura Chambers, Bill Dempsey, Mark Dunlea, Jim Drake, Dave Fleischer, Erica Foldy, Janet Keating, Stephanie Golden, Paul Gorman, Stephanie Hankey, Ron Hayduk, Andy Hsaio, Sandra Killett, Marian Krauskopf, Richard Louv, Gerry Mannion, David Maurasse, Katherine McFate, Matt Montelongo, Maria Mottola, Joye Norris, Sonia Ospina, Larry Parachini, Martha Parlitsis, Diane Reese, Kathleen Sheekey, David Tobis, Deborah Walter, Sondra Youdelman, Aaron Zimmerman, the boys of FI Morning Woods 2005–06, Kingkole 5, the Brooklyn Writers Space, and social work students at Columbia University.

Several editors at the Chardon Press Series at Jossey-Bass helped us bring this project to fruition. We are grateful to each of them for their guidance and insights: Johanna Vondeling worked with us to conceive the project and Dorothy Hearst shepherded the initial stages of writing. Allison Brunner brought us through writing the final manuscript, offering clear, patient, and helpful direction to help us achieve our goals, which we greatly appreciate.

We are grateful to Kim Klein and Stephanie Roth for supporting this book and we thank Rinku Sen for first recommending us to Jossey-Bass. We thank Nancy Adess for her thorough and thoughtful copyedit. We are very grateful to Jesse Wiley and Xenia Lisanevich as well as to our production editor, Nina Kreiden, and all of the terrific Jossey-Bass staff who helped get this book on the shelves and let people know about it.

May 2007

Joan Minieri
Brooklyn, New York

Paul Getsos
New York, New York

THE AUTHORS

JOAN MINIERI is a cofounder of Community Voices Heard (CVH). She has served on the board of directors of CVH and as a project consultant.

Joan was the founding codirector of the New York City Organizing Support Center, where she trained community leaders and organizers and supported developing organizations. She was the communications director for the National Religious Partnership for the Environment, an alliance of religious institutions that promotes environmental sustainability and justice. She managed the Catholic Bishops' Campaign for Human Development in the New York Archdiocese, a fund for community organizing. She has organized homeless people and conducted mass mobilizations for housing justice. She has also done congregation-based organizing and neighborhood organizing in New York City and in Pennsylvania's Lehigh Valley, and she has participated in national movement-building. She has taught social welfare at Borough of Manhattan Community College and LaGuardia Community College.

Joan's recent publications, written with the Research Center for Leadership in Action at New York University's Robert F. Wagner School of Public Service, include *From Constituents to Stakeholders: Building Organizational Ownership and Providing Opportunities to Lead,* and *Transforming Lives, Changing Communities: How Social Change Organizations Build and Use Power.*

Joan's awards include a Charles H. Revson Fellowship and a Union Square Award from the Fund for the City of New York. She is a graduate of Muhlenberg College and holds a master's degree from the Columbia University School of Social Work.

PAUL GETSOS worked on myriad issues during college and after, including fighting President Reagan's budget cuts, doing anti-apartheid work at Rutgers University and antinuclear work in New York City and Boston. His first paid organizing job was as a canvasser for Greenpeace. He worked on electoral campaigns in the Bay Area and in a statewide environmental organization.

Paul was downstate director of the Hunger Action Network of New York State (HANNYS) when he cofounded Community Voices Heard with Joan Minieri and Gail Aska. He served as CVH's executive director and lead organizer for ten years. Paul also volunteered with the National Gay and Lesbian Taskforce's Statewide Ballot Initiative Project, training more than sixty-five people in electoral and organizing skills.

Paul has been a key strategist for national and regional coalitions, including the National Campaign for Jobs and Income Support, and has participated in the World Social Forum in Brazil.

Paul teaches Community Organizing at the Columbia University School of Social Work. He has taught at the City University of New York in Social Welfare Movements and Human Service Administration.

Paul is a graduate of Rutgers University.

Joan and Paul received the Ford Foundation's Leadership for a Changing World award as part of a six-member leadership team from Community Voices Heard.

INTRODUCTION:
THE POWER OF PARTICIPATION

We live at a time when the dominant culture, including the media, elected officials, and corporate advertisers, herald individualism. The stories we hear in school focus on the heroes and heroines of history, rarely on the collective power of organized groups. Although it is true that good stories rely on strong characters, promoting individuals helps those in power to play down the stories of how mass movements, collective struggle, and community-based campaigns have moved resources, shifted power, and improved the lives of many people.

CHANGE THROUGH COLLECTIVE POWER

This book is about the power of participation.

If you want to make a difference, you're not alone—and you can't do it alone. Individuals make a big difference when they act together strategically, peacefully, and in large numbers. Our aims are to give you the tools to engage in your own struggles against social and political forces and to continue the long-standing tradition of radical social change through collective power-building.

If you are willing to take on those who make decisions that have negative effects on the many while benefiting the few, this book is for you.

What Is Radical Democracy?

Radical means going to the source or the root; democracy is rule by the people.

In radical democracy, people at the base of society participate in all aspects of the political system, from holding elected officials accountable to running for their local planning boards. Radical democracy is ordinary people participating in active community institutions where they discuss politics and ideas as they work for a better neighborhood, city, state, nation, and beyond.

How Do We Build Our Power?

The fundamental way you build power is by getting people to understand the source of their social or political problems, then devise solutions, strategize, take on leadership, and move to action through campaigns that win concrete changes.

Although anyone can use the techniques we describe in this book for any purpose, we hope you use them in the spirit we intend: to build the power of people who have been shut out of or turned off by the political process—people in low- or middle-income communities who are disaffected, disillusioned, and overextended. We are explicit about the need to create communities in which rights, resources, and opportunities extend to everyone, equitably and peacefully.

Throughout this book, we refer to organizations that do this work as "community power-building organizations."

What Are the Components and Principles for Building Community Power?

The following are what we believe to be the essential elements for building power that is strong and deep, regardless of the problem, issue, or setting. These are core components that we think organizers and leaders need to incorporate into their work in order to be effective. We explore all of these components in greater detail throughout this book.

1. Build a base of members: more people means more power.

   • *Get people involved.* An organizer gets people involved. This is ongoing work and it never stops. You go to their homes, their jobs, the institutions and agencies where they congregate, and you talk with them. You don't tell people what they should do, you help them figure out what they want to do and can do to address problems collectively in their communities. You get people to see that it is worth their time to talk to their neighbors or coworkers, come to planning meetings, think, learn, and evaluate. You align them as members of your campaign or organization, keeping track of what they do and what support they need. You build their confidence and help them realize their potential, both for their own personal development and for a larger, collective good. You support their participation and recognize and respect them.

- *Move powerholders with numbers.* In democratic societies, powerholders respond to large numbers of people making demands of them. By powerholders we mean those decision makers, such as elected officials or CEOs, who are the targets of community power-building campaigns. Numbers are ultimately the bottom line, so you keep many people involved and active in campaigns and the organization.

- *Get members to make decisions.* You engage members in making decisions about how to move campaigns forward and how to develop their own organization. They come to meetings and give their opinions; you also call them periodically to check in. When people have a stake in the outcome and others are listening to them, they stay involved.

2. Get members to understand what organizing is: action fosters commitment.

- *Guide members to see the roots of problems.* An organizer helps people understand how their problems are based in policies, programs, or practices. You convene people with others who have the same problems as theirs so they can see what connects their experiences.

- *Move members to action.* Action shows people what organizing is all about. It is essential to engage members in direct actions—planned, collective activities in which you confront, challenge, and negotiate with a person who can give your community what it wants. You run actions that have clear objectives to move a campaign forward.

3. Develop members to be leaders: leaders learn by doing.

- *Let leaders do the work.* An organizer develops members to be leaders by training and supporting them to facilitate meetings, manage campaigns and their own organization, and by engaging them in the social justice movement. You make sure that members and leaders represent the organization publicly to allies and the media.

- *Conduct political education.* An organizer moves leaders to understand who has power in society and how government, corporate, and private powerholders operate. With this knowledge, leaders make better decisions and engage in more effective planning and campaigns.

4. Implement strategic campaigns: campaigns deliver wins.

- *Run winnable campaigns.* A campaign is a planned series of strategies and actions designed to achieve clear goals and objectives. You guide members to enter into a campaign based on extensive research and a carefully considered strategy. When people get involved in community power-building campaigns, they understand what the objectives are, and they see and understand how their involvement makes a difference.

- *Analyze power.* Power analysis is a distinct process fundamental to an effective campaign. It is a systematic way of looking at who is with you, who is against you, and how important their support or opposition is to the campaign. Members use this information to make honest assessments of their own power and their ability to achieve their objectives. If you implement a campaign based on an inaccurate power analysis, or worse, with no power analysis, it is likely to fail. This only burns members, leaders, and organizers.

5. Engage members in the social justice movement: neutrality is not an option.

- *Build the movement.* Successful campaigns and organizations engage in the larger social justice movement. You build relationships with other community leaders and organizations and expand your community's base of power. An organizer guides members and leaders to engage in movement-building in order to develop them more deeply.

- *State an ideology.* Corporations, the military, the wealthy, and elected officials all have a clear vision of the world they want to create. They put this vision forth as an explicit ideology or worldview and galvanize support for it. An ideology includes not only the world you envision but how you believe you can realize it. Organizers work with members and community leaders to put forward their own view of the world, including people who are struggling to articulate what they believe or who agree with the vision of your organization but have been convinced by misinformation or lack of access to information to support an ideology that is not in their interests.

What Are Some of the Main Concepts of Organizing?

The following is an overview of the some of the main organizing concepts we refer to throughout this book. Keep in mind that this is an overview, not an inclusive checklist.

Action. A collective action, which we often refer to simply as "an action," is a public showing of an organization's power, such as a march. Actions take place during campaigns. In addition, a person can "take action" as an individual to support a campaign or organization, such as signing a membership card or writing a letter to an elected representative.

Mobilization. The essential process of moving people to action.

Power. Power is the ability to act and to make things happen.

Strategy. In a campaign, strategy is the way or ways that a community power-building organization uses its power to win what it wants. Effective organizations are strategic in everything they do.

Public relationships. Community power-building organizations exist to build members' collective political power, not their personal social status. The result is a network of "public relationships."

Political education. Political education is a form of training about issues as well as about social movements and history that you do both formally in workshop sessions and informally in daily or regular contact with members and leaders. Through political education, you communicate and develop the ideology or worldview of the organization.

Winning. Organizing focuses on winning. It results in positive, concrete change in people's lives.

Evaluation. Evaluation is the process of assessing your actions and determining what worked, what didn't, and what you would do differently next time. Evaluation takes place after every substantive event, from a day of recruitment to a phone conversation with an ally. Frequent and honest evaluation builds the skills, standards, and excellence of everyone in the organization. We sometimes refer to an evaluation that follows a specific activity as "debriefing."

Movement-building. In movement-building you use your resources to engage in broader social justice activities that are not solely connected to winnable campaigns or the self-interest of community members.

EFFECTIVE MOVEMENTS

The impact of organizing on the social and political landscape is evident both historically and into the present. In our view, organizing has been critical to creating major socioeconomic shifts through nonviolent means, both in the United States and across the globe. In this book we talk broadly about the social justice "movement," which encompasses the work of individuals and groups worldwide. At specific times the organizing that causes these socioeconomic shifts is deep and sustained, skillfully riding a wave of public unrest and engaging mass numbers of people in leadership and action. When these kinds of movements for justice arise, the types of organizations we describe in this book, community power-building organizations, provide leaders and the institutional base to seize the moment and actualize its potential. By justice we mean expanding rights and economic and educational opportunities that include everyone, as well as preserving natural resources, ensuring that government fulfills its role of providing public services and protections, and using a peaceful approach to resolving conflict, locally and around the world.

Here are some examples: In the United States in the 1860s, the Civil War and the abolition of slavery were preceded by radicals organizing to raise public consciousness to the need to end slavery. The socialist and populist organizing of the late nineteenth century across the industrialized world won, in the United States, the eight-hour work day, child labor laws, and the minimum wage. Also in the United States, the civil rights movement of the 1950s and 1960s galvanized leaders and activists who had been training and organizing for years in their own communities. This movement expanded the right to vote to African Americans and caused a seismic shift in domestic social policy. It also laid the groundwork for the movement to end United States military involvement in Vietnam. In the 1980s, across Eastern Europe, student and labor organizing led to the dissolution of totalitarian governments. Currently, movements in Latin America, led by indigenous communities and workers, are gaining control of governments, changing local politics, and challenging globalization.

Additional campaigns of the last twenty-five years that have galvanized into movements include the following:

Living wage and corporate accountability. Starting in the 1990s at the local level across the United States, these campaigns have used strategic alliances among community organizations, labor unions, and religious organizations to win fair wages that allow low-wage workers to live above poverty as well as additional improvements in their lives. Growing out of this work, local community organizations have spearheaded campaigns to ensure that economic development is equitable and includes community members—winning jobs, community benefits, and more community control in development decisions.

ACT-UP. In the 1980s, amid one of the greatest health crises in the century, ACT-UP speeded the development of treatments for AIDS while working to end discrimination and vilification of those who suffer from the disease. It used creative, massive direct actions focused on clear targets and a combination of other strategies, including media, not only to get the nation to understand and feel compassion for those with AIDS but to change the drug-approval process. This activity led to saving and extending the lives of hundreds of thousands of people with AIDS. Even today, AIDS activists across the globe, inspired by ACT-UP, work to ensure that AIDS drugs are available to everyone who needs them.

Student and community movement for corporate divestment from South Africa. The United States movement to divest from white-governed South Africa grew from student organizing in the late 1980s. Students demanded that their colleges and universities stop investing in companies that were doing business in South Africa. This movement soon expanded beyond campuses to include religious and community-based organizations, galvanizing the general public. While it eventually became a celebrity cause, the students who organized on their own campuses were an important component in getting the United States government and U.S. corporations to understand that investing in apartheid was unacceptable. Their efforts also supported local movements in South Africa.

THE RIGHT-WING RISE TO POWER

Right-wing Republicans in the United States have successfully used grassroots organizing to gain power to implement their agenda, using techniques similar to the ones we describe in this book. The right wing has successfully shifted the parameters of the debate, resulting in moving both moderate Republicans and Democrats to target low-income people, people of color, women, and the lesbian, gay, bisexual, transgender (LGBT) community. We've seen the federal government as well as state and local governments abandon their role to provide for people in need while providing huge tax relief to corporations and the wealthy. We've seen the government limit individual rights while allowing corporate power to consolidate in ways that not only influence the political process and the financing of electoral campaigns but also drastically curtail the rights and benefits of the workers whose cheap labor feeds corporate profits. We've also witnessed the expansion of United States military and police power across the globe.

The right wing has been strategic, focused, and well financed. In addition to grassroots organizing, it has worked extensively with membership institutions such as churches. It has funded and supported public-policy think tanks and conservative media outlets and focused on winning electoral and appointed positions of power at the local, state, and regional levels. The fact that the right wing uses organizing tools to advance its agenda only supports the need to identify, train, and activate the broadest possible base of people for our own work.

THE FIELD OF COMMUNITY ORGANIZING

The following provides a basic framework for understanding the field of community organizing in the United States. A review of Saul Alinksy's work provides a way to understand how community organizing has evolved in the United States since World War II. In her Introduction to *Stir It Up: Lessons in Community Organizing and Advocacy,* published in 2003, Rinku Sen describes how Alinsky, an organizer based in Chicago starting in the late 1940s, was the first to devise and write down a model of organizing that others could replicate. The first organization he built, the Back of the Yards Neighborhood Council, was an "organization of organizations," including churches and labor union and service organizations. The established leaders of each of these organizations brought their own membership to the Neighborhood Council, which won expanded services and educational access for the mostly southern and eastern European immigrants working in the meatpacking plants and stockyards in the Back of the Yards community. Alinksy presented his organizing ideas in two books, starting in 1946 with *Reveille for Radicals.* In 1970, he wrote *Rules for Radicals,* in which some of his directives include the need to establish a clear distinction between the role of an organizer and that of a leader, the importance of addressing issues that reflect the self-interest of community members, and focusing on winning over adhering to an ideology. Both books promote the use of bold, creative direct actions to show the power of the people. Sen also describes the feminist and antiracist critique of Alinksy's principles, focusing on his reliance on formal leadership, the kinds of issues he worked on, and the lack of a deeper analysis to look beyond specific issues.

Alinsky's ideas continue to be a force in organizing. To form your own opinions about them, it is worth reading his books, especially the concise and provocative *Rules for Radicals.*

Community organizing groups operate either as independents or as part of a network. In an independent community organizing group, the individual members of the organization make decisions about all aspects of the organization, including how to raise and distribute resources, what kind staff they need, how to run actions, what principles they want to guide their work, and the issues they want to take on.

Sometimes power-building organizations affiliate with one another through an organizing network. A network is different from a coalition, which builds power on a single issue. A network offers ongoing affiliation and provides additional support to the organizations it includes, such as staff, or formalized training in a specific model of organizing and funding, or access to funding.

Sen reviews the oldest of the organizing networks, the IAF (Industrial Areas Foundation), which Saul Alinksy founded. The IAF now focuses on creating groupings primarily of religious congregations and established religious institutions that engage people in large numbers and have explicit, shared values. The IAF includes dozens of organizations representing tens of thousands of families. IAF organizations have secured many victories, including affordable housing, job creation, and schools. Sen notes that other networks include ACORN (Association for Community Organizations for Reform Now) and CTWO (the Center for Third World Organizing). Wade Rathke founded ACORN in 1970 in Little Rock, Arkansas, as an organization that individuals, not institutions, could join and lead. Now with organizations in more than two dozen states, ACORN has reached out to include those who are traditionally unorganized, winning victories that include local living-wage ordinances and reforming public schools. Gary Delgado and Hulbert James founded CTWO in 1980 in order to pay explicit attention to issues of race. It has trained thousands of organizers and leaders of color and successfully tested new forms of multiracial organizing.

Groups also affiliate with one another through national organizations, alliances, and campaigns, either for ongoing support or to win on an issue. Organizations that engage groups in these kinds of national affiliations include the Center for Community Change and the Northwest Federation of Community Organizations.

In *Democracy in Action: Community Organizing and Social Change,* published in 2004, Kristina Smock describes five types of community-organizing approaches: the power-based model, the community-building model, the civic model, the women-centered model, and the transformative model. Smock observed these models as she examined the experiences of ten community organizing groups in

Chicago and in Portland, Oregon, in 1998 and 1999. The following is an overview of the models, which offer a way to understand the spectrum of strategies and techniques that organizations are using to achieve change at the community level.

Power-Based Model. In this model, the community views its problem as a lack of power within the political decision-making process. Therefore, it builds its clout so that it can get its interests better represented in the public sphere. In a power-building model, organizers and leaders create a large, formal people's organization and use conflict and confrontation to demonstrate their power and pressure powerholders to concede to their demands.

Community-Building Model. In this model, the community views its problems as stemming from the deterioration of its social and economic infrastructure. Therefore, it rebuilds itself from within and connects to the mainstream economy. In a community-building model, organizers and leaders create collaborative partnerships among stakeholders, including businesses, nonprofits, and government entities, in order to be publicly recognized as a legitimate representative of the community as a whole.

Civic Model. In this model, the community views its problems as being based in social disorder. Therefore, it restores stability by activating both formal and informal mechanisms of social control. In a civic model, organizers and leaders create opportunities for neighbors to meet and problem solve in order to get the city services system to respond to neighborhood problems.

Women-Centered Model. In this model, the community views its problems as stemming from institutions at the core of the community that are unresponsive to the needs of women and families. Therefore, it conceptualizes household problems as public issues and builds the leadership of women to pursue collective solutions. In a women-centered model, organizers and leaders create small support teams and provide safe, nurturing spaces for community members to gather and build shared leadership. From this base of support they can interact one-on-one with staff and administrators of public institutions and get them to be more responsive to community concerns.

Transformative Model. In this model the community views its problems as symptoms of unjust political institutions that especially disempower low-income people. Therefore, it challenges the way institutions work. In a transformative model, organizers and leaders develop an ideological foundation within the community so that a broad-based movement for social change can emerge and change the terms of public debate.

In our view, an organization can incorporate elements from more than one of these models—with independents being more likely to experiment with different techniques and strategies. For example, Community Voices Heard uses a power-building model with a substantial emphasis on shared power and decision making, building the leadership of women and transforming political institutions—thus creating a hybrid organization with the characteristics of at least three of the models.

The conditions for organizing on your issues and in your community differ from those in other communities and issue areas. Especially when starting out, you examine the various models of organizing and the tools you can use. Understanding how different organizations work is very helpful when you start to build your own campaigns and, potentially, an organization.

WHO THIS BOOK IS FOR

This book is for anyone who wants to learn about or engage in organizing for social justice. Although we use examples from our own experience organizing low-income constituents, we believe you can use this book to build organizations, develop community leaders, and win campaigns on the range of issues facing your community. The book will be useful for people new to organizing who want to address a problem in their community; organizers and leaders who want a deeper analysis, particularly of campaigns and of getting members and leaders to participate more fully in running their own organizations; students and teachers of community organizing, public policy advocacy, and political engagement; people working on political campaigns who want to learn how to build effective community-based electoral campaigns; and activists in developing democracies working to expand democracy and build community institutions in their own countries.

WHAT THIS BOOK INCLUDES

The book is organized in four parts. Part One describes how to build community power. In Chapter One we introduce the components and principles of building community power and in Chapter Two we clarify the types of power that exist and why organizing groups must understand and talk about power.

Part Two describes the steps in building a base for power. In it we explore how to recruit people to join your campaign or organization (Chapter Three), how to get them involved (Chapter Four), and the absolutely essential task of developing many different kinds of community leaders (Chapter Five). In Chapter Six we describe how to use technology to build your base and your organization, including why you need a database and how to use it.

Part Three describes how to develop and manage campaigns. We explore how to work with community members to identify an issue they can win (Chapter Seven), how to engage in campaign research in order to understand the power dynamics and the politics of an issue (Chapter Eight), and how to choose and develop the best strategy for your campaign (Chapter Nine). In Chapter Ten, we describe how to write a campaign plan with clear objectives you can later measure and evaluate.

Chapters Eleven, Twelve, and Thirteen cover implementing and evaluating campaigns. We suggest organizational systems and structures for managing a member-led campaign; look at what actions are, how to run them, and why; and describe campaign evaluation and how to involve members in it.

Part Four is devoted to building a movement. In Chapter Fourteen we explore partnerships—when to use them and how to function within them. Chapter Fifteen describes how to engage in movement-building in order to sustain leaders and staff and take on larger social issues. We conclude with ways to put your principles into practice and build power over the long term. At the end of the book the Resources provide overviews of several ways to support your organizing, including fundraising and electoral organizing.

Each chapter ends with an overview of challenges related to the topic and how to address them as well as a checklist of essential elements. Throughout the book we include sample agendas of sessions to engage members and leaders in a meeting or training related to the topic. At the end of each chapter we include Tools you can use directly in your own work or adapt, including handouts for trainings, worksheets, checklists, and training exercises.

Activists and organizers, whether in the United States or in a developing democracy, can apply the skills, tools, and strategies laid out in this book to build community-controlled institutions, which lead to the development of vibrant and active democratic cultures at the local and regional levels.

THE STORY OF
COMMUNITY VOICES HEARD

The main source of examples we use throughout the book is Community Voices Heard (CVH). For more than a decade, CVH has won successful campaigns to improve the delivery of antipoverty programs to tens of thousands of welfare recipients, make jobs available to help them transition off of welfare, and bring thousands of low-income people into the policy-making process. This is the story of how a group of fewer than a dozen poor women in New York City built a powerful organization while raising children, participating in a challenging and sometimes dehumanizing welfare system, and facing an alignment of powerful political, intellectual, and media forces against them. We use it to illustrate the strategies, skills, and techniques that any group of people can use to build their power to address social injustice.

CVH's focus from 1994 to 1997 was primarily to stop proposals to cut welfare programs at the federal, state, and local levels. Both Republicans and Democrats in the federal government were dismantling the country's antipoverty programs for women and children. State and local governments started cutting public assistance programs and imposing harsh limitations on benefits and access. Corporate and conservative media outlets were demonizing poor people, targeting "welfare mothers" with particular venom.

The advocacy organizations that had lobbied for years around the fine details of federal welfare policy had no power to resist. They had no base of people to lobby legislators and politicians. They could not effectively mobilize mass numbers of people to demonstrate opposition to the cuts. They had no trained and effective leaders who were on welfare, who could provide living proof that welfare mothers were hardworking mothers who cared for their children while trying to hold jobs. In some cases, advocates believed that they could negotiate with policymakers to preserve components of welfare programs, which proved to be unsuccessful. And they were not asking mothers who relied on welfare either to make ends meet or as a safety net for their families what they wanted and how they felt about the cuts.

People may have different views of the role or importance of these programs. But the fact that there was no organized opposition, no organizations, no leaders, no movement, meant that a Democratic president signed legislation ending the entitlement to federal assistance to poor women and children in the United States. Programs created by the Democratic Party and that had existed since the Great Depression and expanded in the 1960s' War on Poverty were gone. It was in this political climate that CVH became one of several organizations of women on welfare to form during this time.

Allies in CVH's early campaigns included advocacy groups such as the Hunger Action Network of New York State and the Welfare Reform Network, labor organizations such as AFSCME DC 37, CSEA, and the New York State AFL-CIO, and policy groups such as the Fiscal Policy Institute and the National Employment Law Project. We had limited success in the policy arena, but we began to educate and train women on welfare and build an organization.

Between 1996 and 2001 CVH focused on workfare organizing and getting paid jobs for participants in New York City's workfare program, called the Work Experience Program (WEP). Workfare requires people to work at jobs for no pay—they work in exchange for their welfare benefits. A vast majority of WEP assignments were in city agencies where WEP workers performed tasks traditionally done by paid city employees.

CVH's Transitional Jobs Campaign or the "jobs campaign" is the main example we refer to in this book. It sought to create paid transitional jobs for welfare recipients. A transitional job is a temporary job that combines a paid wage with on-the-job training and assistance in finding work after the program is over. These jobs often target low-income and hard-to-employ individuals. The campaign started in 1997 when CVH and its allies created and introduced the Transitional Jobs Bill; it ended in 2000 when the New York City Council passed the bill. Allies included AFSCME DC 37, CWA Local 1180, National Employment Law Project, and the Fifth Avenue Committee/WEP Workers Together, along with other organizations that signed on to the Ad-Hoc Coalition for Real Jobs.

These organizations also helped CVH in its simultaneous attempts to win the Empire State Jobs Program, a state program to provide transitional jobs, on which the city program was based. In addition, CVH worked with NY ACORN on workfare and WEP organizing, and it continues to partner with ACORN on a variety of campaigns.

Mayor Rudolph Giuliani vetoed the New York City Transitional Jobs Bill. Even after the City Council overrode the mayor's veto, he refused to create transitional jobs. CVH began another campaign and mounted a legal challenge. Finally, in 2001, Mayor Giuliani created a slightly different program than the one outlined in the Transitional Jobs Bill, but in the end, the city created thirteen thousand transitional jobs.

In 2002, Michael Bloomberg became mayor of New York City. While he continued many of Giuliani's policies, his administration created a dialogue with community groups and advocates, opening up opportunities to affect policies and program administration.

CVH focused on the national level, working with national alliances such as the National Campaign for Jobs and Income Support, the Welfare ENGINE, and Center for Third World Organizing to affect the reauthorization of welfare reform legislation; locally, CVH continued to organize workers who were participating in transitional jobs programs.

As more of our members moved into the low-wage workforce, we took on new issues and campaigns, including working to improve education and training programs for welfare recipients and equitable and accountable economic development. We began forays into global justice and movement-building work. Some of the campaign allies we refer to include AFSCME Local 983, Fiscal Policy Institute, Good Old Lower East Side, Central Labor Council, University Settlement, and the Hudson Yards Alliance.

After a major leadership and membership strategic planning process in 2003, the organization decided to engage more actively in the electoral arena and in new issue campaigns as well as to begin a plan to build statewide power. In 2005, CVH initiated a campaign to organize public housing residents and to address workforce development issues. In these recent years, more men have become active and assumed leadership roles at CVH.

In Chapter One we describe how we met Gail Aska, who channeled her anger at raising a young son on welfare into remarkable leadership for justice and co-founded CVH with us. Throughout the book, we use examples based on other leaders and organizers we've worked with. With the exception of Gail, public officials, and the names of ally organizations, we do not use real names. In some cases, we combine campaigns for the purpose of illustration. For instance, the examples we use that refer to the Transitional Jobs Campaign are in fact based on two campaigns for jobs at the city and state levels.

Although the examples we use are based on real people and events, this book is meant as a tool to teach people about the basics of organizing and strategy development, not as a documentation project or promotion for any campaign or organization.

By no means has the success of CVH been ours alone. We have worked with hundreds of strategic and powerful leaders and collaborated with dedicated allies and supporters as well as dozens of committed staff—all willing to work hard, put in long hours, and strive for excellence, often under intense pressure. Without these people, there would be no story of CVH.

If you are interested in learning more about CVH's campaign for transitional jobs, including an evaluation of its strategies and tactics and documentation of its work through the perspectives of its staff, members, and allies, we recommend reading the report Community Voices Heard: Changing People and Public Policy Through Low-Income Organizing. *You can use this as a case study for teaching and training. It is available through Community Voices Heard (www.cvhaction.org).*

Tools for Radical Democracy

part one

Building Community Power

When you set out to build the power of a community—particularly a politically marginalized community—you are explicit. You propose that the community can build power in addition to winning on issues, and you are strategic about establishing a team of community leaders who can drive the process of doing so on their own behalf. You include training and political education and get agreements on fundamental goals and principles for how the community will use collective action as a way of achieving solutions to its problems. You are clear about the role of an organizer and how that role differs from the role of members of a campaign or organization. You take action. You do not wait for people to come to you. You find partners, go out, listen, learn, and build a network of public relationships.

In Chapter One we outline the steps we took to start Community Voices Heard. We touch on how we and our cofounder, Gail Aska, tapped our anger at injustice, our personal experiences in social justice work and in our own lives, and a sense of humor in order to stay energized, overcome obstacles, and keep moving forward. We describe the qualities and main tasks of organizers as well as the choices organizers and leaders face in taking on the challenges of building community power. In Chapter Two we explore the concept of power itself—what it is and why you define it, understand it, and build it in order to achieve social change.

Taking It On:
Starting to Build Power

A SEAT AT THE TABLE

In 1992 it looks as though the Democrats have their first chance in twelve years to regain the presidency of the United States. Bill Clinton, a moderate governor from the state of Arkansas, is the Democrats' presumptive nominee to face an increasingly unpopular incumbent, George H. W. Bush. One of Clinton's promises to voters is that he will "end welfare as we know it," a rallying cry to conservatives in both parties. Joan and Paul meet for the first time when we join with a group of other activists and service providers to organize an action at the Democratic Convention in our home city of New York. The goal of this action is to show Clinton and the Democrats that this cannot be the campaign centerpiece. In planning this action we deepen our commitment to a key principle that we believe is essential to building community power: constituents and community members need to be in control.

Our group plans to close all of the soup kitchens and emergency food programs in New York City. We plan to direct people instead to get their meals that day at a huge soup kitchen at the convention. We reason that this will dramatically communicate the effects of welfare cuts and stand out in the array of convention protests by various interest groups.

This plan takes shape until Anita Adams comes to one of the organizing meetings. Anita and her children live at the Brooklyn Arms, a notoriously mismanaged, abusive welfare hotel in Brooklyn. Many of us know about Anita's work as the leader of an organizing campaign to make improvements at the hotel and ultimately, to shut it down. Anita comes to the meeting because she has heard rumors of the plan to close the kitchens and the pantries. She is incensed: What does a group of white advocates think we are doing *for* poor women of color and their children?

She derides us not so much for the plan as for not including poor women in the planning process: How could we take such a drastic measure without bothering to ask people in the community how it will affect them?

Anita is confrontational in the best possible way. She agitates our group. She makes us uncomfortable so we will think about what we are doing and move to a different form of action.

We change our plan. Anita works with us to bring low-income people to the convention by offering political education, providing transportation to the site, and giving them roles in the action. Although these had all been elements in the planning prior to Anita's involvement, they would have been rendered completely meaningless by coercing people to come by shutting down their emergency food services.

As the two of us move on to start an organization, Community Voices Heard (CVH), in order to address the same concerns that activated us at the '92 convention, we draw from many organizing experiences.

But we have both heard Anita Adams's call to action loud and clear: work *with* people, don't do *for* them.

How Do We Get Started?

You find partners and get to work.

We started organizing together in the 1990s out of outrage and a belief that through collective action we could make a difference. We found in each other, and our colleague Gail Aska, potential partners for doing something constructive and necessary to fight back against policies to reform the welfare system in the United States that we knew would be devastating. We started talking about the need to bring the people who would be most affected by welfare reform to the table with decision makers. No one else was organizing this constituency in New York City and many thought it would be impossible to do so. From our experiences of organizing other low-income constituencies, we believed it was critical to try.

Here we describe how we started building CVH. For your situation you may need to move at a different pace or implement the steps in some other ways. However, we offer our experience as an example to show that if you want to build the power to make sure that you not only get what you want, but you do so in a way that is resilient in the face of opposing interests, you do not just start engaging in action. You proceed intentionally.

Step One: Go out and talk to people. Before we did anything else, we conducted more than fifty one-on-one meetings with a variety of people. We met with organizers who had organized low-income people in the past; service providers who provided services to women and children; advocates with national, state, and local organizations; funders; religious leaders; union leaders; and well-established and powerful local organizing networks. We also included some key constituent leaders we had heard of or whom we met at meetings in the community, most of whom were engaged in some form of activism in a service organization.

In these meetings we asked the following questions:

- Are you addressing problems with welfare reform?
- If so, how? For instance, by providing services, pursuing legal strategies, or engaging in advocacy? (For more on different approaches to addressing community problems see Resource E.)
- We're thinking about trying to organize to bring welfare recipients more firmly into the welfare reform debate. Are you or anyone else you know doing this?
- Do you think what we want to do is needed? Why or why not?
- What are your questions for us?
- If we move forward, how would you support us or get involved?
- Who else should we talk with?

Although the investment in time was substantial—we did these meetings over the course of about ten weeks—it was essential for our success. We learned that no one else was doing what we planned. We learned about the politics surrounding welfare reform and the potential challenges and opportunities we faced. Although some people encouraged us, many told us we were crazy. We had one meeting, for example, with a professor and respected activist on welfare issues whom Joan particularly admired. We were eager to get her perspective—expecting to hear enthusiasm and get important contacts. Instead, we sat cramped in her office while she literally blew cigarette smoke in our faces, dismissed our ideas, and ended the meeting early when someone else came to her door. We left and stood, stunned, in the hallway. Rather than walking away dejected after this and similar experiences, we tapped into our anger. And since the situation was so ridiculous, we had to laugh. We kept reminding ourselves that we believed in what we were doing. We started to build relationships with organizations and individuals who were with us and who we would call on later. Tool 1.1 at the end of this chapter offers a sample phone rap to schedule these meetings and Tool 1.2 provides a guide for conducting them.

Step Two: Identify an initial organizing committee. Once we knew that no one was organizing people on welfare, we began the real work of building an organizing committee. We started to meet welfare recipients. Because changes in welfare would affect women and children most of all, we reached out to these constituents, a term meaning the people directly affected by the problem we wanted to address. We conducted "Welfare Reform Teach-Ins" in community organizations that served mothers on welfare. These teach-ins educated women about their rights, given the proposed changes. We asked how they would reform the welfare system. We did civics education about how they could affect policy making. We spread information, built a list of people we could engage, and learned who had "fire in the belly" to organize.

Not everyone we met and invested in turned out to be a leader. For months we worked closely with Cynthia, a low-income woman active in social justice campaigns in the city. We thought she had potential to be a great leader and eventually a staff organizer. When it turned out that her life circumstances would not allow this level of involvement, it was very difficult for her and for us to face.

Around this time, we also met Gail, and she and we moved forward together.

Gail Aska—CVH Cofounder

When Gail was pushed out of her job as a data entry supervisor by a United States economy driven by corporate downsizing, like many other single mothers, she needed support. She and her son lived in a New York City shelter for a short time and received welfare benefits. At a local family services center, she formed Sister Circle, a self-help group of mothers. They were aware that something dramatic was unfolding politically and that they were at the center of it. Gail moved them to action. "Let's get out of the house and see what everyone is talking about," she told them. "Cutting us off welfare, [putting our children in] orphanages. I was angry and upset, and [I] wanted to get women involved in something." When Paul met Gail at a meeting of welfare rights advocates, Gail had just moved to an apartment and was ready to start organizing.

"When I got involved with Paul, we worked to educate, educate, educate—not about welfare rights, but about who has power," Gail said. After meeting with Gail's group, Paul invited the participants to a full-day organizing meeting that he and Joan were organizing with other advocates, organizers, and people on welfare. At that meeting, Gail stood out. She sat in the middle of her group. She didn't raise her voice or wave a fist, but when she spoke, everyone listened. She was a presence. She was angry, but a hearty smile was her most prominent expression. She was hopeful. She could imagine and see a better way and draw people into believing in that vision too.

From that day, we moved forward with Gail as partners in starting CVH. Gail became the chair of the board of our new organization. Her leadership was grounded in her direct experience, especially her resentment of the lack of respect given to women, particularly women of color, who were on welfare. "They didn't know the power they had, the power they possessed," she said of the women. "We kind of pulled that out of them, we showed them they had power and you have to learn how to use it."

Gail often recalled how frequently others in the welfare-reform fray told us that we would never be able to organize low-income people effectively. The fact that we eventually built a base and won real legislative and administrative changes was a source of tremendous satisfaction for her. "I think we showed them exactly what we could do," she said. "Nothing is more dangerous than an angry mother," she liked to say, with a smile, of course.

Gail became a great public speaker. She first addressed public officials and the media in her role as a leader. Later, she became a CVH staff member and continued to speak out to a different audience of CVH funders and allies. She helped train members of CVH to step up and be heard. Guided by her desire to bring respect to women on welfare, the welcoming, family-like nature of the organization is another product of her steadfast vision. Gail died in 2005 of complications from diabetes. In her journey from the shelter system to the halls of power, she helped to build a political institution of low-income people.*

---

*Quotations are from an interview conducted for the New York Foundation, used by permission of the foundation.

Step Three: Make a proposal for power. We engaged in deep discourse about the politics surrounding welfare reform with the women we were meeting. We agitated them, asking why they thought people considered them lazy or believed they didn't want to work. If they had solutions to fix welfare, why would no one listen to them? We asked people outright: Do you want to build power with other people in the same situation as you are in so policymakers will listen to you? We found women who did. They wanted to organize, and they wanted to build an organization.

Step Four: Develop principles. Once we identified about twenty people who wanted to form a core group, we began to discuss what the organization would look like and how it would operate. Because we had been building relationships and trust, we could have honest conversations. We considered various approaches. We agreed that the low-income leaders would represent the organization publicly, make decisions about what it would do, be the majority of its board of directors, and hold each other accountable for their actions on the organization's behalf.

Step Five: Kick it off—engage the broader community. We did not move forward with just the desire and buy-in of twenty people. Working with this core group as well as some advocates and staff from service groups, we held a series of meetings over the course of five months and met with more than five hundred mothers on welfare. Their resounding response was, "Yes. We want to build our power." Tool 1.3, Six Ss for a Successful Meeting, provides a template for holding meetings that get results.

Step Six: Train an organizing committee. By now people had come in through three ways: the personal networks of original leaders like Gail; referrals from other organizations that worked with welfare recipients, making our initial research meetings pay off; and teach-ins and some initial, small direct actions.

We identified the twenty-five best potential leaders and brought them to a three-day training about one thing: power. Organizers from the IAF (Industrial Areas Foundation) network conducted the training. We raised money so that the women could bring their children to the training and have good child care while they did their work. We went to a nice, comfortable retreat center. We set a culture of respect. The women reached a shared understanding about the purpose of the organization while deepening their relationships with us and with one another. Many who attended the training went on to play significant roles in the organization.

Step Seven: Establish a leadership team. We established a leadership team to manage the building of the organization; most of those on the team had attended the power training. (See the next section for an example of how to establish a leadership team.)

Step Eight: Ramp up the work. A wider group of members began to work together more effectively and got more focused. They met regularly and clarified and agreed on goals and objectives. The leadership team oversaw those of us who were playing staff roles. The group engaged in more significant actions, including marches in the state capital with hundreds of people. In one dramatic action, one of our core leaders, surrounded by two hundred people, posted an eviction notice on the door to the governor's office to dramatize the effects of his proposals to cut the state welfare budget. We also brought mothers on welfare to the nation's capital to talk directly to their elected representatives. These women were, in some cases, the first actual welfare recipients that architects of welfare reform or their key staff had ever talked with. Exercise 1.1 at the end of the chapter offers a way to help a group of people begin to see what they want to accomplish together. Exercise 1.2 offers some questions to guide a discussion of how to move forward.

What Is a Leadership Team and What Does It Do?

A leadership team is the group of people at the core of the organization who make key decisions about campaigns and the development of the organization. They represent the organization publicly and help raise money to support it. You can also establish a leadership team for a specific campaign.

The leadership team has a core and a shape, but it is not static. While you start out with a fairly defined team of leaders, the team evolves over the life of the organization. These leaders have a variety of skills and qualities. If all the leaders of the organization just want to do actions, then the organization is perpetually in action, but not necessarily effective. If the core leaders are always analyzing things, then the organization may never move to action.

In some organizations the leadership team and the board or steering committee are the same group. In other cases, the organization decentralizes leadership responsibilities throughout the organization, with leadership teams for specific campaigns running at the same time.

The following story shows how we built the initial leadership team at CVH:

Paul met Gail at a meeting of welfare advocates. At that meeting, Gail introduced Paul to her friend Phyllis, a member of Sister Circle. A few weeks later, Gail brought Phyllis and her longtime friend Dina, also active in Sister Circle, to an organizing meeting that we convened with other activists and service providers. Through doing welfare reform teach-ins, we met Karen, a low-income mother who wanted to organize and who said she would try to get her friend Betsy involved too. We also met Janet, a college student who relied on welfare to raise her two young sons, and Laura, who needed a range of benefits to care for her school-aged daughter who had some health concerns. Janet and Laura were frustrated that women on welfare did not have a voice in the organizations where they'd been going to find out about welfare reform.

Working along with Gail, we convened a series of initial meetings to talk about starting an organization. Phyllis, Dina, Karen, Betsy, Janet, and Laura regularly attended. We were impressed by the different strengths these women brought, and we worked with them to develop their leadership skills (see Chapter Five for more on developing leaders). Their different strengths served the organization well over time:

- *Vision.* Gail was both a visionary and caretaking leader who kept the focus on gaining respect for women on welfare while fostering a sense of family in the emerging organization. She became a presence at the office, took leadership in meetings, and personally motivated other women who felt powerless to come out and get involved.

- *Recruitment.* Laura recruited other students on welfare to join us.

- *Facilitation.* Dina moved us to make decisions and regularly chaired meetings.

- *Agitation.* Karen challenged others to step up to responsibilities and also confronted public officials and other people with power in our direct actions.

- *Involvement.* Phyllis made phone calls to turn people out for meetings and actions.

- *Representation.* Betsy often represented the group at community meetings and conferences.

- *Relationship-building.* Janet built relationships between us and the more established organizations in which she participated. Janet was the one to place the eviction notice on the Governor's door.

When we created a formal organization, these women became the board of directors.

As CVH gained power and expanded its work, the leadership team decided to recruit some allies with professional skills to join them on the board. The leadership team gave the board specific powers and responsibilities while decentralizing decision making throughout the organization. They created organizing committees to direct the course of individual campaigns.

Because of the nature of the issues we were addressing, many of the leaders in the early days of our organization had frequent life-changing circumstances. While we retained a solid core, Paul and the other organizers we hired were continually building our leadership team, bringing out the capacity of individuals and helping them function effectively as a team.

A leadership team is not an insider club. It is a group of people who consistently have the time and space in their lives to build power and make a difference—which is often a challenge in the intense period of starting an organization. In order for the team to be effective, the members need to challenge each other and at times themselves to take on different responsibilities, change roles, and make room for newer leaders to participate and develop.

Do We Have to Create an Organization in Order to Build Power?

In order to achieve a true shift in power, you often need not only to win a campaign but to establish an organization. You can, however, use power-building techniques to win free-standing campaigns that make a real difference in people's lives.

We built an organization because that's what people directly affected by the issues wanted, and we agreed with them. Member-led organizations like CVH become community institutions for political engagement. They are essential for creating substantive, long-lasting, radical change. These organizations continue a long tradition in the United States of making democracy work.

From the beginning, the women we were organizing were clear that they wanted an organization, not just a single campaign. They wanted an organization that followed the following organizing principles:

- *Power.* They wanted to build an organization with as many members as possible that would represent their interests, not only on welfare reform but also on other issues, such as job creation, education and training for jobs, and improving their children's schools.

- *Action.* They wanted to directly engage and negotiate with powerholders and were willing to be confrontational, if necessary.

- *Self-Determination.* They were clear that they needed to build, manage, and represent the organization. They did not want to cede these roles to staff or to professional advocates.

- *Shift the parameters of the debate.* They did not want to talk about minor improvements in policies. They wanted to shift the public and political debate to include what they believed would make a real difference in their lives.

These core principles were central to the development of Community Voices Heard over the next decade and beyond. We believe these are critical for all community power-building organizations. In addition, the original CVH leaders explicitly wanted an inclusive organization for all people on welfare—all ages, racial and ethnic groups, and personal circumstances. Clarity about who the organization is for is a critical early decision.

Most of what we describe in this book assumes the resources and goals of an organization because ultimately, organizations consolidate and perpetuate community power.

Should We Build an Organization to Address Our Issue?

This decision is both personal and collective. The following general questions can help guide you.

Do I (or we) have the appetite to engage in organization-building? It takes hard work, a lot of time, and financial resources to build an organization. It can be extremely rewarding and lead to very real and important changes, but you need to be hungry for it, not doing it because you feel that you "should."

How complex is the problem? It is important to understand the difference between a problem and an issue. Although people often use the term "issue" very broadly, we use it in a specific way throughout this book. An issue is a solution to a problem. For example, for us, the attack on welfare policy was a problem. It took some time to identify the initial solution women on welfare wanted to pursue—stop the governor from cutting welfare programs in New York State. (For more information about the difference between problems and issues and how to identify issues, see Chapter Seven.) As in our case, you may need to build an organization if the problem has many fronts and the solutions are complicated. For example, we eventually had to define and pursue issues on the local, state, and federal levels in order to have a real impact on the problem of the destruction of the welfare system.

Sometimes you can resolve a problem with a free-standing campaign. For instance, a developer wants to destroy your local park to build luxury housing. People in the community clearly define their issue: save the park. As we lay out in Part Three, you initiate a campaign to achieve your goal, a lot of people from the community get involved, and you win. Whether or not this victory will ultimately save the park depends on how intense the development pressure is in your community. Will another developer come along shortly and try the same thing? Even problems that seem relatively easy to solve can recur if you don't address the root causes.

Is another community organizing group working on the problem? Take the time to meet with people to find out if anyone else is addressing what you want to address with the same constituency. If someone is, it does not necessarily mean you should not. It does mean that you need to find out more and make an assessment about the effectiveness of others' efforts. Knowing who else is working on the problem not only gives you information about whether or not you need an organization, it also shows people that you are serious, strategic, and respectful of the community and its leaders, especially if you are from outside of the community.

Is the issue winnable? It is hard to build an organization around something the community cannot win, even if people feel passionately that it is the solution to their problem. (For more on determining if the issue is winnable, see Chapter Seven.)

Do the people affected by the problem want an organization? Do community members say they want an organization? If so, do they come out over a sustained period of time to build one? If people meet consistently and follow through on their commitments, there is some potential that they are ready for an organization. You don't need thousands of people to start, but you do need a core group of leaders and people moving to action.

Are there resources to address the issue? Are individuals and foundations willing to give you money to pay for staff, travel, mailings, and a full range of expenses? If you run a campaign, then disband, you are more able to get by with volunteers serving as organizers and people contributing goods and services. If you decide to build an organization, you need to raise money. See Resource B for more on raising money for organizing.

How Soon Do We Need to Establish a Structure and Raise Money?

You need some internal structure early on, but do not get bogged down.

In starting CVH, we kept our initial fundraising and approach to management simple. We began as a project of the advocacy organization Paul worked for, which gave us office space and some staff support. We did not focus on hiring more staff; instead we cultivated the skills and commitment of the constituent leaders. Work got done, and it solidified their engagement—they saw that what they did made a real difference. As we ramped it up, we raised money and established some management systems. We got members involved in soliciting in-kind donations for things like materials and travel, and with the leadership team, we started cultivating long-term funding sources. We also developed relationships with technical assistance providers who would help us, over time, to establish a legal organization. Our recommendation is that in the beginning, as in the life of the organization or campaign, get people involved and don't get bogged down—move to action!

In the Conclusion and in Resource F, Creating a Legal Community Power-Building Organization, we review other things to consider about structuring your organization.

What Is an Organizer and What Is the Role of an Organizer?

An organizer builds a group of people or institutions to address a common problem through collective action. An organizer plays the role of convener, agitator, teacher, student, motivator, and coach.

An organizer can be unpaid or paid. An organizer can gain formal training in an academy or be taught by his or her life experience. Some organizers start early on in their lives, others get into organizing later. Some organize for a short time, others for their entire careers. Organizers are students, mothers, fathers, young people, and seniors. Organizers are leaders themselves in the broader social justice movement.

Throughout this book, we describe the specific role of an organizer and how it is different from the role of member or leader of an organization. Essentially, an organizer meets people where they are and plays the role of an agitator, trying to get people to move to the most fruitful actions. For example, if a group of people working to stop a hazardous waste plant only want to write letters and circulate a petition, an organizer probes and questions their ideas. The organizer helps them evaluate their thinking and come up with actions that they feel comfortable doing that, unlike just holding a petition drive, have the potential to have a real impact.

If your organization is deciding what to do about a new economic-development project that will displace hundreds of families but promises to provide jobs, you get people to think critically. You ask enough questions and provide enough options that they engage in a serious conversation to weigh the costs and benefits of the proposal. Moreover, you don't sit back when a member makes a racist, sexist, homophobic, or other discriminatory remark. You engage that member in critical thinking and reflection.

As you move people in these ways, you bring them together, learn with them and from them, and like the coach of an athletic team, help them to achieve all that they are capable of.

Do I Need to Be from the Community I Want to Organize?

No. There are pros and cons to being from the community or being from outside of it.

During welfare reform many women, particularly women of color on welfare, became leaders in local organizations and eventually, organizers. They brought new perspectives and tactics as well as urgency. They could motivate women on welfare in ways that other organizers could not. However, sometimes when a person organizes in her or his own community, it can be hard to move out of the role of being a member or leader to be in the role of an organizer.

On the other hand, organizers from outside the community can bring years of experience on other issues, a new perspective, fresh energy, and a more objective view of an issue or the political landscape. The challenges they sometimes face can include the need to take time to build trust and acceptance in a community and not understanding an issue at the gut level. Some organizers try to impose an organizing model on a situation where it just does not fit, or they may avoid experimenting with new ideas and the tactics that the community would like to use.

What Are Some of the Core Skills of an Organizer?

Throughout this book, we highlight the role and the skills of an organizer. You engage in fundamental tasks, such as facilitating meetings, conducting research, or developing strategy. The following are some of the core skills that make it possible for you to do these and other organizing tasks effectively.

Agitation. Agitation is the skill of engaging in a dialogue that moves a person to action. You ask questions or suggest ideas that make someone a little uncomfortable. People "move" when they are uncomfortable—they do something to make the discomfort go away. They think or act differently. Effective agitation is both a core skill and an art. It brings out tensions in a healthy and useful way. It is not meant to threaten or humiliate. Agitation gets to the motivations for change and empowerment that lie within individuals, meetings, organizations, and communities.

Listening and learning. Listening—to those with whom you agree and those with whom you don't—is necessary for creating social change. When you listen, you learn. You refine your ability to ask good questions that give you insight into people, relationships, problems, and issues. An organizer does not have all the answers. Organizers, members, and leaders learn from each other.

Critical thinking. You seek out information and think about what you hear and see. You look at all the angles to see where they lead. You form opinions, ideas, and insights. You learn to think on your feet and how to adapt when plans do not go perfectly well.

For example, although you can go to a training to learn the elements of a meeting agenda, you help members create the meeting they need to have by thinking critically about what they most need to get out of the meeting and assessing which members and leaders can develop by taking on different roles at the meeting. A simple tool to help you to develop the skill of critical thinking is to keep an organizer notebook. You can use this like a journal to write down thoughts and ideas as they come.

What Are Some Qualities That Organizers Have?

Since organizers are people from all walks of life, they bring a range of qualities to their work. The following are some we've observed in good organizers:

- *Anger.* Organizers are angry about injustice. They channel anger to move people to action.
- *Flexibility.* Organizers are able to refocus and adapt to changing situations.
- *Sense of humor.* Having a sense of humor helps to diffuse conflict, relieve tense situations, and keep an organizer going for the long haul.
- *Fearlessness.* When organizers seek to dismantle institutions and systems that perpetuate inequality, they take real risks and must be unafraid of the consequences.
- *Ability to hear.* Good organizers are able to hear what people say and reflect on it.

- *Awareness of their own self-interest.* Organizers understand what they want to get out of a situation.

- *Ability to be self-critical and reflective.* Organizers are acutely able to think about what they've done and what they are doing and consider what could potentially happen if they take a course of action.

- *Willingness to share power.* Organizers have to be willing to give up power, let members make decisions, and ultimately be willing to win or to lose if that's where members' decisions lead.

CHALLENGES
TO GETTING STARTED

"Other groups are working on the problem." Investigate how other groups are addressing the same problem and if they are seeking a similar solution to the one you want to pursue. Keep in mind that people sometimes use the term "organizing" to describe methods other than base-building for power. You have to do your research. If they are using an approach other than organizing, your efforts could complement their work. If they are organizing effectively, make sure that your efforts do not replicate theirs. For example, focus on a different constituency or a different neighborhood.

"People do not want to meet with us or don't think we can do what we say we want to do." Start to build a track record. Do small-scale, limited action and bring constituent leaders into the meetings. Incremental accomplishments will help you get in the door.

"We have no money for staff or other expenses." If you are addressing a locally based problem, you need an issue, a focus, and people in order to raise money. Assess the amount of work you need to do and how much of a crisis you are in. If the problem needs to be addressed immediately, start with volunteers, build some accomplishments, and use these to leverage your fundraising efforts.

ESSENTIAL ELEMENTS
FOR GETTING STARTED

☑ *Get out in the field.* Don't sit in your home or office alone. Go out and talk to people. Connect with as wide and diverse a group as possible.

☑ *Be clear about what you want to do.* Both allies and constituents will respond more positively to a clear idea and vision than to something that is not well thought out or that is too complicated.

☑ *Ask for feedback and comments.* Having a vision does not mean that your project is static, especially in the beginning. Engage people with conversations that elicit their ideas and feedback.

☑ *Bring a leadership team together early.* Don't wait for the perfect leadership team. Start engaging constituents early, bringing people to meetings, having them lead discussion groups, and doing both short-term planning and long-term visioning.

☑ *Don't replicate good work.* If another organization is doing a good job of addressing your issue, position your efforts in a way that adds to the mix.

Tool 1.1
Sample Phone Rap to Schedule Assessment Meetings

You can use the following to schedule one-on-one meetings to assess whether or not you have a potential campaign or organization.

My name is _____ . I am calling because I am doing some work on _____ in the community. I've been working with a group of people who might want to organize to address this, and before we go deeper, we want to find out what others are doing and what they think about the problem. For example, how do you think this is all unfolding? Is there a need to organize people, or would a different strategy be better? Can we set up a meeting in the near future to talk about this? It would take between thirty minutes and an hour.

If the person is tentative, mention who you have met with or how many people you are working with. Share any knowledge you have about the problem or about the person you are calling. If your initial group has done anything you can cite, talk about it.

Get a meeting commitment.

Tool 1.2
Sample Community Organizing Assessment Tool

You can use the following as a guide for organizing assessment meetings:

- Introduce yourself and thank the person for taking time to meet.

- Tell the person you are interested in working on a community problem but that before you do, you want to know who else is working on it and what they are doing. If you have met with other people, mention who you have met with, but don't talk about what these others have said. You want to hear what this person thinks.

- Engage the person in the following questions: What do you know about the problem? Who is currently working on it? Who else has worked on it in the past?

  - If anyone (including this person) is working on the problem, ask about how and what the goals are. Ask for specifics of what this person has accomplished, how, and with whom.

  - Ask for this person's analysis. What has worked, what has not, what could help address the problem better?

  - Ask this person for any other thoughts.

- Say briefly what you have done and what your thoughts are for addressing the problem. Remember, you are there to pick this person's brain, not to talk about your own work! Be clear if you are just exploring or if you are moving forward.

- Ask if there are any challenges you can expect moving forward.

- Ask if she or he is interested in being involved or helping to build the campaign or organization you are thinking about.

- Get her or his contact information: name, address, phone, e-mail.

After the Meeting

- Make sure you put the contact information in a database, including any notes you don't want to forget. (For more about keeping track of information using a database, see Chapter Six.)

- Set up meetings with anyone the person suggested.

- Send a thank-you note via e-mail or postal mail, telling the person how you will follow up.

Tool 1.3
Six Ss for a Successful Meeting

You hold many meetings in organizing. Incorporate the following into every meeting. You can use this as a guide, handout, or checklist to train staff or members.

1. **Sign in.** Everyone writes his or her name and contact information on a preprinted sheet with blank boxes or on a pad of paper. Signing in at the beginning of every organizational gathering not only brings in up-to-date contact information, it also reinforces the importance of *getting* contact information from everyone. It demonstrates to people who are there for the first time that the organization cares if they come back.

2. **Say "welcome."** At every meeting, a member or leader has the specific role of welcoming new people, both as they come in and when they are together as a group.

3. **Say names.** Everyone goes around and says their name to open the meeting, even if there are a lot of people there. This brings everyone into the room, establishes equal footing with the facilitator and among experienced and new members, and helps people learn each others' names. If time permits, people say why they are there, their role in the organization, what they hope to get from the meeting, or other orienting information. Name tags may not be necessary at every gathering, but if there are new people there, it helps orient everyone.

4. **Sit in a circle.** When people look at each other during the meeting, it supports dialogue and relationship-building.

5. **Secure the right space.** The meeting environment matters. For example, if the room is too big, people feel like the turnout is too small. If it's too small, they want to leave. If it is clean and well ventilated, they're at ease. If the floor is so dirty they don't want to put their bags down, they may not come back. If the phone rings in the background, it gives the meeting a buzz. If the phone rings right next to the participants, it's distracting. Pay attention to what will create the right space for the specific meeting.

6. **Share food.** Even if it's only a plate of cookies, food bonds people, gives them physical energy, and creates a homey feeling. If the meeting occurs at meal times, try to serve real food of some kind or ask people to bring something to share.

Exercise 1.1
Visioning Exercise

You can use the following exercise to help a group of people begin to see what they want to accomplish together.

Time: About one hour, depending on the number of people.

Materials: Props for the sculptures, such as hats or items connected with the issue.

Roles: Overall facilitator and facilitator for each group.

Room set-up: Movable chairs so small groups can gather. Enough wall space to tape the headlines to the wall or floor space for the sculptures.

- Facilitator puts participants into small groups of at least five and not more than seven people and asks someone to facilitate in each small group, possibly having prepared them in advance.

- Facilitator describes the goal: To create a vision of what we hope to do together to address the problem or issue we have identified.

- Facilitator describes the basic exercise: Participants will depict a vision of what the group will have accomplished in one year, in three years, and in ten years.

There are two versions of this exercise:

You can use "headline futures," in which each small group writes a headline that the largest daily newspaper will write about the work of those who are gathered in one, three, and ten years. One advantage of this method is that you can post the headlines and really compare and dissect them. Alternatively, you can use a more active exercise where the small groups use themselves and a few props to create living sculptures of what they will have accomplished in one, three, and ten years. In a living sculpture, the participants arrange themselves in some formation, usually with one person serving to direct and place people in position.

- Participants develop their headlines or sculptures; at the end of thirty minutes, each group posts and talks about its headlines or sculptures with the larger group for about three or four minutes.

- Debrief the exercise. The facilitator guides participants to go into what each headline or sculpture says and what it indicates more deeply. It can help people to see common issues or approaches. If people develop products that are about just winning the issue and less about continued work, this could give them a sense that they may want to focus on a campaign, not on building an organization. The facilitator uses what people create to ask pointed and clarifying questions such as, Does this word or gesture mean you see an organization forming out of the campaign? Why or why not? If you see an organization, what will keep this group working together into the future?

Exercise 1.2
Where Are We At?

You can use the following questions to guide a discussion with others in your community—or with a partner—about where you are at:

- What have we done so far? Who have we talked with?

- What is our vision? Our worldview? What do we share and where are there differences?

- What have we learned from our actions and conversations?

- What more do we need to know in order to move our work forward?

- Who can gather this information?

- What specifically will each of us do? What are our individual and collective goals?

- What is our timeline for moving forward?

Powering Up

In 1993 a small margin of voters elects Rudolph Giuliani as mayor of New York City. Despite his limited mandate, he is in a position of power and can change the way New York City operates, not only during his tenure but well into the future. He creates a police force that increases the harassment of people of color and the poor. He changes zoning laws, which allows for a new kind of development, which transforms Manhattan. He adds layers of onerous procedures and rules to New York City's welfare system. Instead of negotiating the difficulties of accessing welfare benefits as a source of support, families and individuals make the decision to turn to friends, family, and charities in order to survive.

The mayor's power, while significant, is not absolute. People organize to oppose his policies. Welfare mothers start building an organization. They take on the mayor and demand that the city help them move off welfare into jobs. The leaders of Community Voices Heard (CVH) recruit thousands of members and mobilize hundreds of people into the city's streets and auditoriums. They challenge the mayor's policies and his appointees, lead discussions with church and labor leaders, and direct lawyers who represent their interests in court. They strategically and methodically go from having no power to having enough power, with other organizations, to challenge the mayor's policies and force New York City to create jobs for welfare mothers.

What Is Power and Why Is It Important to Understand It?

Power is the ability to act and to make things happen.

Power is a neutral force. How you use power—to do good or to do harm—determines what kind of effect it has. Understanding power makes members of an organization more comfortable wanting power. Through leadership development and training in the context of a campaign, people come to understand what power is, who has it, how to build it, how to use it, and how to talk about it.

Can One Person Have Power?

Power often manifests in a single person, but this person is accountable to others.

In a democracy, individuals derive their power from the people they represent or the financial interests and resources they control. This structure is as true of elected officials and corporate executives as it is of community leaders.

What Are the Forms of Power?

The following are ways that people use power in our society:

Power over. People exert power over others, to expand rights and resources or to limit them. This type of power includes everything from a company deciding how much to pay its employees to a state using organized violence to control dissent.

Power for. People use power at times for others, to act on their behalf. This type of power includes actions that benefit others, such as a social service organization providing free food or an advocate securing housing for a homeless family.

Power with. People also build and share power with others. This is the kind of power that comes from collective activity. It requires nonviolent tactics or peaceful direct action rather than guns. Martin Luther King, Jr., the U.S. Civil Rights leader, called this combined power, "The strength required to bring about social, political, and economic change."

In community organizing, "power with" exists in the form of a base of members who make decisions together and run their own organizations and campaigns.

How Does Power Manifest in Society?

Power manifests as organized violence, organized money, and organized people.

The following types of power exist in some form in nearly every human community:

Organized money. Power represents itself in this way through institutions such as banks, multinational corporations, trade councils, and other business interests. A lone business person with an individual company or a single millionaire does not have much power, except over her or his own workers. But when millionaires or business people organize, they amass power that they can wield over others. This is the power of organized money. Such power can also come from organized resources, such as oil cartels or landowners.

Organized violence. Organized violence can be seen in the power of the state, as expressed in the military or police, which use violence or the threat of violence to maintain power over individuals or groups. This type of power can also be used by organized groups of people who use violence to maintain their power in a community, such as gangs, organized crime, or vigilante groups. Organized violence can also lie with groups seeking to overthrow or destabilize governments, such as insurgents, terrorists, and violent revolutionary groups.

Organized people. Nonviolent movements rely on organized people for their base of power. People can be organized through political parties in elections or in institutions with members. They can also organize through mass mobilizations in strikes, marches, rallies, and protests. Oppressed people by themselves do not have power; when they are organized or in collective movement together, they do.

How Do We Show and Exercise Our Power?

You show your power through numbers: members, leaders, and collective action.

You exercise your power when you get things done. You show your power through actions that move your campaign forward. For example, in the Transitional Jobs Campaign (See "The Story of Community Voices Heard"), CVH showed its power in the following ways:

Mobilizing thousands of WEP workers and welfare recipients every year. Potential allies and the city council speaker saw CVH's numbers and their roots in the community.

Executing effective actions based on a well-researched strategy. When people came out for actions—both mass demonstrations and smaller events and meetings— they knew the issue, what they wanted, and the plan for getting what they wanted.

Promoting leaders who can speak to and challenge powerholders. Scores of CVH leaders, almost all women, led meetings and discussions with the allies and public officials who CVH had to move. They were not just spokespeople, they were strong leaders who could challenge, agitate, and move those they engaged in public and private discussions.

CVH exercised its power when it followed up and when, for example, it got a powerful ally to join the campaign or a city councilperson to introduce a bill.

How Do We Check the Power of Individuals in Our Organization?

You build accountability into your structure.

Accountability is essential for building community power. If your campaign or organization is not accountable to the people it represents or its allies, or individuals are not accountable to a larger group of people, you only replicate the oppressive, unfair power dynamics of other parts of society. In organizing, you base your accountability in having constituents as members and leaders who are making decisions about the organization and its campaigns. They have a stake in its success and the impact of its work. Throughout this book we describe ways to build accountability into the decision making of your organization. The following are some of the main ways to structure accountability into your work:

Board or steering committee. The board or steering committee is an oversight group of members and leaders of the organization. Sometimes they invite a small number of individuals to join them who are not from the constituency but who have specific skills. Although organizations and campaigns establish different ways of staffing their work, in most the board is the group that hires, oversees, and can fire the lead staff person. Other members and leaders usually elect or appoint board members. (See Resource E for more information about when you must establish a board.)

Keep in mind that even though the organization is member-led, most organizations empower a lead staff person to hire, supervise, and fire other staff and to report to the board on his or her activities. Members do not randomly direct the staff, and staff are accountable for their work to their supervisors, leadership teams, and committees, not to individual members.

Organizing committee. This is the group of members who oversee the development and implementation of the campaign plan. The organizing committee ideally includes both new members and experienced leaders who are directly affected by the issues. An organizer builds the committee and helps the members to do the committee's work successfully. For more on organizing committees, see Chapter Eight.

Memos of Understanding and operating principles. These documents are ones you create and use in partnerships. They clearly delineate how the partnership will function; what the goals and objectives of the partnership are; the activities, responsibilities, and tasks of each group and any central body; and how the members of the partnership will share resources. The documents also spell out the ramifications of what happens when people violate them.

Open meetings, minutes, transparency, oral and written documentation. In organization meetings and in partnerships, these elements all help ensure that those involved have come to their decisions together. The written documents outline the action steps to which participants can later hold each other accountable.

Why Is It Essential to Build the Power of Our Community, Not Just Win on Issues?

It is not enough to win policies or concessions. What is won can easily be lost. It is not enough just to react to bad situations. You seek to shift power and proactively create the world you want.

What you win can go unrealized if the pressure isn't there to make sure it gets fully funded and implemented. Lapses in implementation may be caused by turnover in political, agency, or corporate personnel; the lengthy process of legal appeals; or the lack of resources to do the proper oversight. For these reasons and more, getting a judge to order a corporation to engage in an environmental clean-up may not be enough. You need a base of people in the community who can monitor the clean-up, demonstrate on the CEO's lawn if they have to, or go back to court and make sure the job gets done.

Much of what we now take for granted in the United States, from labor laws to environmental regulations and free public education, all came from the steady demands of community leaders over time. Organizations continue to this day to fight to sustain these rights.

In the CVH campaign to win transitional jobs, although the campaign won the passage of city legislation to create the transitional jobs program, it had to run several subsequent campaigns over the course of several years in order to get the mayor to implement the program. If CVH had just celebrated a victory, there would be not be a transitional jobs program.

How Do We Shift Power?

You shift power by developing and implementing a strategy to do so.

There is a difference between strategic use of power and tactical use of power. Tactical use of power is exercising your power for a single or short-term win, as you do in a campaign. In strategic use of power, you shift power from one group of people to another group of people. You do this through a long-term strategy that includes building multiple organizations and developing the infrastructure to support these organizations. It includes not only creating community power-building organizations but establishing other kinds of organizations and securing positions of power and influence.

For example, as we described in the Introduction, right-wing conservatives strategically shifted power in the United States in the last twenty-five years through more than just winning campaigns. They used base-building, electing people to a variety of offices at different levels, developing and funding research and advocacy organizations, and securing judicial appointments.

What Are Some Other Ways We Exercise Power to Achieve Social Change?

Mass mobilizing, electoral organizing, labor organizing, and movement-building are other ways to achieve change. You can also use these strategies as part of your community organizing.

Mass mobilizing. In these events, large numbers of people move into action, usually to oppose something. Although there is some organizational structure behind the action, most of the people who come out into the streets are not connected to any specific organization; rather, the problem or issue moves them to action. Examples of mass mobilizations include protests against the Vietnam War, which helped move the U.S. government to pull out its troops. Other mass mobilizations were the large protests against nuclear weapons and nuclear power in the 1970s and 1980s.

Electoral organizing. Organizations engage in electoral organizing to build political power. If their tax status allows them to do partisan work, they work to either elect or reject candidates for office. This kind of work can include training and developing community leaders to run for office. Although connected to community organizing, electoral organizing is different, as we explain in Resource C.

Labor organizing. This strategy includes organizing unorganized workers and building the power of specific workers to achieve better working conditions, pay, and benefits. Although community organizations that do labor organizing often focus on immigrant groups, they do not do so exclusively. Examples of community organizations that do labor organizing include CVH's Transitional Jobs Campaign, the national movement to organize day laborers, and efforts in various cities to organize taxi drivers and part-time and temporary workers.

Movement-building. Many organizations also see themselves as part of a broader social movement that seeks change beyond the direct self-interest of any one group.

Whether or not a certified "movement" exists at any particular time is always a matter of debate among activists and organizers, but within local organizations many people come to see themselves as part of something that reaches beyond their own issues. They often refer to this something as "the movement." They may see their own organizations as being connected to others that represent similar constituencies. Many form alliances in order to consolidate the power to move their agendas forward. In addition, individuals take the experiences they gain at one organization and apply them to working with other social change groups. (For more on movement-building see Chapter Fifteen.)

CHALLENGES
TO POWERING UP

"*Our members do not like the term* power." This type of objection is why participants in your campaign or members of your organization need to define what power means to them. You talk about power in trainings and political education, in recruitment, and in developing a mission statement and operating principles. Exercise 2.1 offers a way to reflect on what power means, Exercise 2.2 helps members reflect on different forms of power, and Exercise 2.3 presents the views of some political leaders on power.

"*We are just getting started. How do we set up strong internal accountability systems?*" Throughout this book, we describe ways to build accountability into your decision making and into the way your organization operates. In addition, we suggest that you seek some technical assistance to set up the best type of organization for your situation.

ESSENTIAL ELEMENTS
FOR POWERING UP EFFECTIVELY

☑ *Talk about power.* You are explicit in your materials, trainings, and organizational culture that you are building power and that you understand the power that others have.

☑ *Build in accountability.* You ensure that individuals within the organization are using their power in ways that represent everyone's interests and that build trust with allies.

☑ *Move to action.* This is the way you show your power.

Exercise 2.1
What Does Your Power Look Like?

This exercise gives participants, primarily organization members, a way to start thinking and talking about power in their own lives. It is a good warm-up exercise for a longer session about power.

Time: About thirty minutes.

Materials: Chart paper and enough multicolored markers for each person to have three or four to work with. Sample power pictures.

Roles: Facilitator.

Room set-up: Tables where people can draw pictures. Enough wall space to hang pictures.

- Facilitator distributes chart paper and asks participants to take about ten minutes to draw pictures of when they have felt powerful. Facilitator offers a couple of samples, one political, one more personal.

Giving examples invites people to draw from whatever experiences feel most relevant to them to begin a discussion of power. It should also show that people don't have to be artists to draw these pictures! The facilitator can use samples from past workshops or pictures she prepares herself.

- Facilitator asks people to post their pictures on the wall when they're complete.

- Facilitator asks people to find a partner and talk about each of their pictures for five or ten minutes each. Facilitator flags people after the first five or ten minutes to switch, so that each partner gets to share.

This "partner share" technique allows for everyone to participate and creates a buzz of voices in the room. It also keeps the exercise safe for people who don't want to talk about themselves in front of the full group, especially if this is the first exercise of a longer workshop. The exercise also progresses more efficiently than if everyone talks about their pictures to the full group.

- The group comes together to hear some samples of what people shared.

- As participants debrief as a large group, the facilitator writes down some key words that describe power, its characteristics, or its applications.

Exercise 2.2
Power in Community Organizing

This exercise invites participants, primarily organization members, to reflect on different forms of power in their lives and to understand better what power means in community organizing.

Time: 45–60 minutes allows time for in-depth discussion.

Materials: "Forms of Power in Our Lives" diagram on a chart. "Forms of Power in Our Lives" handout. Photographs of people in the organization exercising their power. Other pictures of power (preferably copied on letter-sized paper).

Roles: Facilitator.

Room set-up: Any seating will work, although enough room to have people sit around a table or with their chairs in a circle is preferable. Wall space or easels to display charts.

- Facilitator writes a definition of power in community organizing on a chart: "Power is the ability to act and to make things happen."

- Facilitator then shows a large diagram on chart paper titled "Forms of Power in Our Lives" that looks like this:

Forms of Power in Our Lives		
Power Over	**Power For**	**Power With**
• Some authority has the power (boss to employee)	• An advocate has the power (caseworker at a shelter)	• You build and share power with others (what power means at our organization—the power that comes from organizing!)
[room for graphic]	[graphic]	[graphic]

The facilitator can add a graphic or photo that corresponds to each of the forms of power.

Ideally, give each participant a sheet of paper with these forms of power listed on it so that they can listen and participate rather than be writing what they see on the chart.

- Facilitator reviews the forms of power listed on the diagram.

Exercise 2.2
Power in Community Organizing, Cont'd

- Facilitator asks: "What do you think of this?"

- Facilitator asks: "What have you done or seen at our organization that illustrates what it means to have 'power with' others?"

In the course of this conversation, the facilitator shares two examples she's thought of in advance. She also has pictures available that illustrate the examples—such as leaders sharing the stage at an accountability session or members talking at an organizing meeting.

- Participants choose pictures and add them to the Forms of Power in Our Lives diagram on the chart. If members are present who participated in those actions, they talk about their experiences.

- The facilitator passes out other pictures of power, such as demonstrators at a rally, political leaders speaking to the press, money changing hands, a church building. She asks participants to each choose a picture and add it to the Forms of Power in Our Lives diagram on the chart. Some members of the group can then talk about why they chose their pictures and what the pictures mean to them.

Asking people to get up and do something gets them involved and keeps the energy up in the room.

- The facilitator shows another chart with the following three points listed on it:
  • Organized people • Organized money • Organized violence.
  She asks: "What's the role of each of these in the different forms of power?"

If there is adequate time, people can turn to the person next to them or quickly gather in groups of three or four to discuss this question for ten minutes, then come together and share samples of what they talked about.

- The facilitator says: "At our organization, we mostly have organized people. Because we're building power with others, we can never have too many people involved in our organization. We raise money so that we have the resources to hire staff, run an office, and things like that, but we'll never win changes in public policy simply based on how much money we have. We don't use violence in any form."

- The facilitator reviews the main points and addresses any questions people may have.

Exercise 2.3
What Do Some Political Leaders Say About Power?

This exercise offers a provocative way to get people thinking about power. It also incorporates political education by noting the lives and contributions of political leaders. It is best used with members of your organization as part of a larger training on power or to incorporate a discussion on power into other trainings or meetings. The exercise is to read and discuss quotations about power. We provide two sample quotations. You can change these or add quotations that will interest your membership.

Time: 20 minutes to discuss two or three quotations.

Materials: Quotations written on chart paper. Tape to hang the charts.

Roles: Facilitator.

Room set-up: Enough wall space to hang quotations, and room for participants to walk around the room and view them.

- The facilitator posts quotations about power and the names of the people who said them, written on chart paper, around the room.

- The facilitator asks people to get up, go around, and read the quotes together.

- The facilitator offers some information about the quoted leaders and invites others to contribute to the discussion as well. Sample questions: "What's meaningful to you about this leader? What's meaningful about what she or he says about power?"

  o "Now power, properly understood, is nothing but the ability to achieve purpose. It is the strength required to bring about social, political and economic change."—Martin Luther King Jr.

  o "Power concedes nothing without a demand. It never did and it never will."—Frederick Douglass

- The facilitator guides the discussion, which is adjusted to fit the purpose of the training.

- Alternatively, participants can go around and read the quotations silently. They can stand in front of the quotation that is most meaningful to them, and engage in a discussion with others who identify with it as well. The participants then come together to share what they discussed in the small groups.

part two

Building a Base for Power

Base-building is the work of engaging people in a campaign or organization and developing their ability to collectively address issues they care about. Your power comes from the ability to attract, mobilize, and develop large numbers of people who are in relationship with your organization, not just names on mailing labels or in e-mail groups. People do not come to you. You go out and find them.

Base-building is the core strategy for building community power. Once constituents—people directly affected by the problems your organization addresses—become members of your organization, they are your base. A base is not a fixed, static thing. It grows and changes as your campaigns grow and change.

Base building is

Continuous. You constantly build your base, even while engaged in other activities.

Non-Linear. Base building steps do not always follow each other in the same order. People enter the organization in a range of ways, and organizers adapt to that.

Analytical and nuanced. You exercise judgment about how much time to invest in each person, to deepen his or her involvement.

Persistent. You call people many times to get them to commit and to remind them to turn out to actions. You contact them in-person, by mail, and by phone.

Time intensive. You spend a great deal of time bringing people into the organization, keeping them involved, and developing their leadership.

About relationships. You talk to dozens of people on a regular basis. Everyone you recruit and develop has a relationship with you, with other members, and with the organization.

Directive. You have a focus—you bring information and people into the organization—you are not an outreach worker taking information out to the community. You do not seek people to help—you look for people who want to build power.

You can never have too big a base. A large base keeps your organization powerful, both internally and externally. A large base helps show the people with institutional and political power that your power is broad and deep in the community and that your leadership comes from knowledgeable, strategic community members.

A large base that you are constantly replenishing connects your organization to the community. You know what is going on at the ground level, you understand how people are experiencing the issues, and you know what will move people to action.

Because base-building is a core organizational concern, everyone in the organization is involved in the base-building activities of recruitment, involvement, leadership development, and tracking. The person in charge of fundraising needs a broad base of donors, administrative staff need volunteers, and any policy or research arms need relationships with a broad group of allies.

We describe each of the components of base-building in detail in the chapters in this section.

Recruiting Constituents for Collective Action

SIGN ME UP—I WANT TO LEARN MORE

Lorena, a single mother working for minimum wage, can't make her rent and goes to the welfare office for help. When she gives her application form to the caseworker, the caseworker yells at Lorena in the middle of the office, telling her she should learn to manage money—it's her own fault she's in trouble.

At the same welfare office, Renee, a Community Voices Heard (CVH) organizer, is signing up people for a new campaign to create jobs for people on welfare. After Lorena finishes with the caseworker and starts to leave, Renee stops her and starts a conversation, asking Lorena what happened. Lorena tells her and asks if Renee can help with her case.

Renee explains that she is not a caseworker, but that she works with a group of people on welfare who just stopped the governor from cutting welfare benefits by protesting in Albany and meeting with legislators right here in the Bronx. Even though Lorena is thinking about the money she needs, she's angry. "I've worked for eight years at every job I could so I wouldn't need welfare," she tells Renee. "My rent went up three months ago and I had to come here. But she made me feel like I don't deserve help." Renee asks Lorena why she thinks caseworkers do that and what she thinks would make the system better. They talk for a few minutes. Renee pulls a postcard from a stack on her clipboard. "These are for the mayor," Renee says, "telling him we want jobs with decent wages so that people on welfare can really support themselves." Lorena readily agrees to sign a postcard. Renee invites Lorena to come to a meeting at CVH to work on the campaign, but Lorena is unsure about doing that. She agrees to give Renee her name, address, and phone number and says it's OK if Renee wants to call her.

As Renee walks away, she jots a number "2" next to Lorena's name, meaning that on a scale of one to three, Renee's quick assessment is that Lorena's potential to move to action is in the middle. Lorena was engaged, angry, and asked questions, all signs of interest, but since she didn't say she wanted to get involved, maybe she will or maybe she won't. Renee will call Lorena the next day to explore her potential further.

What Is Recruitment for Base-Building and Why Is It Important?

Recruitment is the process of meeting people, assessing their potential to get involved in collective action, and recording their contact information. You can only build a base for power by constantly going out and bringing new people who are affected by the issues into your campaign and your organization.

Recruitment includes not only building a list of names, but also starting to "work the list" by following up with people so they become members of your organization. In addition, issues change over time, so you keep bringing in new people who are affected in new ways.

How Do We Conduct Recruitment?

You conduct recruitment by going out to find constituents where they live, work, socialize, or spend time, or by inviting people to teach-ins, house meetings, and other small-group events.

The first process, which organizers refer to as "going out in the field," is described here. Later in the chapter we discuss recruiting people through teach-ins and house meetings. See Tool 3.1 for a handout covering dos and don'ts of successful recruitment in the field.

1. Before You Go Out

- *Understand the campaign.* When you conduct recruitment, you are building not only the organization but usually a campaign as well. Before you go out, be clear about the goal and demands of the campaign, how many people you need to recruit, and which constituents are directly affected. (For more about campaigns, see Chapters Seven through Thirteen.)

- *Identify good points of entry.* A point of entry is a place where you can meet people affected by the issue your organization is addressing. A good point of entry allows you the freedom to talk to many people in a short period of time. At most points of entry you meet "cold contacts." A cold contact is someone who has no knowledge of your organization. A point of entry could be a social service site, a workplace, or a park. In a rural setting, it is likely to be a church, a school, or a gathering in someone's home. You go where constituents are at the time they are most likely to be there, not just where and when it is most convenient for you. For example, doorknocking, or going door-to-door to talk to people at their homes, can be a good point of entry. The best time to knock on doors, in most communities, is Sunday evening, between 5 P.M. and 9 P.M., clearly outside what many people would consider a regular work week. Finding a good point of entry takes some research, trial, and evaluation. See Tool 3.2 for a sample worksheet you can use to guide organizers to plan where, when, and how they will do recruitment.

Identifying Points of Entry

For the CVH campaign to win real jobs with good wages and benefits for people on welfare, CVH uses Work Experience Program (WEP) worksites as the main point of entry. (See the Story of Community Voices Heard for background information about the jobs campaign and WEP program.) WEP workers, the constituents of the campaign, must perform work activities in exchange for welfare benefits, but they do not receive a paycheck. They often work right alongside union members and others who are doing exactly the same thing but are getting paid a full salary.

CVH organizers use investigative skills to find WEP workers, going to parks, recreation centers, and office buildings and asking where the workers are. They learn that the WEP workers usually do cleaning and maintenance. Because outsiders can only legally talk to workers before their shifts, during lunch hours, or after the work day, the organizers learn when these times occur. They find out where workers take smoking breaks and where their locker rooms are. Sometimes they enter buildings and organize impromptu meetings while people are working. This action violates city regulations but ends up recruiting a lot of workers, using the setting of group meetings to get people to think collectively. For example, when at City Hall for a public hearing—a building that is normally off limits for organizing—an organizer may go up to some WEP workers who are cleaning the bathrooms and try to recruit them.

- *Set numeric goals.* Organizing is all about numbers. You set goals for the number of people you need to sign up every time you go out. At the start of a new campaign, an organizer, preferably someone with experience, may try to recruit people at different points of entry in order to establish the average number of people he or she can sign up in an hour. This is one way to determine a standard that everyone who is doing recruitment can follow. Whether you start with an end goal, such as five hundred contacts, or with a site-specific goal, such as ten people at a worksite, clear numeric goals give you the ability to evaluate the effectiveness of your daily and weekly recruitment.

- *Practice a rap.* Construct the outline of a rap, a five- to seven-minute conversation that prepares you to talk with someone you don't know and helps you assess if a person you're speaking with will move to action. More on this important tool follows later in this chapter.

- *Prepare materials.* Keep materials to a minimum so you don't overwhelm people. If you want to distribute anything besides what we describe here, such as a brochure, keep it simple and highlight any accomplishments you have.

Adapt the following materials based on the campaign and its progress or by evaluating what gets people to respond.

> *Data-collection sheet.* A data-collection sheet, also referred to as a sign-up or contact sheet, is a sheet (usually carried on a clipboard) on which you record name, contact information, personal characteristics, and your assessment of whether or not a person will move to action.

> *Commitment cards.* A commitment card or pledge card is a good engagement tool. It is a form of collective action. A commitment card is a sheet of paper that states a commitment to come to an action or support a campaign: "I will be at City Hall on October 5th to fight for jobs!" It includes information about the time and place of the action that you give to the contact as well as a tear-off sheet that the person fills in and gives you. Another kind of commitment card is a "membership card," set up in a similar way, stating that the person wants to be a member of the organization or be considered a participant in the campaign. A commitment card gives you something concrete to follow up on in a phone call:

"Thanks for signing our pledge yesterday. I'm calling to remind you to come out to City Hall on Friday!" It gives you something to show allies and people in power as you implement your campaign: "More than five hundred people have signed our action pledge to fight for jobs now!"

Flyer. Create a simple, attention-getting flyer about the campaign or an upcoming event that conveys three points. First, it highlights an organizational accomplishment to show people that others just like them won something that made their community better. Second, it agitates people with a bold heading or question, such as, "What does your drinking water smell like?" Third, it includes your contact information.

- *Determine a call to action.* Decide on a concrete act a potential member can take. It could be writing a letter on the spot, calling a local legislator on an offered cell phone, completing a survey, or signing a petition to a landlord. (Tool 7.2 in Chapter Seven provides a sample survey.) Taking such an action deepens commitment, helping a person to feel that she did something useful. If she does take such an action, it clearly indicates to you that she wants to do something to change her condition. Like signing a commitment card or pledge, taking an action is an initial form of collective action.

- *Show you are proud of your organization.* You don't need ID cards or credentials, your legitimacy comes from your organization's accomplishments and the power of collective action. A button or t-shirt with the name of the organization on it can help people understand that you are part of an organized group and show that you are proud to be a part of it. Do not wear buttons or t-shirts if you do not want your presence to be known by those who don't want you talking to people at the site.

2. Out in the Field

- *Listen for readiness and potential.* You look for people who have an appetite to do something with others and who openly question the way things are. You also look for people who are ready but hesitant, due to fear or inexperience from not knowing what to do or feeling like there is no use. It is the role of the organizer to move people who feel this way—to get them to see that collective action makes a difference. You offer people a chance to participate in something big and exciting. This offer starts with your rap. You offer possibilities for real change.

- *Explore self-interest.* A person's self-interest is what she needs to get out of the time and energy she puts into being involved. Having self-interest is different from being selfish. Self-interest is a natural, guiding force. If someone really wants and needs something—a job, a place to live, a good education for her children—she puts time and energy into activities that get those needs met. Self-interest also includes wanting to learn new skills or build personal networks. When you understand someone's self-interest, you can use it to get her involved.

- *Conduct research.* By listening, you learn more about the issues and how they are affecting people. You note trends and common concerns, not individual anecdotes.

- *Get a commitment.* Getting a commitment is the key to follow-up. If someone just says, "I'll call you," chances are she won't. If someone says she will do something, you can call and ask her to do it. You can use a commitment card or make a direct request you determined in advance. Keep in mind that recruitment commitments are "soft commitments." The person has conveyed interest but you have to confirm it. Some organizations ask for member dues during recruitment as a way of not only raising money but also getting a commitment. Giving money is a stronger commitment, but still requires follow-up.

- *Form assessments.* Throughout the conversation, you look for the person's analysis of the issues and a desire to get involved, not just wanting to talk or get help. You form an initial assessment about the person's potential to get involved, using the tips described in Tool 3.3. Many groups use a rating system such as the following to evaluate the likelihood that a person will get involved:

  1: Very likely to get involved. A "1" engages in a dialogue. She understands the need for collective action to address community problems. She is deeply concerned about the issue. You prioritize "1s" for immediate, intensive follow up.

  2: Maybe will get involved. A "2" has self-interest in the issue but lacks urgency or deep connection to your offer for collective action. You contact "2s" to follow up, but may not do so intensively, especially if you have many "1s."

3: Unlikely to get involved. A "3" gives you her contact information but does not express any fire. She would rather resolve the problem alone. You do not prioritize "3s" for follow-up, but keep them on your list for surveys and similar efforts.

Making an assessment is not about whether or not you like a person. It is not about who is the most talkative or whether or not you think someone has a good heart. It is an objective assessment about the potential of that person to move to collective action with your organization.

- *Record contact information.* On your data-collection sheet, you clearly write down a name, address, phone number, rating, and comments for everyone who stops and has a conversation with you. It is better for you to do the writing, going through each category for thoroughness, rather than have people fill out their contact information themselves. You write legibly so you can read the information later. Without records to which you and other organizers can later refer, it is not worth having the conversations.

- *Keep moving.* It can be tempting to stay with someone you think has a great analysis of the issues, or someone you think you can convince if you can keep the conversation going, but limiting the time you spend with each person is absolutely essential. If someone has potential, you will follow up later. If someone is not interested, say thanks and move on. With experience, you learn to assess real interest in two or three minutes. You stay with one person for no more than five to seven minutes. You can accomplish a great deal in that short period of time. Always remember your numeric goals. There are other people you need to meet.

- *Don't promise what you can't deliver.* You don't get involved with people's personal problems or promise that if they get involved in a campaign, they will definitely win. The only promise you can make is, "If we don't act, nothing will change."

3. Back at the Office
- *Reflect on your field work.* If you have someone with whom you can debrief, do so. A debrief is a conversation in which you review the facts of what you

experienced and then look at the implications. If you are alone, think critically for a moment and make notes in your organizer notebook. Who was a good potential leader and why? (For more on leadership identification, see Chapter Five.) What did you learn about the issue? How well did your rap work? How was the turf—the geographic area where your organization's members live or where you are looking for new constituents? Were the constituents you were looking for actually there and could you talk with them? Has another organization tried to organize people there? Talk or think about whether or not you met your numeric goals and why. Reflect on the positive experiences—the people who said yes, not just those who said no.

- *Enter contacts and assessments into the database.* You put the information from your contact sheets into the database. A database is a computer software program that keeps track of information about people. (For more on establishing and using a database, see Chapter Six.) You are building your list, which refers to the names and information you have about constituents. Your job is to work this list—to turn names and numbers into members.

- *Use visual aids to share information.* In addition to entering contact information into the database, writing on wall charts the numbers you contacted helps communicate progress, shares information with other staff and with members, and visually highlights the importance of doing ongoing recruitment.

- *Reflect on your assessments.* As you put your assessment notes in the database, you reflect further: Why do you think a person is likely or not to get involved? What did she specifically say or do? This reflection is part of the critical thinking that an organizer develops. It helps you to decide realistically how much time you will spend trying to involve each person.

- *Follow up.* Adhere to a twenty-four- to forty-eight-hour rule: Within twenty-four to forty-eight hours, you call people with potential and have a deeper conversation. If you wait too long, people are likely to forget about your conversation and the interest they experienced when speaking with you face-to-face. Send a follow-up letter and information about your organization. Immediately schedule to visit anyone you ranked as a "1."

Bringing Information and People into the Organization

In recruiting for the Transitional Jobs Campaign, CVH organizers leave the office in the mornings with clipboards stacked with pledge cards people can sign saying they support the campaign, information about WEP workers' rights, and flyers about upcoming meetings or actions. Organizers urge people to come out to actions. They get signed pledge cards so CVH can show city officials and labor unions that WEP workers are organized and want real jobs.

At the end of each day of recruitment, organizers come back to CVH with their pledge cards, their notes about WEP sites, assessments of the people they met, and notes about what people agreed to do. They talk with each other about what they experienced in the field. Organizers are learning what affects WEP workers on the ground.

What Are Some Other Ways We Find People?

Sometimes people come to you, but you still have to do the work of recruiting them.

Constituents you have never met before may attend your actions, such as public meetings or rallies. They may call the office or stop by. These are potential members. No matter where or how you meet a potential member, the process is always the same: you make an assessment and get contact information so you can follow up.

Recruiting Someone Who Contacts You

Jacqueline is a WEP worker in a city agency. She is angry that she has been pulled out of college and forced to work for free, and she is struggling to get child care for her son. One day she sees a flyer about a meeting of WEP workers and she calls the number on the flyer. An organizer answers the phone. Instead of just telling Jacqueline what time the meeting will be, he talks with her about CVH and the campaign and finds out where she works. He tells her someone will be there the next morning to talk with her about her WEP site. He takes her name and contact information. The next day, an organizer goes to her site. Jacqueline talks with the organizer and agrees to organize a meeting at her site. Even though the other workers do not get involved, Jacqueline goes on to play a core leadership role at CVH, speaking out in public, doing strategic planning, and eventually serving on the board of directors—all because a staff member engaged her in a chance phone call and got the information to follow up.

How Do We Talk with Someone We Don't Know?

Effective initial recruitment, the first time you talk with someone, is characterized by a strong rap.

A rap is the five- to seven-minute conversation that introduces you and the organization. It is your tool for approaching a person you don't know and engaging him or her in a dialogue.

You approach a person confidently. Never ask, "Can I talk to you?" The best approach is: "I'm Mary from Community Voices Heard and I am here talking to people about their thoughts about _____. I'd like to know what you think." Introducing yourself, the organization, and your reason for being there immediately clarifies why you are stopping this person to talk or why you need him to keep the door open. Anything you can say about the accomplishments of your organization—"what people like you have already won"—encourages him to talk with you.

In your rap, you test whether or not the issue resonates. Does it affect this person and does she care about it? You listen for the connections she may have in the community—through a workplace, neighborhood association, or institution such as church or school. A rap includes political education, so that you can both motivate someone to engage with you and assess how she analyzes the problem.

You talk *with* each person and show that you are listening—make eye contact, smile, reflect back what you hear. You don't talk *at* people or lecture them. You only ask questions to engage a person in a conversation. If you want something, don't ask. Instead, you say, for example, "Let me write down your name and number."

A rap is not a script. It is nuanced, directive, yet fluid enough to accommodate responses. A rap is somewhat like poetry. It encompasses the voice of the organizer and organization. It sounds real and natural. A great rap motivates people to engage with the larger world. The more you do a rap, the more skilled you become at having this conversation with people.

The sample rap in Exhibit 3.1 shows the elements of a rap in the order that is most effective. You can refer to this sample to create a rap that works for you. See Tool 3.4 for a blank form for writing a rap and Exercise 3.1 for a scenario to train people to think about elements of a rap in relationship to other recruitment tools. See Exercise 3.2 for how to train people to do a rap.

Exhibit 3.1
Sample Rap

Introduction	I am Mary from Community Voices Heard, and I'm talking to people today about the mayor's proposal to provide $600 million in city funds for a new stadium in Manhattan.
Self-interest	Do you think the mayor should be giving the wealthy owners of a sports team city funds to build a stadium—while he proposes cutting city services in this neighborhood?
Accomplishments	The members of Community Voices Heard, who are all people just like you, successfully pressured New York City to create ten thousand jobs for people on welfare and improve services at city antipoverty programs.
Political education	The mayor says he wants people on welfare to get jobs and that's why he is giving this money to the sports team to build the stadium. Yet there are no job guarantees or any legal commitments to hire unemployed people on welfare or to pay living wages with benefits. Why do you think that is?
Agitation	What do you think about city money being given to sports teams and tax breaks to wealthy developers while our neighborhood schools are overcrowded and don't have enough textbooks?
Call to action	These petitions will go to the mayor, showing him that people are opposed to this funding of the stadium. It would be great if you'd sign one.
Commitment	We are having a meeting in two weeks to talk more about this issue and how it affects our community. I hope you can come.
Data collection	I'd like to write down your contact information: name, address, phone number, e-mail, and best time to reach you.

What Makes Someone "Recruited"?

You consider a person to be recruited when she or he publicly aligns as a member of your organization.

Recruitment *begins* when you get someone's name and contact information and *continues* as you move the person to take a step that your organization recognizes as indicating "I am now part of this organization." In some organizations the step is going to a meeting or participating in a collective action. In others, it is attending an orientation. In some organizations the step is signing a membership card or paying dues. Whatever the step, once the person you are recruiting takes it, she becomes part of your membership and you work to involve her, as we describe in Chapter Four.

What Are Some Additional Tools to Recruit People?

You bring people into your organization through group meetings.

CVH uses two different types of group meetings to recruit people: teach-ins and house meetings. A house meeting or teach-in provides you with a ready-made group of people. These settings allow you to spend more time with people and see how they act in a group. You explain the campaign and issue in more detail and hear more about people's thoughts and ideas. You begin the process of getting people to think about the systemic reasons for their problems. House meetings and teach-ins offer roles for members and leaders of your organization, providing excellent opportunities to develop their skills. In rural areas or in organizations where constituents are spread over a large distance, group meetings also serve as a way for organizers to meet and recruit new people. Exercise 3.3, the Community Voices Heard Community Teach-In, provides a sample teach-in curriculum. (See Chapter Seven for more information on how to conduct a house meeting.)

Tool 3.5 provides a summary of key recruitment tools.

CHALLENGES TO RECRUITMENT

"We keep interrupting people who are having dinner." This is good. You're reaching people when they are home. Ask for a specific time to return and go back at that time.

"Workplace security won't let us in." You don't ask for permission. You walk in confidently and start talking with the people you want to recruit. If someone blocks

your access, you engage the person rather than demanding your rights. For instance, you politely say why you're there and that you'd appreciate a space to talk to people on their break.

"Isn't it easier to find people through the Internet?" Web sites, e-mail, and other technology, such as text messaging, are not for recruitment. These are tools to help you mobilize people *after* you meet them, just like the telephone. You recruit people face-to-face.

"Everyone says no." Check your rap and the skills of the organizers. More likely, if everyone is saying no, the campaign may be seeking something people don't want—or something they don't want enough to fight for. Or you might be recruiting people who are not being affected by the issue. In these cases, you make changes to the campaign.

Sometimes people just won't talk with you. They may have been burned in a previous campaign that ended badly or by an organization that betrayed their trust. The community may be intimidated by someone in power, such as a landlord or employer. In these cases, you can usually find someone you can probe to assess if the campaign is possible. If you recruit the right people for the right issue with a positive, open attitude, you will get names and numbers.

ESSENTIAL ELEMENTS
FOR EFFECTIVE RECRUITMENT

☑ *Set numeric goals.* Set realistic but ambitious goals for the numbers of people you need to meet and bring into your organization.

☑ *Go out and talk with people.* Talking with hundreds of individuals face-to-face on a regular basis is the only way to build the power of ordinary people.

☑ *Get a commitment.* Getting people to commit to something you can follow up on is the key to effective recruitment.

☑ *Assess potential and get contact information.* No matter how or where you meet a new person, whether it's in the field or through a phone call at the office, the fundamental process is the same: make an assessment about her potential to get involved and get her contact information so you can follow up.

☑ *Follow the twenty-four- to forty-eight-hour rule.* Contact a person with potential within twenty-four to forty-eight hours of meeting her.

Tool 3.1
The Dos and Don'ts of Successful Recruitment

You can use the following as a handout for training people to conduct recruitment.

DO!

Do know why you are talking to this constituent. Why are you recruiting members at this site, and for what purpose?

Do use a rap. Before you go out, practice a rap. Play out different statements and questions, with someone else if possible.

Do listen. Good listening helps you to learn about the issue and make a connection with each person. Smile, make eye contact, stay cheerful.

Do agitate. Ask probing questions to elicit a person's true feelings about an issue and how deeply she cares. Look for anger, an important indicator that someone may move to action.

Do offer an immediate opportunity for action. Many people want to get involved but don't know how. Provide an opportunity to do something now.

Do be clear about collective action. Make sure a person knows you are offering an opportunity to build power, not one-on-one help with her problems.

Do get a commitment. It is harder for an individual to get out of something she commits to. If she makes a date to come to something, then all you do is follow up with a confirmation call.

Do write down contact information. Write down a name, address, phone number, and your assessment of this person's potential. Write clearly and neatly on a uniform contact sheet.

Do follow the twenty-four to forty-eight-hour follow-up rule. Good follow-up is the key to effective recruitment. Within twenty-four to forty-eight hours, make a thank you or reminder call and send a note.

Tool 3.1
The Dos and Don'ts of Successful Recruitment, Cont'd

DON'T!

Don't start with, *"Do you have a minute?"* Always begin with a confident statement: *"I'm here talking with people about . . . and I would like to know what you think."*

Don't carry too much material. Too much written information overwhelms people and is ineffective. Take only what you need. Be sure you can be physically relaxed and able to easily write on a clipboard.

Don't be a salesperson. Organizing is about relationships and working together, not selling a product. People are turned off if you sell the organization too aggressively.

Don't spend time convincing someone who isn't interested. If someone is clearly not interested, say thanks, and walk away. If she wants personal help and your organization offers referrals, give the person a phone number and move on.

Don't spend too much time with anyone. Don't stay with any one person for more than five to seven minutes. If someone seems great, make a note and follow up later!

Don't offer empty promises. Be honest. Don't tell a person that you or your organization will do something you can't do.

Tool 3.2
Point of Entry Recruitment Chart

You can use the following worksheet as a training exercise with a group or as an individual planning tool. Individually or in staff teams, it guides organizers to think about and record where, when, and how they will do recruitment. In a group training with members and staff, it enables members to contribute information about where to find other constituents and to understand the recruitment process better. Participants fill in the following information:

Tool 3.2
Point of Entry Recruitment Chart, Cont'd

Site:	One	Two	Three	Four
Where will we go?				
Who will we meet?				
How often will we go? (daily, weekly, etc.?)				
What time? (10 A.M., 3 P.M., and so on)				
How many contacts needed in that time?				
Who will go?				
What is the call to action?				
What is the commitment?				
Rap points:				
1.				
2.				
3.				
4.				
Tools we'll bring: (survey, other?)				

Tool 3.3
Tips for Assessing Interest and Potential

Look for "we" versus "me." Does she say "me" throughout the conversation, or does she say "our community," "us," "my neighbors," or "the building." Does she suggest collective solutions? Plural language communicates that she understands that the problem and the solution are bigger than her own individual condition and that she has potential to get involved.

Listen for hope. Does she say things can improve and that she wants to play a role in making that happen? If so, she could have potential.

Watch for active listening. Active listening is a very good indicator of interest. To find out if someone is participating in active listening, ask a focused, direct question and see if she responds. Does she ask about your views? Does she refer back to what you say?

Make eye contact. Look directly at the person. If he looks you in the eye, smiles, and nods, he is interested in the conversation. Don't assume that if his arms are crossed or he looks stern that he is not engaged.

Acknowledge distractions. If he is looking at something else, he might not be interested. If he does give you his contact information, he might just be distracted. You take the information and ask for a better time to come back.

Notice how the conversation ends. Once you get contact information, the end of the conversation ultimately determines how you assess a person. The following are common responses and what they generally mean:

"Put me on the mailing list." Many people say this. Without a commitment, this usually means a person won't get involved, especially not soon. Sometimes she will say "I can't get involved until a certain date, call me then." Take note of the date and contact her then.

"I'm not sure." You try to agitate someone who is hesitant and see how she responds in order to make the best assessment.

"I have my own plan." She is unlikely to get involved.

"I want to get involved." This statement, along with a commitment to do something, is the best indication that someone will get involved.

Tool 3.4
Rap Outline

You can use the following outline as an individual planning tool to prepare organizers to conduct recruitment. Participants write phrases, in their own words and voice, for each point. Ideally, they should practice the rap before using it.

Your name:

The name of the organization and why you are there talking to people:

An open question that assesses self-interest:

A follow-up question:

Organizational accomplishment:

Information about the problem—political education, agitation, proposed solution:

The call to action:

The commitment:

Name, address, phone number:

Thank you and follow up:

Quick notes and rating:

Tool 3.5
Tools for Effective Recruitment

The following table provides a summary of key recruitment tools.

Tool	Contact Type	What It Is	Purpose	Where You Do It
Collective action	Cold contacts and general members	An invitation to participate in a collective action—rally, march, accountability meeting.	Introduce people to the organization and get them involved	At a point of entry, over the phone, through a mailing
Community survey	Cold contacts	A series of questions you can ask people about an issue—a questionnaire	Identify or better understand issues and new constituents	At a point of entry, especially door-to-door
House meeting	Referrals—friends of current members	A one-hour meeting at someone's home	Bring people together to identify issues and introduce the organization	The home of a member
Teach-in	Cold or referral; people associated with a community organization	A one- or two-hour training session about policy issues	Educate people about issues, build a list of people to follow up with	A service, advocacy, religious, or educational group

Exercise 3.1
The Fundamentals of Recruitment:
Develop, Don't Destroy! Part One

You can use the following as a training exercise to review the fundamentals of recruitment. Part Two of this exercise, which reviews how to involve members, follows Chapter Four.

Scenario: Your organization wants the state legislature to adopt its plan to develop affordable housing and locally controlled stores in an up-and-coming area of your state, just outside the small city where your constituents live. At the same time, a rich developer is proposing to build luxury housing and big-box stores in the same area, with no commitment to hire locally and a weak promise of including some affordable housing units. Your organization is planning a mass meeting with Speaker Morgan, a key legislator, in three weeks. You need to sign up 150 new people for your organization in order to get enough people to the meeting and to build the campaign.

Task: Answer the following the questions:

- What do you need to know before you go out to recruit people?

- What's your point of entry—where will you go to recruit people and why?

- What are the main elements of your rap?

- What is an engagement tool you can use?

- How many days will you have to spend doing recruitment?

Exercise 3.2
The "10 in 60" Organizational Rap

(Used by permission of Community Voices Heard)

The following exercise trains people to be focused and to see how much they can say in a short time.

Time: About 45 minutes for small groups of five.

Materials: For each group, one-minute hourglass timer or other simple device that can clearly mark a minute in a way that everyone can see. Watches or clocks are not the best choice. Handout or chart with the ten questions. Paper and pens for each participant to write a "10 in 60."

Roles: Overall facilitator, timekeeper, and facilitator for each group.

Room set-up: Movable chairs or break-out rooms. If everyone will be in the same room, needs to be large enough for each group to talk without interfering with the others.

- Participants form small groups of at least three and not more than five people.

- Facilitator describes the goals: To practice being focused; to see how much can be said in a short time.

- Facilitator describes the basic exercise: Participants will say 10 things about themselves and their organization in 60 seconds.

- Facilitator posts or hands out the following topics. Based on these topics, each person takes ten minutes to write a "10 in 60."

    1. Your *name* and *role,* and the *name of the organization.*

    2. The *problem* the organization addresses.

    3. The *solution* the organization proposes.

    4. *Why* the organization addresses the problem.

    5. *Primary constituents* and *location* of the organization.

    6. Why you are *involved* in the organization.

    7. A *strategy* the organization uses.

    8. One *accomplishment* of the organization.

    9. One of the organization's greatest *challenges.*

    10. An engaging *question* to the group members who are listening.

Exercise 3.2
The "10 in 60" Organizational Rap, Cont'd

- Facilitator tells the group that everyone will take turns delivering their "10 in 60" to their small group. A timekeeper in each group keeps track of the sixty seconds for each rapper as well as the three-minute debrief following each rap. The small-group facilitator keeps the process moving and makes sure the group addresses each of the debrief questions (see below).

- Each group selects its own timekeeper and a facilitator.

- Each person delivers a "10 in 60." After each rap, the group debriefs for three minutes, using the following questions:

  - To the group: *What did you like about the "10 in 60"?*

  - To the rapper: *What was difficult for you about doing the "10 in 60"?*

  - To the group: *Did the presenter cover all ten points? Were the points logical and connected?*

  - To the rapper: *What would you do differently?*

- The groups come together to talk about what participants learned in this exercise.

Exercise 3.3
The Community Voices Heard Community Teach-In

(Used by permission of Community Voices Heard)

The following discussion and example of the community teach-ins used by Community Voices Heard (CVH) can serve as a sample teach-in curriculum. The curriculum illustrates just one way to use this tool. You can use the model for a range of purposes, including sharing specific information about a law or policy, as well as for broader political education.

Time: About one hour.

Materials: Chart paper and markers. Pledge cards, notepaper, and pens. Flyers for upcoming actions, with the name and contact information for the organization.

Exercise 3.3
The Community Voices Heard Community Teach-In, Cont'd

Roles: Facilitator.

Room set-up: Any arrangement of chairs or tables placed in a circle or half-circle if possible. Large, empty space on the wall for hanging the problem tree.

A CVH teach-in is a participatory education workshop, meaning that participants are active in learning, not just listening to a lecture and taking notes. The goals of CVH teach-ins are to recruit new CVH members and develop a network to mobilize for collective actions. Usually, a teach-in is one to two hours long. Although organizers usually facilitate, experienced CVH leaders sometimes take on key facilitation roles. CVH's first teach-ins were about welfare reform proposals in the early 1990s. Organizers went to community groups, including shelters and social service programs, and educated people on welfare about what was happening with the reform proposals. They asked what low-income people on welfare truly needed.

CVH teach-ins now include a discussion of how CVH is led by its low-income members. They also include power analysis, looking at who can make decisions about the policies being discussed and how much power these decision makers do or do not have to provide what the members of CVH want. Facilitators usually offer people a Call to Action, such as writing a letter to an elected official, and ask participants to sign a pledge card to come to a collective action.

As in any recruitment effort, facilitators write down names and contact information and note if participants want to get involved with CVH. Organizers often build relationships with staff at the sites where they hold teach-ins to invite participants to collective actions.

The following shows a sample format for a basic one-hour teach-in designed to introduce people to CVH and get their contact information.

Introduction: What is CVH?

- On chart paper the facilitator writes five things about CVH, noting these are based on core organizational principles developed through an extensive board, staff, and member planning process. Examples: led by low-income people; fights to change public policies that its members choose to focus on; has a core value of respecting all people equally.

- Facilitator notes that, at CVH, the focus is on "member led" and "wins." ("Member led" especially gets people interested and builds credibility.)

Exercise 3.3
The Community Voices Heard Community Teach-In, Cont'd

Exercise: Problem Tree

- On extra large chart paper, facilitator posts a simple outline of a tree.

- Leaves signify individual problems: Let's hear what your "leaves" are. Call them out as "I" statements ("I need a job").

- Trunk and branches are immediate causes: Let's hear your "trunks" and "branches." Call them out as "We" statements or problems ("We need more decent jobs in this city").

- Roots are "big picture" causes: Let's hear what's at the root of these problems. Example: "The government is not for the people" or "racism." (Some will be "isms," but not all.)

- Facilitator reviews the components of the tree and guides participants back over the process—beginning with root causes to "we" problems and then to "I" problems. Talks about how CVH focuses on the "we" while keeping in mind the "I" and "roots." Gives examples of the tools CVH uses, such as member-led campaigns and creative actions.

Our Campaign: What Are We Trying to Win?

- The facilitator reviews the goals and objectives of the current campaign, including providing political education on the political or economic source of the problem. The facilitator asks about participants' experiences related to the issue.

- Participants engage in a discussion about the issue and the campaign.

- The facilitator offers a Call to Action, such as signing postcards to elected officials.

Closing: Collect Contact Information

- The facilitator distributes pledge cards where participants can commit to come to a future meeting or action and fill out their names, contact information, and interests. (The facilitator can later call and follow up. If she is building for an action, she may also call the person who invited her to do the teach-in and ask for help mobilizing people.)

Involving Members in Building Their Own Organization

OK, I'M READY—LET'S GET TO WORK

Walking along 116th Street to the Community Voices Heard (CVH) office, Lorena looks up and sees the words on the green awning, "CVH—Fighting for Families, Fighting for Ourselves." She likes that. As she guides her son up the long flight of stairs, she can hear voices coming from the second floor. Renee comes over and says, "I'm so glad you're here!" and then helps Lorena settle her son in a room with another child and a babysitter. Her son picks out a toy and seems at ease. Lorena sits at a table with about a dozen people. Around her, phones are ringing, a copy machine is humming, and people are walking around, talking in English and in Spanish. On long lists posted on the faded blue walls surrounding the meeting table people's names handwritten in marker indicate sign-ups to do things.

Lorena accepts a slice of pizza and writes her name and contact information on a sign-up sheet that people are passing around. A woman who introduces herself as a CVH member starts the meeting and asks everyone to introduce themselves. Everyone seems to be in the same situation as Lorena, trying to get by. The woman talks about the ways that they want to improve the way the welfare system works and how they are fighting to get the city and state to create paid jobs, with education and training, for welfare recipients. She talks about the progress they made in getting people to support their bill, and Lorena recognizes the name of her local city council person. She thinks to herself that this group must be important if they got him to do something. At one point, the woman running the meeting says they need to pick three people to go into a meeting with the mayor's staff while a larger group of people will hold a press conference outside. She asks Lorena what she thinks. Lorena comments, but feels a little uncomfortable.

61

By the end of the meeting, Lorena has not learned anything to help her with her case, but she feels less alone than when her caseworker screamed at her just a few days before. She doesn't want to bring her son out at night, and she isn't sure if she likes talking in meetings, but when Renee tells her afterward that it would be great if she'd come to the press conference, Lorena says she will try. Something is happening here, and Lorena wants to be a part of it.

What Is Member Involvement and Why Is It Important?

Member involvement is an evolutionary process in which organizers develop the participation and ownership of constituents. Members do the work of a community power-building organization, so their participation is essential. When members are deeply involved, they come to feel their own power and start to demystify the concept of community engagement.

Organizers move members to take on tasks, make collective decisions, and turn out for actions and organizational activities.

Involvement does not just happen. You think strategically about how to use each member's abilities to greatest effect and how to motivate each of them to act—and to continue to act.

What Are the Different Types of Members We Need?

You need an active membership with people taking different roles.

General members. General members come out to mass actions, large annual membership meetings, and sometimes planning meetings. You contact general members at least every three to six months. You test ideas for new campaigns with them and ask them to help make decisions about potential campaigns.

Working members. These members actively build the campaigns and the organization. You ask them to come to the office, make phone calls, do mailings, talk to their neighbors, and attend organizing meetings. They often exercise some leadership by making decisions on campaigns and actions. The more working members you have, the greater the potential you have for a large turnout.

Leaders. Leaders are core organizational decision makers. They also bring their own networks of people into the organization. You engage them in deep strategy planning for campaigns and for the organization. Leaders represent the organization to powerholders—decision makers such as elected officials or CEOs—who are the targets of your campaigns. Leaders negotiate on behalf of the organization. They are accountable to the rest of the membership.

"Paper" members. These less active members have taken a formal step to connect with your organization. For instance, they may have signed a membership card or even paid dues, but they do not come out to actions or meetings. You may send them newsletters or call to try to move them to come to mass actions, but you do not invest a lot of time into involving them. The power they lend to the organization is that they build your numbers. Labor unions, community organizing networks, elected officials, and the media all respond to these numbers.

How Do We Involve Members in Our Organization?

Simply put, you get members to do things!

As we described in Chapter Three, you start the process of involvement in the first five minutes of meeting a potential member, when you get him or her to respond to a call to action or to sign a pledge card. Some specific ways to continue the process include involving members in the following ways:

Making decisions. When members come to meetings and make decisions about the direction of campaigns and the organization, they develop ownership of its well-being. Decision making is a source of real power. We include sample sessions throughout this book that show how to engage members in decision making.

Mobilizing other members. Members need to send out mailings, call people to turn out for actions, or knock on doors in their neighborhoods to recruit new members. Tool 4.1 shows how to conduct a phone bank evening for getting people out to an action. Exercise 4.1 provides a half-day training on how to do door-knocking for recruitment.

Coming out to actions. Members get most energized when they engage in action that moves the campaign forward. You mobilize them to meet with elected officials, march, form pickets, and participate in a wide range of other exciting actions, which we describe in Chapter Twelve.

Taking on roles. You increase the likelihood that someone will get involved if you give him a role at the meeting or action you invite him to attend. Ask him to greet people at the door, make food, chair the session, or present testimony. You make sure you include time to prep or train him. Tool 4.2 provides guidelines for helping a member prepare testimony.

Paying dues. When members pay dues, they expect the organization to deliver. Dues help pay salaries, rent, and other costs. When members invest their own money in the organization, it becomes their organization.

Meeting membership criteria. Many organizations establish some kind of criteria members need to meet. For example, every member must recruit ten more members or hold one house meeting a year or participate in a leadership training course.

Raising money. When members not only give their own money but also fundraise for the organization, it shows their commitment in a very deep way. Fundraising includes seeking in-kind donations, such as computers or skills. For more on fundraising, see Resource B.

Engaging in public relationships for power. People get involved and stay involved with an organization when they have positive relationships within it. You foster these relationships, for example, when you place new people in working groups with other members, then call to find out how it's going, or when you have members meet with new people before or after meetings. Activities such as general membership meetings, holiday parties, and movie nights also help develop these relationships. The relationship between an organizer and a member can be very strong. Keep in mind that although you truly try to get to know each member, you have a public relationship based in your work together, not a private one.

Getting Members Involved: Two Stories

After 9/11, Community Voices Heard (CVH) participates in a campaign to create an emergency jobs program to put some of the tens of thousands of people who lost their jobs in a range of industries back to work. Organizers recruit temporary workers and WEP workers in city agencies and begin by getting people to come out for a specific action—a town hall meeting and march to the agency responsible for redeveloping Lower Manhattan. The march will take place during the lunch hour so workers can attend. They will demand a meeting with the head of the agency.

Organizers focus on points of entry downtown and use a rap and materials aimed at turning people out for the action. Many people are not sure if they can come, but most agree to sign pledge cards supporting the campaign as well as postcards demanding that the agency allocate funding for an emergency jobs pro-

---

gram—an initial form of involvement. Organizers call those who agree to come to the action to remind and move them to come out. Some do so, deepening their involvement.

One WEP worker, Paula, tells the organizer she is angry about being forced to work for no pay and that the agency distributing the 9/11 funds is giving the jobs to the friends of its own board members. Since her shift starts at lunch time, Paula cannot march. Assessing that from her anger and interest Paula wants to do something now, the organizer asks if she will recruit the other workers in her office. A Spanish-speaker, Paula can bring in workers with whom the organizer, who speaks only English, has trouble communicating. Paula readily agrees. She collects pledges, postcards, and names and phone numbers from the other workers and gives them to the organizer. The organizer then asks a Spanish-speaking organizer to call these workers and get them to come to the action. The organizer suggests to Paula that the workers will be more likely to come to the action if Paula walks them to the building lobby. Paula arrives early on the day of the action and does this. She sees her involvement come full circle, as she connects the workers directly with the organizer.

Although this story shows how organizers got several different people involved in different ways within two weeks of meeting an organizer—signing pledges, coming out to an action, recruiting others to participate—another campaign offers an example of member involvement that took several months of follow-up on the part of the organizer.

In the Transitional Jobs Campaign, an organizer meets Sam coming out of a welfare office one day. She engages him using her rap and gets his contact information. She calls Sam the next day to get him to come to the next planning meeting. He says he will try, but winds up not being able to make it. Based on his interest and good conversations with Sam, the organizer decides to keep calling him. After four months of intermittent conversations and attempts to move him to action, Sam finally comes to an organizing meeting at CVH.

At the meeting, members identify a small number of people to testify to the mayor at a public hearing to urge him to sign the Transitional Jobs Bill the city council has passed. Although the mayor vows to veto the bill, members want to offer the best possible testimonies to try to sway him at the last minute.

Sam tells the other members that he is a veteran, disabled in the Vietnam War. In addition, he worked for twenty-five years before he was fired from his job due to downsizing. He then had to turn to welfare. Based on this compelling story, members decide to ask Sam to testify, even though this is only his first meeting. The organizer preps Sam and Sam gives an excellent testimony. Although he does not move the mayor to sign the bill, Sam feels his power. The organizer immediately offers Sam additional opportunities for action. Sam becomes very involved and two years after attending his first meeting, he becomes a CVH board member.

How Do We Identify Where Members Fit in the Organization?

You call, visit, and use every interaction to assess where a member is in relation to the organization and the campaign.

The following are assessment tools:

Assessment phone calls. In assessment calls, you determine how comfortable people are in their roles, see how they are doing, and assess if they want to step up their involvement or step back. These calls last about fifteen or twenty minutes, so in an evening you can speak with between nine and twelve people. Assessment calls help you to update your lists: you remove people who are no longer interested.

Home visits. You do home visits with people you have identified as "1s" during recruitment. You also do them with people with whom you want to solidify a connection because they have come out to some meetings or actions. You arrange the visit in advance or you drop by, and you have a goal for the visit, such as getting people to come out to an important action or to host a house meeting. Home visits generally last fifteen to twenty minutes, and you have to account for the time to travel from one home to another. The face-to-face contact helps you assess body language and build deeper relationships. People are more honest in person. They consider a home visit to be a more serious gesture on the part of an organization, increasing the likelihood they will get involved.

Organizing meetings. Organizing meetings offer ideal ways to assess how people can be involved. You ask them directly to do things, both in preparation for meetings and at meetings, such as making reminder calls, photocopying, and facilitating. At the end of meetings, you review the tasks that members need to complete before the next meeting or action so that people can volunteer right there.

One-on-one meetings. Through one-on-one meetings with individuals, you identify people who are ready to take on more significant leadership roles. A one-on-one is a specific type of home visit, which lasts thirty to forty minutes. We describe how to do one-on-ones in Chapter Five.

Database. Especially in larger organizations, you may not notice everyone who comes out. A database that tracks involvement can be useful for identifying these people. You can produce lists of members who have come to many events, people who have been consistent over a number of years, or people who have taken on some ongoing activities, and follow up with them.

How Do We Increase the Involvement of Members?

You are strategic and deliberate about moving people from one type of membership to another in order to increase and deepen their involvement.

You make choices about which member is right for which role, who is likely to follow through on her promises, who needs to be challenged, who requires training, and who is not going to progress. You engage people in conversations and use intuitive skills to determine when they are ready to get more involved. You observe, watching to see which members are taking on tasks and responsibilities. Once you determine that someone is ready to do more, especially to move into a leadership role, you ask him to do so and support him as we describe in Chapter Five.

Moving a Member to Be More Deeply Involved

After meeting an organizer at her welfare office, Lorena becomes a general member with Community Voices Heard. For years she occasionally participates in strategy meetings, but CVH can best count on her to attend major actions. When Paul decides to leave his job as executive director of CVH, leaders consider whom to approach to serve on the board and shepherd this transition. Zelda, a long-time leader and board co-chair, has seen Lorena participate in meetings and actions. She is impressed with Lorena's judgment and commitment. Zelda and Paul agree that they will each approach Lorena and ask her to consider joining the board.

They meet with Lorena and talk with her about the time commitment as well as what she can bring to the organization in this new, deeper role. After several discussions and time to think about it, Lorena agrees to join the board. Lorena did not just decide one day, "I want to be on the board." Instead, a leader and staff person guide her movement from one type of membership to another.

You assess members every chance you get. Opportunities include when a member drops by, when you are driving to a meeting together, or when you are waiting for a meeting to start. A good organizer juggles a lot of relationships and responsibilities, making it important to form assessments whenever the opportunity arises.

The biggest mistake is not to try to move someone. If you think someone is ready, ask. Member involvement requires being direct with people, honest with yourself about their potential, and both challenging and flexible as you support them. Exercise 4.2 provides a scenario and questions for getting people to think about opportunities and ways to engage new and existing members more deeply.

How Do We Make Sure Members Do What They Commit to Do?

The following describes how you can increase the likelihood that someone will follow through when she agrees to do something.

1. Before the Activity

   - *Make confirmation calls.* In these calls you remind the person about what she said she would do and when she needs to do it. You make three confirmation calls. The first call is the day after she makes the commitment; the second is halfway between the time she made the commitment and the activity; the third is the night before the activity. Leaving a phone message is not enough—you need to speak with her directly.

   - *Offer support, training, and technical assistance.* Here is an example of offering your support in a confirmation call: "Hello, Lorena—this is Renee from CVH. You agreed to pull together people from your tenants association on the 28th to talk about CVH and our campaign for jobs. Are we still on for that meeting? Yes? Great! Is there anything you need to do to prepare for that meeting? Do you need me to come and go over an agenda with you? Help you doorknock? No? Great. Well, I'll call you a week before the meeting to check in with you again, get a list of people who will be coming, and to go over the agenda. Talk to you then!"

   - *Send a reminder by snail or electronic mail.* A written reminder firms up commitment, particularly for group activities such as a mailing or phone bank. You include the date, time, place, activity, information about food or child care, a thank you, and a contact number.

- *Make a final reminder call.* Even if you have to keep trying on the day of the activity, make that final live call to turn the person out!

2. During the Activity

- *Make the member feel comfortable.* Tell her how this activity is critical for building the organization and winning the campaign. Offer training and support.

- *Observe the activity.* Make sure the member is being effective.

- *Thank the member.* Acknowledge and thank the member publicly and get her to commit to doing something again, right there.

3. After the Activity

- *Ask how it went.* Ask the member how the activity went and how she feels she performed.

- *Ask if she has questions.* Answer any questions she has and assess if she will continue to work on the campaign and in what capacity.

Is Paying People a Good Way to Get Them Involved?

No. We strongly believe that paying people to engage in power-building activities with an organization does not ultimately build power.

You could never raise enough money to pay for all the work required for building an effective organization. If you pay members, you also risk seeming to reward certain people and not others, which creates instability. In addition, you foster an atmosphere of serving and helping individual members rather than building their collective power. If members get paid, they are accountable to whoever is signing their check, not to other members, which limits their ownership in the organization. In years of organizing with no-income people, CVH has not paid constituents. Power is the payoff.

Sometimes, particularly with constituents who are unemployed, those who put in a lot of time—and feel they are doing the same tasks as a paid organizer—want to get a stipend or move into a paid position. Some just feel entitled, others would really like to become organizers. In this case, you can try the following:

- *Provide material support.* Provide food and child care at meetings and work activities and arrange for transportation if needed, so that coming out does not cost people money.

- *Clearly explain how organizations build power and why you don't pay members.* It is easier to enforce the organization's position when everyone knows, up front, what it is and why it exists.

- *Don't be afraid to lose a member.* If someone disagrees and wants to stop participating, you let them. You are not resentful, just clear. Never make a special arrangement for one member. It will definitely cause problems with others in the future.

- *Provide opportunities for members who want to organize or work in a social change organization as a career.* Establish clear policies and programs for training people within the organization and for considering members who want to apply for job openings along with other qualified candidates. Refer members to look outside the organization as well, to training programs, entry-level jobs, and short-term jobs that will expose them to the career of organizing or administering an organization.

Organizations do sometimes hire people from the membership and some cultivate members to learn to take on staff roles. This can work out well, but when a member goes on staff, his or her role changes. For example, after about three years of being a member and serving as board chair of CVH, our colleague, Gail, accepted a job on staff. She went from representing the organization in public to developing other people to do so. She no longer had oversight of the organization's director, but instead was accountable to him and to other staff. This is not always an easy transition. Although hiring members can seem like the perfect solution to staffing needs and to address the interests of members, it requires clear guidelines and oversight to make it work.

CHALLENGES
TO MEMBER INVOLVEMENT

"Our lists are overwhelming." Although this is a good problem to have and the result of effective recruitment, a huge list can overwhelm an organizer and lead to losing potential members. You can address this challenge by doing the most effective assessment possible during recruitment, so that the numbers of people with whom you have to follow up are real and you do not waste time calling people who are not interested. You also train members to assist with assessment phone calls, calling the "2s" or those you have not contacted recently. You clean up your list by choosing an upcoming event or conducting a survey that provides

an opportunity to call through the entire list and see who is still interested. Finally, you invest in people who say they are going to come out, and do, not those who keep promising but don't show up. Try a "three strike" rule. If someone says he is going to come and three times in a row does not, put him lower on your priority list or take him off.

"Our members are burned out." Although burnout is normal, you don't want to lose people. Be sure to acknowledge and recognize members for their work by holding volunteer and member parties that recognize people's contributions and help energize them. Similarly, CVH recognizes those members who put in a lot of time by prioritizing them to participate in exciting movement-building activities in other states and countries. Having social time, such as sharing dinner before or after a volunteer shift, is another way to build solidarity and a sense of mutual support. In addition, taking on varied roles and tasks energizes people. Directly ask members if they would like to do something new or different and what kind of training or support would they need to do it. Make sure that you are not over-asking the same members to do things. It is easy to go to those who do the job well. You don't have to prep them, you know they will show up. Check in periodically so you know these members aren't feeling burned out.

ESSENTIAL ELEMENTS
FOR INVOLVING MEMBERS

☑ *Get them to do things.* Moving people to action early and often is the best way to get them involved and keep them involved.

☑ *Engage them in making decisions.* People feel that the organization is their own when they come to meetings not just to talk, but to make decisions that move the work forward.

☑ *Call, visit, and continually assess how and when to involve them.* Staying in contact with people and directly asking what they can and want to do builds their involvement.

☑ *Make at least three live confirmation or reminder calls.* When a member agrees to do something, you call at least three times to directly speak with her, remind her, and offer your support.

☑ *Acknowledge and thank them.* When you acknowledge and thank members publicly for the work they do, it builds your relationship with them and encourages them to do more.

Tool 4.1
Phone Bank Evening

Phone banks are a great way to get members involved in doing something that really helps the organization. In the example here of an agenda for such an evening, the purpose of the phone bank is to get people to an action.

Sample Phone Bank Training and Phone Bank Evening

6:00   Callers arrive and help themselves to refreshments.

6:15–6:45   **Training**

Introductions: Everyone says their name, how they are involved with the organization, why they came out tonight.

Goals of the evening: On chart paper, facilitator writes out how many phone calls we need to make tonight, how many hours we have, how many calls a person can make per hour, and our goals for contacts and yeses. This is important for evaluation and a sense of accomplishment at the end of the evening.

Review phone bank materials: List of people to call, instructions, sign-up sheets, rap.

Review campaign material: Campaign one-pager, action flyer and location, goals of action.

Review "Five Things to Remember for Callers"

Five Things to Remember for Callers

1. Figure on five minutes per contact (actual live person).

2. Remember to get a firm commitment, Yes or No.

3. Convey urgency—Why this action is important.

4. Smile! Your face shows over the phone. Grumpies and tired people convey a grumpy, lazy organization.

5. Keep good records.

Rap: Review rap and answer questions.

Role play: Two people role play a couple of phone calls. They do different types of calls, both good and bad, and ask the volunteers what they think: what worked, what did not?

Break up into pairs and role-play: Organizer or phone bank leader listens to pairs and gives positive feedback.

Tool 4.1
Phone Bank Evening, Cont'd

6:45   Start phone calling. Organizer or phone bank leader checks in with volunteers constantly, listens to their rap, and gives positive reinforcement.

7:15   Organizer goes around and engages volunteers in brief conversations to get to know them.

7:30   Light food available. People take a short break.

8:00–9:00 One-hour push—best time to call!

9:00–9:15 Convene for evaluation. Did we reach our goals? What were people's experiences?

Tool 4.2
Preparing Testimony

When members who are affected by an issue speak truth to power in public hearings, as media spokespersons or while trying to engage other groups in a campaign, their words can move people to change their opinions and to act. Providing testimony also builds member skills and buy-in. You can use the following guidelines and the sample that follows when helping a member to prepare testimony.

Guidelines for Helping a Member Prepare Testimony

Don't write a person's testimony, provide an outline (see the example below). An outline lets the member develop her own ideas about what she wants to say. Include the length of time the person has to speak.

Clearly identify and state the goals for the speaker. Each speaking engagement should have a goal and a clear ask. Help the member to be as specific and targeted as possible and to develop testimony that fits the audience.

Connect personal experience to systemic problems and structural solutions. Stay away from horror stories or sob stories. Help the member connect personal experience to a larger community problem and state a solution to address it. Include facts.

Always include a call to action or a demand. Testimonies can make people uncomfortable or can make them more open to listen. Either reaction can get them to move on an issue. The member uses the opportunity to directly call for what the organization wants the listeners to do.

Practice, practice, practice. The member should write and practice her testimony so she does not read it from a piece of paper. It is best to practice at home in front of a mirror or with other members who can give feedback.

Sample Outline for Testimony

Introduction, hello, and thanks

My name is Helen Smith and I want to thank you for coming out to hear about the important issue I want to talk about today.

Credentials and organizational background

I have been a member of _____ for five years. In that time _____ has accomplished these three things: _____, _____, _____.

Why you are here

We are here today to . . . (present testimony, educate the congregation)

Personal experience

I have lived in this community for twenty-five years and remember what a wonderful place it was. Like many of you, I came here to raise a healthy family in a beautiful setting. But that is the past. Today members of my family are sick, and one family friend has passed away from a rare form of cancer. The woods that once were a paradise have become a toxic waste dump.

Connection to the larger problem

I am not alone. Hundreds of other families in this community have family members who are seriously ill as a result of this dumping.

State the problem

Corporation X has been dumping toxics into the river for two years and the state EPA has not done anything to address it. The company's behavior has caused increased incidences of cancer in our communities and many of our children are at risk of severe illnesses.

State the demand

We are asking that the Chair of the Assembly Health Committee hold hearings on Earth Day to find out why the state EPA is not doing its job to protect our community from corporate polluters.

Ask for action

Please call and write the chair of the committee to demand that he hold public hearings to find out why the EPA is doing nothing and the pollution is allowed to continue.

Express thanks

Thank you for hearing me today and allowing me to represent the hundreds of other families affected by this issue.

Exercise 4.1
Doorknocking Training

The following is a training you can use to train members and volunteers to knock on doors for base-building or other organizing purposes. It includes seventy-five minutes of training, two hours in the field, and fifteen minutes to debrief. Because people go out into the field together to accomplish a goal, this kind of training is also a form of collective action. It is a group of people acting together to inform and move community members and to build your power. You evaluate it like an action, have goals like an action, and make it a group activity like an action.

Materials:

For training: Handout—basics of a rap; easel, pad, and markers.

For field work: Rap sheet, pledge or membership cards, surveys or petitions, pens, clipboards (with a rap sheet and staff phone number taped to the back!), maps or directions to the places where the outreach is taking place, organizational information or action information, organizational buttons or hats.

Room set-up: Chairs in a circle. Have drinks and snacks available when people return from the field.

Preparation for the Training

- Scout the area where people will doorknock—if people have a bad experience, they will not come back.

- Map out the quickest ways to get people from the training site to the field.

- Use the training as a membership development opportunity. Identify members to take on the role of team captain, gathering their group and working with people out in the field. Set the teams in advance and prep the team captain.

- Make sure all materials are ready to go.

The Training

- Facilitator leads a round of introductions, in which people say their names, how they got involved, and why they are there. (5 minutes)

- An organizer or leader presents the basics of the campaign, also written on chart paper, and explains the goals for the doorknocking, including numeric goals for the number of contacts for the day and what this will mean to the campaign. For example, if the goal is for each person to get six commits an hour and twenty people are going out, they will get 240 commits in a two-hour canvass. Also review any other relevant goals, such as getting people to sign a pledge to vote. (10 minutes)

- Facilitator reviews the following basics and writes them on a chart: (10 minutes)

  ○ Spend only about five minutes with each person. You need to talk to lots of people and get their names and numbers.

  ○ Doorknocking without getting names and numbers is not useful and does not build your lists. Get contact information and write it down yourself.

  ○ You do not need to know every situation and policy in order to doorknock. If you don't know an answer, tell the person to call or stop by the office.

- Facilitator asks what concerns and fears participants have about talking to people at the doors. She writes down and addresses each fear, giving the overall message that most people will be receptive at the doors. The following are the fears you might hear: (20 minutes)

Doorknocking Fears

Fear	Facilitator Response
People will say no.	Give the number (or percentage) of people who usually respond yes at the doors. Also tell them that if someone says no, say thank you and move on.
Generally afraid of knocking on a stranger's door.	Have a leader prepped who has done this before and talk about the experience. Frame this as an opportunity to build trust with people and build community.
Don't want to bother people.	If people are busy, say that you are sorry for bothering them but you only need them for five minutes. If they are too busy to spend five minutes, ask them when you can come back.
Afraid for own safety.	Explain that the people we work with live in these areas as well and that fear is something that is real—but in reality the threat is not. Tell people we are also going out in teams that will keep an eye out for one another.

Exercise 4.1
Doorknocking Training, Cont'd

- The message of the facilitator and leaders is that most people will be receptive at the doors.

- Facilitator distributes the rap and reviews the basic components of a rap and the recruitment tools (contact sheet, clipboard, and other tools). Participants read the rap to themselves and ask clarifying questions. (10 minutes)

- Rap practice: In the larger group or in pairs if the group is large, participants practice giving the rap and using the tools. Leaders or staff work with people to make sure they are using the rap and the tools effectively. After people have a chance to practice, ask for volunteers to model for the group and use the volunteer modeling to reinforce what people need to do. (15 minutes)

- Participants ask brief clarifying questions and form teams. Facilitator reminds people that they will be out for two hours, then come back to debrief as a group. (5 minutes)

- When people return, they debrief for fifteen or twenty minutes. As they come in, the facilitator has them mark down their numbers on a big sheet and write a word or two about their experience. As people grab something to eat, the facilitator talks to them about the experience. When everyone has returned, the facilitator brings the group together and evaluates with the following questions: What were our goals? Did we reach them? Why or why not? What did you learn?

- Close by asking people what they liked about the experience and relate it back to the fears they discussed earlier. Facilitator asks who was the best person each doorknocker met and why.

Things to Remember:
- People will find reasons not to go or delay hitting the streets. Get people moving.

- When calling people for a reminder, tell them not to bring things they need to carry, such as a large purse, bag, or backpack. They should come light on their feet and wearing comfortable shoes.

- Depending on what you are signing people up to do, in addition to practicing the sign-up, have a large copy of a filled-out form for participants to view. Reinforce that the doorknockers fill out the information themselves.

Exercise 4.2
Develop, Don't Destroy! Part Two

You can use the following as a training exercise to review the fundamentals of involving members. For Part One of this exercise on how to recruit members, see Chapter Three.

Scenario: Your organization wants the state legislature to adopt its plan to develop affordable housing and locally controlled stores in an up-and-coming area of your state, just outside the small city where your constituents live. At the same time, a rich developer is proposing to build luxury housing and big-box stores in the same area, with no commitment to hire locally and a weak promise of including some affordable housing units. Your organization is planning a mass meeting with Speaker Morgan, a key legislator, next week. Over the last two weeks, you met your goal of signing up 150 new people who say they will come and you have followed up with a phone call to each of them to confirm.

Task: Answer the following questions:

- How can you use this as an opportunity to assess if some existing, working members of your organization can get more involved?

- What kinds of roles can you give these members to increase their involvement and work this new list?

- What can you do with two or three of the "1s" you're recruiting to involve them as deeply as possible?

Developing Leaders from All Walks of Life

During the Community Voices Heard (CVH) campaign for transitional jobs, labor union members and officials need to see and hear the workers out front in order to support the campaign. Organizers set out to find rank-and-file WEP workers who will not just be involved, but who have the potential to be leaders. They train WEP workers to run meetings, lead actions, give testimony about the impact of WEP, and engage in discussions with elected officials, labor leaders, and the press. Training takes place at organizing committee meetings, in Saturday sessions, in one-on-one meetings in people's homes, and right before actions. Trainings include a combination of readings about political ideology, discussions, presentations, and role plays covering the potential scenarios leaders can expect to face in action. Organizers also bring potential leaders together for a three-day leadership-training weekend that focuses on team building, skills development, and critical thinking. This new base of leaders helps win the campaign. (For more information about WEP, workfare, and the CVH jobs campaign, see "The Story of Community Voices Heard," p. xxxi.)

What Is Leadership Development and Why Is It Important?

Leadership development is a strategic and deliberate effort to educate and train members to strengthen their skills so they can apply these skills to campaigns and the work of the organization. Leadership development gives members the knowledge and skills to run their own organizations effectively, hold staff accountable, and manage campaigns that address the issues they care about.

Leadership development significantly deepens the involvement of members. It is one of an organizer's primary responsibilities. You develop a broad base of leaders to ensure that decision making, knowledge, and responsibility do not become concentrated in one or two people. Because organizations across communities develop leaders, it builds the base for democratic movements for social change.

How Do We Develop Leaders?

You develop leaders following a specific process.

The following describes the process of leadership development by following the development of Angela, who became a core leader at CVH. We begin with Angela's recruitment (see Chapter Three for how to recruit people) and move through her initial involvement (see Chapter Four for involving members) in order to show why and how the organizer identifies her as a potential leader and starts to guide her development. Although we number the steps in sequence, you sometimes do them in a different order depending on the situation.

Step One. Angela gets recruited. While Angela is cooking dinner one night, Jackson, a CVH organizer who is out surveying people to identify new issues for CVH to work on, knocks on her door. He explains that he is talking to everyone in her housing project to learn about community issues.

Even though Angela is busy making dinner, she is excited that someone actually wants to know what she thinks about problems in the community, and invites him in. She turns off the flame and says her husband and daughter can eat a few minutes later. She sits at the table with Jackson. She tells him she has been active in the past and that preserving public housing is her biggest concern. Jackson completes the survey with her and takes down her contact information. He hands her a flyer for the next CVH meeting and says, "I'll call to remind you about the meeting, I hope you can come!" When he leaves the apartment, Jackson is enthusiastic about Angela. After his two weeks of doorknocking, someone finally stands out. Angela has a political analysis of her problems, she's been involved in collective action, and she wants to do something. He writes a "1" next to her name—very likely to get involved—and makes a note to call her the next day.

When Jackson calls Angela the next day, she says she can't make it to the next meeting. He tells her that CVH members are still considering whether or not to work on public housing, but she can get involved right away with other activities. She says she might. He thanks her for her time and says he will call her soon.

Jackson calls Angela a week later to invite her to attend an accountability session with the newly elected city council person from her district. CVH wants the council person to commit to working with CVH on a range of community issues. (For more about accountability sessions see Chapter Twelve.)

Step Two. Angela moves to action. Jackson calls Angela two more times and sends Angela two mailings about the accountability session. She is interested that this group is trying so hard to get her to come to something. She also wants to hear what the new city council person has to say. Even though she is very busy, she decides to go to the action.

Step Three. Angela enters into a relationship with the organization. At the accountability session, Angela talks with Jackson as the meeting room fills with people. He introduces her to Susan, a board member and core leader at CVH, who asks Angela about what concerns her in the community and urges her to get involved "because we need a lot of people to get those in power to give us what we want!" At the end of the accountability session, a CVH member whom Angela recognizes from the neighborhood gets up and invites everyone to come to the next CVH meeting to plan a Lobby Day in Albany to fight the governor's proposed budget cuts. When Angela goes over to this member after the meeting to say hello, he urges her to come to the meeting and she agrees.

Angela goes to the meeting and participates in brainstorming about places to do more recruitment in her neighborhood. At the end of the meeting, Jackson asks if he can come by Angela's house again to talk a little longer. Angela says yes and they figure out a time and date.

Step Four. Angela moves toward leadership. When Jackson visits Angela, she enjoys answering his questions about her interests and her family. She then tells him that she had to go on welfare when she lost her long-time job. She was only on welfare for a short time before getting a job at a social service organization. She tells him that when welfare reform was happening a few years earlier, she tried to get some of the women using services where she worked to sign letters to the governor, but no one really cared. This turned her off from trying to do anything. Instead, she got more involved in her church and focused on her family. She is now looking for another job after being laid off.

In response to Jackson's questions about what she cares about, Angela says that she is most concerned about losing her housing because of the rumors she's heard that the city is getting ready to sell her development. She also says that she'd like to improve her housing project. After about a half-hour, Jackson thanks her and says he will contact her soon. He was focused and intentional about guiding this one-on-one meeting, and now has a better sense of Angela's leadership potential.

Step Five. Angela participates in a leadership training. Although Angela has come to some activities and met with Jackson one-on-one, she has not gotten more involved. She is focused on getting a job. She is most concerned about housing, and CVH has not yet chosen an issue for its next campaign. One day, Jackson stops by her apartment to invite her to the Saturday School—a training day to educate new members about power, self-interest, and the approach CVH uses for organizing, and a way for organizers to initiate the process of leadership development with specific individuals. Angela says she will come if she has time. When Jackson calls to confirm that she'll come, she's swayed by his persistence and decides to go.

At the training, Angela sits in a group with others to discuss when they felt powerful in their lives. One woman describes leading a meeting with a city council person, another talks about addressing a group of union leaders. In the afternoon, Angela plays the role of a state senator who refuses to fund a new after-school program. Angela learns that the Saturday School is just one kind of training that happens at CVH. She also learns that CVH requires a lot of people to make a decision to take on a campaign, which is why it has not started to work on public housing. Another member of CVH agitates her a bit, saying that if she wants to see the campaign get started, she has to do something to help make it happen. Later, on her way home, she reflects on the training. She learned about how to move a person with power, but also about the people in the group. She feels connected to something and thinks that her participation could help move CVH to work on public housing. She wants to do something to help not only herself and her family, but her friends and neighbors as well. Angela decides to work with Jackson a few hours a week to survey people in her building about their concerns.

Step Six. Angela participates in decision making. Four weeks later, Angela joins about forty other CVH members to analyze data from CVH's recent surveys and meetings to decide what the organization will work on for its next campaign.

Participants in the meeting vote on six possible areas to focus on. The top three are public housing, public education, and gentrification. Although all of these are important, they learn that in a few weeks the city's housing commissioner will be deciding whether to approve a proposal to raise public housing fees. The group decides to engage in a campaign to stop the fee increases. Although Angela has given her opinion at CVH meetings before and even helped make some basic decisions for actions or events, she has entered a deeper level of decision making at this meeting on something she really cares about.

Step Seven. Angela takes responsibility. At a follow-up meeting, Jackson and some core leaders ask Angela to take on a leadership role. She agrees to facilitate an important meeting at CVH the following week at which members will decide on what kind of action to run at the housing commissioner's office and begin to plan it out.

Step Eight. Angela receives leadership prep. Angela meets Jackson at her house for a leadership prep session. They develop an agenda for the planning meeting. They come up with a list of ideas for what the action at the commissioner's office might be that she will use to start the meeting off. They review who will be at the planning meeting, what she can expect, and some tips for facilitation.

Step Nine. Angela assumes a leadership role and puts the training into practice. The action planning meeting is packed because of the proposed fee increases. Angela starts off the meeting well, but it soon gets chaotic. People have a wide range of opinions about what to do at the action. A couple of new people keep interrupting, saying, "We should get Oprah to cover the issue on one of her shows." The senior organizer needs to help facilitate the decision making. The group settles down and decides to hold a picket and deliver a letter to the commissioner asking to meet with him. Angela closes the meeting on her own.

Step Ten. Angela reflects and evaluates. After the meeting, Angela, Jackson, and the senior organizer evaluate. At first, they review what happened and how Angela feels about it. Although Angela feels generally good about how the meeting went, she is concerned about the portion of the meeting that she could not manage alone. As they move into evaluating what worked, what did not, and what she could have done differently, she learns how to deflect people who want to sidetrack decision making and how to neutralize people who come with their own agendas. She tells the organizers, "I learned, but I am exhausted." She says, half-jokingly, "I never want to do that again!" However, she commits to playing a leadership role in the action and to working with Jackson to improve her facilitation skills.

Step Eleven. Angela participates in direct action, confronting and challenging people with power. On the day of the action at the agency, Angela is a core decision maker and a press spokesperson. She works along with Jackson, whom she first met only four months ago, and another long-time community member. She makes critical decisions about how close to the entrance to do the picket and negotiates with the police to get there. She makes sure the group is chanting while a television crew is filming the action. Toward the end of the action she talks to a reporter, making sure that the demand to eliminate the housing fee increase is the key message she delivers.

Angela is a developing as a leader. After this action, Jackson talks more with her about the skills she wants to develop and the role she wants to play. He writes up a leadership plan for Angela, like the one in Tool 5.1 at the end of the chapter, so he can be strategic about developing her.

How Do We Make Leadership Development an Ongoing Process?

After the campaign that initially engages a leader is over, in addition to involving her in additional campaigns that interest her, you use a range of organizational functions to keep that leader engaged and to deepen her skills. These methods include leadership retreats, strategic planning sessions, and joining the board or one of its committees.

For example, engaging Angela again and again allows her to get more comfortable with different leadership roles, learn how to deal with real-life scenarios, and improve her ability to think on her feet. The more Angela does, the stronger she becomes as a leader. She also experiences the following characteristics of leadership that CVH builds into the organization:

- *Sharing power.* Leaders rotate through different roles. They practice working in teams. They step aside at times or challenge themselves to take on new forms of leadership so that emerging leaders can play key roles. Power-sharing also prevents individual leaders from taking on too much and burning out. This understanding begins for Angela when she realizes that she cannot do everything at the action. While she is talking to the press she has to allow other leaders to make decisions about when and how to end the action.
- *Remaining accountable.* Leaders understand that they represent a larger group of members, not just their own interests. The organization builds accountability into its structure. For instance, leaders formally report back to one another about their activities on behalf of the organization. When Angela recruits tenants in her building to join CVH, she has to report back to them about the campaign's progress and bring their ideas back to the organizing meetings she attends.
- *Getting recognition.* When the organization publicly recognizes the contributions and accomplishments of leaders, it affirms that they make a difference and that the organization values them. Recognition happens at organizing meetings, public actions, meetings with partners, and other venues. Displaying pictures in

the office from actions and celebrations also recognizes people. It helps everyone who comes there to know the story of the organization and the people who make it work. At the end of the action at the commissioner's office, members cheer when Susan, the CVH board member Angela met at the first CVH activity she attended, publicly thanks her for her work on the action. The next day, Angela feels even more acknowledged when a neighbor comes over with the newspaper in which Angela is quoted. The neighbor reads Angela's quotes out loud and hugs her, thanking her for fighting for all of the residents of the building.

Why Do We Develop Many Leaders?

More leaders mean more power.

The power of having many leaders shows up in many forms:

- *You have more members.* Because each leader has a following or is building one, the more leaders you have, the more members they can each mobilize.

- *Powerholders perceive you as strong.* People in power assume that leaders have followers. When powerholders interact with many different leaders from your organization, they know that the organization must have a strong base.

- *The work gets done.* An effective organizer builds a team of people with a variety of strengths and skills to meet a range of responsibilities.

- *The work is sustainable.* Success does not rely on one person. If a key person leaves or pulls back on her or his involvement, the work continues because other leaders can take on the roles and responsibilities that person fulfilled.

- *There is increased accountability.* With a team of leaders who are trained and experienced in collective action and decision making, the organization can make democratic decisions and people can hold one another accountable.

- *The group's roots are in the community.* When an organization has more leaders based in the community, it more fully represents the community's experiences and ideas. Also, like a tree with deep roots in the ground, an organization with a broad base of leaders is able to withstand harsh conditions.

- *New opportunities arise.* When you have a broad base of leaders, some leaders can engage in activities outside of the core campaign, such as movement-building or alliance-building. With a lot of leaders available for these activities, you don't burn out the leaders who are working intensively to win the campaign.

- *There is a stronger movement for justice.* The strength of the movement becomes especially clear when a crisis ignites a community. For example, in 2006, when the U.S. Congress was considering changes in immigration policy, community-based leaders from throughout the country organized a series of walkouts, marches, and other actions in support of specific pieces of legislation that would support immigrants. These actions involved millions of immigrants as well as supporters of fair immigration policy. Their precision, cohesion, and sheer numbers showed the depth and breadth of both highly experienced and emerging leadership in immigrant communities. Communities that had built their leadership and their power over many years were able to mobilize when they needed to.

What Do We Look for in a Leader?

You look for potential—basic skills you can develop as well as the ability to get involved in collective action and bring others into the campaign or organization.

You can develop anyone with potential who is directly affected by social and political issues and who is ready to step up and act. Leaders are the people in your base. They are taxi drivers, janitors, lawyers, homemakers, teachers, unemployed people, and office assistants. Leaders are ordinary people of all races, ages, economic, and ethnic backgrounds. These are the qualities you look for in a potential leader:

- *A following.* One important sign of leadership potential is a following. A following is an active base of people that a leader can turn out. Leaders either have a following, or they have the appetite and ability to develop one.

The Appetite to Build a Following

Gail Aska, the cofounder of Community Voices Heard, was a leader not only because of her sharp political analysis, excellent public speaking, and agitation skills, but also because she had a following. She brought a base of women on welfare to the initial organizing project. These women came from her network of friends and her colleagues at various community organizations. She continued to build her following by engaging women she met at CVH actions and meetings. She talked with individual women about their lives, their frustrations, their children, and their dreams. She offered herself as an inspiration—someone who was speaking out to gain respect for women on welfare. She did not do this for her own personal ambitions but to have relationships with a base of women she could motivate to build the organization.

• *Different styles.* Not all leaders are alike. Although some people have more than one type of trait in their leadership style, you rarely find everything in one person. The best teams of leaders include a range of interests and strengths. See Tool 5.2, Qualities of Leaders in Community Organizing, for an outline of some of the traits, contributions, and key words related to these styles. Tool 5.3, Leadership Styles, and Exercise 5.1, What's My Leadership Style? provide more resources for thinking about and balancing the styles of individuals on a team. The following chart provides examples of the kinds of activities people with different styles of leadership like.

Leadership Style	Leader Likes To . . .
The doer	Get things done. Move to action.
The thinker	Analyze every option.
The visionary	See how things should ideally be.
The caretaker	Make sure everyone is included and respected.

• *A range of skills.* Within a range of styles, leaders have a variety of skills. These include skills that move the work of the organization forward, such as conducting recruitment and researching issues. They also include skills that help constituents run their own campaigns and the organization itself. These are skills such as facilitating meetings, planning and strategizing about campaigns, talking with reporters and interviewers, confronting and negotiating with powerholders, reviewing budgets, and raising money.

When assessing whether or not you will invest in developing someone as a leader, you look not just at how a person experiences the problem, but also at how she or he views the issue—the solution to the problem that the organization can focus on in a campaign. For instance, Angela and other CVH members are experiencing a problem—their housing is unstable. They decide to create a campaign around a solution that will help address this problem—stop the fee increases. (For more on the difference between problems and issues, see Chapter Seven.)

You can use the following questions as guidelines for thinking critically about a person's potential:

Assessment Guidelines: Is This Person a Potential Leader?

- What is this person's worldview? How sharp is her political analysis of the problem?
- How clearly does she understand and support our strategy (base-building and community organizing)?
- Does the issue affect her personally? What is her self-interest?
- What are her skills and abilities? What can she do, what does she want to do better?
- What networks and connections does she have?
- How effectively can she talk about the issue?
- Does she see beyond her own immediate circumstance?
- How much time and desire to work collectively on the issue does she have?
- How well does she listen? How will she work with others?
- What sustains her? How can she keep going for the long haul?

What Are Our Tools for Identifying Potential Leaders?

One-on-one meetings and observation of members in real-life scenarios are the two best ways to identify leaders.

One-on-ones are "agendaless" meetings in which an organizer or trained leader explores the kinds of questions we list above. In addition, watching how members participate in meetings and actions and how they respond to real-life situations helps you see who acts as a leader and who you can follow up with one-on-one for further assessment.

In a one-on-one meeting, you sit down with a person for thirty to forty-five minutes to build a stronger relationship and to assess her or his leadership potential. You meet one-on-one with a person who has done something that makes you want to invest more time in her. She may have played an important role at an action, come out for actions consistently, or told you about her network of people in the community.

In a one-on-one meeting, you listen much more than you talk. This meeting is not to chat or for you to solve an individual's problem. You are not there to sell your organization or convince someone to join you. You are there to learn and to build a relationship. As with a rap, you are very focused in a one-on-one meeting. Doing effective one-on-ones is among the true arts of organizing. The following scenario illustrates a conversation for setting up a one-on-one meeting.

Organizer: Angela, I'm really glad you came out to the accountability session. I'm wondering if I can come by your house again to talk with you, maybe for about a half-hour this time.

Angela: I have to go out and meet with a man about a job. I can stop by your office afterwards.

Organizer: I'd rather come to you. How about the next day? *(Best to meet in her home. You get to know her better. Also, meeting her in the office feels like "intake.")*

Angela: I'm usually home in the mornings. You can just stop by.

Organizer: Why don't we say Wednesday morning, at 10 A.M. at your house. *(Specific about the date, time, and place.)*

Angela: OK. What do you want to meet about?

Organizer: I want to learn more about what you've done before in the community and what you think needs to happen to improve things. *(Be clear that this meeting is about getting to know her and what she thinks, not about getting her to do something.)*

How Do We Conduct a One-on-One Meeting?

Use the following guidelines and sample statements to structure a one-on-one meeting:

State very clearly why you are there. Within the first few minutes, after exchanging greetings, let her know the purpose of the meeting: "I'm here to listen to you. I want to find out more about what's important to you and learn what you think should be done to improve the community."

Note what you see in her home. Are there family members around or pictures on the walls? Does it seem she has a support system to support her organizing? Is she financially comfortable? Struggling? What else do you notice?

Ask open-ended questions that require more than a yes or no answer. Listen for lead-ins to her story. Explore different areas, touching on her personal experience, what she knows about her community, and her view of the world: "Whose responsibility do you think it is to prevent your housing project from being sold?" "What do other people in your building have to say?" "Who do you think would want to buy out the projects?"

Use her comments to learn, not to offer advice. Build the conversation off of what she raises, by asking questions related to what she says: "Why do people join the tenants' association?"

Share some common ground. Sharing during a one-on-one helps build a relationship. The organizer or leader conducting the meeting primarily listens, but does talk about 25 percent of the time. During this time, you share some of your views about the world and the issues at hand as well as how the organization approaches community problems. You can talk about why you got involved in organizing. Just remember, you share your perspective to build a relationship, not to tell someone what or how to think: "I took a job with CVH because my mother needed welfare to raise us. Growing up, I saw that rich people are organized. I believe we have to be organized too, and the city can do more to help regular people raise their families instead of giving all the tax breaks to rich people."

Identify self-interest. What does this person get excited about? Ask follow-up questions to confirm your hunches: "It seems like you're most concerned about your housing. What other things are you concerned about, besides the rumors you've heard that it's for sale?"

Assess if her views are generally similar to the vision of your organization. Ask a question that will get at whether she believes in the more just society your organization envisions: "Why do you think the city shouldn't sell off the housing projects?"

Clarify her understanding of collective action. Does she embrace a long-term struggle, or is she looking for immediate answers? Does she respond to the idea of joining with others, or does she think individuals should take care of their own problems? "What do you think is the best way for our community to make sure we preserve public housing and improve the projects?"

Introduce agitation into the conversation to find out how she responds to uncomfortable situations. If a person shuts down or gets too angry in the face of agitation, it gives you information about her potential to handle situations that are difficult or require negotiation. Agitation helps to get people thinking about the world, their situation, and their role in the situation: "In Chicago, when the city came in with a plan to sell public housing, people were outraged. They called their representatives and the press, and basically went down to City Hall and demanded the mayor stop his plan. But in this community, there has been hardly a whimper. Excuse me for saying this, but if the mayor knows he can get away with it, he can just start the bidding for public housing."

Find out her networks and other leadership roles. Begin to develop a picture of the people she knows: "What other organizations do you work with? Are you active in the PTA or at your church? Let's talk about other friends or family members you can bring with you to the next meeting."

State the follow-up. Be clear about what will happen next: "I'll call you to remind you about the next meeting."

Solidify the commitment. Suggest a role she can take at the next opportunity: "Maybe at the next meeting you can greet new people at the door."

Always thank the person for her time! Tell her you will be in contact.

After the conversation, write down a few points such as the following:

- Three things that impressed me about this person.

- What motivates this person?

- Do I think this person will really get involved with our organization? Why?

When doing one-on-ones, keep the following points in mind:

Avoid taking notes during the conversation. You need to be listening and making eye contact, not writing.

Let the responses guide the conversation. Don't work off a checklist of questions. Just make sure you hit all the points you want to somewhere during the conversation.

Start doing one-on-ones with a more experienced organizer. Especially in the beginning, debrief with someone so that you can improve your skills.

What If We Do Not Have Time to Do One-on-Ones or We Have Too Many People to Meet With?

You do "mini" one-on-ones during times such as travel and when people are engaged in volunteer activities like mailings and phone-banking. You ask the same kinds of questions as in a one-on-one meeting and practice careful listening.

We strongly encourage you to invest some time into doing one-on-ones out of the office and in people's homes. But when you are short on time and cannot do one-on-ones with everyone, you incorporate one-on-one questions and listening into your regular interactions with members. If you are taking a train to a meeting with a member, you don't pull out the newspaper or your laptop. You ask about her story. Use all opportunities to engage people in conversations about their interests, networks, experience of collective action, and their skills.

How Many People Do We Need to Contact to Find One Leader?

You cast a net that is wide enough to catch people with a range of skills and interests as well as those people who may not strike you as potential leaders right away.

It is hard to quantify exactly how many people you need to recruit to develop leaders. It depends on factors such as the constituency, the issue, and how you recruit people. In any case, the more people you talk with, the more likely you are to find a leader to develop. Here are how many contacts we find it typically takes to bring in a leader:

- Four hundred contacts for whom you have a name, address, and phone number
- One hundred who express an interest
- Thirty who attend a meeting or action
- Ten who come back again and continue in some form with the organization
- Between one and five who engage in a leadership-development activity through attending a training or taking on a key role in an action
- One or two who continue to develop as leaders

These numbers may look daunting, but you get hundreds of contacts by continually doing recruitment at good points of entry and involving people in the organization in meaningful ways. This is really the work of effective base-building.

Can an Organizer Be a Leader?

The role of an organizer is different and distinct from that of a leader. Organizers are not the leaders of the organization. Instead, they exercise leadership.

For example, organizers step up to take on job responsibilities or gain expertise on the issues to help guide member decision making. We describe the distinctions among the roles of organizers, members, and leaders throughout this book, but the following are some essential differences:

Salaries. Assuming that you have some resources, organizers get paid by the organization, leaders do not. (See Chapter Four for why we strongly recommend against paying stipends to members and leaders to ensure their involvement.) If you do hire a leader, her role changes. Her job is to develop a broad base of members to become leaders, not to function as a leader herself.

Decision making. As we describe earlier in this chapter, decision making is a primary building block of developing leadership. Organizers help guide decision making, which is a critical and skilled role, but they do not make organizational decisions.

Representation. Leaders publicly represent the organization at actions and with the press. We recommend that organizers do not speak at public actions at all—and that they speak to the press on background only. This press policy can sometimes be particularly challenging. Reporters want to talk with someone now, and if you can't reach a leader, you can lose the chance to have your organization in the press. In our experience, the trade-off is worth it to ensure community empowerment.

It can be easier to have staff work the press, but it keeps you from the important work of training a broad base of people to do so. We have seen public attention intoxicate even the most committed staff, and before you know it, member voices are reduced to providing anecdotes while the organizer takes the mic.

It is absolutely essential to prioritize having leaders out front as spokespersons. In our own work, there have been clear boundaries between organizer and leader roles, supported by organizational policy. However, others handle these distinctions somewhat differently. For example, at the Ohio Valley Environmental Coalition, an organization in West Virginia that fights mining companies, codirector Janet Keating says that, although they bring the media to talk to people in the coalfields, and members of the organization are the speakers at public actions most of the time, she and other staff also take on these roles at times. According to Janet, a fear-driven "culture of silence" has existed for a long time in their community. "People have not spoken out here," she says. "There is so much poverty, and the only good jobs are through these corporations that are doing the destruction." Janet, who was born in the community where she now organizes, sees part of her staff role as providing an example of "a regular person who challenges authority."

In addition, organizers often exercise leadership in coalitions and other types of partnerships, attending meetings, strategizing, and engaging in negotiation with staff of other organizations while remaining accountable to their own leaders and members.

What Is Leadership Training?

Leadership training is the tool you use to make sure that people have the knowledge and skills to be effective in their leadership roles. Leadership training is different from leadership development, which is happening all the time.

Most training in community power-building organizations is popular education. This is a form of adult education that incorporates what people already know from their direct experiences. Popular education engages participants in hands-on activities, not lectures. For example, to learn how to identify community issues, participants might spend a day out in the community talking with people. Popular education also includes small-group discussions and other formats that invite everyone to participate. It emphasizes reflection as an essential learning tool. So, for example, after going out into the community to talk with people, participants reflect on and talk about what happened, what they thought of the experience, and how it made them feel.

The following are different types of trainings you do with members as well as with leaders. Since members and leaders often participate together, we include the full range of trainings here. Although staff generally design and facilitate trainings, leaders can learn to do so as well. See Resource D for training tips. In addition, there are training exercises throughout this book that you can use or adapt to your needs.

Training in organizational ideology and culture. Ideology training includes an overview of the strategies the organization uses to create social change as well as the mission and values that drive the organization. Topics include an overview of the organization's history, how organizing is different from social service delivery, and an introduction to power.

Skills building. Skills training includes two areas: doing the work of organizing and developing leadership skills. Topics for doing the work of organizing include door knocking, recruitment, phone calls, and mobilization tasks. Leadership skills topics include how to facilitate meetings, how to conduct power analyses, and how to negotiate with powerholders. Skills trainings help ensure that constituents can truly lead the organization.

Political education. Political education includes two main areas: issues and education about social movements and history. In issue training, you broaden people's knowledge about the issue—why it is necessary to pursue, whom it affects, and who makes decisions related to it. With this knowledge, members and leaders can make the best decisions about campaigns.

You offer a clear ideological bent. You seek to change or broaden people's understanding, make connections between their local issue and larger social issues, and see where their struggles fit into a historical perspective. Sample topics include the history of the squatters movement worldwide, the impact of the U.S. Civil Rights Movement, how the U.S. Electoral College disempowers voters, key changes in public health policy since the AIDS epidemic began, and an overview of capitalism.

Civics education. In these trainings you review how government operates, the lawmaking and policymaking process, and how decisions are made. From this base of information, members can look at policy and analyze it. They can discuss policy with reporters and in meetings with powerholders. Topics include how a bill becomes a law, the process for zoning and redevelopment, and who represents us.

In addition to building knowledge and skills, each of these kinds of trainings increases the capacity and confidence of leaders and helps them to think critically and engage in vibrant, challenging discussions.

Leadership "prep." Leadership preparation, or "prep," is training that you target to a specific role that a leader takes on. When a leader agrees, for instance, to facilitate a planning meeting, to give testimony at a public hearing, or to engage in a legislative meeting with a public official, the organizer walks the leader through the role and provides background, including the goal of the activity and the main players. The organizer preps all the leaders who will have roles in the activity. Prep includes reviewing what the leaders will do or say, considering the what ifs, and role-playing their parts. Leadership prep provides the opportunity for leaders to do the best possible job and to learn from their actions. They have the chance to make sure they understand the dimensions of the issue, how it plays out in this activity, and other things that do not get covered in more general trainings.

Before a large action, it is best to have some one-on-one leadership prep, then small-group prep, and a final larger-group prep before the activity. Depending on the activity, if these sessions are not possible due to time considerations, you meet together one-on-one. Keep in mind, however, that group prep helps people practice and evaluate how they work as a team. The following offers examples of when to do leadership prep sessions; see Exercise 5.2 for a sample leadership prep session.

Sample Progression of When to Do Leadership Prep Sessions

1. Organizing committee decides to do an action.

   Assigns ten leadership roles.

   Quick meeting of leaders to set date of first prep and final prep meeting.

   Organizer schedules individual prep meetings.

2. Individual prep meetings.

3. First group prep meeting.

4. Final pre-action group prep meeting (on-site run-through, day of the action).

5. Leadership group evaluation.

CHALLENGES
TO LEADERSHIP DEVELOPMENT

"We don't seem to have the time to develop leaders and do new recruitment." If you just develop leaders, you will not bring in enough members to win campaigns. If you focus only on recruiting new members, you will not have leaders to run the organization. Finding the time to prep leaders before an action can be an especially difficult challenge, as you juggle that activity with turnout, getting press coverage, and other demands. If you struggle with this situation, you are not alone, but you can't let any of the pieces slide. You can try to address the challenge of managing a range of base-building activities by training members to help with the phone calls and mailings needed to get people to meetings and actions and by scheduling your base-building activities. For example, during CVH's Transitional Jobs Campaign, organizers recruited WEP workers in the morning and early afternoons. They did one-on-ones and leadership prep in the late afternoons when the workers were just getting off work and going home. They did more formalized group trainings in the evenings and on weekends when workers could come to the office. Finally, between campaigns or when recruitment is slow, prioritize one-on-one leadership development.

"We seem to focus on people who don't work out." Identifying leaders takes practice and experience. In addition to learning how to recognize a leader, you can eas-

ily spend time developing someone you like who really does not have the potential. Sometimes you have a dearth of leadership, so you focus on someone who is not ready. You can address this challenge by being aware of it and by challenging yourself to be as objective as possible. Evaluating with others, such as senior staff or experienced members, can help.

"Everyone who works hard in our organization thinks they're leaders." Although people might be doing important work, they may or may not be leaders. For example, if a member who comes to every meeting is great at motivational speaking but cannot effectively engage with other members to make decisions, it may not be appropriate to develop her as a leader or place her in leadership situations. You can try to challenge her one-on-one on her weaknesses to see if she is willing to address them. You can also try directing her to other kinds of responsibilities. In the end, you don't focus on developing people who are not leaders.

"We develop people, then they leave." Many organizations, particularly those that are organizing fluid and transient communities such as parents, unemployed people, or students, experience this challenge. Sometimes the reason is positive: a homeless person gets a home or a student graduates and goes off to college. Sometimes it is not positive: a person loses his job and has to move to get a new one, or you call and the number is disconnected. The best way to address leadership turnover is simply to develop a lot of leaders who are doing different kinds of things. When someone leaves you lose "a" leader, not "our" leader, and there is someone available to take on his or her role.

"Our leaders act like a clique." Especially in organizations that value leaders highly, those who become leaders may acquire a sense of privilege, which is a natural result of the time and energy they put in, but is not good for sustaining a collective spirit. Cliques can form naturally among founders and people who have worked intensively together for a long time. Sometimes the feeling of there being a clique is less about wanting to keep people out and more about functioning within an unwritten culture that new people can find hard to enter or understand. To address the problem of cliques, honor and reward leadership openly, honestly, and with clear reasons. Be clear that people receive benefits, such as opportunities to travel on behalf of the organization, based not on who they are but on what they have done. Make sure that all leaders and members know how people can enter leadership positions, such as board positions or public roles in actions. Remain

accountable, going back to the membership periodically to report on who is taking on which roles and why. It also helps to write out your operating principles so that everyone can see and understand them. Engage experienced leaders in orienting new leaders to their roles.

ESSENTIAL ELEMENTS
FOR EFFECTIVE LEADERSHIP DEVELOPMENT

☑ *Be proactive.* A good organizer is always looking for people who have the appetite and the potential to be leaders and including clear objectives in her or his work plan for developing individual leaders.

☑ *Do one-on-ones.* Take the time to meet with people to assess their potential.

☑ *Provide training and opportunities to apply it.* You not only train people in workshops, you get them to exercise leadership in ways that they can evaluate and learn from. When considering any organizational activity, you ask "How will this develop leaders?" You train leaders in formal workshops, prep sessions, in "quick and dirty" trainings built into actions and meetings, and by evaluating with them after activities.

☑ *Develop different types of leaders.* Look for a range of people who are willing to step up, work with others, and be accountable for their actions.

☑ *Understand your role.* The job of an organizer is different from that of a leader. Do not blur the boundaries of your role or your responsibilities.

Tool 5.1
Leadership Development Plan Template

You can use the following as a sample for developing leadership plans for individuals.

Name:

Entry—how she became involved in the organization:

Issues or campaign she wants to work on:

What is her leadership style?

What are her strengths and weaknesses? How do we build on her strengths and address her weaknesses?

What would challenge and stretch her?

One-on-one meeting—date held or scheduled:

Self-interest:

Skills:

Motivation:

What she likes to do:

Current membership roles or leadership tasks:

Leadership roles goals:

What does she need to achieve these goals (use the following worksheet):

Meeting Leadership Development Needs: Sample

Member name: Maria Storrs

Past membership activity: Participated in eight phone-banking evenings

Leadership Opportunity	Training Needs	How We Give It to Her	When	Who
Phone Bank Coordinator	Phone Bank Coordinator Training; Database Training	Individual training followed by staff leading phone bank with her two nights	One week before next action January 10th	Jackson (organizer)
Meeting Facilitator	Facilitator Training & Public Speaking	Prioritize inviting her to next leadership school training.	Next leadership school is in February.	Henry (lead organizer who runs leadership schools)

Tool 5.1
Leadership Development Plan Template, Cont'd

Meeting Leadership Development Needs: Worksheet

Member name:

Past membership activity:

Leadership Opportunity	Trainings Needs	How We Give It to Her	When	Who

Tool 5.2
Qualities of Leaders in Community Organizing

You can use the following handout as part of a leadership training session. To use this in an exercise, for example, you could ask participants to read the handout, either out loud or to themselves, and circle something—for instance, what is most surprising to them or perhaps what they believe best describes them. They then discuss what they circled with the person sitting next to them, then come together and discuss as a group. It can also be useful to ask participants to add qualities to the list—based on their own experiences—in both categories.

Tool 5.2
Qualities of Leaders in Community Organizing, Cont'd

Leaders are people who:

- *Deliver.* If a leader promises to do something, she or he does it.

- *Have a following (or want to build one).* Leaders know other people in the community who share their concerns. Leaders identify other people who can be brought into the project and welcome new people readily.

- *Are accountable.* Others in the organization or community care about what a leader is saying or doing on their behalf. Leaders check in with the people they represent.

- *Listen.* Leaders have their ear to the ground and take the time to ask other people what they need and what they think.

- *Motivate others.* Leaders bring out the best in other people.

- *Get respect and give respect.* Other people listen to leaders and experience them as trusted colleagues.

- *Rise to the occasion.* In a crisis, others can count on leaders to respond.

- *Are angry.* Leaders are comfortable expressing their dissatisfaction with oppressive people and institutions and are ready to direct their anger at doing something productive.

- *Are hopeful.* Leaders believe that change is possible and that they have a role in creating their own future.

- *Understand self-interest.* Leaders know what's important to them and what they want to get from building the organization. Leaders believe that working with others is how to get what they want.

- *Want to build collective power.* Leaders know that building collective power is the way to create long-term solutions to social problems.

- *Have a sense of humor.* Leaders understand that humor sustains communities and individuals and prevents bitterness and burnout. They may not be comedians or great joke-tellers, but they are able to find the humor in both the good and not-so-good aspects of everyday life.

A leader is not necessarily:

- The loudest person in the group.

- The person who speaks the most.

- The one with the most money or education.

Tool 5.3
Leadership Styles

You can use this handout together with Exercise 5.1 to guide staff and leaders to reflect on how they contribute to the whole—as a member of a leadership team, an active leader in a campaign, or in their role in the organization. We suggest Exercise 5.1 as a sample of how you can use the outline of each style, and the figure presented here, "The Style Wheel," to have a discussion to achieve your purpose.

Leadership Styles

Style	Contributes	Key Words	Traits Include
Visionary	Goal setting	Dreamer. Lofty. Creative.	• Able to dream and think big. • Can describe and bring to life a picture of the world they want to see. • Can become so wrapped up in the big picture, never figure out how to get there. • Others can see them as being unrealistic.
Thinker	Research and strategy	Educated (or self-educated). Grounded. Analytical.	• Able to engage in deep analysis. • Enjoy research, reading, and reflection. • Can get stuck in analysis and be resistant to action. • Others can see them as being inflexible.
Doer	Action	Hands-on. Fun. Confrontational.	• Able to think on their feet and move quickly. • Enjoy challenging others and doing things. • Can get so focused on doing that can act just for the fun of it, or can move ahead without others. • Others can see them as being insensitive and uncaring.
Caretaker	Process	Teacher. Selfless. Warm.	• Able to share knowledge and information. • Enjoy nurturing others and making sure everyone is participating and feeling respected. • Can believe they have all the knowledge; don't like when others confront or challenge them. • Others can see them as being condescending.

Tool 5.3
Leadership Styles, Cont'd

The Leadership Style Wheel: Who Else Do We Need?

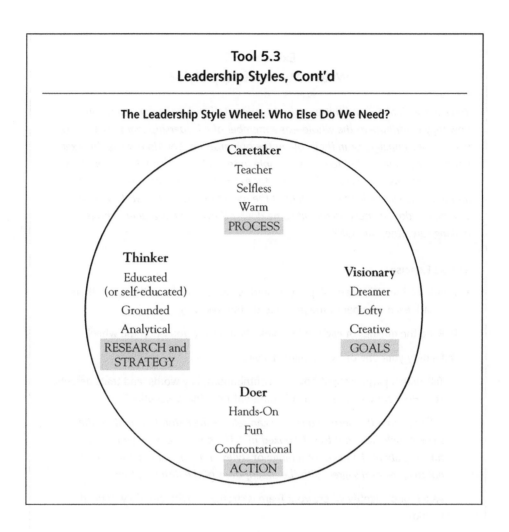

Caretaker
Teacher
Selfless
Warm
PROCESS

Thinker
Educated
(or self-educated)
Grounded
Analytical
RESEARCH and
STRATEGY

Visionary
Dreamer
Lofty
Creative
GOALS

Doer
Hands-On
Fun
Confrontational
ACTION

Exercise 5.1
What's My Leadership Style?

You can use Tool 5.3 and this exercise to guide staff and leaders to reflect on how they contribute to the whole—as a member of a leadership team, as an active leader in a campaign, or in their role in the organization. You do not use this exercise to box people in, but to engage people in self-reflection and discussion. You can also use this exercise in other ways; for example, to evaluate the strengths and weaknesses of a leadership team. If the team members see that they are all visionaries, do they need to recruit some doers? If everyone is a doer, who is making sure others are OK?

Sample Exercise

- Hand out Tool 5.3, Leadership Styles, and review the grid and the figure there. Then ask each member of the group to do the following:

  ○ Read the outlines of each style. Think about where you fit on the wheel.

  ○ Identify your one or two dominant styles.

  ○ Talk with a partner about how the contributions, key words, and traits describe you. How are you possibly a little different from this description?

    Talking about this second question can relieve the natural inclination that some people have not to get "boxed in." The goal here is to get people thinking about the need for a range of styles on their team or committee, not to agree or disagree with the descriptions of the different traits.

  ○ As a group, identify where your team is strongest. Who else do you need to add?

Exercise 5.2
Sample Leadership Prep Session

You can use the following as a guideline for planning a leadership prep session. You can use this guideline for both group and individual prep sessions.

5:30–6:00   **Gather.**

6:00–6:10:   **Introductions.** Leaders say their names, their roles in the organization, and their roles in the activity.

6:10–6:20   **Goal review.** Organizer reviews the goal of the activity: Is it to educate legislators at a hearing about a proposal or an issue, to move a specific legislator to support a piece of legislation, or to plan an action?

6:20–6:30   **Lay out and clarify roles and responsibilities.** Leaders review the different roles that need to be filled and who will do what. They explain what each role requires and the purpose of the role (example: introduce a public official, lead go-arounds in an organizing meeting).

6:30–6:45   **Develop and review speaking pieces.** Each member develops and reviews sample talking points or questions that will prepare him or her to speak.

6:45–7:15   **Role play.** Leaders test their skills, practice what they are going to do, and see how the group works as a team. Later, they will be able to say what worked, what needs improvement, and what problems they encountered.

7:15–7:45   **What ifs.** The organizer and leaders brainstorm everything that could happen and what the group will do in each instance.

7:45–8:00   **Questions.** The leaders raise questions as well as concerns. Sometimes people need to raise things they haven't thought of before that they recognize as they get closer to actually playing a critical role in a meeting or action.

8:00–8:15   **Meeting evaluation and close.** The leaders evaluate this session and identify when and where they will evaluate the activity for which they just prepared.

chapter
SIX

Uploading Technology

**WHO WE NEED, WHY WE NEED THEM,
AND HOW WE GET THEM**

The Community Voices Heard (CVH) lead organizer is meeting with Jackson and Renee to identify potential leaders to invite to an issue-identification meeting. The lead organizer lays out what they should search for when they conduct queries on the database: "We want to find out the problems people are having with child care. Let's to do an initial search of people who have come to three or more actions this year and are currently in WEP and have children." (For more on the Work Experience Program [WEP] and CVH, see "The Story of Community Voices Heard," p. xxxi). Renee asks if all welfare recipients should come. "Only if they have ever done WEP or are in WEP," the lead organizer says. "This is a workfare and childcare issue ID meeting, and we should only have people in WEP identifying the issues at this point." Jackson comments that he meets a lot of good people at WEP sites who have been organizing meetings, getting pledge and action cards signed, and with whom he has had good phone conversations, but they have never come out to an action. The three discuss the pros and cons of including people who are doing things at their sites but have not come out to actions. The lead organizer asks if they have been making notes in the database on who these people are. Both Renee and Jackson have been doing so in the memo box on each person's file. "OK," the lead organizer says, "include them in the search, as well as anyone you have done a one-on-one with, if you think they are good." The two organizers go back to their computers and in twenty-five minutes return with the total number of people they could invite to the meeting—486 meet the criteria. They all agree it's a good number to start with, and Jackson goes off to print out the labels for a mailing that will go out later that day.

What Is Technology and Why Is It Important?

Technology is an instrument, or set of instruments, you use to do activities more effectively and efficiently. Technology expands the capacity of your organization and your ability to be more effective.

When you use it strategically, technology can help you engage more people, do more research, and reach more allies, supporters, and elected officials. Technology is an important base-building tool. (In this chapter, we assume you have some basic knowledge of technology terms.)

How Have Organizations Used Technology?

Organizations have used every new tool that draws people in.

With the invention of the printing press, people could, for the first time, print documents for distribution. Telephones enabled people to contact others without going to their doors. Photocopying machines allowed people to print flyers and information cheaply. The Internet has helped people to distribute and access information instantaneously and on demand.

However, each change of technology was useful to organizers only when it was either cheap enough or in wide enough use that they could use it to reach allies and potential members. So, for example, even though the Internet is in wide use today, in our experience it is not the most effective way to reach very-low-income people on a regular basis, since many cannot afford to have computers in their homes. In addition, once a communication tool becomes an effective way to reach people, a variety of interests, from mass marketers to a range of activists, use the technology, inundating people until they no longer pay attention it.

"Internet organizing" has arisen in recent years, with activist hubs such as MoveOn.org targeting the middle class. This organizing strategy is clearly different from the method of organizing we cover in this book. In the approach we describe here, any technology-based method of communication is simply a way to enhance the ability to reach people, but it cannot replace the power of face-to-face contact.

How Can Technology Improve the Capacity of Our Organization?

Technology improves your capacity to target your communication, organize and present information, and conduct research.

The following are some essential ways that technology helps organizations to build power and the tools appropriate for each objective. More on each of the essential tools we introduce here follows later in this chapter.

Targeting communication. Technology increases your ability to contact more people more strategically, using the following methods:

- *Database.* A database is a software program that keeps track of information about people. With it you can record a person's contact information, what they have come out for, and what they are interested in. An easy-to-use database that is set up to meet your needs helps you to be more targeted when you mobilize members or when you contact donors, allies, and other supporters. Within minutes, you can identify the people who have participated in your organization's activities over the last year. Or you can contact people for Saturday actions whose database file notes them as having Saturday availability. In another situation, if a reporter calls to talk to someone who is a low-wage worker, you can find someone who fits that description because you have noted job status and media skills in the database. When the reporter calls, you search the database for a member who is in a low-wage job and who is trained in media skills. Rather than going through a whole list of people who may or may not be able to do the task, you contact the best person immediately. You can use the technology assessment that we describe later in this chapter to help decide what kind of database will meet your needs.

- *Internet connection.* A reliable Internet connection allows you to access the Internet for research and e-mail. For organizations whose members are spread out geographically, the Internet offers ways to communicate and share information. With a networked system and a common domain name, staff and leaders can have their own e-mail accounts (jenny@neighborsunited.org).

- *Web page.* A Web page geared to a target audience, with a well-thought-out promotion plan, helps to get information out quickly to people interested in learning more about your organization, including the media, volunteers, job applicants, and potential members.

- *E-mail.* An e-mail list gets information out to many people at once. An e-mail listserv facilitates communication among people interested in an issue or among allies in a campaign.

- *Shared calendars.* A calendar that everyone on a computer network can access helps people both within and external to the organization schedule and notify each other about meetings and events more efficiently.

Organizing information. Organizations need to catalogue and organize a great deal of information about members, donors, and funders as well as organizational information such as reports, research, flyers, and sign-in sheets from meetings.

Technology makes this material readily available. In addition to organizing information in a database as we note earlier, we recommend that you establish a computer network with a centralized file server. A file server is a computer on your network that you use to store and access files. Each computer in the network can access these files. A networked set of computers saves time. It allows information, such as the database, to be established organization-wide and easily shared. With a network, a set of computers can use the same printer or other equipment.

Adapting information to present to a variety of audiences. With cheaper laptops and projectors now available, you can present complicated information more easily. The following introduces some tools you can use to present and adapt information:

- *Presentation software.* With software such as PowerPoint or by using slide shows, you can produce innovative, visually engaging political education and training programs.
- *Multimedia productions.* By putting your trainings or presentation on DVDs or CDs you can reach a larger audience. You can also include mapping, music, photographs, and other media to engage people in presentations.
- *Desktop publishing software and a good printer.* It is increasingly affordable for organizations to produce their own high-quality, accessible training and educational materials as well as information for targets and policymakers using desktop publishing software and a good, high-volume color printer.

Conducting research. You use technology to research campaigns and public policies. Using Internet search engines, you can get information about targets, planning and decision-making processes, and about local, state, and federal levels of government. The following outlines some of the possible research tools technology provides:

- *Internet-based search engines.* Search engines include tools such as Google and LexisNexis, which is an archive of information that you pay to access. Search engines help you to search the entire Internet for information on a topic, key word, or during a particular time period.
- *Statistical analysis programs.* Programs such as SPSS help you to sort through and analyze data. These are tools for developing effective research reports about public policy or program evaluation or for engaging in statistical research projects.

- *Mapping*. Mapping creates a visual picture of socioeconomic and land-use data. Maps can help to build your case about proposals for policy change. For example, you create a map of where asthma rates are high or where drinking water is contaminated and overlay it with a map of where people live in poverty. You use the map to make a strong visual argument to an elected representative of that area that she needs to support antipoverty programs for those residents.

What Is a Technology Assessment and How Do We Do One?

In a technology assessment, an organization reviews its organizational objectives and technology capacity in order to determine the technology it needs to purchase and use. You review what you need the technology to do, then lay out what technology you will use, who will use it, and how. The assessment and planning take about six to eight weeks to complete, using the following steps.

Step One: Assemble a team. Gather a small team of people who will be involved in both doing the assessment and developing the plan. This team usually includes one or two staff people and one or two leaders who are among those who will use, purchase, and manage the technology. Secure the assistance of someone who understands the latest technology to conduct the assessment. You may adjust the members of your team as you move through the steps of the assessment.

Step Two: Review your organizational objectives. Consider what you want to accomplish during the next one to three years. If you have a strategic plan or an organizing campaign plan, you use it to identify objectives.

Step Three: Examine your current technology capacity. Review what you currently have, including your software and hardware, what shape your equipment is in, and what staff, members, and leadership know and can do with the technology you have now.

Step Four: Identify users. Consider the full range of staff, members, leaders, or volunteers who use or will use the technology and which staff people or volunteers are responsible for managing it.

Step Five: Determine who will develop and implement the technology plan. Once you complete the assessment, will you have the capacity, expertise, and know-how within your organization—through staff, members, volunteers, or board—to develop a plan? If not, consider the resources you may need, such as intermediary groups, technical assistance providers, or funds sometimes available through small "technical assistance" grants from your existing funders, to hire a technology consultant.

Step Six: Develop the technology plan. Review your assessment and your objectives for the coming one to three years. If membership development and recruitment are key components, a strong database program is important. If effective political education and trainings are key, prioritize good presentation programs and hardware. A plan includes an inventory of skills and equipment you need, the steps you will take to meet these needs, a budget, and a timeline. The technology plan focuses on building your capacity to do the work you laid out in your organizing or strategic plan. You don't add technology that will only add to the work of the organization.

Step Seven: Develop a realistic budget. Consider how many computers you need, which software programs you need, and incidental costs such as Internet connections, cable or DSL lines, and telephone lines. If you are adding a major piece of technology, figure in staffing needs not only for the plan and its implementation, but for any training needed in using the technology and for managing it after the implementation is in place.

Step Eight: Prioritize what you need. People sometimes want to go out and buy everything they think can expand their work. Most organizations cannot afford everything, so you make your decisions about technology based on your priorities.

Step Nine: Designate or identify resources or funds. Once you make a plan, you either designate the resources you need to implement and manage it, or identify how you will get the resources. Some foundations and corporations have special funds for technology and equipment purchases. A clear, comprehensive plan is key for raising money. In addition to raising money, you can sometimes secure donated equipment and software to achieve your goals, but make sure you get what you need. Donated equipment that is outdated or will not meet your needs will reduce your effectiveness, not enhance it.

Step Ten: Implement the plan. Implement the plan according to the priorities you establish. Keep track of whatever is measurable and review benchmarks for evaluation. If the plan takes longer to implement than you think it will due to fundraising delays or learning curves among users, stay on track and manage problems as they arise.

Step Eleven: Evaluate. At times you establish in your technology plan, evaluate if the technology is helping you to reach your organizational or campaign objectives. For example, has your database allowed you to track member involvement more efficiently? Have the fields in your database allowed you to target mailings and phone calls more effectively? Does your Web page meet the needs of its intended users? Make adjustments to your plan based on detailed evaluation, not just because you hear about new technology.

Why Is a Database So Important for Organizing?

Organizing is ultimately about building and managing mass numbers of relationships. A database offers the most effective way to track and manage relationships.

With a well-organized and well-managed database, you keep track of everyone who comes into contact with the organization. You also ensure that the relationships an individual has are organization-wide. It is no longer a question of whose name is in my Rolodex or on my cell phone or computer address book, but rather who is in the organization's database. Of all the technologies available for large-scale base-building, mobilizing, and leadership development, an easy-to-use database is the one technology that most effectively builds the power of an organization in the following ways:

Producing lists for mobilization. With a database, you can produce a list for calling members to come to meetings, for mailing announcements and calls to action, and for producing walking lists to reach your members more efficiently. A walking list is a sheet with names, addresses, and phone numbers that you have sorted based on where people live. For example, you produce a list of members who live on specific streets or on the floors of a building. When you go out to doorknock, you follow the list and check off people's names as you contact them.

Conducting targeted searches. Depending on what kind of information you gather and put into the database, you can conduct quick and easy searches for specific categories of members, donors, or allies. For example, if you want to contact mothers with children for a meeting about public schools, the database can produce a list of mothers with schoolchildren if organizers have been entering that data. If you want to send a special mailing to your hundred largest donors, you can produce a mailing list of those donors. If you want to contact people in a certain legislative district, you can use software to identify all the members active in that district.

Tracking members and other organizational relationships. When you collect information about who comes to meetings, actions, and events, and who gives money or pays dues, and enter that information into the database, you can then analyze this information. If a donor has been giving the same amount of money for ten years, you can engage that person in a targeted conversation, thanking her for her long-term support and asking her to give more. You can identify members who have come out over the years and target them for leadership development work. You can produce a list of people who come to meetings and a list of people who come out for mobilizations.

How Do We Maintain an Effective Database?

You implement the following procedures in order to maintain the most effective database:

Everyone tracks relationships using the database and enters their data immediately. Only people who use the database have access to it. Every staff member and if appropriate, every core leader, tracks all of their relationships through the database. As soon as someone makes a contact, he or she enters the information into the database. The information you enter into the database depends on the primary relationship you have with the individual. Is he a donor, a member, or an organizational ally? Keep only the information you will use. Because the database contains critical and sensitive information, only people the organization trusts and who are doing the organization's work use the database.

One staff person or volunteer is the database point person. One person, with a second person for back-up, is responsible for ensuring the database continues to fit the needs of the organization and addresses any necessary structural changes. The point person also sees that files are backed up and that the database is functioning properly.

What Information Should Be Entered into a Database for Base-Building?

A database for base-building includes the following types of information on each contact:

- *Name.* Full name, nicknames, and salutations. (If you are doing voter work and will do a match with voter databases, you only use the name that the person has registered under.)

- *Contact information.* Mailing address, street address if different, phone numbers (home, work, cell, and best contact), e-mail address.

- *Entry point information.* Date of contact, who met her, how she became involved, point of entry.

- *Member status.* Is she active? If so, how? If the organization has dues, has she paid? Is she a board member, leader, working member, general member?

- *Issue area or campaign.* What campaign or issue does she care about?

- *Personal information.* What personal information you keep depends on what your organization does. For example, a parent-organizing group includes a field for what schools people's children attend.

- *Activity or participation, including the date.* What actions or events has the person attended and when did these activities take place?

- *Skills and interests.* What does she like to do? What volunteer activities should she be targeted for? Does she like to be called to participate in mailings or phone calls? Has she been prepped for press contacts?

- *Donations and gifts.* Separate from dues, you keep track of how much money people donate and when.

- *Miscellaneous.* Use a "memo" box in the database to catch information you cannot categorize.

Table 6.1 shows how such a database is useful.

Why Is a Networked Computer System Important for Organizing?

A networked computer system gives everyone in the organization access to one another's campaign files, documents, and most important, the database.

With a networked computer system, staff members can access all relevant information from their own computers. The network can include computers in one location, or you can set it up so that people can use the Internet to access parts of it from other locations, such as from home or while traveling.

How Do We Establish a Computer Network?

Depending on the technological expertise of your staff or volunteers, you probably need to have a technology consultant set up your system.

Once the system is set up, you will need access to assistance when the system encounters problems. Figure 6.1, A Sample Networked Computer System for a Community Organization, depicts a sample computer network.

How Can We Use Technology for Political Education and Training?

Technology offers an increasing and diverse assortment of affordable tools you can use to educate community members, allies, funders, donors, and even targets of your campaigns.

Table 6.1
Tracking and Developing Members Using a Database

Base-Building Task	Data-Management Task	What the Tasks Produce
Jackson recruits at housing development. Meets Angela. Rates her a #1.	Collects contact information accurately. Notes potential for moving to action.	Data for database.
Jackson evaluates recruitment at office. 15 new members, five #1s.	Enters member contact information in database. Completes any missing information. Puts rating in database category, "Has potential to move to action."	Prioritized people to contact.
Next day Jackson makes follow-up calls.	Generates phone lists of contacts from database he met previous week focusing on #1s and 2s.	Lists of people to call.
Target list is to new members and potential members.	Enters results of phone call assessments into database—17 yeses for organizing meeting—8 maybes.	Additional data on members and contacts.
Jackson does a one-on-one meeting with Angela. Notes issue and volunteer interests.	Enters information in appropriate fields of database—checks off housing and welfare issue fields. Identifies Angela in the memo box as a potential volunteer.	Fuller picture of member that anyone in organization can access through database.
The organizing committee Jackson staffs is planning an accountability session. The turnout goal is 100 people.	Searches database for a variety of contacts to build a large enough list to call to get 100 people at the action. Queries include searches for active members in the district, general members, and new contacts. Jackson produces a list of 650 people to mail to and call.	List of people to call prioritized by relationship to organization and prior participation.
Jackson organizes a mailing party.	Searches database for members who like to do mailings and produces a call list.	List of dependable volunteers to call to do mailing.

Table 6.1
Tracking and Developing Members Using a Database, Cont'd

Base-Building Task	Data-Management Task	What the Tasks Produce
Jackson recruits people for a phone bank.	Does a search on database to produce a list of people he met over the last three months in the district who said they would volunteer to do phone bank.	List of new people who said they would like to volunteer.
Angela coordinates phone bank. Volunteers accurately update contact information on their written sheets and note who says they will come to the action.	Jackson inputs all the responses into the database—yes, no, maybe—by the end of the night.	Preliminary list of people who say they will attend action.
Jackson organizes a reminder phone bank canvass the night before the action.	Produces a call list of yeses and maybes for the phone callers to use when they make their calls.	A list of all yeses and maybes for callers.
Jackson inputs yeses for the final count.	Yeses and maybes are put into the database at the end of the night. There are 158 people confirmed for the action.	A final confirmation list of people who say they are coming.
At the sign-in desk on the night of the action, volunteers check people off lists and sign people in who did not say they were coming.	Before the action, Jackson produces a list of people who say they are or may be coming. Volunteers will use this list and sign in anyone who is not on it.	A registration and preprinted sign-in sheet.
After the action, staff debrief turnout and analyze where people came from.	Staff members input names of action attendees into the database and compare it to the list of yeses and maybes they started with on the night of the action.	List of attendees—where they came from and how many had said they were coming.

Table 6.1

Tracking and Developing Members Using a Database, Cont'd

Base-Building Task	Data-Management Task	What the Tasks Produce
Staff review lists of members who participated to identify new members to develop.	Staff analyze members' prior participation (turn-out history) in database to identify members to follow up with. Members who have come to 3 events in the last 4–6 months will be prioritized for a home visit.	List of people to do home visits with.
Staff begin to track newly involved members.	Track new members or first-time participants in action in database and prioritize people for meetings and actions.	A track record of participation for newly engaged members.

Technology provides opportunities to reach people who learn in different ways. For example, people who like to read rather than listen can see the main points during a presentation that uses presentation software. People who respond to visual imagery, sound, and media can watch documentaries or multimedia presentations. People who need experiential education can engage in interactive exercises on computers or in simulations. These types of technology are described here.

Hardware. The lowering cost and easy availability of digital cameras, video recorders, laptop computers, projectors, and other equipment means that more tools are more available even to low-budget organizations. In addition, this equipment is getting smaller and easier to transport, allowing organizers to bring equipment out of the office and into people's homes and communities.

Presentation software. You use software such as PowerPoint with a laptop computer and projector. By lifting out and projecting on a screen the main points of presentations, such presentation software helps to reinforce key concepts and lessons. Presentation software does not guarantee a good presentation. You use software to illustrate main points, not to put entire presentations on a screen.

Multimedia presentations. You use videos, graphics, mapping software, and other applications to help educate and move people. For example, you videotape an ac-

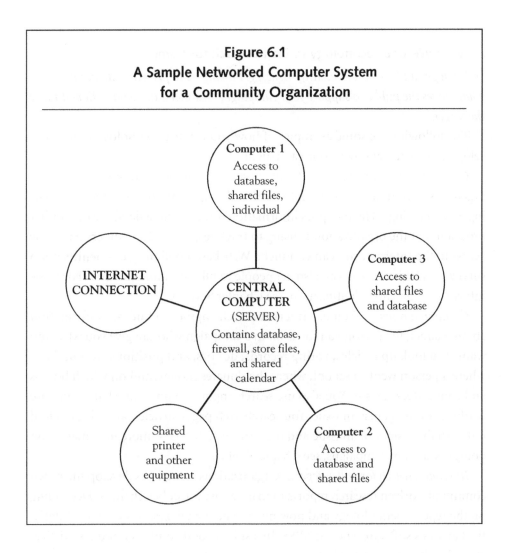

Figure 6.1
A Sample Networked Computer System
for a Community Organization

Computer 1
Access to database, shared files, individual

INTERNET CONNECTION

CENTRAL COMPUTER (SERVER)
Contains database, firewall, store files, and shared calendar

Computer 3
Access to shared files and database

Shared printer and other equipment

Computer 2
Access to database and shared files

tion, press conference, or other event, then analyze it to see what worked or did not. A group of members watches a documentary together about an issue, policy, or target, and then has a conversation about campaign strategy. An elected official watches a graphic representation of how changing zoning laws would affect community development, or sees a map projected on a screen during a town hall meeting or accountability session that shows how different school districts receive different levels of funding or which school districts get the highest percentage of military recruiters visiting them. Potential donors watch a video of an action, members' testimonies, or highlights of a visit to another country.

How Do We Use Technology to Do Research for Campaigns?

Technology can help you to identify issues, get members to prioritize demands, know what moves the public to support your campaign, or understand what will best move the target.

The following are some examples of how you can use technology to help develop, implement, and win your campaign:

Community issue identification. Scanning software, laptops, and similar tools allow organizers or volunteers to enter information they get while doing surveys or holding issue meetings. The tool puts information directly into a database or another program that the organization is using to track responses. If members have easy access to the Internet, you can conduct a Web-based poll or issue-identification survey on a Web site. You can also get people to fill out online surveys. (For more information on issue identification, see Chapter Seven.)

Campaign research. You use Internet search engines to find out information about a target, the person you focus on in a campaign who can give you what you want. You look up articles, voting records, donors, and positions. You find out where a person went to school, where she donates money, and on which boards and committees she sits. You also use search engines to find out what groups are working for or against an issue. You search Web pages, articles, and blogs to find out both the history of an issue and the current status. (For more information on doing research in campaigns, see Chapter Eight.)

Internal research for policy reports. Organizations sometimes develop their own community-driven research reports to make a case for policy changes. Depending on the report methodology and how much data it analyzes, you may need statistical analysis software, such as SPSS. Invest in a good computer and a statistical analysis software program if you are going to engage in this kind of research.

Mapping demographics and data. You use mapping programs to move targets, educate members and constituents, and help determine where to do base-building. You identify where members live or pinpoint where you need to recruit new members for a campaign.

Mapping software can be expensive and difficult to use. It may require a more powerful computer than the ones your organization can afford. Check to see if there are any intermediary organizations or technical assistance providers that help with mapping data. Be clear about the information you need to map and analyze.

It may require that you access specific databases and information that can cost money. You know exactly who your audience is and how mapping will move your campaign forward before you invest in a large-scale mapping project.

CHALLENGES
TO KEEPING DATA SAFE

"We lost all our data!" You lose data through malfunctioning equipment, staff or volunteer mistakes, or computer viruses. To avoid these problems, back up your information weekly. You copy all of your files onto removable devices so that if something crashes or records get deleted, you can retrieve the information from another source. One person in your organization should be responsible for choosing a day and time and doing back-up every week. How long backing up takes depends on how much data you have and whether or not the back-up can be automated. Also, you need virus protection on the file server and all computers.

"A former staff member downloaded all our data and is using it for another organization." It does not take long for someone to download data and files onto a removable storage device. The following are some potential ways to address this challenge:

- *Memo of Understanding.* Create a Memo of Understanding to share with everyone who has access to the data, stipulating that it cannot be shared, sold, or given without proper authorization from whoever is responsible for those decisions in your organization. (For more on Memos of Understanding, see Chapter Fourteen.)

- *Security codes and passwords.* Computers should have passwords or security codes that users need to know to gain access. In practice, these protections can be burdensome, but in active community offices where there is not a lot of oversight, they protect computers from potential data stealers as well as from viruses and misuse.

- *Separate computers for volunteers and members.* Have separate computers, not linked to the network, where members and volunteers can do research, write flyers, or draft testimony. Having separate computers also helps avoid problems when children who are waiting for their parents to finish a meeting want to use a computer to do homework.

"Someone hacked into our network." People hack into computer systems via the Internet and through wireless connections. Although you may think that this situation would never happen to you, it can. Again, don't underestimate the value of your information. In addition, some hackers just like to cause problems for fun. A software program that provides good firewall protection is the only way to protect your organization from hackers. A firewall protects your data by blocking outside information from coming into your computer. Without a firewall, anyone can come in.

ESSENTIAL ELEMENTS
FOR EFFECTIVE USE OF TECHNOLOGY

☑ *Assess your needs.* Do a clear assessment, with an expert if necessary, of what you need.

☑ *Work off a plan.* Don't just add gizmos or expect technology to substitute for face-to-face contact.

☑ *Have every staff person and organizer use the database.* A database is an absolutely essential piece of technology for effective base-building and campaign implementation. Organizers should do their own inputting of information about people they have met.

☑ *Network your computers.* Keep everyone connected to shared information.

☑ *Establish safety procedures.* Be clear about who uses the organization's technology and data. Make sure you invest in firewall protection of your data.

part three

Developing and Running Campaigns

A campaign is a planned series of strategies and actions designed to achieve clear goals and objectives. Campaigns are the life-blood of organizing. Community power-building organizations conduct campaigns to win the administrative, institutional, or policy changes their members want. Organizations also build their power—their numbers, strength, and influence—through campaigns.

Campaigns make specific demands of a person with power. In a proactive campaign, the organization sets out to win something new. The demand is: *We want you to do this.* In a reactive or defensive campaign, the organization tries to stop something from happening. The demand is: *We want you to stop this.*

Through creative, strategic campaigns, organizations show their strength, deepen their capacity, develop community leaders, win changes in the lives of their members and constituents, and shift political power.

Every campaign has three phases: campaign development, campaign implementation, and campaign evaluation.

Campaign development includes identifying an issue, conducting research to collect data, analyzing power, developing strategies, and writing a campaign plan. This phase generally takes one to six months. Campaign implementation is when the organization runs the campaign and engages in collective action. The length of this phase depends on the issue, but it can last for a few months or a few years. In the third phase, campaign evaluation, staff and leaders review the campaign and reflect on what they did and did not accomplish in order to learn from their mistakes and build on their strengths.

Figure P3.1
The Flow of a Campaign

Issue ID	Research	Demand Process	Campaign Planning	Campaign Implementation	Campaign Evaluation
Identifying collective problems, base-building	Landscaping, goal development	Developing and choosing demand	Developing and approving campaign plan	Implementing actions, new base-building, mobilizing membership base	Assessing if met goals and how well organization performed
High Degree of Action Internal actions: town hall meetings, focus groups, issue ID meetings, mass canvasses	**Low Degree of Action** Research meetings, including with allies and stakeholders	**Medium Degree of Action** Solidarity actions, mobilization of members, and support for potential allies; surveying members and constituents	**Low Degree of Action** Campaign strategy meetings and sessions; limited action to test message and demands	**High Degree of Action** Ongoing direct action	**Low–Medium Degree of Action** Limited action that tests whether campaign demands actually implemented; evaluation of full campaign
(All Membership Types + Impacted Constituents) →	(Leaders, Working Members) →	(All Membership Types) →	(Leaders, Working Members) →	(All Membership Types (including new recruits)) →	(Leaders, Working Members)
CVH surveys WEP workers, holds worksite meetings, teach-ins, and house meetings to ID issues with WEP and engages in small-scale actions on WEP.	CVH meets with allies to find out politics of WEP. Works with advocacy groups to find out who decision makers are on WEP and workfare.	CVH develops transitional jobs program based on campaign research and development activities. Talks to WEP workers about transitional jobs program demand and decides on demand.	Leaders and members engage in campaign planning sessions.	CVH organizes action, intensifies WEP worker recruitment, and mobilizes WEP workers. Moves union to join campaign and gets press. Wins passage of program in city council.	CVH evaluates campaign process and outcomes with leadership. Talks to WEP workers and allies to see if program is implemented and assesses need to engage in a campaign to implement the program.

Chapters Seven through Ten lay out the details of developing and planning a campaign, from identifying the right issue and researching the politics of the issue through developing a winning strategy and writing the campaign plan. Chapter Eleven focuses on how to implement the campaign, and Chapter Twelve discusses the actions and tactics you use to do so. Chapter Thirteen details how to evaluate both the actions you have taken and the campaign as a whole.

Figure P3.1 illustrates how activities, action, and membership involvement flow over the course of a campaign. Rather than growing steadily from a small base of people to a larger one, the numbers of people active in the campaign expands and contracts according to the activity and the degree of action. It is important to remember that the different phases are not equal in length. In general, you will spend a vast majority of time on the implementation of your campaign.

Identifying the Right Issue

WHAT DO WE WANT?

With the passage of new federal welfare reform, Mayor Rudolph Giuliani is free to put thousands of welfare recipients into the largest workfare program in the country, the Work Experience Program (WEP). The welfare office starts calling in welfare recipients who are also members of Community Voices Heard (CVH) to give them their assignments. (For background on WEP and CVH, see "The Story of Community Voices Heard," p. xxxi.) They will have to spend up to thirty-five hours a week doing maintenance and office jobs in city agencies or nonprofit organizations, along with a combination of other work activities, for which they will not receive a salary. If they don't agree to take these assignments, they will lose their minimal cash and other benefits.

Mothers with young children scramble to figure out child-care arrangements. Many students have to leave college and educational programs. In Central Park and other city parks, the sight of older women stooping down to pick up garbage, wearing baggy orange vests and a pair of flimsy gloves as their only equipment, becomes commonplace.

CVH organizers go out into the field to talk to WEP workers before and after their work shifts and during lunch breaks. In conversations and impromptu meetings in locker rooms and lunchrooms, workers sign pledge cards and fill out surveys. At meetings at the CVH office, they say they like working and want to work, but the issue is starting to become clear: WEP workers want a paid job with living wages, education, training, and access to a better life.

What Is Issue Identification and Why Is It Important?

Issue identification—or issue ID—is a research and data-collection step. It is the first step an organizer and leaders take when they are ready to take on a new campaign. By engaging in issue identification, you ensure that you choose issues that truly matter to members and constituents, so that you can mobilize and build your membership effectively.

Through issue ID, you go beyond recognizing that a problem exists to focusing on how constituents want to address it. You begin to assess how willing people are to come out and make a specific solution happen and how possible it is for them to achieve what they want.

What's the Difference Between a Problem and an Issue?

An issue is the solution to a problem.

A community power-building organization never organizes around the problems of individuals. It organizes to advance solutions to collective problems that have a systemic cause.

For example, if you are a college student and the finance office does not send your work-study check on time, you have a problem. In order to resolve it, you make a phone call and get the check, or a student advisor advocates for you. But that is not organizing. You organize when you talk to other students and learn that no one gets her or his check delivered on time. You have begun to identify a systemic problem. The office will probably not get your next checks out on time either. When you find out you all have this same problem, you can identify an issue. You can set out to make the finance office function correctly.

Table 7.1, Problems or Issues? further illustrates the differences between problems and issues. In addition, Exercise 7.2, Issue ID: The Problem Tree, trains people to distinguish between a problem and an issue.

Who Does Issue ID?

To guide the ID process, the organizer assembles a leadership team of people who are directly affected by the issue and able to spend some time developing the campaign.

The team includes both experienced leaders and newer people. It is not a closed group. (For more on how to develop a leadership team, see Chapter One.) The leadership team works with the organizer to help set up a framework for engaging in issue ID, including identifying the best tools to use, how many people to talk to, and what issues and demands to test with a broader group of people.

What Makes an Issue the Right Issue?

The right issue moves people to participate and inspires them to lead a successful campaign.

Table 7.1
Problems or Issues?

	Problem	Issue
What is going on?	A local company is dumping toxic waste in a local lake.	The state Environmental Protection Agency needs to hire more staff so it can investigate the site.
Who deals with this?	Someone with power, resources, or access, such as an elected official or reporter who can bring attention to the problem.	A group of residents who live near the lake and use it and are concerned about the environment and their health.
What is the goal?	The dumping stops.	A system or institutional change occurs that stops the dumping and ensures that the dumping does not happen again.
What gets fixed?	The current dumping stops.	The system for investigating and responding to toxic waste dumping and other environmental issues changes and improves.
Who holds power?	Elected official or reporter.	The community residents affected by the toxic waste dumping can make a difference.
What power change takes place?	None.	The community gains strength and influence.
End result	The problem gets addressed, but the system that addresses and stops toxic waste dumping and spills does not. If it happens again, the community has to start over.	When the community addresses the dumping by getting more agency staff to investigate and stop toxic dumping, there is a greater chance that if the problem happens again, it can be addressed quickly.

Here's how you know if you have chosen the right issue:

- *It resonates.* The issue is important to the people who experience the problem it resolves. It makes them animated and angry.
- *It delivers.* Winning on the issue delivers a concrete, positive change that will make people's lives better.
- *It's winnable.* It is possible to win what you want.
- *It has a clear target.* There is one specific person who can give members what they want. This person is known as the target of the campaign.
- *It builds power.* The issue strengthens your organization and brings in new resources—members, relationships, allies, and funds. It unites rather than divides people in the organization.
- *It supports your mission and values.* The right issue is within the parameters of your organization's work.

How Do We Identify the Issue?

You identify the right issue by going out, talking to people, and asking questions.

There are three main tools to identify issues: surveys or questionnaires, individual meetings, and small group meetings.

Surveys or questionnaires. These tools ask people clear and pointed questions about problems in the community. You administer short surveys or questionnaires in person or over the phone. Surveys offer a good leadership development activity when you train working members, leaders, and volunteers to administer them. They also help you get updated information about members. See Tool 7.1 for tips on how to do a phone survey and a sample phone survey conversation. See Tool 7.2 for a sample issue survey.

Individual meetings. When you sit down and talk with individuals, you can probe and have deep discussions. Individual meetings take time, but they give you better information than phone conversations. You can ask more open-ended questions, get people to talk more about problems and issues, and engage in political education. In the following example, Michael, the organizer, probes in a number of areas to help Robert hear things that resonate with his experience. Michael makes choices about how to steer the conversation based on the focus of the organization and what he and the leadership team have been hearing from other people.

Robert (Constituent):	I called my landlord five times about my leaky roof. My apartment is full of mold and the kids are getting sick.
Michael (Organizer):	When it rains, can you tell me what happens in your apartment and how it affects other people in the building?
Robert:	My neighbor across the hall has it too. Her walls are starting to crack. And Number Five downstairs—their ceiling is falling down from the water.
Michael:	What other buildings in the neighborhood does the landlord own?
Robert:	He's all over town. He goes from building to building in his fancy car . . .
Michael:	The city just passed a new law increasing penalties against landlords who repeatedly violate health and safety codes. Has the city filed a complaint against him before?
Robert:	I don't know.
Michael:	We have to find out. If the landlord does not respond to your phone calls, what do you think he might respond to?

Small group meetings. These meetings bring people together to share and discuss their ideas and concerns. Small group meetings give people an opportunity to see their connections on an issue. Small group meetings can be house meetings in people's living rooms, or they can take place at the organization's office or at other community sites. Tool 7.3 gives details on house meetings, along with a sample house meeting agenda. Here's an example of how a small group meeting might happen at a work site.

Identifying an Issue Using Group Meetings

In the offices of a cramped city agency overlooking 125th Street, twenty women on welfare move files from one cabinet to another. Water leaks from a ceiling pipe in the center of the room, splashing loudly into a plastic bucket. Dust fills the air. With the windows sealed shut, the women cough repeatedly. Just two weeks after being forced into this workfare assignment, some have already suffered asthma attacks.

When Paul, organizing for CVH, meets with them during their lunch break, he talks with them about their right to a healthy work environment. Even though conditions are bad, most of the women believe they are on the path to work so do not want to cause a stir.

Their feelings soon change. When Paul returns a few weeks later and asks about what is going on at the work site, the women vent their frustrations. "I have been working here for five weeks. They told me I would get a job, but all I am doing is working for the city for free," says a young mother. "They just make you work to work—for no reason," another woman complains. She says that she doesn't even mind coming in every day if she learns some skills, but all she is doing is carrying wet boxes from one room to another. "This is not helping me get off welfare. It's keeping me stuck on welfare," she insists. Several of the women are visibly sick from the dampness and dust. When Paul asks why they think they are there, they say they understand two things: "They either want us to leave welfare or do city work for free," as one woman explains. "Either way, the mayor saves money for his rich friends," she continues. Paul asks them what they want the city to do, and their discussion leads them to agree: they want paid jobs with training. When Paul passes around a sign-up sheet, eighteen of the twenty women write down their names and phone numbers so he can call them about the next CVH meeting.

How Do We Make Sure We Get to the Issue and Not Just Talk About Problems?

When using issue ID tools, you lead the dialogue and use issue probes in ways that accomplish the following:

Get specifics. If a person says "housing" is an issue, ask what he means by housing. Try to get as specific an answer as possible. Does he mean building more affordable housing or problems with housing conditions?

Identify commonalities. Guide people to distinguish between problems and issues. Where have they identified similar problems? Do they see the same potential solutions?

Prioritize issues. When the individual or group has come up with some issues, have people vote or prioritize what they would like to work on.

Test potential demands. Once the leadership team starts to get a sense of the issue, it drafts a campaign goal and potential demands. When on the phone or out in the field, you start to test these demands with people you talk with.

How Many People Do We Have to Talk To?

Good issue ID requires hundreds, sometimes thousands, of conversations.

You don't rely on the perspectives of a handful of people or the opinions of "experts" who are not directly affected. You go out and talk with people. Exercise 7.1, What's the Issue? offers a way to train members to practice identifying an issue.

If People Identify an Issue, Will They Organize for It?

Not necessarily. Sometimes people identify an issue that is immediate and important, but this does not mean that it is the issue they will put the time and energy into addressing.

For example, at the early CVH welfare reform teach-ins at social service organizations, homeless shelters, schools, and Head Start programs, Gail Aska repeatedly heard mothers on welfare identify the low level of the welfare cash benefit as the biggest welfare-related problem in their day-to-day lives. Finally, she asked people directly, "Would you come to meetings and work with other women to raise the welfare grant?" Their answer was clear: no. Probing, she learned why they would not organize for a benefit increase. Some did not think welfare would be around for much longer. Some bought into the argument that welfare was essentially bad. Overall, most of the women believed that getting a living-wage job was the best thing they could do for themselves and their children.

What If People Identify an Issue That's Different from What Our Organization Usually Works On?

You make decisions about the issues you take on based on the mission of your organization and what you can and cannot do.

Even though community power-building organizations are constituent-led, this does not mean the organization changes its focus every time new people get involved. The organization has a mission as well as members, funders, and supporters to whom it is accountable. Everyone doing recruitment for the organization and inviting people into the issue ID process is clear about the parameters of the work. You don't just start in a whole new direction, even if an issue is important.

Sometimes the members look to another organization that works on an issue that is affecting them. For example, an organization that works on low-income housing development engages in issue ID and learns that most of the people surveyed identify classroom overcrowding and poor conditions at the local public school as something they are concerned about. The housing organization, due to its mission statement and limited resources, refers these individuals to a neighborhood organization engaged in a campaign to improve public schools, rather than develop a new campaign. When there is no other organization working on an issue members identify, they can make the strategic decision to expand their organization's issue focus. But this should be an organization-wide decision that includes board and other leadership.

How Long Does It Take to Identify an Issue?

One organizer working full-time with a leadership team and a base of members should be able to develop an issue in four to ten weeks.

For a reactive or defensive campaign, the time frame for issue ID may be shorter. If, for instance, the community has just learned of a cell-phone tower being erected near an elementary school, the issue gets defined very quickly as stopping the tower. The length of the issue ID process depends to some extent on the immediacy of the problem.

Table 7.2 shows how and when you generally use the issue ID tools. You can use this as the basis for establishing a plan for engaging different types of members, leaders, and potential members. You set goals for the numbers or activities you will undertake, such as small group meetings, as well as the number of people you will reach in each category of membership.

Once you identify the issue, you draft a goal and define concrete demands for a campaign, as we describe in the following sections.

What Is a Campaign Goal and How Do We Develop It?

The campaign goal is a statement about the issue that addresses the big-picture change you want to see. Members develop the campaign goal as they understand why the problem exists and who benefits from it.

A good goal provides a hopeful vision. It gives the campaign a clear focus. You are explicit about where you are heading so you do not bounce from activity to activity. In a community power-building organization, the goal is often a statement

Table 7.2
Using Issue ID Tools

Who	Issue ID Tool	When in ID Process	Goal
Leadership	One-on-ones Small group meetings	Beginning and end	Identify potential issues and demands.
Working members	One-on-ones Small group meetings	Beginning and middle of process	Identify potential issues and demands.
General Members	Surveys (phone) Small group meetings	Beginning and middle of process	Develop issue and make sure it resonates with organization's base.
New potential constituency/ membership	Surveys (face-to-face)	Middle	Identify issues a community cares about and ensure that issues resonate with potential new members.

for change, not just for reform. For example, in CVH's Transitional Jobs Campaign, the goal was "End WEP." It was not "Improve WEP" or "Reconsider WEP." CVH staked out a position that would shift the debate on the issue and clearly state what members wanted.

Political education helps stimulate conversation about what people ultimately want to reach for. In meetings and one-on-one conversations, members discuss the big picture and decide on the statement they want to make about the issue.

What Other Goals Does a Campaign Have?

You establish goals to build your organization internally, especially membership and resources.

Internally, a campaign may seek to organize a new constituency, develop new leaders, raise your profile, or build your influence with allies and stakeholders. For example, if your organization decides to improve transit services so that children can get to school safely, but your organization only organizes parents of public school students, you set a goal to bring in public transit riders.

What Is a Campaign Demand?

A campaign demand is the actual program, administrative procedure, or policy that you want to create or change.

A demand is a concrete, measurable request that you make of an individual person. Every campaign must have a demand.

A demand can be for a social policy: We want you to support a bill that will create jobs for 3,500 people. It can be an administrative demand: We want you to release funding for a jobs program that has been in the city budget for the past three years, or we want you to update the college computer systems so that work-study checks arrive on time.

A demand can be proactive: We want you to require the company to clean up its toxic waste. It can be reactive: Stop the plan to store toxic waste at this location.

"Jobs Now!" is not a demand. A statement like this is a slogan.

A demand requires a clear yes or no answer. This component is essential for evaluating whether the target, who is the person who can give you what you want, supports you or not. A demand that requires a yes or no answer is effective, in part, because it is not what most elected officials, administrators, and corporate executives usually experience. They can usually avoid saying yes or no and instead dance around the question.

A campaign can have more than one demand but generally not more than three. Multiple demands need to be extremely focused. Presenting a laundry list of demands is no more effective than chanting about broad social problems.

How Do We Develop Campaign Demands?

You do effective research to find out what will fix the problem. The leadership team talks with members and leaders to create a solution that truly represents what they want.

Throughout demand development, you do political education with members so they understand how agencies and institutions work. Sometimes, particularly with policy and legislative demands, you work with intermediary or technical assistance groups that help you develop a bill or program to fight for. You always include members in working with these groups. Following are the steps in developing campaign demands, with an example of how they play out.

Members identify the issue. Through extensive issue ID, members say they want more social service programs for seniors.

Leadership team researches the issue, determines potential demands. The leadership team talks with the city's department of aging as well as local senior groups and elected officials. Team members conduct Internet research on models for senior service programs.

Team develops a list of possible demands. Team develops possible demands based on its research and discussions with a group that specializes on public policy and the aged. Possible demands include more funding for current programs, more senior programs in public schools, and funding and a request-for-proposals process for community organizations to develop and run new senior service programs.

Team surveys members about possible demands. Organizer and leaders call members who would benefit from this campaign, such as seniors and people with senior parents. Organizer conducts one-on-one visits with people in their homes. The goal is to identify the priorities people have, given the range of possible demands. The team also directly asks people if they would work on a campaign to get the demands they name.

Team surveys additional constituents. The team surveys seniors in the community. It may decide to use a written survey form as a tool for having organized conversations. The goal of this survey process is to get information about the demands. Similar to recruitment, you collect names and contact information. But because the purpose is data collection, you usually do not follow up with people immediately, as you do in recruitment. Eventually, you contact the people you surveyed to try to get them involved with the campaign. But this step may be three weeks or three months after you meet them. It will be harder to recruit them after so much time has lapsed, so the numeric goals and your time and effort are different.

If the team is using a written survey, it may survey current members of the organization as well by calling them or talking with them when they come to the office for meetings.

Team analyzes survey responses. The team meets to analyze responses. They guide their analysis with some pointed questions, including asking if they themselves would come to meetings and work over the long term to win the demands. Would their friends, family, neighbors work on this issue? Why or why not? The team members also consider what they experienced while surveying and talking with people. Were the people they spoke with agitated or neutral? Did they name what they wanted right away, or did the team members bring them to the demands?

Members meet to choose demands. The organization holds a meeting with members and constituents the team met during the demands-development process. The leadership team presents the proposed goal, the survey responses, and the proposed demands. It either puts the demands forward as decisions already made, or it asks the fuller group to make decisions about what the demands will be. In either case, staff and leaders explain how they came up with the demands and educate people about the reasons behind their recommendations.

By the end of this meeting the organization agrees on one demand: more funding for existing senior programs. Like everything in campaign development, a full group of members will ratify and activate this decision later, when the organization writes its final campaign plan.

What Is a Target?

The target is the person who can meet your demands.

Once you decide what you want, you figure out who can give it to you. You analyze how much power your organization has to move this person. The target is always the person who can give you what you want, the lowest-ranking person who can meet the demands, an individual—not an organization or a group of people— and someone your organization has or can build enough power to move.

You always select a primary target of the campaign. In addition, you may choose a secondary target or targets. A secondary target can influence the target in ways your organization cannot. More on secondary targets follows later in this chapter.

How Do We Do Target Identification?

Target ID is a research process. You answer the following two questions as thoroughly as possible:

Who has the power on your issue? Who can pass the bill you want, create your program, or stop the practices that are harming members of your community? Who is the lowest-ranking person who has the legal administrative power to give you what you want? The target is not necessarily the person with the most power. Someone much lower in a structure may be the person who can make the decision and who your organization can move. You may start out thinking you want to go after the governor, but when you look more closely at the issue, you realize that a commissioner is actually the person who can deliver on your demand.

To whom is the potential target accountable? If it is an elected official, is she accountable to other elected officials, interest groups, campaign contributors? If it is a private citizen, is she accountable to shareholders or trustees? The answer to this question starts to tell you if you have the power to move this person. It also helps determine what secondary targets you might need to establish.

To do target research read the newspaper, go to the library, use the Internet, and talk to colleagues and allies. Review laws, administrative practices, or statutes. Explore which city government agencies control programs, finances, and administration relevant to your issue. Talk to lawyers, government officials, or staff of agencies and departments. For corporate issues, examine materials such as organizational charts, reports, or company Web sites.

In Chapter Eight, we describe how to analyze your ability to move a target and more fully explore where to find information about targets. See Tool 7.4 for questions to use to begin to identify your campaign target.

What Is a Secondary Target?

A secondary target is a person who can get the primary target to do what you want.

Sometimes you do not have enough power to move the target. Instead you can move someone who does have power over the person who can ultimately meet your demands. This person is a secondary target. You must have the ability to get him to do two things: take a position on your demands and move the primary target.

Just as you need to understand the power, accountability, and position of the primary target, you need to know the same things about the secondary target. In addition, you must be totally clear about what you want that secondary target to do.

For example, the speaker in the state legislature is the person who can give you what you want. But you do not have any members in his district, so it will be hard to influence him. Instead you look at who chairs the committee that handles your issue. Both the speaker and the committee chair hold positions of power. The speaker listens to the committee chair. You have a member base in the chair's district. The chair becomes your secondary target. You do not build an alliance or partnership with the committee chair. You exert constituent pressure on him to take a position on your demands and to get the speaker to do what you want.

How Can We Act Quickly in a Crisis
and Still Develop a Successful Campaign?

Accelerate the steps laid out above—but do them while you take advantage of the galvanizing force of the crisis.

In a crisis campaign, you immediately hold group meetings so that people can come together and talk about what's happening. The organizer may meet with key individuals rather than embarking on a time-intensive process of meeting individually with many people.

If the crisis is public, constituents often mobilize themselves. They come out to meetings and actions much more readily. But you still have to go out and talk to people and engage them in order to build the base beyond those people who self-identify.

You don't just hand out flyers or start an e-mail list. You follow the same steps we laid out in Chapter Three: know who you are looking for, calculate how many people you need to talk with, identify where to find them, and practice what to say to them. Get their names and contact information, add them to your list, go visit them, or call them on the phone.

In a time of crisis, it is easier to do issue ID and demand development than it is to identify the target, especially if the campaign involves corporate responsibility. In a crisis it is tempting to start protesting against the person who is most immediately associated with what's going on. Instead you need to research who can actually stop the budget cuts or the pollution.

Accelerating the Steps

At CVH, after the city implements the transitional jobs program, members and organizers hear rumors that the city plans to cut wages for the new workers by almost $2 an hour. The newly elected mayor, Michael Bloomberg, soon confirms the rumors, announcing that he will implement a directive from outgoing Mayor Giuliani not only to cut wages but to privatize the jobs as well, eliminating many of the union and wage protections.

Within two weeks, CVH organizes a meeting of workers to see what it can do about this, and fifty people come out. These workers tell other workers about the organizing and the CVH phones start ringing off the hooks. Fifty to sixty people come out for each organizing meeting and quickly focus on the target, Mayor

Bloomberg, and their demands to stop the wage reduction and privatization plans. The organizers and leaders don't know much yet about Bloomberg, except that he does not like bad publicity. CVH decides to use direct action and a media strategy to get what members want. Three weeks after CVH first became aware of the issue, the workers hold their first action, a protest at City Hall. Almost one hundred workers show up. Within six weeks of the announcement, the mayor agrees not to implement the wage and privatization proposals.

Keep in mind that a reactive crisis campaign is probably only the first campaign you will run. Once the crisis is averted, you engage in a more in-depth issue ID process to get at the systems behind the crisis. If you have built your base, you build power with a victory. Then you develop and mobilize the community to make sure it never happens again.

LEADERSHIP DEVELOPMENT OPPORTUNITIES
DURING ISSUE ID

- *Survey others.* Leaders conduct surveys and lead discussions and focus groups with other members, constituents, and community groups.

- *Conduct online and policy research.* Leaders get on the Internet, talk to policy groups, and read about the issue to help develop talking points or presentations for members.

- *Organize research meetings.* Organize and facilitate meetings with groups that may either potentially work on the campaign or have information on the issue.

CHALLENGES
IN ISSUE ID

"We thought we had the right issue, but no one is coming out to meetings." Sometimes you identify an issue that seems right only to find that you can't sustain a campaign around it. You don't go from hearing something in individual conversations to developing demands without seeing if people will come out to work on the issue. When people don't come out, you have more conversations and forums and probe more deeply.

"People keep identifying the issue but they won't move on it." Sometimes the issue is correct, but you have to cut it a different way—that is, to change your approach and the way you talk about the issue with constituents. Members work together to try different approaches in explaining the issue and demand. Cutting the issue may or may not be the solution. If you try a few different approaches and people still will not move, you don't have the right issue, no matter what they are saying.

"We've been identifying the issue for months, but we still are not sure about it. A core of people are ready, though, and getting restless." Move to limited action and set a timeline for a final decision on the issue and demand. Do small-scale action as you continue base-building and issue ID. In addition to motivating people to stay involved, you may more clearly identify the campaign issue.

"Our members want to make a demand we can't win." Or *"Our members want to make a demand that is really insignificant."* The organizer helps people to think through their decisions. You probe and agitate members to look more realistically at the impact of the demand they want. You directly ask how likely it is that they can win the demand or even aspects of it during a campaign. If members ultimately want the demand, you go with it, but you make sure the campaign has clear objectives and points where they can evaluate their progress.

ESSENTIAL ELEMENTS
FOR EFFECTIVE ISSUE ID

☑ *Choose the right issue.* Identify something that resonates with the community, fixes the problem, and moves people to action for something they can win.

☑ *Consider how the issue builds your power.* Be clear about how the issue builds your organization. Does it bring in new members, new alliances, new knowledge?

☑ *Make sure one person can resolve the issue.* The issue has one clear target, not a variety of different targets.

☑ *Choose the person who can actually meet the demand.* Identify the lowest-level person who can give you what you want.

☑ *Test the issue and demand.* Hold extensive conversations with individuals and groups, including possibly doing small actions to make sure these people want a campaign.

Tool 7.1
Sample Phone Survey

The following are the steps in conducting a phone survey, along with an example of how such a conversation might go.

Identify yourself and why you are calling. Hi, Jackie, this is Michael from Neighbors United. Jackie, you were involved with our Campaign for Safe Housing a few months ago, do you remember that campaign? Great. I'm glad that together we were able to get the commissioner to hire more housing inspectors and keep the landlords in check. I'm calling to follow up with people involved in that campaign.

Ask open questions to engage in a conversation about the problem. How are things with your apartment? Did your landlord make the repairs the inspection turned up?

Find out specifically what her problems are now. How responsive has your landlord been since the inspections increased? Are the repair and safety problems you are still experiencing affecting you alone, or are your neighbors having these problems too?

Ask general, open-ended questions to see what's important to her. I am calling people to find out what they think we need to work on next. What issues would you like to see us address?

Assess what's most resonant. Out of the following issues you've mentioned, and some that others have been mentioning, which would you say is the most important to you and your family: adding additional housing inspectors, having the city take over the landlord's buildings, or building more affordable housing?

Determine her interest in moving to action. Which of these would you work on, maybe come out for a couple of hours a month to address?

Establish a next step. Thanks for this information, Jackie. Could I set up a time to talk to you more after we figure out what our next potential campaign is?

Tool 7.2
Sample Issue Survey

The following is a sample survey that Community Voices Heard has used as a tool to identify the issues people most want to work on. You can also use this kind of survey as a tool for recruitment, as we describe in Chapter Three.

CVH Issues Survey

(Used by permission of Community Voices Heard)

Name _____

Address _____ Apt. #_____ Zip_____

Phone _____ E-mail _____

We'd like to know what issues New Yorkers are most concerned about in 2005. Please rank the following in order of importance to you:

Economic development _____

Children and youth _____

Jobs, education, and training _____

If Economic development, please identify the most important issue to you:

Stopping the use of public money for a Jets Stadium _____

Construction and preservation of affordable housing _____

Getting low-income people more involved in the distribution of public money _____

Other _____

If Children and youth, please identify the most important issue to you:

Affordable, accessible, quality childcare _____

Quality of public schools _____

After-school and community programs for children and youth _____

Other _____

Tool 7.2
Sample Issue Survey, Cont'd

If Jobs, education, and training, please identify the most important issue to you:

Living-wage jobs for low-income New Yorkers _____

Paid jobs programs for people transitioning off of public assistance _____

Access to education and training programs for low-income people _____

Other _____

Other issues or comments: _____

Would you identify yourself as economically self-sufficient? _____

_____

What is your current employment status?

Public assistance _____ Low-wage worker _____ High-wage worker _____

Unemployed _____ Retired _____ Stay-at-home parent _____

Comments _____

Thank you for your participation!

Tool 7.3
House Meetings

You can use the following as handouts or discussion tools to help people do house-meetings for issue ID.

What Is a House Meeting?

A house meeting is a small gathering of people (approximately five to ten). A member or leader invites community members to her home, including family, friends, and neighbors. You use house meetings for a variety of purposes in organizing, including base-building, fundraising, and committee discussions, but they offer an excellent way to investigate problems and identify issues. They help members and leaders to build networks of community relationships that the organization can then mobilize. Staff attend to support the host, but house meetings take the emphasis off the organizing staff.

What Does It Take to Do a House Meeting?

You need to have a list of people to invite to whom you are willing to pose questions about their experiences and probe about what they think should be done about their community problems. This is not a time to gather people to tell them what's on your mind. You need to be ready to really listen to the people you invite.

Once you have a list, it takes about six to ten hours of time to prepare for the house meeting over the course of about three weeks. Call people to invite them, then make follow-up calls to make sure they are coming. Keep in mind that about half of the people you invite will say no, and of those who say yes, only half are likely to come. So to get a group of five people, start with a good list of fifteen. Before the meeting, talk with staff to plan an agenda, prepare what you will say, and get materials such as sign-in sheets or organization newsletters. If you have not facilitated a meeting before, build in a half-hour for a staff member to train you in basic facilitation skills. Get some refreshments and put chairs in a circle. The house meeting itself requires a four- to five-hour evening to set up, hold the meeting, debrief, and clean up.

You need to be able to accommodate five to ten people in your home or at a private, comfortable community location.

House Meetings: Frequently Asked Questions

"What if I do not have a list of people to invite?" Staff can help you think about your contacts and build a list of people, including organization contacts close to

where you live. You only need a group of about five people to have a successful house meeting.

"What if my friends and neighbors are not activists or organizers or don't understand why I am involved in organizing?" A house meeting is a great way to introduce friends and families to this work that is important to you. There is not a lot of pressure on them to follow up.

"What if my home is small?" A comfortable space where you can have five to ten people sitting on chairs or pillows is fine. You do not even need a table. You can also ask a local community organization, such as a church, if you can host a meeting there. Or ask staff to connect you with someone else who does have space for a meeting, and invite people together.

"What if I feel uncomfortable facilitating a meeting by myself?" The organization staff will train you on how to facilitate a meeting and will come to the house meeting to support you.

"What if I don't have the time or money to provide food for everyone who comes?" There's no need to emphasize food. Soda or tea, chips or cookies is enough.

"Is a house meeting a party?" No. Although a house meeting is friendly and interesting, it is not a party. You take time before and after the meeting to ask about each other's families and lives, which helps people to get to know one another, like one another, and build relationships. But a house meeting is an organizing tool to help identify issues and people who want to build power.

Sample Housemeeting Agenda

Time	Activity
6:00–6:15	*Guests arrive and have refreshments.*
6:15–6:20	*Welcome and overview.*
	Host says why she asked people to come, briefly what the organization does, her role with the organization, what will happen in the meeting, and when it will end.

Tool 7.3
House Meetings, Cont'd

6:20–6:30   *Introductions.*

People say their names, their connection to the host, and why they are there.

6:30–6:40   *Purpose of the meeting.*

Host says what the goal of the meeting is: to help learn more about the problems people are experiencing in the community (or a more specific topic, based on the organization and where in the issue ID process the meeting is taking place) and to figure out what we might be able to do about it.

6:40–7:00   *Mini one-on-ones.*

People talk with the person next to them about the problems they are experiencing in the community.

7:00–7:15   *Report backs.*

The group comes together and each pair says what problems it identified. The host takes notes.

7:15–8:00   *Issue ID.*

The host suggests what the two or three top problems seem to be. People explore the problems more deeply, see what they have in common, and brainstorm about potential solutions. The host serves as a facilitator.

8:00–8:15   *Organizing and organization overview. Contact information.*

Someone else from the organization, probably a staff person, talks more about how the organization builds power and what it will do with the contact information and knowledge gained from the meeting. Circulate a sign-in sheet for anyone who wants to give their contact information.

8:15–8:25   *Next steps and commitments.*

The host asks who will make a commitment to take a next step, such as hold a house meeting or come to a follow-up meeting. This is not a high-pressure sales pitch; it is an offer for those who want to do more.

8:25–8:30   *Brief evaluation.*

Everyone says what they thought of the meeting.

Tool 7.4
Sample Target ID Questions

You can use the following questions to start to identify the target of your campaign. It requires some advance research so that you can be as accurate as possible.

What, specifically do we want?

Who has some power to do something about this? (Fill out the following for as many people as you think could do something.)

> Name:
>
> Position:
>
> Who this person reports directly to:
>
> Who she or he thinks they need to deliver to:
>
> Is this person the final decision maker or someone whose support would make it happen?

To find who is the lowest-ranking person who can deliver on the issue, ask:

> How do the positions of each of these people compare to the others?

To find who might be a secondary target, ask:

> Who else could we get to influence each of them?

Exercise 7.1
What's the Issue?

You can use the following scenario and the questions that follow as an exercise to train members to practice identifying an issue. You can also use the questions to look at problems and issues in your own community.

Scenario: Your organization recently won its campaign to add 2,500 jobs to an existing public jobs program for people leaving the welfare system. Members of your organization are now getting these jobs and are talking about problems they're having with transportation. Your organization is ready to develop its next campaign. You are the staff organizer. You are starting to investigate the transportation problem.

Task: Answer the questions below, addressing as specifically as possible what you might potentially find as you identify the issue for the next campaign.

Questions for Identifying an Issue

Problem. What is going on?

Potential Solution. How can it be fixed?

Win-ability. How can we get it fixed? Do we have enough power?

Target. Who can fix it?

Secondary targets. Who else has power in relation to it?

Constituents/Base. To whom does this matter:

    Constituents outside our organization?

    Members of our organization?

Goal. What do we ultimately hope to achieve?

Issue. Based on answering these questions, what might be the policy or administrative change our organization can pursue?

Exercise 7.2
Issue ID: The Problem Tree

(Used by permission of Community Voices Heard)

This exercise trains people to distinguish between a problem and an issue. You can use it to convey the difference between a problem and an issue conceptually or you can use it to begin a discussion about the specific issue the organization may want to address in a campaign. (To see how to use this problem tree exercise to review the role of collective action in making social change, see Exercise 3.3, "The Community Voices Heard Community Teach-In.")

Time: About 30 minutes (40–45 if you include partner sharing at each stage).

Materials: A large image of a tree outlined on paper. Post-It notes. Markers.

Roles: Facilitator, timekeeper.

Room set-up: Movable chairs. Enough blank wall space to post a large image of a tree.

- Facilitator places an outline of a tree on the wall. It is simply a trunk, branches, and roots.

- Facilitator describes the goal of this exercise: To see the difference between a problem and an issue. Possibly to identify issues the organization can address in a campaign.

- Facilitator describes the basic exercise: Participants will create a "problem tree" out of the tree outlined on the wall.

- Facilitator hands out Post-It notes and markers to participants.

- Facilitator asks people to take a few minutes to write on the Post-It notes "problems" that they are facing in their communities or in relationship to what the organization works on—one problem per note. These notes will form the leaves on the tree. Facilitator asks participants to write clearly enough so that others can see it when it's posted on the tree. Facilitator creates an example and posts it as a leaf on a branch to illustrate what the participants will do. Facilitator encourages people to think personally, such as, "I'm about to lose my job," "My child is always sick from the poor air quality in our neighborhood," "The traffic on my street is getting dangerous." Gives participants five minutes and asks them to wait until everyone is done before posting their problem-leaves.

- If time allows, facilitator may ask people to turn to the person next to them first and talk through what they are thinking of writing down, taking two minutes each. You can do this partner-sharing at each or any stage of the exercise. It helps create a buzz in the room, helps people to go deeper in their thinking, and builds relationships.

- Facilitator asks people to call out what they've written and come up to place their Post-Its as leaves on the branches of the tree.

- Facilitator leads a discussion of the "issues" that could arise from these problems, asking *"If that's the problem, what is the solution?"*

- Facilitator writes issues in the trunk of the tree. For example, if a problem-leaf says, "I'm about to lose my job," an issue could be "We need a job training center." Problem: "My child is getting sick from poor air quality." Issue: "The buses need to burn cleaner fuel."

- A visual picture starts to form of the relationship between problems and issues.

- Facilitator leads a discussion about what is at the "roots" of the problems. Encourages people to look more deeply at what creates the issues they face. Examples include racism, stereotypes, unrepresentative government, profits over people. Facilitator writes these words along the roots, or asks people to come up and write what they think. Facilitator leads a group discussion on the issues.

- The group reviews what participants learned in this exercise.

Researching the Politics of an Issue

**LEARNING WHO IS FOR US
AND WHO IS AGAINST US**

Community Voices Heard (CVH) leaders and organizers know that Work Experience Program (WEP) workers want to fight for paid jobs with education and training. They set out to learn the politics of the issue. CVH cofounder Gail Aska attends meetings and coalition events with union leaders and religious leaders to find out where there is agreement on what to do about WEP. Working closely with the organizer, CVH leaders take on other tasks. Betsy facilitates meetings with allies to explore what is and is not winnable at the state and local levels. Janet calls organizations that have developed innovative transitional jobs programs in cities and states throughout the United States. Others explore what Mayor Giuliani's position on job creation would be, determine who on the city council would support the call for jobs, and consider who else will support or oppose a campaign on this issue.

What Is Campaign Research and Why Is It Important?

In campaign research you investigate the forces that shape the issue. Good campaign research empowers organizers and members with information that helps you to choose an effective strategy and create a successful plan to move the target and win your campaign.

In campaign research you get a landscape of the issue and analyze the target and the power dynamics surrounding the issue. You assess the capacity of your organization to take it on.

The history and current politics of an issue can be complex. They can have a negative effect on your campaign if you do not know what to expect. In addition, your ability to develop a winning strategy depends on knowing who the potential stakeholders and opponents are and how they might line up for or against you. Information about how a target acts and reacts helps you choose the most effective actions and tactics.

What Are the Elements of Campaign Research?

Campaign research is made up of the following four elements that inform your campaign plan. We discuss each of these elements later in the chapter.

Landscaping. Campaign research begins with getting an overall picture—the landscape—of the issue. You investigate its history and the possibilities for change in the future.

Target analysis. You know who the target is. Now you acquire an in-depth understanding of the target's position on your issue as well as his pressure points.

Power analysis. You consider who else cares about your issue and how much power they have to support or oppose you. Based on this accumulated knowledge, you honestly assess how much power you will need to move the target and win the campaign.

Organizational assessment. You answer a series of questions about your membership, finances, organizational knowledge, and staffing in order to understand your organizational capacity. This information also helps you determine what kind of strategy you can manage.

Who Engages in Campaign Research?

Staff, members, and leaders who are either part of the organizing committee for the campaign or who form a separate committee to do the research.

You have an organizing committee in place for getting started that will oversee the development and implementation of the campaign. This committee includes both new members of the organization and experienced leaders. An organizer builds the committee and helps the members to do its work successfully. The committee can designate a few members to conduct campaign research, or the entire organizing committee can do research as its main activity.

For purposes of this chapter, we refer to the group of leaders and members who are working with an organizer to do research as a freestanding research committee.

How Do We Conduct Good Campaign Research?

Read, listen, and talk politics with a wide range of people with different perspectives.

The following are some tips to help you conduct good research:

Keep up with the news. Read the newspaper. Watch the news. Listen to the radio. It sounds simple, but local and neighborhood newspapers and magazines, as well as national publications that cover your issues, are important sources of information. Read newspapers and journals that represent the interests of the people involved in your issue. If it's a worker rights issue, read local union papers and business and labor journals. If the issue involves housing or economic development, read real estate papers and journals.

Watch public affairs news programs and television shows, both national and local. Record important coverage to share and discuss with members and leaders. Keeping up with the news tells you where politicians stand. It gives you a sense of public opinion and media interest.

Conduct library research or collect data over the Internet. At the library you can research previous news coverage of the issue or community problem. Ask the librarian how to use the research system there to get what you need. From your office or home, you can use the Internet.

Start with a search engine like Google. At a library you can use LexisNexis, which is an archive of information that requires a fee to access. Search by issue or by people involved in the issue. In addition to reading articles, look at Web pages for other organizations working on your issue. Read their reports and studies. This research tells you the history of an issue and who the players are. (For more on using the Internet to conduct research, see Chapter Six.)

To find out where people who are key to your issue give money and what boards they sit on, talk to researchers in friendly organizations, such as labor unions, or to local political consultants. They can tell you what they know and steer you to current Web pages for public officials or candidates. These pages tell what groups the officials are members of and what issues they care about.

You can go to your local campaign finance board to find out who donates to candidates.

Talk politics. Talk politics with a wide range of people. They may include labor leaders, community leaders, political consultants, elected officials and aides, and people in other community-based or national organizations. Schedule time on the phone or in person and include leaders of your organization. Go to events where you can strike up conversations. Get different viewpoints and positions. Much of what you hear will be officially off the record. You hear people's opinions, not objective facts. That's why you talk to a lot of different people.

Use government resources. Many government Web sites offer information about how the political process works and the hierarchy of an agency. For example, in New York City the Web page for the Department of Planning shows the entire process for changing zoning designations.

Larger advocacy organizations and government watchdog groups, particularly those that work with community organizations, frequently have advocacy guides on their Web sites.

Check out local political meetings. If your issue is related to building or zoning, go to the planning board meeting. If it is social services, go to the social services board hearings. Most local governments have "sunshine laws" that require them to provide information about upcoming hearings and meetings. When you attend community meetings, you meet people, see who the players are, and get notice of other important meetings or events.

If you have trouble finding out about meetings, go to the Web site for the local legislative body. Find out who sits on what committee and who the chair is of each committee. This research will lead you to the chairperson's office, where a constituent liaison can tell you when meetings occur.

Another way to find information about government resources is to call your state representative. Talk to her liaison or go to her office and ask for what you need.

Communicate with the target. Sometimes the target or the target's staff may give you the information you need up front. This meeting is a research meeting, not a place to make a demand. It should be attended by two or three of the strongest leaders of the campaign who come with clear goals of what you want to get out of a meeting. This meeting is different from collective public action because it is not using agitation and power to move the target. Rather, its goal is to find out the target's position.

Meeting with the Target

A group of neighborhood parents working to improve the park in their district decides to find out how the district prioritizes neighborhood parks for capital improvements. First, someone from the leadership team asks for a meeting on behalf of the group with the person the team believes is responsible for approving capital improvements in the parks department. The leader puts a request in writing and then follows up with a phone call. This meeting may take place with the target or the target's key staff.

The letter says something like the following: "We are interested in improving the parks in District 12. We would like to meet with you as the District Parks Manager to find out what needs to be done to improve the administration of services in the park and how we could work together to improve the system."

At the meeting, the leaders ask questions: "What is the process to get what we want done?" "Do you support what we are trying to accomplish?" "If not, what would need to happen for you to support it?"

If the target supports your position or demand, keep in mind that voicing support is different from actually doing something. Campaign development continues, but the campaign research takes a different path. You focus on key questions: Does the target usually follow through on what she says? If not, what makes her follow through? If yes, how close to the actual demand will the target deliver what she promises? The campaign also develops differently, stressing goals and objectives that ensure implementation.

Your ability to get a meeting with the target depends on your issue, the target's position, and your relationship with that person. It can be easier to get than you might think, and it can often be an extremely effective way to get the information you need to begin the campaign.

Throughout campaign research, you spend time thinking about the answers to the questions you pose to yourself and others. Look at the relationship of the answers to one another to see how they fit together.

What Is Landscaping?

Landscaping is the process of developing a full picture of an issue.

You landscape either a major policy issue, such as creating more affordable housing, or a local issue, such as repairing a dilapidated park. In landscaping you look at how the issue has changed over time and what interest groups, organizations, and individuals have been involved in it.

You do landscaping to see your issue's history and potential future. If it's a public policy issue, how is it playing out in your state or at the national level? For example, if you are seeking to create more affordable housing, what kinds of state and federal financial support can your city access? If it's an administrative, corporate, or agency issue, how does it play out within its organizational structure? For instance, if you are seeking an environmental clean-up, has the board of the polluting corporation supported clean-up elsewhere? If it's a community issue, how does it relate to what others are doing? For example, if you want to increase services for people with AIDS, what other public health groups are looking to build their programs as well?

Landscaping tells you what the campaign could look like and what potential opportunities and barriers exist. In an established organization, landscaping tells you if it's worth having a core group of leaders pitch it to the membership.

How Do We Do Landscaping?

In landscaping you get answers to some very specific questions by analyzing the information you get using the research tools discussed earlier.

In landscaping, an organizer working with a research committee explores the following questions:

What is the history of the issue? What has happened on the issue in the past? Who was involved? Was the issue addressed? How has it evolved over time?

What is the current status of the issue? Who is involved now? What is currently happening on the issue?

How could the issue develop? What could create some movement on the issue? For example, would things move on this issue if there was more money in a city budget or if the issue began to affect a new constituency?

Are there any clear patterns and how could these patterns affect our campaign? Over the history of an issue, do patterns occur? Does an organization or individual always get involved at a certain point and shift things? Does a campaign always end in an election year? Do groups in a coalition always get distracted by other things? By identifying patterns you can make sure they do not derail your campaign or you assess how to use them to your advantage.

You take detailed notes and develop lists of stakeholders. You keep track of this information on the computer and with large sheets of paper on the wall so that others can understand and respond to it. The following example shows how to landscape an issue, in this case with a draft demand in place.

Landscaping Employment and Training Issues in New York City

Drafting a demand. CVH starts to develop a campaign to improve the coordination among agencies that provide workforce development services, such as job search, job placement, and basic training. The welfare agency manages some of the services, the youth services agency controls others, and the economic development agency manages some as well. Different city commissioners oversee each of these agencies.

The draft demand is to get the mayor of New York City, Michael Bloomberg, to create a new position, Deputy Mayor for Workforce and Human Development, to oversee all workforce-development programs rather than this oversight being distributed among different agency commissioners.

Learning the history of workforce development. The research team focuses on learning the history of workforce development in New York, including the terms and jargon people use in the field. They meet with staff people from city agencies to find out how the system has worked in the past as well as with people who operate locally based employment programs. They find out which of the city agencies have done a good job and which have not, as well as the dynamics among different agencies. They test the demand of creating a new deputy mayor position to assess resonance and to see who would support or oppose this idea.

Identifying the current status of workforce development. The research team meets to brainstorm about who is affected by workforce-development programs. At the meeting, a member puts a big sheet of paper on the wall. The team creates a list of stakeholders, including specific service providers, clients and consumers of services, business people, and labor and advocacy groups. Later, leaders and staff schedule meetings with some of these key people as well as with friendly people CVH knows inside City Hall to understand how the creation of a new Deputy Mayor for Workforce Development might affect a range of stakeholders, and again, who might support or oppose the campaign.

At the end of this process, CVH realizes that the commissioners who oversee the welfare, youth, and economic development agencies very much want to keep their power. Although CVH has the support of some potential allies, this support is not strong. If CVH runs this campaign, it will have to do so alone. At the same time, no allies oppose it.

Finding out how the issue could develop. The research also tells CVH that it is not the only organization concerned about the division among agencies and commissioners. Some people inside are trying to improve the coordination of city agencies. One commissioner is particularly difficult and does not work with others, but she is close to the mayor. Others are trying to get her to work more as a part of a team. CVH knows now that its issue is at least on the radar screen of some people in City Hall.

Staff meet with program officers in private foundations that fund workforce development to find out if there might be resources for this campaign and to ask if they know of others in the country who are using this kind of coordinating position effectively and if so, how it works.

Looking for patterns. The mayor is up for reelection in the coming year. There is a very strong likelihood that he will win. After analyzing the landscape (and doing a power analysis, which we describe later in this chapter) members and leaders decide it is better to pressure the mayor to address the situation in his next term. In addition to what CVH has learned about this particular issue in the landscaping, it has found in the past that new terms offer opportunities to shake up administrations. Once the mayor gets reelected he is likely to change some of his commissioners. Job creation is a part of his campaign message. CVH can appeal to his need to fulfill this promise and his desire to have a legacy by addressing the need for a more coordinated approach to workforce development in New York City in his next term.

What Is Target Analysis?

Target analysis tells you how a target thinks, acts, and reacts and why.

Once you determine the lowest-ranking person who can meet your demands using the issue ID process we describe in Chapter Seven, you do a thorough analysis of this person and his motivations. This analysis tells you what is most likely to get him to concede to your demands. You are looking for how to use your power to move the target to give you what you want, whether he or she likes you or not.

How Do We Do Target Analysis?

You dig deep and gather the following information about the target:

Clarify basic information about the target. Make sure you know the target's name, title, and place in the organization as well as how long he has held this job.

Understand the target's position. Research what his position currently is on your issue and if it has changed over time. Even if the target's position is generally in your favor, it does not mean he will deliver on your demand. For example, a public official might support government funding of job training programs, but that does not mean she will support your demand for a training program that pays a wage.

To learn the target's position, read past media coverage, review any official correspondence or record keeping, talk with people who understand the politics of the issue, or directly ask the target if she will support your position.

Learn where the target derives his power. Targets generally derive their power from voters, wealth, members, and organizational or government structures and regulations. Many times, agency officials and commissioners derive their power from elected officials.

Politicians derive their power from voters. This group goes beyond who they see as their base of supporters in the general electorate. Politicians get power from the votes of other legislators as well as from their tenure in office or their skill at political maneuvering. Politicians get their power from campaign contributors as well.

Commissioners, high-level bureaucrats, and their key staff derive power from the person who appoints them, who is usually an elected executive such as a mayor or governor.

Lower-level government staff and bureaucrats draw their power from the structures and regulations of an agency and from their tenure with that agency.

Private-sector targets, such as landlords and corporate executives, usually get their power from personal wealth, including cash, property, companies, or stock holdings. They may also derive power from the trustees who oversee their activities.

Heads of unions, community organizations, and similar locally based groups obtain their power from either a board of directors or their membership.

Dig deep. Don't assume you know where the target derives his power based only on cursory information.

Review the policies or issues the target is currently working on. Look at the target's speeches, especially a governor's State of the State or a mayor's State of the City address. For a politician, review the laws he is sponsoring or what he's recently sponsored and what committees he sits on. You can get copies of laws, sometimes for a fee, from the offices of legislative bodies or from the legislative committee. You can get the text of some laws on the Web. Elected officials have newsletters and constituent mailings that outline what they have been involved in. City and state agencies sometimes have reports and Web sites that outline what they accomplished over the year.

Find out who he listens to. You find out who the target listens to and trusts for counsel by reviewing press coverage and asking people who study him.

Investigate self-interest. Figure out what motivates him. Where does the target put his energy? What boards does he sit on, what professional organizations does he belong to? What are his career goals and what does he want his legacy to be? Are members of his family prominently involved in charitable causes or businesses? Sometimes a target's self-interest is clear—elected officials want to stay elected, many politicians want higher office. Sometimes the self-interest is more nuanced. For instance, some politicians are most concerned with making government work. These officials are often quite movable if you are willing to engage in a constructive relationship.

You can't assume that a person's political leanings or identity will tell you if she will be with you or against you. Her politics or identity alone will not tell you where she will stand on your issue, or even more likely, your demand. Political self-interest often rises above everything else. People you see as friends may not do what you ask of them and people you think would never be with you may be willing to support good policy that improves a community problem. You have to do your homework on everyone.

Tool 8.1, Target Analysis Chart, provides a guide to getting and understanding the types of information discussed in the target analysis so far. Tool 8.2 offers a worksheet to use when doing target analysis.

Find out what has moved the target in the past. Knowing what has moved the target in the past helps you to develop your campaign strategy and to identify tactics that will work. (See Chapters Nine and Twelve for a more in-depth look at strategy and tactics.) People who have engaged in recent campaigns with the target are a good source of information. Does the target respond and react to press coverage on an issue, to direct actions and public meetings, to lobbying by important stakeholders? Does she respond to rational policy arguments based on facts and research?

People in power learn to understand tactics and may respond differently over time. For instance, CVH moved Mayor Bloomberg on a campaign within six weeks of his election by going unannounced to City Hall and demonstrating. But while he responded to this tactic early in his first term as mayor, he got used to it. On later campaigns, it was no longer effective.

As with landscaping, you keep careful notes about everything you learn. Tool 8.3 shows a sample chart depicting what moved a target on specific campaigns. Tool 8.4 offers a blank worksheet you can use to record what has moved your target. Exercise 8.1, Getting a Target Snapshot, will help train leaders and members in doing all of this initial target research.

What Is Organizational Assessment?

Organizational assessment tells you two things about your ability to move the target: your organizational power and your internal capacity.

You do this assessment in two steps. In the first step, you look at your organizational power. After you do a full power analysis and choose your strategy, you do the second step, which is to assess your internal capacity and your ability to implement the strategy. We examine the second step in Chapter Nine.

Organizational power is the result of your numbers and your track record. How many people can you move to action, directly or through alliances? Have you won other campaigns that increase your skill and your clout?

Internal capacity is the degree of your financial and human resources for running the campaign. Do you have enough money and staff, or do you have access to these resources? Do you know enough about the issue?

In addition, organizational assessment includes looking at whether or not members buy in to the campaign and if it moves the organization's mission forward.

How Do We Assess Our Own Power?

You review your past campaigns to identify your successes and failures, your strengths and weaknesses.

The leadership of the organization, including the board, the organizing committee members, and the staff, conducts the assessment by asking a series of questions, listed below, and answering them as honestly as possible. In addition to answering questions, they may gather more objective views from allies and other people in the field.

If you use a database to track attendance at meetings and actions, you can easily find the answers to some of the questions.

The following questions will help you begin to assess organizational power:

Who are the constituents in our base?

Who are the constituents who could be in our base?

How many members do we have?

What have we won recently (during the past one, three, and five years)?

When did we win it?

Who was the target?

How long was the campaign?

Did we win on our own?

Who were our allies?

Which of these allies has a stake in our current issue?

Who will stand with us right now?

Who will stand with us if we put some work into bringing them along?

Which allies are we willing to call in on this campaign?

How many constituents outside of our organization did we move to action?

How many could we move now?

How many people with political power can we get to act with us or on our behalf?

Don't forget to evaluate the campaigns that you may not have won. In those cases, did the organization win incremental gains or build limited power? Did it gain knowledge or develop a new base of members? You factor in all of your organization's achievements when assessing your power.

In addition, you use a more nuanced analysis to look at other factors. For instance, do other allies and stakeholders return your calls? Are they willing to meet with your organization? Do they want to know your position on their issues?

How Do We Understand Our Power If This Is Our First Campaign?

You try to get some people involved and see who comes out by engaging in action early.

In an established group, internal mobilizations, such as meetings, outreach days, and trainings, all help you assess when you have enough members who will move on the issue and enable your group to be taken seriously. In a new group, try to get some people involved. For example, a group of homeowners on a block want to stop the building of a high-rise. They do some research and learn the local city council can stop it. They go door-to-door throughout the neighborhood and readily get contact information from people. They hold two well-attended community meetings. Many homeowners are willing to meet with their council representatives and attend actions at their offices. In a small city, this new group has some power.

In a larger city the group's power may not be clear until it engages in action. There are likely to be more forces lined up in opposition or support of the homeowners. The group would have to send ten homeowners unannounced to a council member's office or somehow challenge powerholders collectively in order to know if the group can have some effect.

Working in coalition can also increase the power of a new group. The homeowners may find that the PTA of the local school is also interested in the issue, since the high-rise will lead to overcrowding in the school. If the homeowners work with the parents, they will have more power.

Engaging in public collective action early helps you both to assess your power and show your target, potential allies, and other stakeholders that you have some base that you can mobilize. At what point you do this action is an important judgment call. Do it too early, without a reliable base, and your target won't take you seriously. Do it too late, and the fight might be over. Also, if you wait too long, other organizations become the legitimate representatives on the issue.

Assessing Organizational Capacity and Power: Opposing Pay-Cuts for Parks Workers

The newly elected mayor of New York City, Michael Bloomberg, announces he is cutting the pay of workers in a jobs program in the parks for people transitioning off of welfare. CVH board members, leaders, and staff meet to assess whether or not CVH should develop a campaign with these workers to oppose the cuts. They look at CVH's resources and what the organization is currently working on. CVH has an experienced organizer on staff who worked on the jobs campaign, some uncommitted funds, a base of members who want jobs, and knowledge of the parks system and where workers hang out from doing WEP worker organizing.

CVH understands and has some relationships with unions, particularly the union representing the workers whose pay the mayor is cutting. What CVH does not have in its base are workers from this particular program or a deep understanding of how the program works.

However, according to Zelda, a CVH leader who worked hard to win the jobs campaign, "We organize welfare recipients, and the women who are about to lose their pay are welfare recipients in a program we won. We have to bring them into CVH and work with the union to fight the wage cuts."

Despite what they do not have, leaders, members, and staff assess that they have enough in the form of experienced staff, resources, knowledge about the type of organizing needed, and a connection to the issue. Even without any base or leaders, CVH moves forward to develop the campaign. The campaign ultimately succeeds in stopping the cuts and improving services and education for the workers.

What Is Power Analysis and How Do We Conduct It?

Power analysis is an examination of the external forces surrounding the target. It uses a systematic approach to look at who is with you, who is against you, and how important their support or opposition is to the campaign.

Power analysis tells you the power you have, the power you could have, the power that might support you, and the power that is aligned against you. Initially, power analysis gives you essential raw material for choosing a strategy. Throughout the campaign, you do power analysis as the dynamics of the issue shift.

To do power analysis, you lay out the data you've gathered so far in landscaping, target analysis, and assessing your organizational power and look for pressure points, potential alliances, and likely opponents that will influence the outcome of your campaign activities.

The core work of power analysis is to look honestly and realistically at your organization's power and the power of others. You analyze what it will take to accumulate enough power to win, including what it will take to neutralize the opposition.

Power analysis is a group process that includes leaders and members as well as staff. In the initial power analysis, you lay out the campaign research. You hash out how people view the power surrounding the target. You revisit these topics throughout the campaign.

In your power analysis meeting or a series of meetings you look at the following information:

- Current organizational power—your base of members and leaders
- Potential new constituents who can be part of your base
- Other power players, stakeholders, and potential stakeholders
- Potential allies who could support you in your demands
- Potential opponents who could oppose your campaign

You usually need the two meetings to have a good initial power analysis. In the first meeting, a smaller group of members that includes one or two leaders and one or two people from the research committee sorts out the information the research committee has gathered so far in campaign research. It identifies what to bring to a larger group discussion. In the second meeting, you conduct your power analysis. The power analysis meeting includes the organizing committee members. In this meeting, you post charts and collectively fill in the Power Analysis Grid, as shown in the sample in Tool 8.5, using information the organization has accumulated through its research. Tool 8.6 contains a Power Analysis Grid worksheet you can use for your power analysis.

You look at facts, think about them, and figure out what they mean. Power analysis is not a job for any one person sitting behind a closed door. Power analysis is a skill that some people have a knack for and that most people get better at the more they do it. It draws on the best thinking of those who will implement the campaign.

You can sometimes apply the same questions you use for target analysis to looking at other potential allies or opponents. For example, power analysis shows you that an agency commissioner can make or break your campaign. She is not the decision maker, but if she says no the issue is dead. The campaign then has to include either neutralizing her or gaining her support. Your research tells you whether she will respond to an editorial or to five people arriving unannounced at her office.

You do civics education during this process. People need practical knowledge about how the system works and about past experiences the organization has had on campaigns. They need to know what's in the grapevine about an individual or organization.

You do the initial power analysis grid to get the raw material to choose a strategy that will move the target.

Does Our Power Analysis Change Over Time?

Yes. Power analysis is a focused process at the beginning of the campaign, but continues throughout the campaign as conditions change.

Power analysis is not static. The power dynamics of a campaign are like a chess game. As the players move their pieces, everything adapts and shifts. You start organizing a group of workers to fight for living wage legislation. You succeed in raising the issue's visibility. When a major union gets involved because it sees workers the union can organize, the power dynamics shift. The organization again puts the grid up on the wall. It engages in power analysis to see how to move forward.

What Other Questions Should We Ask Ourselves?

Before moving ahead with the campaign, the board or other governing body of the organization does a brief mission check to make sure the campaign will build the organization in line with its mission and values.

An organizational mission check ensures that a campaign fulfills and is aligned with the organization's mission. Two questions are crucial to ask at this point: How do the campaign and issue match our organizational mission and values? How will the campaign unite or divide our members?

LEADERSHIP DEVELOPMENT OPPORTUNITIES
DURING CAMPAIGN RESEARCH

- *Conduct literature review.* Members and leaders read news articles, journals, and other periodicals, and share information with the research committee.

- *Collect television and radio coverage of an issue and analyze it.* This is an especially good task for members with limited reading skills.

- *Set up and attend meetings with others.* Leaders meet with people who have worked or are working on the issue. They make phone calls, write letters of introduction, and follow up.

- *Analyze information.* The research committee meets to analyze information after it is initially gathered. Leaders identify what information to bring to the power analysis meeting. Then, they hold a power analysis meeting.

- *Facilitate research meetings and power analysis meetings.* Leaders develop skills to guide members to understand the information they are analyzing.

CHALLENGES
IN CAMPAIGN RESEARCH

"We are finding very little information on our issue." If you are breaking new ground with your issue, you may find little information. In that case use what information you can get to choose a strategy and to plan and implement a campaign. If you need to proceed in this way, engage in action either internally or externally, and build points of evaluation early into your campaign plan. These steps will expose you to more information.

"We can't identify who has the power to deliver on our demand." You try to find the person closest to the issue and start doing some small-scale action to find out who the target is.

"The target is unmovable." Everyone can be moved. You just have to find out how. If you cannot move the target you have chosen, try another way to address the issue with other demands and targets in order to achieve the same result.

"Our power analysis shows that no one else is interested in our issue, and we do not have enough power to move the target." This challenge especially happens if you are in a geographically based organization, such as a neighborhood group, and the target is a statewide official. Sometimes you can cut the issue to appeal to other partners or include demands that might not be important to your members but are important to others. If you decide to engage in a campaign alone, you have honest, internal conversations about how long it will take, how you will build the power you need, and ultimately decide if the campaign is worth it.

"Our power analysis shows that there is no way we can win the campaign." Not all campaigns are winnable. Sometimes conditions, laws, and the political climate make it very difficult to win on the demand that members want. You can decide not to waste resources and time by taking on an unwinnable campaign, or you can try to cut the issue differently or choose different demands. Other times, you might decide to take on the campaign just because it is right, taking a movement-building approach. (For more on movement-building, see Chapter Fourteen.) If the organization decides to take on something it can't win, you make sure members understand why it is doing so and the potential impact it could have on the organization. You build in goals and objectives that you can measure and evaluate to make sure members and leaders can evaluate any impact, such as getting one editorial supporting your organization's position or moving six legislators to support your program.

☑ *Be honest with your assessments.* Do not engage in wishful thinking. You don't misread the research team's data and assessments or convince members that the campaign will be easy or winnable if it is not.

☑ *Do be optimistic.* Believe in the ability of your organization and leaders to build power to win something.

☑ *Get a variety of viewpoints.* Don't just go to friends and people who are going to tell you what you want to hear. Go to people with different views and those who may even oppose you.

☑ *Think about different ways to cut the issue.* Your organization does not just look at how the issue affects its own members. The research phase is the time to identify other ways to cut an issue and to figure out ways to engage other constituencies and allies.

Tool 8.1
Target Analysis Chart: Sample Questions

The following chart outlines the main points of exploration for target analysis. You can use this as a tool to train staff and leaders. Tool 8.2 provides a blank Target Analysis Chart Worksheet for you to use in doing research on your specific target.

	Target Analysis	Where to Find Answer	Why It's Important to Know
Power			
Where does the target derive power?	Is she elected or appointed? Does she have power due to wealth or organizational status?	Law, state constitution, city charter, legislative codes, organizational structures, trustee rosters. Conversations with allies, political strategists, friendly politicians.	Tells you the pressure points the target will respond to.
How much power does she have?	Is she accountable to other legislators, to donors, trustees, or others?	See above.	Tells you how much power your organization will need to move the target.

Tool 8.1
Target Analysis Chart: Sample Questions, Cont'd

	Target Analysis	Where to Find Answer	Why It's Important to Know
Issue			
What is the target's position?	Is she for or against or doesn't have a position?	Ask the target in writing and ask for a response. Review policy documents and campaign materials.	Tells you she may support your demand or not have a position.
How big a priority is this issue to the target?	How high up in her priorities is the issue—is it high or low?	Ask the target directly. Review policy documents and campaign materials.	If it's a low priority and her moving to action gets you out of her hair, she might meet your demand quicker. If it's a higher priority, it might take longer, as many groups might be working on the issue, requiring negotiation among them.
Is her position open to change and what would make that happen?	Is she open to change her mind on this issue? What has previous work on this issue with the target been like?	Research previous campaigns or work the target engaged in on this issue.	If she has a history of being moveable or flexible this will help determine your strategy.
Who Does the Target Listen To?			
Who are the people the target listens to?	Does the target have special advisors or friends that she listens to? Family members? Political people or mentors who are important to her career?	Read newspaper coverage of the target and how she operates, looking for names of advisors. Look at agency charts and organizational flow charts. Talk to people.	Helps determine who a secondary target or potential allies might be.
Motivation or Self-Interest			
What is the target's self-interest?	What does she ultimately want to achieve in her position?	Read personal accounts and stories about the target, ask allies and others.	Tells you what to appeal to with the target.
What is the target's motivation?	What does she want for herself now and in the future?	Same as above.	Helps you better understand what may move the target.

Tool 8.2
Target Analysis Chart: Worksheet

Fill in the blanks here as a guide to help you develop a portrait of your target. Complete the second column (Step One), then add the information to the third column (Step Two) as you acquire it.

Target's Name:

Target's Title:

	Step One: Where and How Will We Find the Answer?	Step Two: What Do We Know?
Power		
Where does the target derive power?		
How much power does she have?		
Issue		
What is the target's position?		
How big a priority is this issue to the target?		
Is her position open to change and what would make that happen?		
Who Does the Target Listen To?		
Who are the people the target listens to?		
Motivation or Self-Interest		
What is the target's self-interest?		
What is the target's motivation?		

Tool 8.3
What Moves the Target: Sample

The following chart shows sample information about three campaigns that organizations have conducted over the last three years that moved your sample target. Tool 8.4 provides a blank worksheet you can use to fill in information you learn about what has moved your target on previous campaigns.

Target's name: Mayor Anders

	Issue	Strategies Used	What Worked?	What Did They Finally Have to Negotiate?	How Long Did They Run the Campaign Before Winning?	Why Did the Target Move?
Campaign 1	Smoking Ban—Pass ordinance ending smoking in bars	Alliance Advocacy Media	Alliance Advocacy Media	Allow bars in operation more than 25 years to keep smoking areas.	2 years	Rational policy and self-interest on health and smoking issues
Campaign 2	Bus Route Campaign—Increase numbers of bus routes in low-income communities	Direct action Media Advocacy	Direct action Media	Elimination of 3 routes that were underused	1 year	Media coverage Nuisance campaign at public events
Campaign 3	Food Stamp Campaign—Add 3 Food Stamp offices in city	Direct action Media Advocacy	Direct action Media	Nothing	8 months	Media coverage

What strategies worked in all three campaigns? Media, Direct Action

What strategies might have worked? Advocacy

What did we learn about the target? Cares about media image and likes health issues.

Tool 8.4
What Moves the Target: Worksheet

Fill in the chart using information about three campaigns that you or others have conducted over the last three years that moved your target.

Target's name:

	Issue	Strategies Used	What Worked?	What Did They Finally Have to Negotiate?	How Long Did They Run the Campaign Before Winning?	Why Did the Target Move?
Campaign 1						
Campaign 2						
Campaign 3						

What strategies worked in all three campaigns?

What strategies might have worked?

What did we learn about the target?

Tool 8.5
Power Analysis Grid: Sample

The grid shows sample information for a power analysis of the CVH campaign to create a deputy mayor for workforce development.

	Names of Groups or Individuals	How Much Power Do They Have?	Do We Want Them Involved in Our Campaign?	How Will We Get Them Involved in Our Campaign?
Core Constituency Who is directly affected by the issue?	Unemployed and downsized workers. Welfare recipients, youth of color, and disconnected youth. Members and leaders associated with CVH jobs campaign.	They have the potential to have some medium power on the issue if organized and if they can interject their experiences and perspectives into the media.	Yes.	Recruitment and base-building, especially leadership development and ongoing organizing meetings.
New Constituency Are there new constituencies that have not been working on this issue but who now are being affected by it?	Youth of color and unemployed men.	If organized, there is the potential for strong power since there are many of these constituents. However, these are hard groups to organize.	Yes.	Recruitment at training sites, unemployment sites, and at the neighborhood level.

Tool 8.5
Power Analysis Grid: Sample, Cont'd

	Names of Groups or Individuals	How Much Power Do They Have?	Do We Want Them Involved in Our Campaign?	How Will We Get Them Involved in Our Campaign?
Stakeholders Who are the people who have identifiable self-interest in the outcome of the campaign?	Commissioners and deputy mayors. Businesses looking to hire people. Service and training organizations. Clients of services. Other advocacy groups working on the issue of workforce development.	Employers: some of the biggest have some power. Commissioners and deputy mayors have the mayor's ear and control city agencies. Larger training providers have some power.	Employers: Yes/Maybe Human Services: Yes/Maybe Commissioners/Deputy Mayors: No	One-to-one relationship-building with our key leaders and staff.
Allies Who will support our campaign demands, but do not have a vested self-interest in the outcome?	This campaign does not have allies who do not have self-interest.			
Opponents Who will oppose our demands?	Commissioners and deputy mayors.	Commissioners and deputy mayors are close to the mayor and have his ear.	N/A	Make them irrelevant by getting others to move the mayor, including press and mayoral advisors.

Who or what has successfully moved the target in the past on an issue? The target, Mayor Bloomberg, responds to press—wants a good public image.

Tool 8.6
Power Analysis Grid: Worksheet

You can use the following grid to train staff and leaders to do power analysis.

	Names of Groups or Individuals	How Much Power Do They Have?	Do We Want Them Involved in Our Campaign?	How Will We Get Them Involved in Our Campaign?
Core Constituency Who is directly affected by the issue? Members. Constituents outside the organization.				
New Constituency Are there new constituencies that have not been working on this issue but who now are being affected by it?				

Tool 8.6
Power Analysis Grid: Worksheet, Cont'd

	Names of Groups or Individuals	How Much Power Do They Have?	Do We Want Them Involved in Our Campaign?	How Will We Get Them Involved in Our Campaign?
Stakeholders Who are the people who have identifiable self-interest in the outcome of the campaign?				
Allies Who will support our campaign demands, but do not have a vested self-interest in the outcome?				
Opponents Who will oppose our demands?				(How do we keep them out of our campaign or neutralize them?)

Now, answer this question based on your campaign research as recorded in Tool 8.4: Who or what has successfully moved the target in the past on an issue?

Exercise 8.1
Getting a Target Snapshot

You can use this exercise to begin to get a picture of who the target is, and train or engage leaders and members in doing initial target research. Much more detailed research will follow, but this can be an interesting starting place.

Time: 30 minutes.

Materials: Enough copies of news articles and other materials about the target for each participant to have one. Flip chart and markers for debriefing.

Roles: Facilitator. Readers.

Room set-up: Enough room for everyone to see the flip chart clearly and enough light to read small print.

- Facilitator distributes copies of news articles about the target. *You can search back to when the target won her election or was appointed to her position. These are times when there is usually a flurry of news coverage about a person. You may also include printouts from the target's Web site, campaign literature, or other information that is easy to read.*

- Participants take a few minutes to read the material. Volunteers read a few samples.

- Using a flip chart to write people's responses, the facilitator lists some questions about the target based on what the group has just read. Some sample questions include the following:

  What is her power? What does she do? Where does her power come from?

  Who is she? What is her self-interest? What issues does she care about?

  What has she done before the position she now holds?

  With whom does she ally herself? What is her style or approach?

  Given this information, what's our snapshot of this target?

  What will she respond to?

This exercise can stretch people to look beyond someone's more obvious characteristics. For example, someone who is gay or lesbian may not necessarily have a record on LGBT issues. A man may have a substantial record on women's issues. Reading what reporters have to say about targets can create an interesting and useful starting place to learn about them.

Developing a
Winning Strategy

HOW ARE WE GOING TO WIN?

After spending two months doing research to develop a campaign for transitional jobs for people leaving welfare, Community Voices Heard (CVH) members meet to reflect on what they have learned and to consider the strategy they can use to win the campaign. The meeting includes fifteen people from the research team and the CVH leadership, as well as the organizer, Martha.

Betsy, a leader who has been meeting with allies and other stakeholders, reports that key community and policy organizations are in favor of the CVH Transitional Jobs Bill. She writes their names on a flip-chart and circles the half dozen or so that say they would support the campaign. They are mostly small organizations without a lot of power.

She lists the unions and says they have been reluctant to support the bill. They may even oppose it. They fear the jobs program will solidify a second-tier workforce in city government and cut wages for union workers. "We have to work to get them involved, because without the unions—it will be hard to win this program," Betsy concludes.

Members start talking about what strategies they could use to move the target of the campaign, the city council speaker. Gail hands out a sheet that describes what the research team has learned in its target research. The speaker represents a working-class district in Queens. He does not have a record of championing progressive legislation or focusing on poverty. He is, however, planning to run for mayor, so he may be more open to supporting a jobs program in the coming year.

He is also seeking the support of the city's largest union—which is affected by WEP. "Many of the groups we talked to says he shuts down in confrontational settings," Gail continues. "He won't work with groups that he sees as attacking him, and when he gets mad at a group he stays that way. He will kill any legislation the group proposes in the council."

Members consider their capacity to use various strategies. They are clear that a disruption strategy will not work with the speaker, but they do think that with a direct action strategy of worker actions, culminating with a mass rally at city hall, they can convince the speaker to support the jobs program. Karen, a WEP worker leader, says, "We can do this on our own, we don't need the unions. There are forty thousand WEP workers. Let's show everyone how powerful WEP workers are." Others agree. "It shouldn't be hard," a new leader says, "I have thirty women at my site, and they are all angry. I'm sure I can get them to go."

As they move toward deciding on a strategy, Martha, the organizer, asks people to evaluate the last five CVH actions. She writes the names on a flip chart, as members yell out: Albany Lobby Day! Ground Hog Day! Labor Day Action! City Hall Picket! WEP Worker March! She asks how many people came out for each of these actions. As she writes the numbers on the chart, the mood in the room slowly changes. Twenty-five people, forty-three, sixty-five, ten, and finally the largest action—250 for the Albany Lobby Day, which CVH did jointly with another organization. "How can we move the second most powerful person in New York City," she asks, "when we have an average of forty people at an action—and two organizers?" The members look at each other. Betsy stands up and turns back to the flip chart page where she wrote the list of organizations and unions. "We need more groups involved if we are going to win, especially the unions," she says. Everyone reluctantly agrees.

What Is Campaign Strategy and Why Is It Important?

Campaign strategy is the way or ways that a community power-building organization uses its power to win a demand. An effective strategy provides the framework and method for the campaign.

You figure out the best way that is within your capacity to move the target to give you what you want. This strategy determines the actions and tactics you use in the campaign. You start by asking, "Will a disruption strategy move this target?" and "Do we have the capacity and ability to use disruption?" You do not start by saying. "Let's take over offices."

If the organization just plunges into action with no clear strategy, it goes from event to event with no deep payoff. Targets are strategic. They don't become powerful by doing things without really thinking them through. Organizations need to be strategic to create change. Exercise 9.1 helps people understand what strategy is.

Is Our Constant Base-Building a Strategy?

Yes! Base-building is the core strategy of community power-building organizations.

Through base-building, you bring more people into the political life of a community. You build the power of the community so it can do more than engage in defensive campaigns. It can set the agenda. Sometimes organizations do use strategies without base-building and achieve short-term wins. For example, a media campaign defeats a bill to lift regulations on toxic materials. But corporations are likely to lobby for that bill again. Although you might see some immediate results without base-building, only when those families and individuals who want a clean, toxic-free community have power will corporations stop advancing the pro-toxic law.

What Are the Various Strategies We Can Use?

There are seven main strategies: direct action, disruption, legislative, advocacy, alliance-building, media and public education, and legal strategies.

Tool 9.1 summarizes the following material in a handout, and Tool 9.2 provides a checklist to help evaluate if you have what it takes to implement a particular strategy.

Direct action. In a direct action strategy you engage a target in controlled confrontation. You are in direct negotiation with the target. You mobilize constituents and members of your organization in well-organized, nonviolent events where they directly make a request of a target. This strategy is a show of power. It also builds your power by engaging new people. To use this strategy the organization needs to have a good understanding of when and how to mobilize its base.

Direct actions include accountability sessions, which are mass meetings in which constituents publicly ask yes or no questions of a person with power, the answers to which they can later hold her or him accountable. Direct action also includes target meetings. In a target meeting, a small group of people who represent the larger organization get a meeting with the target because the organization has demonstrated its power. For example, the target agrees to meet with five people in his office because of the five hundred people chanting in his lobby. In these meetings, leaders elicit statements from the target that the organization can hold him accountable to.

Controlled confrontation through direct action requires that an organization has enough juice to turn out a mass number of people, get the target into a room with you, and control the agenda and the target. That control requires advanced constituent leadership and a large team of leaders who can each play a specific role.

Disruption. In a disruption strategy you interrupt the target's day-to-day schedule or interfere with the normal operations of an agency, business, or the state. Actions include sending a group of members to a corporate or government office or establishing a daily picket. This strategy does not require mass numbers of people. Depending on the specific action you choose, you can be effective with ten people or one thousand.

You use this strategy when the target or secondary targets will not acknowledge your presence or when the leadership team decides disruption is the best way to achieve a clear objective, such as getting press coverage or raising the issue in the public eye. A disruption strategy can help to move a target who is concerned about maintaining order.

Disruption is strategic, not chaotic. It is carefully orchestrated and nonviolent. To do effective disruption an organization needs a core group of leaders and a broader membership base who are willing to confront and challenge the power of the state, police, or security officers, and at least some of whom have some experience doing so. It also needs a well-informed, trained, and disciplined membership and a strong tactical team of leaders who can make quick decisions and negotiate with authority figures.

Legislative. In a legislative strategy your organization works with legislative and executive branch leaders to change public policy. This strategy is distinguished by the fact that it usually includes writing a bill as well as passing it. It also includes making sure the bill gets funded and implemented. Each of these elements is essential for making a real policy change.

Constituents meet with legal advisors or other allies to create legislation. Then they meet with legislators or members of a local governing body in their offices to directly ask them to support a bill or program. A legislative strategy usually includes lobby days. These are day-long actions where members descend on a state or city capital and meet with many legislators. You usually hold a march or rally along with a lobby day to get press coverage on the issue and energize participants.

When community power-building organizations use a legislative strategy, they train members to participate in a process that professional experts from advocacy and citizen organizations usually dominate, such as running the lobbying meetings and speaking to the legislators.

The timing of the legislative session can limit when you can use legislative strategies. For example, in New York State the legislature is only in session from January to late Spring. Therefore, a campaign that includes getting sponsors for a bill, passing it through the legislature, and getting it signed by the governor has to take place in this period of time.

You choose a legislative strategy when legislative action or a new law will remedy the problem. You usually prioritize one or two key legislators to work with, such as a committee chair or other powerful legislator, and do basic support work with other legislators. Legislative strategies require the following:

- The ability to move people in decisive legislative districts to move their own legislator
- Enough people in enough districts to get a critical mass of support for the legislation
- The ability to move the legislative leaders, such as committee chairs, who must play a role
- A staff person or leader who can dedicate the time needed to follow up with legislative staff on the status of the legislation and related matters
- Leaders with the skills to negotiate and compromise over policy issues
- Knowledge of the process for city, state, and federal budget development and bill making
- The ability to write legislation or relationships with groups who could help do so
- Time to work the resolution of the issue through the slow process of legislation

Advocacy. In an advocacy strategy your organization improves public or private systems and administrative procedures that affect the issue. You may also get elected officials to create new public programs. This strategy assumes that a target wants systems to work and wants communities to get what they need, she just needs to know there is a problem and a solution to it.

With this strategy you engage in activities such as serving on advisory commissions or surveying the people who use a social service program. You initiate research projects that examine programs, the impact of policies, or other social and economic indicators that may help to convince targets to do the right thing.

Groups that successfully use advocacy strategies usually have some significant wins that give them access to decision makers. They have passed legislation, created programs, or built enough power through direct action or disruption strategies that targets directly respond to them, bringing them, to some extent, inside the decision-making process.

You do not need a lot of people to use an advocacy strategy, but you do need a developed membership base that is experiencing the problem first-hand. You also need a strong leadership team that understands complex issues. The team communicates with bureaucrats who can make something happen and who want and need the organization's on-the-ground information.

Organizations choose an advocacy strategy when a change in systems or procedures will resolve the issue. Advocacy strategies require the following:

- Access to targets, policymakers, and decision makers
- Knowledge about what is happening in the field or in the community that shows your credibility as community representatives
- The capacity to do effective research and to develop easily understandable policy recommendations—either internally or with outside assistance—that deal with an issue
- A target who responds to rational and good-government arguments as opposed to ideology
- A base of organizational power that will make the target listen to your ideas

Alliance-building. In an alliance-building strategy, the issue requires more power than your organization currently has, so you get enough power by forming partnerships with others, including labor, community groups, citizen organizations, and religious-based networks. You use this strategy to combine organizational strengths. You move a target to deliver on a set of goals, objectives, and demands that all the groups agree on. You may run a coordinated campaign, create a formal partnership for the long or short term, or develop a joint project.

An alliance-building strategy is not a sign-on coalition. Although you may participate in coalitions that exist to address a finite set of problems, such as hunger, jobs, or housing, you form strategic alliances to change power structures. You establish a strategic set of relationships and set them in motion to take advantage of the power of each partner in specific ways that move a target to respond to a demand.

Alliance-building strategies take time to develop. You need to have the power to move influential organizations to work with you. Developing this power can take on the elements of a campaign as you learn their self-interest and target the pressure points that will move them to work on your issue.

As you work together, you build trust, honesty, and clarity about the self-interest and needs of each organization. These alliances are not quick-fix solutions to immediate problems. They are strategic remedies to complex problems. (For more about alliance-building, see Chapter Fourteen.)

Alliance-building strategies require the following:

- The ability to compromise and negotiate with other groups working on the issue

- Especially for smaller, grassroots groups working with larger organizations, the ability to bring some power to the table and to be able to use that power when needed

- The ability to find other groups that have power, want to work on your issue, and will make it a real priority for their organization

- The organizational capacity, including staff time, to engage in both the base-building needed to remain powerful as well as the alliance-building needed to have an effective partnership

- The membership support to move slowly on an issue and to devote time to sharing control with other institutions

- Members and leaders who can regularly participate in alliance-building activities

Media and public education. With a media and public education strategy, your organization develops a comprehensive and detailed plan to use public opinion and the media to move a target. You also use this strategy to raise an issue in the public consciousness.

The goal is not to get media coverage. The goal is to move the target. You establish measurable objectives to achieve your goal, such as getting three editorial boards to support your organization's demand. You move reporters and people with influence to write articles, editorials, columns, and special features in support of your issue, or you get them to use their platforms to challenge the target to address the issue. You not only get coverage of your own actions, you also initiate a public dialogue about the issue. Once the target has to respond to both the community and your organization, you use additional strategies to engage in direct negotiation with him.

An effective media and public education strategy requires a comprehensive media plan with clear goals and objectives, including target audiences and a clear message; organizational capacity and commitment to deal with the multifaceted components of implementing a media plan; and leaders and members who can deliver a message about complicated issues in understandable sound bites to both reporters and live audiences.

Legal. In a legal strategy, your organization uses the legal system, the courts, and judicial law to put additional pressure on your target to respond to your demands. This strategy can force the target to respond to an issue she does not want to address. It can move a target to negotiate to avoid a lawsuit. It can also attract press attention to your issue. Members and leaders develop new skills through serving as plaintiffs or by learning about the legal system.

With legal strategies, it is especially important to keep in mind that they support but do not replace the main power-building strategies. Winning a legal battle is not the goal, it is a tool to help achieve the campaign goal.

Effective legal strategies require an in-house legal team or a partner organization that has an expertise in legal matters, a leadership and board that is willing to integrate a legal strategy into the organization, and the ability to respond to the particular requirements of a legal strategy that may affect other aspects of the organization's work, such as city contracts or conflict-of-interest laws.

How Do We Determine What Strategy to Use?

You choose strategies based on two fundamental assessments: will it achieve the goal of moving your target, and does your organization have the capacity and ability to use the strategy effectively.

Members and leaders in a community power-building organization develop strategies collectively in partnership with staff. They assess what strategy to choose by answering the following sets of specific questions. Tool 9.3 presents these questions in a handout. Exercise 9.2 is a quick way to help staff or leaders review the basic considerations for determining what strategy will move a target, and Exercise 9.3 provides a more in-depth strategy exercise.

What strategy will achieve the goal?

- What is the target's position and what does he respond to?

- Does the target support or oppose our demands?

- What tactics does he respond to and what does he not respond to? (For more information on tactics, see Chapter Twelve.)

- Who does he listen to and care about?

- What are some recent examples of what moves the target successfully?

What strategy can our organization implement?

- How much power does our organization have?

- Do we have enough members to get a response from the target?

- Which leaders want to work on this strategy and are they willing to put in time?

- Can we mobilize our members?

- Will the target meet with our organization?

- Does the target feel that he needs to deliver to our members?

- Does our organization have the ability to disrupt the day-to-day business of the target or people connected closely to the target?

What power does our organization need to add?

- What other groups are with us?

- Who will oppose our demands or get involved in the issue once we start to move on it?

- Do we have the power not only to move a target but also to deal with people who oppose us or throw us off track?

What is our organizational capacity?

- Which staff members can we commit to this campaign?

- Do we have organizational experience (staff, board, or leader) to help us develop and implement a successful campaign?

- How much money do we need to conduct this campaign effectively?

- How much money do we have that we can commit to this campaign?

- How can we raise money for this campaign?

- How will this campaign bring in new members and develop our leadership base?

- What other resources or support will we need to put into this campaign?

What Is the Relationship Between Campaign Research and Strategy Assessment?

What you learn in your research, as described in the previous chapter, helps you assess which strategies have the potential to work.

As a result of your landscape research, your strategy deals with the possibility of changes in the campaign and the potential way it could develop.

As a result of your target analysis research, your strategy reflects the target's pressure points and what will effectively move him.

As a result of your power analysis, your strategy reflects your actual power—not imagined or wishful power—as well as identifying other stakeholders who will participate during the campaign, either for or against you.

As a result of your organizational assessment, your strategy is based on your strengths and what your organization can actually do.

Can We Use More Than One Strategy in a Campaign?

Organizations often use a combination of strategies, but keep in mind that the more strategies you use, the more capacity you need, and strategies need to build off of one another.

Your capacity includes the time and energy of members, leaders, and staff. For example, to maintain a ban on toxics, you can effectively build an alliance, which is one strategy, while using the relationships you have with the media, which is a second strategy, but only if you have enough people available to attend meetings, participate in conference calls, and maintain good communication with both allies and reporters.

Keep in mind that multiple strategies always connect and build off of one another. For example, when CVH successfully got Mayor Bloomberg to create the position of Deputy Mayor for Health and Human Services as we describe in Chapters Eight and Ten, he also created a commission to study poverty in the city. The deputy mayor invited CVH to participate in conversations about what the commission should do to address poverty. Using an advocacy strategy, CVH submitted its proposals, then used a media strategy to keep pressure on the deputy mayor to implement its suggestions. CVH increased its power because many of the city's media outlets covered its perspective on the work of the commission and what it should do about poverty. The media strategy also served to strengthen the "insider" advocacy strategy. A different strategy, for example a disruption strategy, would probably have weakened the advocacy strategy.

How Do We Choose a Strategy?

Strategy development is not complicated, but it does require that you look at information, think deeply about it, and decide how to act.

In a community power-building organization, developing strategy is a collective process. Staff and members meet in a campaign strategy session, which gathers the best thinking of everyone who will move the campaign forward and trains people to develop the ability to think, reflect, and act strategically.

Participants in the campaign strategy session include core leaders, board or steering committee members, staff, and working members from the organizing committee and research team. A campaign strategy session is a good way to involve new people who are affected by the issue, as long as they understand the mission and focus of the organization. A trusted ally can also serve as a resource during this meeting.

How Do We Prepare a Campaign Strategy Session?

In order to have a successful session, you thoroughly compile and communicate the research findings and prep the leaders who will facilitate the meeting.

The following are the steps you should take to prepare for a campaign strategy session:

Finalize campaign research findings. Prepare clear, easily digested handouts and large charts with the campaign research findings. You have already organized this information to conduct a power analysis, as we describe in Chapter Eight. One of the charts or handouts for this campaign strategy session is the power analysis grid of potential allies and opponents.

Develop potential strategy scenarios. Prior to the meeting, a small group of core leaders and staff works out a few strategy scenarios for discussion so that the larger group can focus on the "what ifs" and on getting collective buy-in. The small group spends several hours going through the strategy assessment and suggesting different approaches. They look at what they would need in order to take on each strategy and decide if they have it. (See Tool 9.2, Campaign Strategies Checklist.) They show what they think is likely to happen based on taking one route or the other. Sometimes they make a recommendation as to what they think the strategy should be, but their primary job is to lay the groundwork for a good membership discussion and an informed decision. They write up these scenarios so that people can read them before and during the meeting. They prepare to answer questions about the scenarios and about strategies members may suggest that the core leaders do not believe will work at all.

Thinking through strategy approaches is a great opportunity for leadership development. Working out the scenarios challenges experienced people to look at all the angles, talk about their ideas in a small group, and prepare to make a case and be accountable to a larger group of people.

Conduct leadership prep. Staff members prepare two or three of the core leaders to facilitate the session. At least one person is assigned to making sure everyone participates in the strategy session. The facilitators prepare to present and discuss the research findings, the scenarios, the basic concepts of strategy, and all the materials being distributed at the meeting.

Develop and distribute written materials. To summarize, you prepare the following written materials and send them to members in advance of the session: agenda with goals, campaign research findings, power analysis grid, list of all available strategies, and strategy scenarios for this campaign.

Prep members who will be attending the meeting. Staff call members before the meeting and discuss the campaign and the goals for the strategy session. They briefly review the potential strategies and go over the written materials for the meeting. Tool 9.4 offers a sample agenda for a strategy session.

What If Our Organization Can't Implement the Type of Strategy We Need to Win?

Don't undertake a strategy you cannot implement.

Taking on a strategy when you do not have the organizational capacity or the power to implement it can diminish your ability win the campaign. Instead, play to your strengths.

For example, in the CVH jobs campaign, members realized that a disruption strategy featuring a WEP worker strike—forty thousand WEP workers not going to work—would be a significant show of power and would win the campaign. But the organization knew it did not have the staff or money to make such a strike happen.

Instead CVH knew it could build a small leadership team of WEP workers. It could turn out approximately thirty to fifty WEP workers regularly and up to 150 at strategic times. This number was enough to move unions, including a large municipal union that could shape public policy, to support the campaign. CVH also had on-the-ground information about how the WEP program was truly functioning and it had WEP workers who could effectively communicate this information to the press and the public. The campaign strategy therefore included media and public education, alliance-building, and direct action strategies. Rather than trying to organize a weak strike, the organization built its strategy around its strengths and ultimately won the campaign.

You can take on new strategies or a strategy that you may not currently have the capacity to pull off if you have a concrete plan of how to successfully build the capacity to do so.

LEADERSHIP DEVELOPMENT OPPORTUNITIES
DURING STRATEGY DEVELOPMENT

Each strategy offers different opportunities for leaders to develop:

- *Direct action:* Recruit and mobilize; run large-scale actions
- *Disruption:* Make decisions on a tactical team; run actions

- *Legislative:* Facilitate meetings; schedule and hold district legislative meetings and meetings on lobby days
- *Alliance-building:* Represent the organization at ally meetings; participate in meetings with allies; develop and maintain organizational relationships
- *Media and public education:* Develop and manage a media plan; be a press spokesperson; organize and attend editorial board meetings
- *Advocacy:* Develop a research project with staff; help to develop a survey; survey members; conduct research on policies
- *Legal:* Work with legal staff on developing case; serve as plaintiff on the case; negotiate in out-of-court settlements

CHALLENGES
IN STRATEGY DEVELOPMENT

"Our members just want to get everyone they know to write e-mails and letters to the target." Writing to the target is an example of one kind of action you could do, but in itself it is not a strategy. The desire of members to move directly to action or to discussing tactics is a common challenge that they learn from experience is not effective. In Chapter Twelve, we talk more about the importance of connecting actions to strategies in the context of campaigns.

It is the job of experienced leaders and organizers to continually help people to distinguish between actions and strategies, between what really builds their power and what does not, and not to let these kinds of distractions derail a group from effective strategic thinking.

"Since we're an organizing group, our leaders think we should always use disruption first." As with any strategy choice, you only use disruption if your research shows it's the way to move the target, you need to use it, and your organization can do it in a disciplined, nonviolent way.

"Members want the organizer just to go meet with the target." If the organizer meets alone with the target, he or she may get a short-term result, but this action does not build community power. Members may decide that an organizer should meet with a target as part of an advocacy strategy, but they should make every effort to send a leader to this meeting as well. If a staff person participates in a meeting with a target, the goal is to have an impact on a policy or administrative function, not to build the influence of an individual staff member.

"Our strategy is not working." Sometimes you start to work on the campaign and find out that the strategy does not work. You may have overestimated your power or the willingness of other groups to work with you, or you did not do adequate target research. Choosing the wrong strategy does not mean that you will lose the campaign. If the strategy is not working, you evaluate why, then decide if you will start again.

ESSENTIAL ELEMENTS
FOR DEVELOPING A WINNING STRATEGY

☑ *Show your power.* You include mobilizations of members in all of the strategies to ensure that throughout the campaign allies, stakeholders, and targets know that you have power.

☑ *Have all strategies connect to your base-building.* For example, if you are using a media strategy, you develop new members to be spokespeople and include new members on the committee managing the media strategy.

☑ *Use the strategies you need to win.* Organizations often use a combination of strategies, but keep in mind that the more strategies you use, the more capacity you need, and if you use multiple strategies, they need to connect with one another.

☑ *Develop strategy based on a realistic assessment of your own power.* You must engage in an honest evaluation of your own power and capacity. Overly ambitious thinking is not useful in strategy development.

Tool 9.1
The Strategies

You can use the following as a handout for staff or leadership training to help people to understand strategy development. For more about actions, see Chapter Twelve.

Strategy	Goal	Target Responds to . . .	Organizational Capacity Needed	Main Organizing Work	Sample Actions	Training Needs for Members
Direct action	Build enough organizational power to make a target do what you want.	Raw people power in a room.	Ability to turn out large numbers and get target in a room.	Membership recruitment and large-scale mobilization to show power.	Accountability session. Day in the life. Target meeting.	Recruitment. Membership turnout. Mobilization. Running large actions.
Disruption	Disrupt the operations of state power and civil society to get targets to meet with you and cede to your demands.	Nuisance tactics that make his or her life or community uncomfortable.	Ability to coordinate and manage confrontational actions.	Ongoing disruptive actions that apply nuisance tactics.	Office takeovers. Street closures. Pickets. Boycotts.	Recruitment and mobilization. Action training. Political education. Media and street action.
Legislative	Do enough effective work to move enough legislators and elected officials—including their staff—to support a policy or legislative demand.	Lobbying techniques that engage constituents, rational policy, and good government arguments.	Membership base in important districts and the ability to mobilize them in their districts. Ability to generate mass letters, phone calls, and legislative visits.	Organizing legislative meetings with members.	Lobby days. Legislative meetings. Briefings. Work in districts.	How to run house meetings. How to lobby. How to speak to power. Petitioning and letter writing. How government works.

Advocacy	To develop "good government" and good policy arguments to move your targets.	Good public policy and rational decision-making.	Ability to conduct effective policy research and program evaluation either internally or in partnership with another organization.	Research, surveying constituency and developing effective policy reports and arguments.	Briefings for elected officials, policy officials, allies, and media.	How to conduct surveys and do other research.
Alliance-building	Work to build an alliance of organizations that will have enough power to move a target.	The organizations working together and the united power they represent.	The ability to move other stakeholders with power to participate in a deep way on your issues. The resources for staff to coordinate the alliance.	Identifying stakeholders. Relationship-building with allies. Moving allies. Staffing alliance activities.	Actions such as lobby days, marches, or press conferences where all groups participate.	How to facilitate meetings. Power analysis. Negotiating with allies. How unions, religious institutions, and allies operate.
Media and public education	Get media to cover your issues and your position in a way that will move the target. Educate the general public to support your position	Unfavorable press on his or her unwillingness to act on a demand or to act negatively. Positive press on your demand.	Ability to develop and implement a comprehensive media plan. Leaders who are trained to speak. An issue that has the capacity to attract press attention.	Getting press stories, editorial board meetings, prepping members, and creating actions that attract press coverage.	Media briefings. Editorial board meetings. Creative actions. Letters to the editor, op-ed pieces, and press conferences.	Media training—messaging, op-ed writing, press releases, and similar basics. Public speaking training.
Legal	To force the target to respond or negotiate.	Unfavorable press or potential legal hassles.	In-house legal skills or partners, ability to lose a related funding stream.	Working with legally trained allies, getting press for a lawsuit, finding plaintiffs.	Press conference with plaintiffs. Serving papers to the target.	How to serve as plaintiffs, understanding the legal system.

Tool 9.2
Campaign Strategies Checklist

You can use the following points as a guide for the strategy development process to help evaluate if you have what it takes to implement a particular strategy.

Direct Action Strategy. Do we have enough juice to do the following?

- ☐ Turn out a mass number of people.
- ☐ Get the target into a room with you.
- ☐ Control the agenda and the target; this step requires advanced constituent leadership and a large team of leaders who can each play a specific role.

Disruption Strategy. Do we have the following?

- ☐ A core group of leaders and a broader membership base who are willing to confront and challenge the power of the state, police, or security officers, and at least some of whom have some experience doing so.
- ☐ A well-informed, trained, and disciplined membership.
- ☐ A strong tactical team of leaders who can make quick decisions and negotiate with authority figures.

Legislative Strategy. Do we have the following?

- ☐ The ability to move people in decisive legislative districts to move their own legislator.
- ☐ Enough people in enough districts to get a critical mass of support for the legislation.
- ☐ The ability to move the legislative leaders, such as committee chairs, who must play a role.
- ☐ A staff person or leader who can dedicate the time needed to follow up with legislative staff on the status of the legislation and related matters.
- ☐ Leaders have the skills to negotiate and compromise over policy issues.
- ☐ Knowledge of the process for city, state, and federal budget development and bill making.
- ☐ The ability to write legislation or relationships with groups who could help do so.
- ☐ Time to work the resolution of the issue through the slow process of legislation.

Advocacy Strategy. Do we have the following?

- ☐ Access to targets, policymakers, and decision makers.
- ☐ Knowledge about what is happening in the field or in the community that shows our credibility as community representatives.

Tool 9.2
Campaign Strategies Checklist, Cont'd

- ☐ The capacity to do effective research and to develop easily understandable policy recommendations—either internally or with outside assistance—that deal with our issue.
- ☐ A target who responds to rational and good-government arguments as opposed to ideology.
- ☐ A base of organizational power that will make the target listen to your ideas.

Alliance-Building Strategy. Do we have the following?

- ☐ The ability to compromise and negotiate with other groups working on the issue.
- ☐ The ability to bring some power to the table and to be able to use that power when needed.
- ☐ The ability to find other groups that have power, want to work on our issue, and will make it a real priority for their organization.
- ☐ The organizational capacity, including staff time, to engage in both the base-building needed to remain powerful as well as the alliance-building needed to have an effective partnership.
- ☐ The membership support to move slowly on an issue and to devote time to sharing control with other institutions.
- ☐ Members and leaders who can regularly participate in alliance-building activities.

Media and Public Education Strategy. Do we have the following?

- ☐ A comprehensive media plan with clear goals and objectives, including target audiences and a clear message.
- ☐ Organizational capacity and commitment to deal with the multifaceted components of implementing a media plan.
- ☐ Leaders and members who can deliver a message about complicated issues in understandable sound bites to both to reporters and live audiences.

Legal Strategy. Do we have the following?

- ☐ An in-house legal team or a partner organization that has expertise in legal matters.
- ☐ A leadership and board that is willing to integrate a legal strategy into the organization.
- ☐ The ability to respond to the particular requirements of a legal strategy that may affect other aspects of the organization's work, such as city contracts or conflict-of-interest laws.

Tool 9.3

Campaign Strategy Assessment

You can use the following questions to organize what you know about the target and your own power and to choose an effective strategy to move him or her.

What Is the Target's Position and What Does He Respond To?

Does the target support or oppose our demands?

What tactics does he respond to and what does he not respond to?

Who does he listen to and care about?

What are some recent examples of what moves the target successfully?

How Much Power Does Our Organization Have?

Do we have enough members to get a response from the target?

Which leaders want to work on this strategy and are willing to put in time?

Can we mobilize our members?

Will the target meet with our organization?

Does he feel that he needs to deliver to our members?

Does our organization have the ability to disrupt the day-to-day business of the target or people connected closely to the target?

What Power Does Our Organization Need to Add?

What other groups are with us?

Who will oppose our demands or get involved in the issue once we start to move on it?

Do we have the power not only to move a target but also to deal with people who oppose us or throw us off track?

What Is Our Organizational Capacity?

Which staff members can we commit to this campaign?

Do we have organizational experience (staff, board, or leader) to help us develop and implement a successful campaign?

How much money do we need to conduct this campaign effectively?

How much money do we have that we can commit to this campaign?

How can we raise money for this campaign?

How will this campaign bring in new members and develop our leadership base?

What other resources or support will we need to put into this campaign?

Tool 9.4
Sample Agenda for a Strategy Session

The following session requires about three and a half hours, which includes enough time to review all the information as well as adequate time for discussion, evaluation, analysis, and decision making. (See Tool 1.3 in Chapter One for the "Six Ss for a Successful Meeting.")

Step One: Background

Welcome. (10 minutes) The facilitators welcome everyone. Throughout the session, they practice cofacilitation and shared leadership.

The facilitators ask people to introduce themselves, say their role in the organization, and explain why they are involved in planning this campaign.

Research tour. (15 minutes) The facilitators ask people to go around and look at the research information posted on the walls. After a few minutes, everyone finds a partner and talks about what they've read. The facilitators can suggest structured questions or just have people talk for a few moments. The research tour serves as a warm-up exercise for the session.

Review goals for this campaign session. (5 minutes) The facilitators review the following goals for the meeting and answer any clarifying questions:

1. Understand what campaign strategy is and the different types of strategies that are possible. (See Tool 9.1.)

2. Identify the campaign strategies we will use in developing our campaign plan.

Review campaign goals and demand. (5 minutes) The facilitators review the goals and demands for the campaign and make sure everyone is clear about them.

Campaign research overview. (10 minutes) Members say what they think are the most important points from the research. People from the core leadership team say what they think is most important.

Campaign strategy overview. (10 minutes) The facilitators review the various campaign strategies possible and answer any clarifying questions.

Step Two: Choosing the campaign strategy

Lay out the scenarios. (20 minutes) Leaders from the core team present the scenarios for this campaign and answer clarifying questions.

Consider each scenario. (60 minutes) The facilitators use Tool 9.3, Campaign Strategy Assessment, to guide a discussion about the strategy that people want to pursue in this campaign. They point out what is needed to implement each strategy. The facilitators keep the following in mind:

Tool 9.4
Sample Agenda for a Strategy Session, Cont'd

- **Timed decision making.** The facilitators time the discussion and move it steadily toward a clear decision. To get everyone talking and energized, the facilitators intersperse the large-group discussion with questions posed to pairs and small groups.

- **Actions are not strategies.** Depending on the experience of the group, the facilitators may need to clarify the difference between actions and strategies. Campaigns are made up of strategies; strategies are made up of actions. It's common for people to say, "Let's do a march!" The facilitators and other leaders are prepared to talk about how a march is an action, not a strategy.

- **Making a case.** Leaders learn to make a good case for the strategy they think will work, based on their experience and instincts. They talk about campaigns they've participated in and help others to see the clear reality of a political situation.

Break. (15 minutes)

What ifs. (30 minutes) Although the what ifs have likely come to the surface, when the group reconvenes it looks in depth at all the angles for each possible scenario. What if the mayor loses her reelection bid? What if no one comes to our major actions? What if the budget process in the state capital gets delayed? Good strategy decisions require a thorough evaluation of the what ifs.

Going with what the members want. (40 minutes) The facilitators move members toward a consensus decision or, if necessary, a vote. Members may want to try strategies that the leaders or staff do not think will work. In a community power-building organization, you need to listen to what the people most affected by this campaign really want to do. Community Voices Heard has at times gone ahead with strategies the members wanted even when the most experienced leaders or staff in the organization did not think they would work. When this happens, build in clear points for the members to evaluate together whether or not the strategy is moving the target.

Step Three: Wrap up.

Review strategy decisions. (10 minutes) The facilitators review the decisions made during the session and the follow-up steps that need to occur.

Close. (10 minutes) The facilitators conduct a quick meeting evaluation. They go around the room and quickly ask people to say what they thought about the meeting and the plan for moving forward. One way to close a long meeting that leads to an important decision like this is to go around and ask each person to say one word that describes what they are feeling, so you hear a rapid round of "energized," "psyched," "nervous," "exhausted," "can't wait." You get everyone's voice into the room and get a charge for moving forward.

The facilitators thank everyone for participating.

Exercise 9.1
What Is Strategy? The "Give It Up!" Game

The following exercise helps people understand what strategy is. This game is a useful energizer for a long meeting.

Time: 20 minutes.

Materials: Small trinkets, such as books, pens, T-shirts, hats, mugs. (If you can't get these items, use the alternative in the second step.) Give it Up! cards for people to fill out with their strategy. A list on a flip chart for debriefing.

Roles: Facilitator.

Room set-up: Enough room for people to see each other clearly. A flip chart board for debriefing the exercise.

- The facilitator gives each person a trinket.
- The facilitator asks everyone to stand up and check out everyone else's trinkets. (If you don't have trinkets, the facilitator asks people to stand and check out what other people are wearing or holding, such as a pen, a pair of earrings, a sweater.
- The facilitator tells people to decide what someone else has that they want.
- The facilitator passes out Give It Up! cards; each card has five questions on it:

  1. What do I want?

  2. Who has it?

  3. What approach will I take to get what I want?

  4. What am I specifically going to do to get what I want?

  5. What will make the other person give it to me?

- The facilitator asks people to take five minutes to fill out the cards.
- The facilitator reviews the following components of strategy assessment, and jots them down on a flip chart, saying that each component reflects the questions on the Give it Up! cards:

  Demand:

  Target:

  Strategy:

  Actions:

  Pressure Points:

- The facilitator asks a few people to say what they wrote and notes it on the flip chart next to the corresponding organizing concepts.
- The facilitator uses the examples to ask if a person would get what she wants just by starting to act. The debrief points out the difference between specific actions and the plan behind them.

You can use the following as a quick exercise to help staff or leaders review the basic considerations for determining what strategy will move a target.

Target A is the mayor of a major city. The mayor does not have to worry about voters because it his last term. He has no other political ambitions and has a good job in the private sector to return to. He is quite wealthy and not beholden to donors.

He has no politics. He is a manager technocrat who wants things to work well. He very much wants to be known as a problem solver who got things done. He strongly believes in the private sector. He is socially liberal and makes personal donations to a wide range of nonprofit groups in the arts and children's services.

Answer the following questions:

- What is the mayor's self-interest?
- What does he care about?
- What does he respond to?
- What strategy might move this target? What strategy would not move this target?

Exercise 9.3
Using Your Campaign Experience to Train on Strategy

The following offers an outline for doing a strategy exercise using a campaign your organization has conducted or a campaign that someone can talk about in detail. Participants need to have some knowledge about the target or you need to be able to substitute a "mock" target. For instance, we have successfully done the following exercise using the example of the Community Voices Heard Transitional Jobs Campaign and substituting the current mayor of New York City for the actual target of the campaign, who was the city council speaker.

Time: 90 minutes.

Materials: Campaign Strategy Assessment and Campaign Strategies Checklist for each participant.

Roles: Facilitator. Campaign resource person with knowledge of the campaign.

Room set-up: Enough room and moveable chairs for participants to form small groups.

- Participants form small groups (Example: For twenty total participants, five groups of four.)

- Campaign resource person(s) reviews the elements of the sample campaign for the full group: issue, goal, demand, target. **(10 minutes)**

- Facilitator distributes Campaign Strategies Checklist (Tool 9.2) and Campaign Strategy Assessment (Tool 9.3)

- Participants address the first section of the Campaign Strategy Assessment: What is the target's position and what does he respond to? **(10 minutes)**

- Facilitator reviews the strategies and what an organization needs to pursue them, using the Campaign Strategies Checklist. **(10 minutes)**

- Small groups convene and decide what they need to know about the organization, the political environment, allies, media, and so on in order to choose a strategy. They develop a list of questions. They may use the Assessment and Checklist for reference. **(15 minutes)**

- Participants come back together. Each small group asks the campaign resource person(s) their questions. (About **10 minutes,** depending on the number of small groups.)

- Small groups reconvene and choose one or more strategies they believe will work to move the target and win the campaign. **(15 minutes)**

- Participants reconvene and discuss what strategies they chose and why. **(10 minutes)**

- Campaign resource person(s) tells what actually happened in the campaign. **(5 minutes)**

- Participants evaluate the exercise and review what they learned. **(5 minutes)**

Planning a Comprehensive Campaign

**PLOTTING OUR PLAN—
DECIDING WHAT WE WILL DO**

Fifteen Community Voices Heard (CVH) members gather on a Saturday morning. They greet each other and pass around a pot of coffee. They are excited to be ready to make some final decisions and put together the pieces of the jobs campaign plan. They walk around the conference area, read sheets of chart paper posted on the walls, and refer to their handouts. One chart has a large picture of the target, City Council Speaker Peter Vallone. It lists who he listens to, who could move him, and possible actions and tactics that could move him. Another chart is a power analysis that shows the other organizations that support the demand for jobs, which organizations have not yet made a decision, and which organizations could potentially oppose the campaign. Another piece of paper outlines the strategies members have chosen: build a base of workers and an alliance with the city's largest municipal union, and use a media and public education strategy to support the main strategies.

Over the course of this full-day meeting, members develop objectives for recruitment, including working to get the chair of the city's General Welfare Committee to introduce the jobs bill. They identify actions that will help to move the union and raise public awareness. They decide how they are moving forward.

What Is Campaign Planning and Why Is a Campaign Plan Important?

In campaign planning, you plot how you will mobilize your power to move a target to deliver on a demand. A plan helps you reach your goal and implement your campaign strategically and effectively.

209

You also determine a public message that communicates the problem and its solution. You make final decisions about your objectives, and you outline the timing and nature of actions and tactics. Finally, you put all the decisions into a written plan to guide the implementation of the campaign.

Without a campaign plan, you are more likely to engage in unfocused activities that do not contribute to getting targets to meet your demands. A campaign plan also provides benchmarks you use to evaluate the progress of the campaign and the impact of specific actions. The organization uses it to communicate clearly how it is addressing an issue.

What Does a Campaign Plan Include?

The campaign plan includes nine major components:

- A campaign goal
- A demand or set of no more than three demands
- A primary target
- A secondary target, if needed
- Key strategies that will support your primary strategy of base-building
- A series of objectives that you can evaluate
- A preliminary message that you will continue to develop and refine
- The major actions you want to execute
- The types of tactics you either could or should not use, based on your target analysis

Tool 10.1, the Components of a Campaign, provides a handout listing these nine elements and what they are for, along with an example of each. Table 10.1, Components of the Campaign Plan, shows how each of these elements works in the plan.

Table 10.1

Components of the Campaign Plan

Element	At the End of Planning You Will Have . . .	Definition	Action	Example
Goal	An agreed-upon common campaign goal	What you ultimately want to achieve: the big picture.	Structural change in power.	End the Work Experience Program (WEP) for welfare recipients.
Demand	A clear, targeted demand or set of not more than three campaign demands.	The specific programs and policies that you want to change or see happen.	The city council creates and implements a public policy.	Create a paid transitional jobs program for ten thousand welfare recipients.
Primary target	Everyone in agreement and understanding who the target is and why.	The person who can give you what you want.	Target identification determines the target.	Speaker Peter Vallone
Secondary target	If the analysis shows you only have enough power to move a secondary target, you will identify and agree to who that person is.	The person who can apply pressure to move the target to deliver on your demand.	Power analysis combined with target analysis gives you the secondary target.	The head of the municipal union.
Strategy	Identified the key strategies you will use to support your primary strategy of base-building.	The way or ways you use your power to win your demands.	Implement a coordinated legislative, direct action and media strategy.	Get media coverage to move speaker, build public support for transitional jobs, and neutralize opposition. Build a base of workers to move union and speaker. Create and pass a city council bill for transitional jobs.
Objectives	A series of objectives that you can evaluate.	The steps you need to take in order to get what you demand. How you measure progress toward your goal.	A city councilperson who is accountable to welfare recipients and exercises power over the council speaker who can get legislation passed	City councilperson introduces a Transitional Jobs bill.

Table 10.1

Components of the Campaign Plan, Cont'd

Element	At the End of Planning You Will Have . . .	Definition	Action	Example
Message	A preliminary message that you will continue to develop and refine. This message may change as you target it for different audiences.	A short, three- to five-sentence statement that addresses the problem and the issue or the solution you seek.	At a press conference announcing the results of a study of the workfare system, the members who speak on behalf of the organization include the campaign message as part of their statements.	The WEP program is a "public-sector sweatshop" that forces people to work in dead-end jobs with no education or training. The Transitional Jobs Program will replace WEP with a program that provides a living wage to workers and education and training to help them move to full-time employment so they can support their families.
Actions	Identified major actions that you want to execute. You do not plan the actions in this stage, you just identify the type of action and when it will take place.	A collective show of power that directly aims to move a target or decision maker.	The organization exercises power in connection with a demand.	A mass direct action. (Or a more specific action, such as a WEP worker march to coincide with May Day.)
Tactics	Identified the types of tactics that you may— or should not—use, based on your target analysis.	What you do to challenge or engage powerholders and achieve the goal of an action.	The leaders decide on two or three specific components of an action.	The plan may include the following details or more generally say "people power in the streets": A group of CVH members delivers invoices to city hall demanding back pay for their unpaid WEP jobs, and members write letters to the editor about the problems with WEP and the need for a transitional jobs program.

Why Do We Need a Written Plan?

When you write out the plan, the organizing committee has a detailed, time-specific work plan it can use to guide the campaign.

A written plan helps you do the following:

- *Keep on track.* When you outline every aspect of the campaign and place it on a timeline, you stay focused.

- *Conduct effective, ongoing evaluations.* You guide important conversations among members and leaders about problems in the campaign and what you are doing right.

- *Know when you have reached an objective and can move forward.* You avoid getting stuck.

- *Assess and evaluate inevitable shifts.* The plan helps you assess shifts and changes in the issue as well as in power dynamics, public sentiment, or funding.

- *Easily communicate about the campaign with the entire organization.* Leaders, members, and constituents all read and understand the plan.

- *Facilitate political education, training, and leadership development.* People see the reasons for choosing specific targets, strategies, and tactics. Everyone learns about the political process and the real world of policymaking and power.

How Do We Do Campaign Planning?

Campaign planning occurs in a series of meetings between individuals and in small groups, then generally culminates in a larger meeting where members and leaders look at all the pieces together and agree about how to proceed.

You include members and leaders in campaign planning to get their buy-in on the campaign and to choose strategies, objectives, and messages that resonate with them. There are four steps for effective campaign planning:

Review decisions. The organizer and leaders review the decisions about the goal, demands, target, and strategy. They confirm that all the pieces hang together.

Develop objectives. Members develop objectives, the steps to win the demand.

Develop a message. The organizer and leaders develop a campaign message to help make sure that everyone in the organization communicates clearly and consistently about what you want and what you are doing to get it. You devote at least one session and some time to test the message during planning.

Hold a campaign planning session. Once all the information is in and members draft their decisions, you hold a campaign planning session to lay out the plan and have members ratify it.

What Is a Campaign Planning Session?

A campaign planning session is a meeting or series of meetings where members see the results of the research and development phase and use this information to finalize and ratify a plan.

If your campaign planning includes many new people, you may hold a series of weekly evening meetings or a long weekend meeting in order to provide any necessary training and to move through all of the information thoroughly. You address a different question each night: "What is our strategy?" "What is our message?" You then come together on a Saturday for a final campaign planning session where members review and fine-tune the preliminary decisions and ratify them.

This process applies to a proactive campaign, where you have time for extensive planning. For a reactive or crisis situation, you make decisions over a shorter period.

What Are Campaign Objectives?

Objectives are the steps you take to move your target to meet your demands.

An objective has a specific outcome and is measurable. You have several objectives in a campaign. These outcomes in and of themselves have limited effect, but together they create a change. Here are two examples of campaign objectives: recruit two hundred new members; get five articles in local newspapers. Generally, you have the following four types of objectives:

Processes. Periods of time in which you conduct specific activities. In a campaign plan you identify when something starts and when it ends. For example, "On April 1, we will initiate doorknocking to recruit public housing residents; we will end doorknocking on May 30."

Deliverables. Measurable, concrete accomplishments or tangible products. For example, "three hundred new members," "two hundred surveys completed," "a legislative bill," "a research report," "an article in a major paper."

Internal actions. Collective organizational events that test your organization's capacity, leadership, and the resonance of an issue, and that train leaders. Examples include a town hall meeting or a mass canvass. (We describe internal actions in more detail in Chapter Twelve.)

Direct actions. Collective displays of your organization's power. Activities and events you can evaluate that you design in order to get a reaction from the target. For example: "Did we pull off an accountability session in June? Did the mayor come to the accountability session?"

How Do We Determine Campaign Objectives?

A small group of leaders and staff draft objectives that members further develop and ratify in the campaign planning session.

In developing objectives, you continue to conduct some research about how you will meet each objective. There are usually two versions of how things get done. One way is "by the book." For example, the legal process of how a bill becomes a law. You generally find this information in the library or on the Web page of an agency, government body, or for other types of changes, corporation.

Then there is the "realpolitik" version. How do things really work? What are the politics of an issue? Who do you have to move to make sure the right person does what you need him to do? You generally find out this information more informally, through conversations with political people, reading the newspaper, and talking to allies. Balancing "by the book" with "realpolitik" ensures that you develop the full range of objectives you need in order to win.

The following three factors determine the objectives:

The demand. You break down the process for meeting the demand. For example, if the demand is to stop a developer from building on an open space, one of the objectives is to ensure that the developer secures an environmental impact report before moving to bulldoze the area.

The strategies. Strategies also determine objectives. For example, if you are using a legislative strategy to get a bill passed, you establish objectives to get it introduced into the legislature, identify a sponsor for the bill, and secure the sponsor's support.

Organization-building. Because the main strategy is base-building, you include objectives that encompass as many members of the organization as possible and that push the organization to expand its base. For example, if one of the objectives is to bring students into your organization, then another is to move students who are in the general membership to become working members and leaders.

What Is a Campaign Message and Why Do We Need One?

A campaign message is a three- to five-sentence statement that states the problem, its solution, and the way to implement the solution. You need to send a message to the world outside of your organization about what you want and why others should support you.

Members, leaders, and organizers use a message to clearly and consistently communicate about the campaign. You always have a campaign message, even if you decide that the campaign does not have a full-scale media strategy or a media plan. Members include the message when they talk with the media. Leaders and staff convey the message when they recruit members, meet with allies, or directly make a demand of the target.

A campaign message includes the following elements, with examples of each:

A problem. People on welfare are not getting adequate education, training, and paid on-the-job experience in the city's workfare program. They need these benefits to get off welfare and stay off.

A solution. The transitional jobs program will use federal funds to put people to work in living-wage jobs. The recipients will provide important city services while they get the education and training that will help them get the skills they need to get a permanent job.

An action. Tell the mayor to implement the Transitional Jobs Bill today.

A campaign message is essential for the following reasons:

Establishes talking points. The message provides members with clear, consistent talking points for the campaign.

Communicates goals and objectives. The message ensures that the problem, solution, and action you communicate to media, allies, targets, and others reflect the campaign goals and objectives.

Builds understanding of the issue. The message puts complicated campaign and policy details into simple, forthright language, ensuring that your target audience and others whose support you can understand the issue, the solution, and the action. It appeals to a broad audience, beyond your core constituency.

Frames media strategy. If you are using a media strategy or need a media plan for the campaign, the message provides a beginning frame for more detailed media planning.

How Do We Develop a Campaign Message?

You develop a campaign message by drafting and testing phrases with members, leaders, and staff.

If you have the time and resources, you also test the message with people outside of your organization, including allies and your target audience.

You develop a message once you have the components of the campaign plan. You need to know the specifics of what you want and how you will get it, as this is what you need to communicate. You use the following steps to develop a message.

- *Review the campaign.* Review the campaign goals, demands, and strategies.
- *Determine the primary audience.* Whose support do you need in order to win? Who are you seeking to move in order to meet your objectives? Who are the affected constituents, allies, elected officials? Your audience is specific. It is not the general public. You develop a basic message for your audience that you can tailor for others.
- *Draft the message.* Develop and write out the problem, solution, and action in a few brief sentences.
- *Test the message.* Conduct focus groups and one-on-one meetings with the people you want to move. Revise the message if needed.
- *Train the messengers.* Train members and leaders to deliver the campaign message.
- *Refine the message.* Fine-tune and adapt the message over the course of the campaign.

Once you develop a basic message, you stick with it, but you tailor it for different audiences. For example, if you want to use a strategy of alliance-building with unions, you develop a message based on the campaign message that appeals specifically to their self-interest and organizational concerns.

What Is the Role of the Organizer in Campaign Planning?

The organizer offers ideas and possible scenarios throughout the planning process and helps members to clearly consider their data.

Ultimately, however, it is the members' plan. The organizer writes it up but does not have final approval. Organizers do not lead meetings or make campaign decisions—these are activities for the members of the organization. The organizer helps convene a large membership meeting to walk through and ratify all aspects of the campaign plan. In this campaign planning meeting, the organizer helps leaders to challenge members and one another to stretch their thinking.

An organizer is not just a facilitator, but an active participant with a role to play in helping members to make good decisions. Both in the planning process and in ratifying the plan, the organizer guides members and leaders to be realistic in their assessments and asks questions that make them think about what they are planning, saying, or developing.

In the end, it is the members and leaders of the organization—not the organizer—who need to be comfortable carrying out the plan's strategy, actions, and tactics. If the organizer disagrees with the members' decisions, he or she still abides by them.

What Does a Campaign Plan Look Like?

A campaign plan is clear and simple. It is easy to read and to reproduce. It contains each of the elements shown in Table 10.1, with actions and tasks filled in for each objective, along with a time frame.

Tool 10.2 outlines a sample planning session (or series of sessions) that uses Exercise 10.1 (Action, Activity) and Tool 10.3 (Case Study) and Tool 10.4 (Campaign Planning Worksheet) to work through the steps of campaign planning. Tool 10.5 (Getting to a Written Campaign Plan) provides a summary and timeline of campaign development activities up until this point. The following case study provides an example of what a written campaign plan might look like, based on a CVH campaign. The power analysis for this campaign was described in Chapter Eight.

**Mayoral Workforce Development and Poverty Campaign:
July 2005–January 2006**

Goal: (The big picture. What we ultimately want to achieve.) Get the mayor to address poverty and joblessness after the mayoral election.

Demands: (What we want. The specific programs and policies that we want to change or see happen.)

- Create a blue-ribbon commission to research, study, and make policy recommendations on the problems of poverty and joblessness

- Create a new position of Deputy Mayor for Workforce and Human Development

Strategies: (How we will win. Methods for putting our power in motion to win our demand.)

- Direct Action: Getting our target in the room to show our power

- Media: Moving the media to cover our issue and raise our demands

---

- Electoral: Using our political power to move a target who is running for re-election (see Resource G for more on electoral organizing)

Message: (What we will tell the world.) Sample messages:

In New York City, one out of five people lives in poverty. This number is unacceptable in one of the world's richest cities. Unemployment and joblessness affect communities of color particularly hard. We are demanding that the next mayor prioritize addressing poverty and reducing joblessness and unemployment. We believe that the mayor must make ending poverty and joblessness number one on his list of priorities. The next mayor can do this by creating a new deputy mayor position that focuses on these issues and creating a blue-ribbon commission to look at poverty and its causes and to make concrete recommendations to the mayor on policies to address the problem.

Or, depending on the audience:

In New York City, one out of five people lives in poverty. As a result, many people are homeless or at risk of losing their home and going hungry. Many children and youth do not have access to resources, services, and programs that could give them a strong start at the beginning of their academic career. This situation is wrong in a city that has so much wealth and resources. Community Voices Heard is asking that the next mayor create a blue-ribbon commission to come up with recommendations on how to address these issues through concrete policies and programs in his second term. We are asking that you communicate this to the mayor by signing this postcard telling him you are concerned about poverty and that you believe he needs to make addressing poverty a key priority in his second term.

Target: (Who can give us what we want.) The mayor.

Resources: (Staff, money, base):

- Organizing committee of twenty-five leaders
- One staff organizer; one part-time lead organizer, one part-time policy staff person
- Four part-time canvass staff
- Five thousand CVH members and voters
- $1,000 for an event

Objectives

Objective 1. Organize accountability forum with mayoral candidates

    Action: Invite mayoral candidates to forum

    When: (By month, by week) Secure candidates' commitment by October 1

    Tasks: Send out letters

           Call candidates

           Schedule candidates

           Schedule space and identify logistical needs

           ID and train leaders

           Recruit and train volunteers

           Develop mobilization plan

Objective 2. Collect 2,500 pledge cards to deliver to candidates

    Action: Get voters to sign Pledge to Vote on Jobs cards

    When: August 15–October 15

    Tasks: Develop and print cards

           Develop walk lists to go door to door

           Train staff and leaders in gathering pledge cards

Objective 3. Develop media message for CVH media work

    Action: Organize media committee meetings

    When: July–August

    Tasks: Organize meeting

           Train members

           Develop message

Objective 4. Inject issue of poverty in media campaign coverage

    Action: Organize media events and conduct media outreach to targeted media covering mayoral election

    When: August–November

Tasks: Train members in press points

Contact press contacts and reporters to get story placement

Organize two or three media events to get coverage of poverty

Leadership team: Key leaders participating in the CVH jobs campaign

Base: (Describe who, how large, how solid). Base will be CVH core members involved in CVH jobs campaign. Goal is to turn out 100 to 150 people from this base. Target new base of 2,500 East Harlem and South Bronx voters—goal of 100 people turning out from this base for a total of 250 for this action.

Member and leader development activities:

- Media work
- Recruitment, mobilization for event, and to get pledge cards
- Running accountability meeting
- Running organizing meetings
- Organizing media events

Member and leader training needs:

- Public speaking training
- Facilitation training
- Recruitment training
- Phone-banking training
- Target meeting training

How Do We Ratify the Campaign Plan?

You strive for consensus, but eventually a majority vote determines if the organization accepts the campaign plan.

By the time members vote on the plan, they have already had extensive input into developing the campaign. However, sometimes you cannot reach consensus about key elements, particularly on demands, strategies, and goals. The campaign plan is only effective if these elements are clear and concise, not watered down for the sake of reaching an agreement. If you accept the plan based on a majority vote, you may lose those who disagree. But if you use a democratic and fair decision-making process, people usually finalize the plan and move on.

LEADERSHIP DEVELOPMENT OPPORTUNITIES
DURING CAMPAIGN PLANNING

- *Interview, listen to, and engage others.* Leaders make high-level choices where resources, policies, and values are all at stake. They involve as many other people as possible in the campaign through one-on-one conversations with other members to get their views and buy-in on the campaign. They are trained and debrief with an organizer in order to build interviewing and listening skills. Leaders prepare and facilitate small-group meetings, such as those to choose objectives and develop a message.

- *Build ownership.* Leaders make recommendations about the best choices for the campaign and represent the proposed plan to other members in the same situation who are trying to make a difference. Gaining the powerful experience of coming together to make and ratify decisions collectively shows members that this is their organization and that they are building their political power.

- *Develop and test messages.* Communicate effectively with a wide range of people.

- *Ratify the plan.* Leaders play a role in the membership meeting where the organization will ratify the written campaign plan. A team of leaders meets with the organizer in the days before the meeting to review the written plan and any handouts for the meeting, finalize an agenda, review tasks, practice what everyone will say, and gel as a team.

CHALLENGES
IN CAMPAIGN PLANNING

"Our members are skipping some essential objectives in their planning discussions." If members and leaders are planning the campaign based on faulty logic, the organizer helps them get back on track, referring back to research findings or decisions the group has already made. The organizer does not tell them they are wrong but instead probes them to think more deeply.

"The leaders are suggesting realistic pieces, but the total plan is too ambitious." Use your assessment of organizational capacity to guide leaders and members to establish a realistic plan.

"We are not able to do all we need to do in the planning sessions but people are ready to move on the campaign." The most important aspects of the plan—the goals, the target, the strategy, and the objectives for the first three to six months—are critical. Once you establish these elements you can get started and work out how to address the other components of the plan over time. Although it is good to have the message ready, you can test and decide on it after you kick off the campaign.

ESSENTIAL ELEMENTS
FOR EFFECTIVE CAMPAIGN PLANNING

☑ *Don't over-plan.* Leave room to evaluate your work and respond to the changing political environment.

☑ *Build off campaign development.* Directly use what you learned while researching the campaign and developing the main components.

☑ *Prep leaders for the campaign planning sessions.* Prepared leaders help ensure that the campaign plan effectively builds off of campaign development. Prioritize this element, don't let it fall to the bottom of the list.

☑ *Use the campaign planning session to make decisions.* When members and leaders gather for the campaign planning session, they are there to make final decisions, establish buy-in, and lay out what the coming months will look like in the organization.

☑ *Remember—every action causes a reaction.* Once the campaign gets under way, you execute your plan in relationship to how the target reacts to your organization's actions.

Tool 10.1
The Components of a Campaign

You can use the following as a handout or on a flip chart to orient members and leaders during campaign planning.

Goal. The big picture. What we ultimately want to achieve. (End childhood hunger in our community.)

Demand. What we want. The specific programs and policies that we want to change or be implemented. (More food subsidies for families.)

Strategy. How we will win. Methods for putting our power in motion to win our demand. (Media and public education, direct action.)

Objectives. How we will get there. The steps we need to take in order to get what we demand. How we will measure progress toward our goal. (Objective #1: Twenty-five Teach-ins; Objective #2: Turn out one thousand people during state budget process.)

Message. What we will tell the world. A short, two- or three-sentence statement that addresses the problem and the issue or the solution we seek. ("One out of every five children in our community goes to bed hungry, even in families where both parents work. The effects of hunger—on kids and on our entire community—are profound and preventable. Our state is considering a bill to put an end to childhood hunger that costs taxpayers less than their Monday morning coffee.")

Target. Who can give us what we want. (The chair of the state senate finance committee.)

Action. What events we will do. A collective show of power that directly aims to move a target or decision maker. (Pack the budget hearings in the state capitol.)

Tactic. What activities we will do. What we will do to challenge or engage powerholders and achieve the goal of an action. (Conduct mass street theatre on capitol steps during the budget process, hold legislative meetings.)

<h1 style="text-align: center;">Tool 10.2
Sample Campaign Planning Session</h1>

The following campaign planning session totals eight hours. You can distribute planning over a series of evenings, over a day and a half, or do it in one day, as we show here. In this sample session, we assume about twenty people are participating. Core leaders are cofacilitating the meeting with support from staff. When we refer to the facilitator, we mean one member of the small team of people who are guiding this session.

Part One: Introductions and Warm-up. (1 hour—9:30–10:30 A.M.)

Review objectives. People get to know each other, agree on the goals of the meeting, and get in the mind frame for campaign planning.

Introductions. The facilitator asks everyone to go around and say their names and one or two sentences about how and why they got involved with the organization and the campaign. **(20 minutes)**

Warm-up exercise. Action, Activity. (See Exercise 10.1) **(30 minutes)**
The facilitator explains that the purpose of doing this exercise is to help people get further acquainted and to get them thinking about the kinds of actions and activities they might want to plan for the campaign.

Review goals for the meeting. The facilitator reviews the goals for the meeting and confirms that everyone understands and agrees that this is why they are here. **(10 minutes)**

The main goals of the meeting are:

- Develop objectives for the campaign.
- Start to identify the kinds of actions and tactics we will use.
- Agree on the goal, demands, target, and strategy for the campaign.
- Develop the campaign plan.

Part Two: Understanding Campaigns (3 hours—10:30–1:30)

Objective. Participants identify the basic components of a campaign.

The Components of a Campaign. The facilitator reviews the components of a campaign (see Tool 10.1 for a sample handout). If the organization has done campaigns before, the facilitator guides the group through a discussion of each of the components of one of those campaigns. Alternately, she distributes a sample campaign case study. (A sample case study appears in Tool 10.3.) Participants read the case study aloud. In small groups, they identify the components of the campaign in the case study. The groups come together to distinquish the different parts of a campaign. **(30 minutes)**

Actions and tactics. In groups of three, participants talk about actions and tactics they have used in the past or have heard about. The facilitator and leaders give examples from past campaigns. The facilitator also refers people back to the Action, Activity exercise they did earlier. The small groups write about the actions they've used or heard about and post them on the walls. They then walk around and look at what people have written This is raw material for planning the campaign, which participants will do after lunch. **(30 minutes)**

Lunch. (30 minutes)

Campaign goals, demands, and target. The facilitator reviews the goals, demands, and target of the campaign. The presentation includes handouts or charts and pictures of the target. The person doing the overview explains who decided on the goals, demand, and target and how they did so. She then reviews the strategies that members have chosen. The facilitator asks to hear clarifying questions. At this point in developing the campaign, if members have been engaged in the process, the group is likely to agree to move forward with the goals, demands, target, and strategy. **(30 minutes)**

Timeline. The facilitator sets up a calendar on chart paper that looks at four-month periods for the next year. The group reviews important dates that are critical for the campaign, including a timeline of the external factors that may affect the campaign, such as a budget process or a plan to build a new development. The group adds important dates, events, or hooks, such as the first day of school or holidays. **(30 minutes)**

Objectives. The team that drafted the campaign objectives reviews them with the group, connecting them with the timeline where appropriate. The group discusses the objectives. They will further develop these objectives when they develop the campaign plan. **(30 minutes)**

Tool 10.2
Sample Campaign Planning Session, Cont'd

Part Three: Planning the Campaign (4 hours—1:30–5:30 P.M.)

Objective. Participants develop a plan for the campaign.

Developing our campaign plan. Participants form three small groups of six to eight people. The facilitator may assign people to the groups to ensure a good mix of newer and more experienced members. Each group has people in the following roles:

- Strong, trained facilitator
- Note taker
- Person to report back to the large group

Each group also has the following:

- Campaign planning worksheets (Tool 10.4) that include what's been established so far and any helpful information from the campaign research
- Action, Activity sheets to refer to

Each small group develops a proposal for the larger group, using the worksheets as a guide. If there are multiple strategies each group can work on a different strategy, which allows a deeper and more detailed proposal. If each group works on all the strategies the proposals will be broader.

Facilitation in these small groups is important for keeping the group focused. For instance, the facilitator keeps the group focused on objectives as opposed to just talking about actions. **(60 minutes)**

Break. During an extended break, a core group of leaders and staff examine the campaign plans. If the groups worked on the same strategies, they look for similarities and differences. They put the information together, but clarify which group developed each aspect of the proposal. If each group worked on a different strategy, they combine the information. In either case, the group should see a timeline, similar to the one they developed earlier, with the campaign plan applied to it. If you have the technology to project it on a screen and give everyone a corresponding handout, that is best, but you can also do it manually using chart paper and large, bold lettering. **(30 minutes)**

Campaign plan review. Members review the full plan. Facilitators and leaders guide an assessment of what the organization can actually do, using charts and handouts

Tool 10.2
Sample Campaign Planning Session, Cont'd

as needed, to address staffing, resources, and similar capacity concerns. People form pairs and take about fifteen minutes to discuss the proposed plan, talk through any questions they have, and if the plan calls for more than the organization can take on, identify their priorities. The group comes together and makes changes as needed. **(90 minutes)**

Break. This break gives people a chance to digest the plan. **(10 minutes)**

Plan ratification. Members come back together, raise any remaining questions, and ratify the plan. The plan you leave with has to be firm enough that the organizing committee can start to implement it, but it also needs to be open for adaptation and adjustment. **(30 minutes)**

Meeting evaluation. The facilitator reviews the goals for the day and then checks in to see if the participants believe that they met their goals. People say what they will do to follow up on the plan. **(20 minutes)**

Close.

Tool 10.3
Case Study for Identifying the Parts of a Campaign

See Table 10.1 for identified components.

The Transitional Jobs Campaign

In 1997, to comply with the new federal welfare reform bill, New York City expands its workfare program for welfare recipients. Workfare requires people to work at jobs for no pay—they work in exchange for their welfare benefits. New York City's workfare program is the Work Experience Program (WEP). WEP workers often perform jobs right alongside union members and others who are doing exactly the same thing but are getting paid a salary.

CVH organizers talk to thousands of WEP workers about what they are experiencing and what will improve their situations. The organizers learn that people want to work, but they want to replace WEP with paid jobs, with education and training.

CVH starts to talk to other groups working on workfare and welfare issues and soon partners with the Fifth Avenue Committee to explore creating a transitional jobs program. For this program to come to life, the city council needs to pass legislation—the Transitional Jobs Bill. The speaker of the city council can move the bill through the council, and CVH believes it can build enough power to move him. WEP workers meet at CVH to figure out how to get the bill introduced into a city council committee. They learn all about Speaker Peter Vallone and about who else has a stake in the campaign.

The speaker plans to run for mayor. He needs good media and the support of labor unions for his mayoral bid. The unions see WEP as a threat to unionization and a way to cut wages. The unions could ensure that the speaker supports the bill. CVH seeks to build an alliance with the union.

As they develop the campaign, members decide they want to build a base of one thousand WEP workers and develop reports and studies that show the problems with the WEP program. The organization starts to say publicly that WEP is a public-sector sweatshop that forces mothers with children to work in no-wage, dead-end jobs that do not help them get off of welfare. CVH sets out to get five hundred WEP workers to sign pledge cards supporting the campaign that they can deliver to the unions and the media.

During the course of the campaign, CVH organizes a march of WEP workers on city office buildings, where members deliver invoices to city hall asking for "back pay" for their work in WEP. This, as well as op-ed pieces, letters to the editor, and media stories CVH places, helps to put pressure on the council speaker about the failures of WEP to move people into the workforce.

Tool 10.4
Campaign Planning Worksheet

You can use the following as a worksheet for participants in a campaign planning session to complete. In advance of the planning session, fill in any information that members have already decided on. Even if participants in the planning will ratify some of these decisions, they will do so more knowledgably if the information is in front of them. For a sample campaign plan, see the chapter text.

Goal: The big picture. What we ultimately want to achieve.

Demand: What we want. The specific programs and policies that we want to change or see happen.

Strategies: How we will win. Methods for putting our power in motion to win our demand.

Message: What we will tell the world.

Target: Who can give us what we want.

Resources (Staff, money, base):

Objective One:

    Tasks—Actions—Tactics:

    What   When (By month, by week)

Objective Two:

    Tasks—Actions—Tactics:

    What   When (By month, by week)

Objective Three:

    Tasks—Actions—Tactics:

    What   When (By month, by week)

Leadership Team:

Base (Describe who, how large, how solid):

Member/Leader Development Activities:

Member/Leader Training Needs:

ADDITIONAL OBJECTIVES (add as many as needed):

Objective #____:

Tasks—Actions—Tactics:

What   When (By month, by week)

Objective #____:

Tasks—Actions—Tactics:

What   When (By month, by week)

Objective #____:

Tasks—Actions—Tactics:

What   When (By month, by week)

Tool 10.5
Getting to a Written Campaign Plan

A Handout Summarizing Campaign Development Activities

It generally takes a few months before you start to write up a campaign plan, depending on the issue, unless a crisis forces you to accelerate the steps. No matter the time frame, you can use the following overview as a handout for training or orienting staff and members to the full process of campaign development. Seeing all of the steps laid out can help ensure that everyone is clear about all of the activities that have occurred leading up to the campaign plan or can help prepare people to undertake the process from the beginning. If you are responding to a crisis, some or all of these steps can be combined.

Issue ID

Convene Members and Leaders. In a membership meeting or in multiple meetings over a few weeks, members talk about the problems they are experiencing and what some solutions to issues might be. They begin to focus on one potential issue.

Conduct One-on-Ones with Core Members and Leaders. Staff meet with core members and leaders to talk about the potential issue and assess if they will work on the campaign. They discuss how they think it will affect the organization and who else can they recruit to work on the campaign.

Create a Leadership Team. Staff identify a group of members and leaders who can engage in issue ID activities with them, including by conducting surveys and speaking with constituents.

Survey Current Membership. The team calls members of the organization to see if the potential issue resonates with them and if they would work on it. They might ask, What do you want to get out of the campaign? What is the goal you want to achieve?

Speak with Constituents. The team goes out to see how constituents feel about the issue. To determine whether the issue would move constituents to action, they use surveys or other tools to gather information.

Review and Analyze Data. Leaders and staff review what people said in the surveys, during one-on-ones, and in the group meetings.

Develop Demands. What do the members want? The leadership team prepares recommendations for campaign demands.

Identify the Target. Leaders, members, and staff identify who has the power to give members what they want.

Tool 10.5
Getting to a Written Campaign Plan, Cont'd

Campaign Research

Check-In with Organization Members and Community Members. At a membership meeting, the team assesses if the demands resonate with members and the constituency. Members vote to move forward with the demands.

Do a Landscape of the Issue. The leadership team investigates the history of the issue and its potential future.

Engage in Target Research. The team asks, What kind of power does the target have? What kind of power does the organization need to move her or him?

Conduct a Power Analysis. The team asks, Who cares about the issue and has power in relationship to it?

Do an Organizational Assessment. The team reviews the organization's numbers and track record. Staff ask, Will the campaign develop members' leadership skills and build the organization?

Strategy Development

Schedule a Strategy Meeting. The leadership team establishes a date and time for a strategy meeting, at which leaders and members can choose a strategy or strategies for the campaign.

Develop Strategy Scenarios. A core group of leaders and staff develop possible strategy scenarios. They create an agenda and materials, and prepare to facilitate the strategy meeting.

Leadership and Membership Outreach

Reach Out to Core Members. Staff call members and leaders to discuss the issue, potential targets, and strategies, and to start to incorporate what they think into the plan.

Talk with Constituents. Staff and leaders go out into the community and talk to people who are affected by the issue. These conversations include discussions about the issue and campaign as well as briefings on the organization and its past campaigns.

Getting to a Written Campaign Plan, Cont'd

Strategy Meeting and Campaign Planning

Hold the Strategy Meeting. Members meet to choose a strategy for the campaign, which is based on what they've learned from the research.

Assess Organizational Capacity. Members ask, Given the strategy, does the organization have the staff, money, and other resources to conduct the campaign?

Develop Objectives. Leaders and staff develop objectives to achieve the goal.

Craft a Message. What is the consistent, brief message your organization will use to communicate about the campaign?

Engage in Political Education. Staff and leaders ask, What are the systems and forces behind the issue? Why does the problem exist, and who does it affect? Who benefits from it?

Hold a Campaign Planning Session. Members meet to review, finalize, and ratify the goals, objectives, demands, target, strategy, message, and types of actions and tactics they will use in the campaign.

Write the Campaign Plan. A staff member writes up the plan.

Exercise 10.1
Action, Activity

You can use the following as a warm-up exercise for a campaign planning or action planning session or as part of a leadership development course.

Time: 30 minutes

Materials: Brightly colored cards with actions and activities printed in large, bold letters. String or yarn. Action, Activity Chart (see below).

Roles: Facilitator

Room set-up: Enough room for people to walk around and talk in pairs.

Objective. By the end of this exercise people will have matched the different actions they can use in their campaign with the activities these actions require. They will have shared their experiences with actions and begun to name how many people each action requires.

- Facilitator hands out cards prepared in advance. Each card has either an action or an activity written on it with heavy marker or printed off the computer (see chart below for sample actions and activities). If you have photographs of the various actions, ideally from your organization, you can tape those to the cards as well. If you attach yarn or string, people can wear the cards around their necks.

- Participants hold their cards or hang them around their necks so everyone can see the wording.

- Facilitator asks the participants to find the person with the action or activity that matches their own. She holds up a sample card: Postcard campaign. Then she holds up the card that matches it: A group sends thousands of postcards to a target asking him to do something.

- The facilitator asks everyone to walk around the room and find the person with the card that best matches theirs. She encourages people to introduce themselves to each other and talk about the action and activity.

- When everybody finds a partner, the facilitator asks each pair to read their action and activity. If the group disagrees about the match, the facilitator probes with questions about why they disagree. Each time there is a disagreement about a pair, the facilitator recognizes it as a question mark.

- At the end of this process, the facilitator shows a chart or distributes a card with the correct terms and definitions (see the Action, Activity Chart that follows).

Exercise 10.1
Action, Activity, Cont'd

- The facilitator asks how many people have participated in each action. She goes through the list and asks how many people have participated in each type of action, noting it on a chart on the wall. She asks how many people are needed for each action. This gets people thinking about the capacity of the organization.

Action, Activity Chart

Action	Activity
Sit-in	People sit in an office waiting room without being invited and stay until they get what they want.
March	People walk together from one spot to another.
Press conference	An organization holds a meeting for the press about an issue, report, or action.
Legislative briefing	An organization holds an informational meeting for a group of elected officials.
Boycott	An organization asks people not to patronize a service or buy a product.
Strike	A group of people decides to walk out of their job, their school, or other place.
Rally	A group of people participate in an event at a public site with speakers who are talking about an issue.
Demonstration	People show their opposition to or need for something through a mass action at a site of power.
Picket line	A group of people walk in a small moving circle at the entrance of a building to educate people about an issue or discourage them from entering.
Street theater	People create a skit, song, or reading about an issue and perform it out in the open.
Flyering	People hand out leaflets to educate the public about an issue.

Exercise 10.1
Action, Activity, Cont'd

Action	Activity
Town hall meeting	An open meeting about an issue or problem that builds membership and gets the word out.
Accountability session	A large meeting with a target who can make decisions and give clear yes or no answers.
Building or office takeover	A large group of people takes over an office with the goal of stopping it from functioning.
Lobby day	A group of people meet with a large number of elected officials in one day, usually at the state or national capitol.
Lobby meeting	People from a particular district meet with their representative.
Call-in day	People call a target on one day to get him or her to do something.
Disrupting public meetings	A group of people disrupt a public meeting such as a hearing or press conference.
Banner drop	An organization drops or holds a banner with a simple message in a place where the media are present.
Civil disobedience	People willingly and knowingly break the law to get their issue in the news. Their actions may or may not lead to arrest.

Implementing an Effective Campaign

The new members that Community Voices Heard (CVH) organizers have been recruiting at Work Experience Program (WEP) sites are coming out for biweekly meetings. In these meetings, CVH leaders and organizers educate new people about CVH's campaign to create a jobs program that will replace workfare with jobs that pay real wages. The meetings also give WEP workers a place to talk about their difficult work assignments.

At this week's meeting, CVH leaders hand out sheets with the campaign goal, demands, target, and the current campaign accomplishments and activities so people understand that things are getting done. The chair of the city council's General Welfare Committee is ready to introduce the bill to create the jobs program, and tonight the group will focus on preparing for an action connected with this step. Betsy starts with an update about engaging new allies to sign on to the campaign. Members offer ideas and feedback. A new member, Theresa, stands up to facilitate the next part of the meeting, a discussion about turnout for a press conference. "Okay," Theresa says, "How are we going to get fifty WEP workers to City Hall in two weeks for the press conference?" The members start talking and the meeting moves into its action-planning stage.

The campaign is under way.

What Is Campaign Implementation and Why Is It Important?

Campaign implementation is the phase of a campaign when an organization exercises its power publicly to move a target to deliver on a campaign demand. When you implement a campaign, you build all aspects of your organization, including membership, the skills of leaders, and the organization's power.

When you implement a campaign, you engage in action, evaluate the impact of your action based on your campaign plan, and then engage in more action to achieve your next objective. During campaign implementation all of your research, analysis, and decision making come together. Your organization puts it out there: We are taking on a fight. Allies, constituents, targets, general members, and the public encounter your organization as it mobilizes its power to win a campaign and shift power on an issue.

Campaign implementation is when the largest numbers of people intersect with your organization and decide if they want to become members, allies, and supporters. Campaign implementation results in either a win or a loss, which increases an organization's power or diminishes it.

When Does Campaign Implementation Start?

Campaign implementation starts with a kickoff event at which your organization publicly states that it is engaging in a campaign to get a target to meet its demands.

Campaign implementation can begin on the first day you go out and recruit new members to participate. It can begin with a leadership training session, a press conference, a day of coordinated actions, or a large meeting of allies and supporters. It can start with the release of a report or with a call to action aimed at your target.

What Kinds of Activities Are Associated with Campaign Implementation?

The following activities are associated with campaign implementation:

Base-building. You recruit people to get involved through campaigns. (For more on recruitment, see Chapter Three.)

Leadership development. Exercising leadership in public actions is one of the best ways to learn leadership skills. Campaigns offer public opportunities for leadership, such as leading community forums and negotiating with targets.

Mobilization. During a campaign, the organization demonstrates its base of power and involves its entire base. In public actions, in meetings with allies, and in the press, organizations show power in the streets, in the halls of government, and in community spaces.

Collective planning and evaluation. At organizing committee meetings members and leaders plan and evaluate activities, ensuring that you keep to the plan. You ensure that your work remains relevant, given political shifts and the reaction to your actions.

Decision making. Members make decisions primarily at organizing committee meetings. Decisions include negotiating demands, retooling strategies and tactics, and choosing to change the campaign plan.

Target actions. Campaigns need action, usually directed at the target. The action can be a small community meeting in your office with a city agency staff person or as large as a five-hundred-person accountability session with an elected official in a union hall. Other actions include mass canvasses in a neighborhood and street theater to educate community members. (For more on actions, see Chapter Twelve.)

Membership campaign education. Members and new people you recruit during the campaign need to know what's going on in order to be fully engaged. You offer education in all forms of contact, including through mailings, phone calls, home visits, and membership meetings.

Negotiation. Negotiation is the process of determining a compromise between two different positions. Campaign implementation requires a great deal of negotiation. Negotiation takes place during public actions, in small-group meetings, or in negotiating sessions between leaders and the target or the target's staff. Members decide who will negotiate on behalf of the organization, what the final negotiations are, and how the negotiations will take place.

When you are engaged in campaign implementation, this range of activities—many of which occur simultaneously—requires leaders and organizers to use two important skills: the ability to multitask and to prioritize.

How Do We Structure a Member-Controlled Campaign?

Two of the most effective campaign structures that ensure membership involvement and decision making are the organizing committee and the leadership team.

Organizing committee. This group makes sure the campaign follows the campaign plan. The organizing committee is made up of members, leaders, and people involved in the campaign-development process as well as newly recruited members. Although the organizing committee has a core group, it is open enough that others can join in and play active roles. The organizing committee is a tool for building membership. Organizing committee meetings occur throughout the campaign. When you recruit people or want to get them more involved, you invite them to the next organizing committee meeting, where they meet other people who share their issues. They can start doing things immediately. A description of the elements of organizing committee meetings follows later in this chapter.

Leadership team. This core group can represent the organizing committee. The leadership team makes emergency decisions and decisions between meetings. The leadership team works with staff to develop agendas for organizing committee meetings and to chair the meetings. This team also agitates members to see the political aspects of the campaign. Members on the leadership team take the lead in confronting targets. The organization's core leaders may appoint the leadership team, or members of the organizing committee can elect the team. Sometimes the team self-selects, with members offering to take on the responsibility. (For more on leadership teams, including the importance of having a balance of styles on the team, see Chapter Five.)

How Do We Manage the Flow of a Campaign?

The organizing committee manages the campaign by evaluating its progress, asking whether or not actions achieved their objectives, and then deciding how to move forward based on this evaluation.

Even with a comprehensive campaign plan, things change. Every action provokes a reaction that you must analyze and evaluate. Change is good, because it proves that your intervention on an issue is having an impact. But even when you plan and think about potential responses to your organization's actions, things sometimes occur outside of your control or come out differently than you expect. As the organizing committee manages the campaign, it adjusts the campaign plan in timing or tactics. Sometimes the committee decides to change the strategy or the demands based on negotiations or new information.

The organizing committee and organizing meetings offer concrete ways not only to move the campaign forward but also to develop members' skills. You get as many people as possible involved in evaluating and making strategic decisions. You can't really teach people to do these things through workshops alone—they need to do it. Organizations that do not focus on building power tend to use meetings to update people. Participants listen to reports while evaluation and strategic thinking take place among staff or a limited number of people. In contrast, in a community power-building organization many people have these skills. (For more on how to use evaluation to manage the campaign flow, see Chapter Thirteen.)

How Do We Structure Organizing Committee Meetings?

You structure organizing committee meetings to accomplish two main goals: helping people to understand how the campaign is progressing in relation to the campaign plan and getting people to make decisions about the next steps in the campaign.

Because in the organizing committee both experienced and new members are together, you incorporate campaign updates, participatory exercises, and some training wherever possible. Exhibit 11.1 provides a rundown of what happens in organizing committee meetings.

Exhibit 11.1
Elements of Organizing Committee Meetings

Campaign review. Review the goals, demands, objectives, and targets as well as the strategies. Refer to the campaign plan.

Campaign update. What is the status of the campaign? What is the most recent development? How are we doing on our plan?

Evaluation and check-in. Are we doing all that we need to do right now?

Decisions. Conduct any decision making needed.

Training in civic affairs and political systems. Do a short training (fifteen to fifty minutes) on the politics of an issue to reinforce an understanding of power and the dimensions of the issue. For instance, you briefly review the problem the campaign addresses and what political systems perpetuate it. You elicit members' personal experiences of the issue alongside a timeline of significant policy decisions related to it. You put up photographs of key powerholders and their positions. You highlight the sources of money behind their power.

Collective action. Whenever possible, include a collective action in the meeting. For example, everyone makes phone calls to do turnout for a rally or goes out together to do a sixty-minute door-to-door canvass. People do something together to build the campaign, not just sign a petition or a postcard.

Summary, next steps, and evaluation of meeting. What did we decide? Who's doing what? How was this meeting?

What Other Kinds of Meetings Do We Hold While Implementing the Campaign?

Other meetings help develop members and ensure effective actions and a well-run, membership-controlled campaign.

Table 11.1 illustrates the different types of meetings you hold when implementing a campaign. The number of participants may vary based on the size of your organization.

How Do We Make Sure Members Lead a Successful Campaign?

Running a successful membership-controlled campaign requires that an organization provide opportunities for members and leaders to engage in all aspects of the campaign process and that the campaign has clear goals, objectives, and demands.

The following are ten key ways to ensure a successful member-led campaign.

1. *Stay focused.* Maintain a focus on the goals, objectives, demands, strategies, and targets. An effective campaign is an active campaign, but in all the activity, it's easy to get sidetracked. Don't let it happen. Being single-minded and focused is the way to win. Your written campaign plan is the best tool for staying on point. A culture of accountability in the organization is a source of support and helps everyone keep everything on the table.

2. *Get and keep members involved in real campaign activities through the organizing committee.* When members and leaders are making decisions and implementing the campaign plan, they have ownership of it. The more they put into the campaign, the more they make sure that their networks of people get involved and come out for key actions. Regularly scheduled organizing committee meetings are a vehicle for engaging people.

3. *Build a strong leadership team.* A strong leadership team helps the organizing committee manage an effective campaign. As the team gels, it makes quick decisions effectively, engages the broader membership, and is articulate about the campaign to new, general, and working members as well as to allies and the press.

4. *Stay up to date.* Don't implement the campaign in a vacuum. Frequently check in with other stakeholders, allies, and partners, and read up on your issue in the paper. If your target is a public official, make sure you know what he or she is saying about the issue. You can get so immersed that it starts to feel like

Table 11.1

Campaign Implementation Meetings

Meeting	When	Number of People	Length	Who	Goal
Campaign planning	End of campaign development and planning phase.	30–50	6–8 hours	Board, leaders, members, new constituents.	A complete written campaign plan.
Organizing committee	Monthly.	20–40	2–3 hours	Leaders, members, new members, potential members.	Campaign management, decision making, updates, bring in new members.
Leadership preparation	Before meetings and actions.	1–5	1–2 hours	Leaders and members involved in meetings and actions.	Train people to facilitate, lead meetings and actions.
Leadership team	One every two weeks or as needed.	8–15	1–1½ hours	Organizing committee leadership.	General campaign management and decision making.
Action planning	Weekly, prior to an action.	Depends on action.	1–2 hours	Members and leaders involved in action (including new members).	Develop, plan, and execute a direct action.
Campaign trainings	Once a month or as needed.	10–20	1½ hours	New members.	Educate new members on issues and campaign.
Skills trainings	As needed.	5–15	3 hours	Committee members.	Train members to take on key leadership roles and do work such as public speaking or facilitation.

everyone sees and experiences your issue the way staff and members of your organization do. After a series of successful actions, it can start to feel like victory long before you've actually won. Keep current with the reality of your issue.

5. *Ensure the issue continues to be relevant to members.* If an issue does not resonate with members they won't come out. Be mindful of what members say they care about and pay attention to what they turn out for. If the issue stops being relevant, talk with members and constituents to find out why. The organizing committee evaluates if it should continue the campaign or address the issue in a different way.

6. *Engage in frequent, honest campaign evaluations.* Because a campaign is a series of coordinated objectives and actions, if an action does not achieve its objective it will affect the rest of the plan. Engage in evaluations throughout the campaign to make sure the strategy, actions, and tactics are moving the target.

7. *Build your base.* Sometimes during the course of a campaign, organizations and organizers stop base-building to do other things that the campaign demands. This neglect is a mistake, both for the campaign and for long-range organizational growth, health, and development. A campaign needs people. It needs to show power in numbers. And a campaign is the best recruitment tool to bring people into the organization.

8. *Don't shortcut member control.* During the course of the campaign, you may see a chance to use shortcuts, especially when it comes to maintaining membership control and decision making. It seems easier to have one reliable person make a decision or speak to the press. Canceling the leadership training session will allow staff to finish working on a grant proposal. Don't do it. In the long run, if members are not in control and developing as leaders—even if you win on the issue—you are not building community power. The Industrial Areas Foundation, a network of community organizations throughout the United States (that we describe in the Introduction), has what its staff and leaders call an "Iron Rule": *Never do for others what they can do for themselves.* This is an especially useful principle to follow during campaign implementation.

9. *Engage in action regularly.* Well-developed, strategic, and goal-oriented actions galvanize members and allow them to see the results of their work, even when a campaign is difficult or is only slowly moving a target.

10. *Negotiate from strength—don't underestimate your power.* Organizations and organizers often underestimate their own power or their potential for power. But you must make a real estimate of your actual power and deliver on your promises. If you say fifty people will be at the press conference, there are fifty people at the press conference. If you tell a target the organization will end the picket if he meets with its leaders, end the picket when he agrees. This ability to follow through is how your organization comes to command respect. Know what your power is, where it lies, and its real capacity. If your organization fills a room with one thousand people to confront the CEO about a toxic spill, you can make some demands. Operate from your position of strength.

How Do We Negotiate?

In community power-building organizations, members decide who will negotiate on behalf of the organization, what the final negotiations are, and how the negotiations will take place.

Negotiation starts with a demand. You develop demands for the overall campaign and each time the organization engages a target during a campaign. Sometimes the demand is the same as the larger campaign demand, such as "Pass our jobs bill," or it may be something the campaign needs to get from a specific encounter, such as "Meet with our leadership." Demands reflect what members want, how much power they have to move the target, and the personality of the target and of the organization. You establish realistic demands so that targets take you seriously, and you leave room for negotiations. The following example illustrates how to develop such a demand.

> ### Building In Negotiation
>
> In developing demands for the transitional jobs program, CVH members decide they want jobs that will last no less than a year, that at least five thousand jobs will be developed over two years, and that participants in the jobs program will have paid, on-the-job training. Taking into consideration that various allies in the campaign prioritize different things, the partners in the campaign agree to ask for ten thousand jobs over five years, with jobs lasting eighteen to twenty-four months and incorporating education and training. These expanded demands allow room for negotiation without undercutting what CVH members want.

There are three steps to building an organization's negotiations:

Choose the main negotiator. The organizing committee identifies the main negotiator or negotiating team. Negotiators are from the organizational leadership, are directly affected by the issue, and have strong leadership skills. Sometimes the negotiating team includes a staff person. When the negotiation takes place during an action, the negotiating team is usually the tactical team. (For more on decision-making roles in actions, see Chapter Twelve.)

Determine the organization's negotiating position. This is a complicated process that includes understanding the political process and landscape, learning what members will accept as a win and what they will see as a defeat, and knowing when losing is more important than winning—for the long term. The organizing committee establishes the bottom line of what is acceptable to a majority of members and gives this position to the negotiators. It takes time to determine the negotiating position. The organization holds group discussions either within organizing meetings or in meetings it holds specifically for the purpose of planning for negotiations. The organizer later calls members or follows up at organizing committee meetings to make sure the negotiating position includes their opinions and expectations.

Decide when a win is a loss. Sometimes negotiating a win has a negative effect, particularly if you negotiate to get something members do not believe in or have not been involved in determining. Another time a win is a loss is when the negotiators win something that really does not deliver enough to members. The organization determines when it is better to stand by the bottom line of what members want—and lose—than it is to win something that members experience as a defeat. If the members feel burned in any of these ways you can lose them, and the organization may not be able to mount another campaign on the issue for a long time.

You rarely win everything you demand. The organization needs to master how to engage in negotiation to win the most it can. Exercise 11.1 can help train members in negotiation skills.

What Is the Role of an Organizer in Implementing a Campaign?

The organizer provides information, identifies people for the organizing committee, and works in partnership with the committee to manage the campaign—probing and challenging members to do their most effective thinking.

The organizer staffs the committee and takes direction from it. She or he implements the decisions of the committee. In a community power-building organization, staff have no decision-making power in terms of strategy, actions, or tactics and should not directly engage in negotiations. These are roles for the members. If you want to build community power, it is critical that staff members cultivate this discipline.

Nonetheless, organizers do play an important role. They build the organizing committee by identifying people who can get involved, both new recruits and general members. They hold research meetings and conversations with allies and the staff members of targets. Organizers identify training needs and conduct training as needed. Organizers provide information to the organizing committee about research, strategy, and other aspects of the campaign so that members can engage in the best thinking possible. One of an organizer's core skills is offering the committee ideas, proposals, and the information it needs to make informed decisions.

Do Organizers Have Any Power During a Campaign?

Yes, organizers have power, even in a member-led campaign, particularly in what they bring to or raise with the organizing committee.

An organizer is more than a facilitator or a person who helps a process along. An organizer is an active player in the organizing process, but in partnership with members. It is important that an organizer bring information to the organizing committee that is accurate, broadly based, and easily understandable. If an organizer holds back important information, or moves from offering perspectives and experience to giving advice and making decisions for the campaign, she is misusing the power and trust members give her.

What Should an Organizer Do If Members Ask for Advice?

Organizers should not give advice, but they can offer perspectives and possible scenarios for people to evaluate and analyze.

Community members often want to hear what an organizer thinks about a strategy, a decision, or a potential action. This is a good instinct. Professional organizers often have years of experience or a strong perspective. They are thinking about the campaign more than members can. They have a great deal to offer people seeking to build power and make change. Community members seeking this advice are acting in their community's best interests. Organizers can give members information to work with that draws from their experience without dictating what members should do.

If the organizer gives straight advice, one of three things could happen: the members listen to what the organizer thinks and reject it completely, the members take aspects of what the organizer provides, or the members just go along with the organizer's advice. None of these situations builds a strong, independent, free-thinking leadership.

What If Our Campaign Plan Is Just Not Working?

Do deep evaluation of why the plan is not working, seek advice, try different adjustments, and be prepared to go back to the beginning if needed.

There are several ways in which a plan may not be working. If people, particularly new people, are not participating in the campaign, it could be that the campaign message is wrong. You take another look at the message and retool it. If people are still not getting involved, it may be due to the issue or demand. You go back to the issue identification phase of the campaign to figure out what needs to change. Just because people say something is a problem does not mean they will move to action to address it.

If people are getting involved, new members are coming in, and you are doing everything right but not reaching critical objectives, the problem could be the power analysis or choice of strategy. For instance, if the power analysis suggested that more groups would be involved in the campaign and they are not, then you may have to move away from an alliance-building strategy to one that relies more on your own organizational power and strength.

If the actions are not moving the target, conduct more target research or do a deeper target analysis to figure out why the target is so resilient or if she or he is even the right target.

Check in with mentors. Experienced organizers, community leaders, or skilled technical assistance providers who are impartial but committed to you and your issue can help think through what might be wrong with the campaign plan.

How Do We Avoid Getting Stuck in "Meeting Mode?"

Engage in collective public action throughout the campaign.

Meeting mode occurs when members and leaders spend all their time in meetings where nothing gets accomplished. Meetings serve an important purpose, but during a campaign, meetings focus on making sure you are achieving your campaign objectives and that you are planning, preparing for, and evaluating collective public actions. People will not come out just to meet, even if the issue is important to them. During a campaign, use meetings to get into "campaign mode" and direct the energy into action.

Sometimes organizations go into meeting mode because they want member buy-in and community control, not because they are avoiding planning or implementing a campaign. Although this is a good instinct, know when you are holding the same meeting over and over again. For example, Jackson, a CVH organizer, recruited about 150 public housing residents to hold campaign development meetings. For a variety of reasons, the organization got stuck between campaign development and campaign implementation. In each meeting the residents explored the potential issues but got no further. Finally, Jackson realized that the organizing committee was losing people. He brought a leadership team together and they prepared some proposals to move the campaign to a more active phase. At the next meeting, participants voted on those proposals at the beginning, and by the end of the meeting people were excited and finally felt that they were making progress.

What Are Some Elements of Effective Meetings?

Effective meetings share a number of the following common elements:

An agenda. All meetings have an agenda that lays out the goals and objectives, what will happen, and how long each item on the agenda will take.

Introductions and welcome. Everyone introduces themselves.

A purpose. Is the purpose of the meeting to build relationships among people or make sure a key decision gets made? Is it to share information or train leaders? Even if a range of things occur in a meeting, you are clear about its core purpose.

Clear goals and objectives. You can effectively communicate to people what they will do in the meeting and why they should attend.

Participatory activities. Staff and leaders work together to design a meeting that includes participants' voices and leadership. Everyone in the room can feel they are part of the group. You include small-group discussion, collaboration between partners, action, writing, and other ways of having people do more in the meeting than just sit and listen. Good meetings build a collective spirit and identity. Making decisions, giving input, and talking with other members foster this sense.

A strong and prepared facilitator. Someone or a team of people plays the distinct role of moving the agenda along, keeping the meeting focused, helping people make decisions, and ensuring that everyone has the chance to participate.

The right length to complete the agenda. You have enough time to accomplish the goals of the meeting. You respect people's time and other commitments by starting and ending the meeting on time.

A sense of forward movement. People feel they are collectively accomplishing things and the campaign is progressing. When you are implementing a campaign, you connect meetings to concrete activities that move your campaign forward. People want to come back and do something!

A sense of achieving goals. If the goal is to train people to speak in public, to develop a street theater piece, or to make a tactical decision about a campaign, people leave with this outcome.

A summary of decisions and next steps. You review decisions and have a clear statement of next steps and who is responsible for implementing them.

An evaluation. In closing, you identify what worked and what could be improved.

A new learning experience. When people learn something new they feel they are growing as individuals. Meetings can always have even a small part of the agenda devoted to political education or skills building.

Respect for people's other commitments. The timing of meetings also shows respect for the other commitments people have, such as having dinner and putting children to bed. The members themselves decide on these logistics—the length, time, and location of meetings.

Ineffective meetings share these elements:

No agenda, no goals, and no update of accomplishments. A meeting without an agenda or without an update of the campaign and meeting goals leads to confusion. No update on progress leads people to believe that they are not accomplishing anything.

No facilitation or an unprepared facilitator. Meetings where facilitators don't know the goals of the meeting and do not have the skill to facilitate can cause people—particularly new people—never to come back.

No connection to action. Meetings that are not connected to campaign action, to doing activities that help you reach your goals and objectives, communicate to people the organization is in "meeting mode" and not really doing anything. These meetings only repeat what was discussed at the last meeting. They get stuck in process and protocol. They drive people away from a campaign and from your organization.

Do not meet the needs of the people participating in the campaign. You don't design meetings to meet the needs of organizers, but rather to meet the needs of the members who need to be there. For example, if members live in two areas that are far apart, you choose a location between the two or alternate between meeting spots.

Keep in mind that each organization develops a meeting culture. It is important to check that this meeting culture fits members' needs and lifestyles, especially as an organization evolves. For example, CVH started out with a committed but small group of leaders. People were very comfortable with each other. Long meetings became the norm. Once people came to a meeting, the unspoken culture was to get everything done, no matter how long it took. As the organization grew and new people became involved, CVH had to reevaluate how it ran its meetings. What worked with fifteen core leaders who knew each other very well did not work for groups of thirty-five to fifty people with other kinds of demands in their lives and who lacked the deep personal connections the founding members shared.

How Do We Know When the Campaign Is Over?

You win or you lose or you make an assessment that the campaign is not moving forward and you have to end it.

A campaign is over when you get the target to respond to your demand positively, either in whole or in part, or when the target clearly says no and your evaluation and assessment show that you will not be able to move him on the issue. When nothing you do will make a difference, the campaign is over. (For more on ending and evaluating the campaign, see Chapter Thirteen.)

LEADERSHIP DEVELOPMENT OPPORTUNITIES
DURING CAMPAIGN IMPLEMENTATION

- *Recruit others.* Leaders go to points of entry and talk with people about the campaign.
- *Run phone canvasses.* Leaders manage canvasses and phone trees to call members to come out to actions and important meetings.
- *Be a block or neighborhood captain.* Leaders mobilize their neighbors for actions.
- *Facilitate mass mailings.* Get other members to come to mailing parties. Oversee the process of getting out a mass mailing.
- *Conduct outreach to allies.* Leaders talk to and recruit allies to the campaign, often for the specific purpose of increasing the involvement of their constituents. They do teach-ins or speak at other organizations to get their support.
- *Develop actions and tactics.* Leaders play a key role in developing actions and ideas for actions. They produce props, lead chants, and other activities. Make critical decisions during an action.

- *Engage in grassroots fundraising.* Work with other leaders to develop budgets for actions and raise funds, including in-kind donations and donations from individuals.

- *Be a campaign spokesperson.* Make calls to the press to get them to come to actions, speak at press conferences, do interviews at actions, and write op-ed pieces and letters to the editor.

CHALLENGES
DURING CAMPAIGN IMPLEMENTATION

"Our campaign is losing." The leadership team decides how to proceed. It can decide to continue and see what happens, understanding that failure is likely or possible. It can stop the campaign, evaluate the strategy, and develop a new plan. It can decide to cut its losses and end the campaign. Whatever choice the leadership makes, it communicates what it is doing with all who have a stake in the campaign—members, leaders, allies, staff, and even targets.

"Our campaign is progressing well and we are on track, but we are not bringing new people into the organization." Sometimes, even when the campaign is going well, it is not resonating in the community. Community members may think that the campaign is resolving the problem and they don't need to get involved, or the organizers are working so much on the campaign that they are not doing base-building.

Make sure you are not promoting a premature sense of victory—in media work, with allies, or during recruitment. Make sure organizers are following a recruitment schedule and meeting numeric goals. Sometimes the issue isn't as important as the organization thought it was. In this case, the leadership team evaluates and decides how to move forward.

"The campaign is moving quickly from action to action and we do not have time to do adequate leadership development." Particularly in reactive or emergency campaigns where there is a lot of planning and mobilization for action, it can seem hard to do leadership development. In those cases, you do "quick and dirty" leadership development and incorporate it into the work of the campaign. For example, although it may be hard to schedule separate trainings, you include leadership training as part of existing meetings. You also try to do more one-on-one meetings.

"The people who come to meetings are not coming to actions." Sometimes people come to meetings and make decisions but do not do anything else to pull their weight. If this happens, the leadership team comes up with a proposal to reverse

the process to ensure that those people who are doing the work at actions or in the organization are making the campaign decisions. This strategy also provides opportunities for the organizer to agitate people into action, telling them that by coming out to actions, they can participate more deeply in decision making.

"No one is coming to organizing meetings but people are doing other work on the campaign." The organizing committee should be guiding the campaign. If people are not coming but are doing other things, assess if the organizer and leaders are prioritizing organizing meetings, and if not, why not. Try cutting down on the number of meetings; hold fewer but more effective meetings. Another reason for low attendance could be that members feel burnt out on meetings and would rather spend their time doing more satisfying work on the campaign. In this case it is important for the organizer and leaders to communicate to people the importance of organizing meetings as the structure for guiding a truly member-led campaign.

ESSENTIAL ELEMENTS
FOR EFFECTIVE CAMPAIGN IMPLEMENTATION

☑ *Respond to changes in the campaign plan.* When your organization engages in action, there will be reaction and things will change. As the campaign progresses, make changes to your plan to reflect new developments.

☑ *Maximize opportunities for people to get involved.* Include opportunities for member involvement, decision making, leadership development, and mobilization in all aspects of the campaign. Campaign implementation is when the most people, especially new people, get involved.

☑ *Rely on strong leaders, but ensure opportunities for new members to take on leadership roles.* It is natural to get comfortable with the best leaders. Today's new member can one day be a great leader—but only if he or she has a chance to take on that role. When filling roles, such as developing leadership teams and choosing facilitators, create a mix of old members and newer people.

☑ *Keep objectives, demands, and goals clear and present.* Leaders, members, and staff always refer back to the question: Does the proposed action help us achieve our goals and get our demands met?

☑ *Evaluate campaign structures.* Make sure that the way organizing committee meetings work, leadership teams are constructed, and how people are chosen for roles works for everyone involved.

Exercise 11.1
Negotiation Role Play

You can use the following as an exercise to prepare leaders to participate in negotiations or to gain a better understanding of negotiation in a campaign.

Time: 60 minutes.

Materials: Props, such as hats or other costumes to help people have fun with their roles. Chart paper for debriefing.

Roles: A facilitator experienced enough to guide a debriefing session that will likely require weaving together different elements.

Room set-up: Enough room for people to arrange their chairs around a small group and hear their discussion clearly. Ideally, two separate rooms or a large enough space so the teams can prepare without the other team hearing. A table that role players can sit around for the negotiation meeting, and enough room so that everyone else can see and hear them comfortably. A flip chart for debriefing the exercise.

Housing Now! Scenario:

Housing Now! is a community organization that has been working all year on a campaign to get the city to build affordable, subsidized housing near the marina. This run-down area is on the verge of an economic resurgence. The organization wants longtime residents to be able to stay and share in the benefits. Housing Now! demands one thousand units of new housing for low-to-moderate-income families, with one-quarter of these available to its members. The housing units would rent for 50 percent of market value and people could live in them as long as they wanted or needed to. Housing Now! wants the units to be low-rise townhouses scattered throughout the waterfront neighborhood. Its membership had debated all the possibilities for the waterfront. It considers the number of units to be the only point that it is willing to change.

The organization has the following attributes:

- Three thousand general members, defined as people who have come out at least once for an action or meeting in the previous year (Housing Now! members do not pay dues)

- A strong active base of about five hundred working members who have come out several times to campaign meetings and actions on this issue

- An experienced leadership team

Exercise 11.1
Negotiation Role Play, Cont'd

- A track record of public policy accomplishments related to housing
- The ability to move some key members of the city council

The city council supports a different version of this program. They would create six hundred units, with no guarantees for Housing Now! members. The units would rent for 70 percent of market value, and once a family earns more than $35,000 a year, it would have to move. The units would only be built in one section of the neighborhood, but they won't say which one. Some of the housing could be in small apartment buildings. City council leaders say that this is the best they can do and their final offer. If they do not get Housing Now's support for this program, they will not create the program themselves, because housing is not one of their key issues for this year.

Mayor Boden has another proposal. The mayor's program would create one thousand housing units for people with a range of incomes. Half will be for sale at market rate and half will rent at 50 percent of market value for low- and moderate-income families. Ten percent of the rental housing would include support services for formerly homeless families. The mayor would promise Housing Now! five hundred cards for a lottery that will be drawn for the low- and moderate-income units. A total of three thousand cards would be distributed through other organizations. The renters can stay as long as they want or need to stay. The mayor won't say what the style of the housing would be. It would all be in an area near the marina where some nice restaurants and shops have been opening, due to the mayor's economic development strategy for the area.

Mayor Boden ran on a promise to create new housing to relieve the city's problems of homelessness and dilapidated housing stock and to create more housing options for the middle class. The mayor has been meeting with a variety of groups concerned about the marina and has asked the leadership team of Housing Now! to meet with her to see if the organization will support her proposal.

In order to create new housing in the city, the city council and the mayor need to agree on a proposal. Because Housing Now! is the largest and most well-established housing group in the city, if the organization and the mayor agree on a proposal, the city council will likely move to create that program. If Housing Now! and the city council agree on a proposal, that will likely become the program.

The organizing committee of Housing Now! has selected four people to negotiate with a team from the mayor's office.

Housing Now! Team:

- A long-time board member of Housing Now! who lives in the marina area in decent, secure housing. Worked on her own to support the mayor's election campaign.

- An active member whose family has been living in a shelter for the last year.

- A member who is relatively new, of middle income, and lives just outside the marina area.

- A local religious leader from the marina area who helped to found Housing Now! and whose congregants are very active in the organization.

Mayor's Team:

- Mayor Boden, a wealthy former businessperson in the second half of her first term. Ran a populist campaign but has delivered mostly to the business community.

- The Deputy Commissioner of Housing Development, who is in his first city job, and who used to work as an organizer for Housing Now!

- The Deputy Commissioner for Welfare and Homeless Shelters, who has been in city government for many years.

- The political advisor to the mayor who is running the mayor's reelection campaign and is concerned about the mayor's image in poor communities.

Exercise:

- Each group meets for twenty minutes to decide on roles, prepare a strategy, and come up with the statements and positions they think they will need. Each group discussion takes place in a separate fishbowl, with other participants observing the process of the group.

- The groups come together to negotiate. The mayor's office has allocated twenty minutes for the teams to negotiate their differences.

- After the negotiation, the facilitator guides the following debriefing:

- First, the observers who did not participate in either negotiating team answer the following questions:

  How did the group you observed prepare for the negotiation?

  How did they resolve any differences among the team members?

What did each group do in the negotiation at the mayor's office that was effective? How did this action help them get what they wanted?

What did each group do that was not effective? How did this action prevent them from getting what they wanted?

What was the end result of the negotiation? Who got what?

- Next, the facilitator asks the team participants to debrief, asking the following questions:

    What was most interesting thing you experienced in the role you played?

    What was the hardest part of the process of preparing for the negotiation?

    What did your team do in the negotiation that was most effective? Was this effective action something you thought about in advance or did it surprise you?

    What did your team do in the negotiation that was least effective?

    Is your team going back to Housing Now! or to those to whom the mayor feels accountable with good news or bad news?

- In closing, the facilitator guides a discussion of what participants learned from this exercise that they can apply to an upcoming negotiation in the campaign. The facilitator helps draw out some key elements of negotiation that participants need to be aware of. Refer to the section on negotiation earlier in this chapter for a description of these key elements.

Running Kick-A** Actions!

MARCHING THROUGH THE STREETS

"What do we want?"

"Paid jobs!"

"When do we want them?"

"*Now!*"

These chants echo through the canyons of lower Manhattan, as 150 Community Voices Heard (CVH) members march to various Work Experience Program (WEP) worksites on a mild spring day with one clear demand: pass the New York City Transitional Jobs Bill to create real, paid jobs for people in workfare. At Two Lafayette Street, scores of WEP workers are inside, working for no pay. The CVH marchers, most of whom are WEP workers themselves, set up a moving picket that stretches an entire city block. City workers leaving for lunch on this first nice day of spring have to stop on their way out of the building and maneuver through the handmade signs and demonstrators with noisemakers wearing blue "CVH" baseballs caps. The CVH members hand out sheets of paper listing what they want as well as flyers asking people to call the city council speaker and tell him to pass the jobs bill now. Some of the city workers read the materials, pull out their cell phones, and call the number on the sheet, to the cheers of the demonstrators. As the picket continues, a group of women come out, holding signs that read: We work! We deserve a paycheck too! They are WEP workers who are joining the march on their lunch hour.

After twenty minutes at this site, the group heads to the building where city council members have their offices. The marchers carry a huge copy of a letter signed by all the WEP workers who joined the demonstration. The top of the letter reads: "We want real jobs! Pass the TJP bill today!" They plan to deliver the letter directly to the speaker.

What Is an Action and Why Is It Important?

An action is a public showing of your organization's power. Actions show your numbers and the quality of your organization's leaders.

In an action, community members challenge the power of their campaign's target, often in creative, bold, or energizing ways. They make a public demand to which the target must respond either by saying yes or no or negotiating.

Each action helps you get closer to winning the campaign. Actions are the most critical opportunity to flex your organization's muscle with a target.

What Are Some Important Characteristics of Actions?

The best actions have a number of characteristics in common:

Tension. When you introduce tension, you make the target uncomfortable. When a target is uncomfortable, he or she moves to do something to stop being uncomfortable. Introducing tension does not mean yelling or screaming. You introduce tension, for example, when you force a target who is used to doing all the talking to stick to the agenda your organization prepared.

Member-driven. Actions are the best opportunity to develop the skills, confidence, and power of members. Actions have many roles members can fill. The best actions have activities that members are willing to do and are trained to execute and that stretch them to try new things.

Connection with strategies. For example, if you are using a legislative strategy, actions include lobby days and meetings with legislators.

Creativity and energy. Great actions are fun and exciting and become part of the story of your organization. They are public shows. You make them fun to relieve tension and to get your point across in ways that people can hear and understand.

Education. Through actions, members see and learn how political power operates.

Careful planning. Actions require detailed planning and preparation. If an action fails to illustrate your power—few people show up to fill a large room for an accountability meeting or leaders are not prepped to press the target strongly to meet their demands—it can have a negative effect on your organization for a very long time.

Within your capacity. You only choose actions that your organization can run effectively.

Essential for winning. Every campaign requires a series of collective, public actions in order to shift power.

Putting an Alinsky Principle to Work

Saul Alinsky stresses that the best actions are within the experience of members and outside the experience of the target. Here's an example of that principle. Members of A Cleaner Southside (ACS) are concerned about the poor quality of their water. They believe Leather Works, a big manufacturing company, is responsible. They take a bus to the vacation beach home of Jed Brown, CEO of Leather Works. Brown is used to facing protesters, including ACS members, in town meetings or even at his main residence, but no group has ever come to his vacation home. Rather than chanting and rallying like they usually do, ACS members go to the beach. They lay out on blankets while their children play in the sand, just like any other day at the beach. Except on this day, they offer cups of dirty water from their coolers to other beachgoers, explaining how the pollution from Jed Brown's plant is affecting their health. The protest generates a great deal of press coverage and moves Brown to schedule a meeting with a team of ACS leaders.

When Do We Organize an Action?

You move to action when you can exercise your power effectively.

If you wait too long to engage in action, members lose interest. You can start with internal actions, as we describe later in this chapter, soon after you start the campaign development phase. When you enter the campaign implementation phase, the organizing committee refers to the campaign plan to see if a potential action helps reach the campaign objectives and how it will do so. For example, the campaign plan says that in April you need a public show of power to affect the legislative session. In January, members assess their capacity and the needs of the campaign and choose a specific type of action.

Use small actions or joint actions, if necessary. Even if your organization does not have the capacity to pull off large actions, small actions help members to build the skills, confidence, and experience to manage more sophisticated actions. For example, they hold community meetings that bring in new members and prepare them to run large meetings with targets. They organize a small informational picket so they experience what it is like to deal with security guards or police. They deliver something that represents the campaign issue to a target's office.

You can also organize an action with a more experienced group. With larger numbers of people and seasoned staff, members have safe experiences that prepare them to try similar tactics and actions in their own organization.

Some organizations move to action quickly and easily; others take longer. Organizations of people who are in crisis tend to move to action more quickly than organizations where issues—although important—are not perceived to be issues of life or death. For example, when we started CVH, the members were facing severe cutbacks in the social safety net they needed to support their children. They moved to action very quickly and established an organizational culture in which members expect action to take place regularly. Similarly, if an organization has members and leaders who have been in a lot of actions, it is able to organize actions more quickly and easily than a group of people who have never moved into action or who are used to other forms of showing their power.

What Are the Types of Actions?

Actions can be internal or external.

External actions may or may not be direct actions, but the most significant kind of action you undertake is an external direct action that puts you into contact with your target.

Internal action. An internal action is both a test of members' commitment to an issue and a campaign and an opportunity to train members to conduct larger public actions. Internal actions allow you to see how members engage in the work of organizing. An example of an internal action is a survey project. For instance, members of an environmental justice organization go out into the community and ask people about their health in order to detect patterns of disease they can link with a toxic site. You can run internal actions during the campaign development phase as well as during implementation.

External action. An external action moves members to exercise their power publicly. External actions build your campaign so you can move the target. An example is mobilizing members to join a rally for better working conditions organized by a local health workers union whose support you want for your campaign. You do an action that shows your organization can turn people out. If you are focused and confident that you can mobilize people, you can run an external action at any time in the campaign, including during campaign development, to show your power.

Direct action. A direct action is an external action that puts members in direct contact with the target. An example of a direct action is a meeting in your office with the parks commissioner to discuss the budget for a neighborhood park or a large community meeting that you organize to ask the mayor to create a special initiative to build more parks. It can also be a takeover of the lobby of the state agency that funds the local parks system.

You implement direct actions in nearly every campaign, whether or not you choose a direct action strategy as described in Chapter Nine. You only do direct actions when you have a campaign plan in place. You have many ways you can exercise your power through direct action, no matter what strategy you choose. The following sections describe the types of actions you can do in the street, in the room, and in the target's space.

People Power in the Street. These actions disrupt normal business operations where a target lives, works, or is expected, such as at a fundraising dinner. They include picketing, marching, rallying, and taking over a building.

Picketing

- *What it is.* A picket is a moving line of people who are chanting, holding signs, and handing out printed information to the public. The moving line is usually blocking the entrance to a building or is close enough to the entrance that people going inside cannot avoid it. The target of the campaign is usually in the building or closely associated with it. A good picket is as close to the target as possible.

- *When to use it.* Picketing has an element of surprise because it does not require a permit. It also gets you close to the target. Picketing is very effective for public education. For example, members picket outside of a political fundraising event to draw attention to the fact that none of the candidates has taken a clear position on their issue. Picketing gains attention by causing disruption. You slow down entrance to a building or ask people to join the picket or not to cross the picket line in solidarity.

- *Time required.* Usually about one hour.

- *Legal considerations.* Picketing is legal, but learn if there are local ordinances about pedestrian traffic and noise and follow them. You do not need a permit. You occupy a space of your choice without risking arrest of members who stay in the picket line. If the police show up, and often with a non-permitted action like this they will, keep calm and professional. You have the right to assemble. Focus on negotiating with the police how close to the target you can get. In most cases the goal of the police, especially at a small protest, is to stop it and have people leave of their own accord. They do not want to arrest a lot of people and process them. However, police will sometimes target the organizer or leader, hoping that neutralizing that person can end the protest.

Only one person from staff and one person from the tactical team speak to police. Other people are not involved in negotiating. You reinforce this rule in your planning and training before the action. The tactical team makes the final decision about where to move and what to do.

In this kind of action, any illegal activity, such as smoking marijuana or jaywalking, can get people arrested. Stay focused on the purpose of the action. In addition, everyone should bring identification, just in case of any unforeseen problems and possible arrests.

Depending on your local ordinances, you will probably not be able to use amplified sound at a nonpermitted picket.

- *How many people.* With a minimum of just twenty people you can hand out a great deal of printed information. With a larger group of up to sixty, you can force the target to see or hear your organization's presence. You can also do mass pickets that include hundreds of people, but these actions require a lot of coordination with many experienced leaders.

- *Preparation.* Visible clothing or buttons as well as signs that identify the organization and its demands draw attention to a picket and to its purpose. Clear, provocative written materials that people will want to read help reach the public education goals of a picket.

A good picket is lively, colorful, and noisy! A chant captain keeps everyone vocal and ensures that the whole group is chanting the same thing. Cans with pennies inside as well as tambourines and whistles make noise. Members use a clear rap while handing out materials. Everyone knows what to do or say if the target emerges. Leaders have press packets and are prepared to speak with the press.

Four people serve as anchors for the point at each end that people march around, and another three or four people act as picket movers, moving the picket along and keeping picketers close together. All participants hold up signs.

You scout out your location ahead of time. If you are picketing outside a fundraising event, for instance, you know how many doors the candidates could enter so that you can have members picketing at each location.

- *Action tip.* Some things that make these actions fun and attract press include making large puppets resembling the target and using three-dimensional visuals, such as costumes and statues.

Tool 12.1 is a handout on picket rules.

Rallying

- *What it is.* A rally is a static group of people who are standing in a defined area. They are chanting and listening to speakers or music. There is usually one keynote speaker as well as other speakers representing different aspects of the issue.

- *When to use it.* Rallies tend not to cause major disruption and are better for getting out a message or showing your organizational power than for getting a demand met.

- *Time required.* The length of a rally depends on its goals and other actions it is connected with. If it occurs on its own at lunchtime in a local park, for example, it goes for no more than an hour. If it marks the end of a small, local march, it is also about one hour long. National or large marches often end in rallies that are two or more hours long as the marchers wait for everyone to reach the final site. A rally could also be part of a full-day or half-day event to raise awareness about an issue.

- *Legal considerations.* You usually need a permit for the number of people expected as well as for using a sound system. Rallies are common and the police carefully control them.

You negotiate for a visible site as close as possible to some aspect of the issue you want to highlight. It is better to have too many people in a small space than too few in a large space. If you can't get a satisfactory site, you make an issue of it in the local media. For example, organizers unsuccessfully sought a space in New York City's Central Park for a protest against the Iraq war. They raised a great deal of awareness about the event and its goals by getting the press to cover their site negotiations with the city.

- *How many people.* Rallying is most effective with a large number of people, at least one hundred.

- *Preparation.* You organize a rally as far in advance as possible to allow for time to negotiate for a site, prepare speakers, and turn people out. If you want to gather more than a thousand people, you start planning nine to twelve months in advance. Smaller rallies of fifty to several hundred people require three to six months of planning. Exceptions occur when some public event turns the spotlight on your issue, making it easier to galvanize people. In these situations rallies can be organized much more quickly. If you are organizing the rally with other partners, it will take weeks or months, depending on the number of groups involved, to negotiate who will speak, how to deliver a consistent message, and similar aspects of the event.

  Public service announcements, op ed pieces, and radio interviews ahead of time help with turnout and raise public awareness about the issue. Keep up the energy by keeping speakers to a minimum and limiting the topics as well as the length of time each person speaks. Have an engaging emcee and include some music or performance.

  Have press packets available and leaders prepared to speak with the press.

- *Action tip.* At the end of the rally use an energetic, powerful act to build the collective spirit. Examples are a mass die-in, taking over a street, or bringing everyone into the lobby of a building to ask for a meeting with the target. Use cell phones and speaker systems to involve everyone in the crowd to talk with the target.

Marching

- *What it is.* A march is a group of people moving from one spot to another.

- *When to use it.* Marching is an energetic and effective way to get members out and to get issues known in the community. A march can keep people motivated for a longer action. For example, if you need to go to the offices of two targets, marching from one to the other keeps up energy in between. Marching is especially exciting and activating for new people.

- *Time required.* Usually one to two hours, but it depends on the goals and the other actions the march is connected with.

- *Legal considerations.* A march can either be permitted or nonpermitted. In deciding whether or not to seek a permit for a march or other action, research how your local police department reacts to protests and demonstrations. For example, if your local law enforcement agencies are difficult to work with or have little experience with protests or a history of arresting people at demonstrations, it could make sense to apply for a permit.

When seeking a permit for a march, you negotiate with the police about a route for you to march along. You can usually have a permit to amplify sound and a police escort. You also agree with the police on where you will assemble, where you will start your march, and where you will end.

If you negotiate to get a permit, the police may want to put you far away from where you want to be. You may then instead choose a non-permitted march, which could get you closer to the target and has an element of surprise. For instance, if you want to do a building takeover or a picket at a target's office at the end of the march, the police are unlikely to allow you to get that close to the target. If you forgo the permit to get closer to the target, keep in mind that you can legally march on the sidewalk without a permit. If you march on the sidewalk and have enough people, you can try to negotiate with the police to expand your march onto a street or at least a lane of traffic.

When negotiating for a permit or during the course of a march, you try not to let the police steer you into an isolated side street or a wall. These common tactics effectively disperse the marchers or even frighten them off. For example, marches protesting the United States invasion of Iraq drew nearly one million people in New York City. When police on horseback prevented marchers from following the course of the huge march, participants found themselves bottlenecked and pinned against walls and one another. Many panicked marchers just pushed their way out and left.

- *How many people.* The right number of people depends on where you are marching. One hundred people in a small downtown business district will attract attention, while in a large city you may need one thousand people to create the same effect.

- *Preparation.* Members and leaders receive training to serve as marshals who maintain order and give directions in the march. They also serve as communicators in situations such as the police trying to change the course of the march or leaders deciding to try to take the street. A march is often connected to other actions, such as delivering petitions or holding a rally, so members need to be prepared to follow the full course of events.

You have press packets available and leaders prepared to speak with the press.

- *Action tip:* Ask marchers all to wear the same-color shirt or organizational hats or jackets to show your numbers more visually. Also, when people carry flags and banners high above their heads, it is more effective than holding them waist-high.

Building Takeovers

- *What it is.* In a takeover, people enter an office, building, or other significant site. They enter unexpected and with a demand.

- *When to use it.* Takeovers are most effective for getting a meeting with a target who has been refusing to meet with you. Takeovers agitate targets and make them uncomfortable. Takeovers can range from nonconfrontational, with people simply entering an office, to more agitational, with people entering the lobby of the target's apartment building, sitting down, and refusing to leave until the target responds to their demand. Takeovers are a way to radicalize members and empower them to engage in more confrontational actions.

- *Time required.* Building takeovers usually take an hour to an hour and a half, depending on the objectives and the extent to which you push the limits of legal protest.

- *Legal considerations.* If a building is privately owned, you may be breaking the law against trespassing. If you are impeding traffic and the flow of business, you could be cited for disturbing the peace. Depending on the political climate, the target, the issue, and the powers of government at the time of the protest, you may face more serious charges.

- *How many people.* The larger the space, the more people you need. You can take over a small office or lobby with twenty or thirty people. A larger building can require more than a thousand people.

- *Preparation.* Takeovers require a high degree of member buy-in, strong leadership skills, and organizational discipline. Members and leaders are in continual negotiation with the people who work at the site or with security personnel. Members have to be extremely comfortable with tension, disruption strategies, and dealing with police.

- *Action tip:* Balloons, large signs, and props help you fill up a space. Make sure that you investigate the building's entrances and security at least twice so that you do not miss anything that will affect your action.

Building Takeover

An alliance of community groups working on the redevelopment of lower Manhattan after 9/11 organizes an accountability session with the head of the Lower Manhattan Development Corporation (LMDC), the agency responsible for deciding how to use $1 billion in federal funds to redevelop Lower Manhattan. As the date approaches, leaders learn that the target will not come to the session. The organizing committee plans a march to the LMDC's offices a block from the World Trade Center site to demand that the head of the LMDC meet with the groups about their proposals. When marchers arrive at the building, two hundred people enter the lobby holding signs and balloons and shaking noisemakers. They hold the lobby for twenty-five minutes, stopping business. In addition, five members get directly into the LMDC office and sit in. As a result of the disruption and the show of power, when alliance leaders call the head of the LMDC, he agrees to meet with members of the alliance in one week.

People Power in the Room. These actions show powerholders and targets that an organization represents and can mobilize large numbers of constituents and that these constituents can control an agenda. Examples of these types of actions include accountability sessions, meeting with a target, and "day in the life" actions.

Accountability Session

- *What it is.* An accountability session is a public meeting where an organization mobilizes a large enough number of people to pressure a target to deliver on a demand. Community power-building organizations regularly conduct these important actions.

  In an accountability session, leaders of the organization make specific demands of the target, to which he has to answer yes or no. The target does not give you a speech. This is not an occasion for the target to tell you what he thinks. At an accountability session a target tells your organization whether or not he is willing to do what you want him to do.

The organization establishes a clear format. It has timed periods for questions and answers, which it records for public knowledge. Organizations often use a large scorecard to record the target's responses. They give the target the questions in advance so that he can prepare a response and so that he can't say he needs to study or investigate it.

- *When to use it.* You use an accountability session when your organization has enough power or when the political conditions are right to get a target into a room. You also have enough power in your track record and in your membership and alliances that you can mobilize to move the target. In addition, you have a large enough leadership team to take on the roles necessary in a large and structured meeting.

  You use an accountability session when the target will only move because of mass public action. An accountability session offers the opportunity to politicize your members. They see their relationship to a public official from a perspective of power and control, and they witness a powerful person working and managing a public negotiation with his or her constituents.

  If the target will not accept your invitation, you can hold the session with an empty seat. You make it more of a rally, with the press hook that the target does not care about the community. This tactic will only work if your membership is more experienced, as it is depleting to new people to hold an accountability session with no target there.

  If you hold the session near the target's home or office and the target does not show up on the day of the event, you can march over and try to bring him to the session. When doing your phone calls to turn people out, you let leaders and members know that such a march is a possibility so they are prepared for a potential change in plans.

- *Time required.* An accountability session usually lasts around two hours. The audience arrives first, at least thirty minutes before the target, so you can make sure the room is full, that people know the format, and that they are energized with chants or props.

- *Legal considerations.* There are usually no legal considerations regarding accountability sessions. If you are doing a session with a candidate running for office, contact a legal advisor to make sure you follow local election laws.

- *How many people.* In most cases, you need at least two hundred people. More often, you need to pack an auditorium with five hundred or more. Accountability sessions can also have thousands of participants.

- *Preparation.* Before the event, you negotiate with the target's staff about a date, location, and the format. You agree on the format and the amount of time the target will have to address questions. Getting the target to agree to an agenda that your organization controls may not be easy, as most targets are used to being in charge, but it is essential. You forward the questions to the target before the session and communicate that you expect clear responses—yes or no. Having a target respond to the community in this way clearly demonstrates your power.

  If you are organizing your first accountability session, you start at least six months in advance. Getting the target to commit, negotiating about time and format, and mobilizing your membership all take time. Once the organization has experience successfully executing this type of action and it has a well-established base, you may be able to organize a session in three months.

  Members prepare the demands that they will make of the target on the day of the action, usually in the form of yes-or-no questions. For example, if the accountability session seeks to hold political candidates accountable on the organization's issues, a sample question is: "If you are elected, will you require The Big Company to clean up its toxic waste?"

  Organizers prepare strong, experienced leaders and members to ask the questions at accountability sessions. Other members energize the audience by leading chants. Other important roles include giving testimonials or brief motivational speeches, speaking to the press, and greeting the target when he or she arrives.

  If you decide you need an accountability session but can't turn out enough people or get the target there on your own, you might consider working with a cosponsoring organization. The organization must have a proven ability to turn people out and care about the campaign as much as your organization does. Ultimately, you don't do this type of action unless you have a foolproof plan to fill the room with constituents. If you work with a cosponsor, you make sure that members of your organization play key roles in developing and executing the session.

You carefully consider the location and size of the room. If you are concerned about turnout, have a smaller room than you think you will need. If turnout is weak, you will still pack the room. Even if you're certain you can fill a room, never have a huge space that will make hundreds of people look small. It is better to be in a smaller room packed with people than to be in a larger room with empty seats. Keep a couple of rows of chairs folded until you need them. When people see more chairs being set up in a hurry, it builds excitement.

At the session, have press packets available as well as leaders prepared to speak with the press.

Tool 12.2 provides a sample agenda for an accountability session.

- *Action tip:* Always have a plan of what you will do if the target does not come or is late.

Accountability Session

The mayor wants to spend up to $600 million in public funds to build a new football stadium. CVH opposes this plan. The organization holds an accountability session with the speaker of the city council in a church in his district. One goal of the session is to pressure him to come out against public financing for the stadium. Organizers prep four strong leaders to ask him if he will oppose public financing for the stadium as well as to state his position on several other matters. On the night of the session, members place a scoreboard behind the speaker and the leaders ask their questions. He gives a noncommittal response on the stadium funding. The audience of more than three hundred people chants and sings about the folly of tax cuts for wealthy developers. The speaker, visibly upset, tries to clarify his statement. The chair asks him to simply state clearly whether he agrees to come out against public financing for the stadium or not. She reminds him that his time to address this question is almost up. This makes him more agitated. Finally, time is up. Over his objections, a member records that his position is no. Within a week of the event, the speaker comes out publicly to oppose the stadium financing, helping to cement the defeat of the mayor's position.

Target Meeting

- *What it is.* A small group of people who represent the larger organization meet with the target. You show your power to the target by having strong leaders interact with him or her. Your organization sets the agenda. It's best to have the target come to you or to a neutral space you determine. If you rent or borrow a space, you clearly identify it as being in your control with banners, signs, and people.

- *When to use it.* A target meeting is often the follow-up to a previous action, or it may occur because you are in the thick of an issue and have enough juice to get a meeting with a target.

- *Time required.* Target meetings usually last an hour.

- *Legal considerations.* None.

- *How many people.* Eight to ten people usually attend a target meeting. Target meetings can show broader participation through having the representatives bring petitions, membership cards, or letters to the meeting or having additional members waiting outside the office.

- *Preparation.* Target meetings require at least two good prep meetings, with role plays and a discussion of what ifs. It is useful to have a run-through practice the day of the meeting. You practice, for example, what if the target sends a representative? As always, you call members two or three times before the meeting to make sure they will come to the target meeting.

- *Action tip:* Seating placement is everything in small meetings. You don't have a lot of people to create tension, but you do have the organization's best and most courageous leaders. You deconstruct the usual power set-up. Force the target to sit right next to leaders, as people equal to him or her. If the target brings aides, keep them as far away and out of sight as possible. If you have a low chair in your office, make sure the target sits in it. Seat everyone in a circle or around a table. Do not let the target stand or position himself or herself as the head of the room.

Day in the Life

- *What it is.* You introduce the target to an issue and make a set of demands in a place that illustrates the issue. An example is visiting welfare centers to understand what welfare recipients experience or conducting a "toxic tour" of polluted sites that are affecting people's health.

- *When to use it.* You do a Day in the Life when you want a target to understand an issue more personally and on a deeper level. This may help move him to support your demands. This action can also uncover problems that a target does not see. It attracts press, which helps pressure the target to act.

- *Time required.* These actions require six to eight hours from members as well as from the target or the target's representative.

- *Legal considerations.* None, unless you go to places that do not have public access.

- *How many people.* Day in the Life actions need two or three good leaders and two or three "tour guides" at each spot. Having a group of five or ten members available for discussion at the beginning and end of the action also lets the target see your power.

- *Preparation.* You map out the tour and account for travel and other factors. You prep all the participants, both those who accompany the target and meet the target at the sites as well as those who are available to speak with the target before and after the tour. Since this is usually an action that press attend, you prepare press packets as well as leaders to speak with the press.

- *Action tip:* Start or end the day at your office with a larger group of members both to show your power and to include more members in the action. Include a question and answer session with the target over lunch or dinner— even better, a dinner that members cook.

People Power in the Target's Space. You achieve people power in the target's space when you shift the control of a powerholder's space to your organization's members. You make the target uncomfortable and more amenable to your demands by changing the way his or her space operates. Examples of people power in the target's space include packing hearings, altering the dynamics of hearing or meetings rooms, and street theater.

Packing Hearings and Other Public Events

- *What it is.* Your organization fills up the audience in a room where, for example, people are giving testimony about a piece of legislation. You change the hearing from being a show of the legislature's power to being a space that your organization's members control. In another example, you go where the target is giving a speech and fill out the audience.

- *When to use it*. When a hearing occurs or when a target will be accessible to the public. You know when and where this event will occur in enough time to mobilize your members. You can use this action when you can't get the target to respond to your requests for a face-to-face meeting. By going to the target's space with large numbers of people and good messaging, you amplify your power and keep the issue in the target's face.

- *Time required*. Depends on the public event—minimum one hour.

- *Legal considerations*. Depending on the event, you may have the right to assemble there or you may not. If you do not, you prepare to negotiate with police. If you decide you want to break the law intentionally as an act of civil disobedience, you contact local legal resource groups for assistance before the action.

- *How many people*. Enough people to pack or fill out the space.

- *Preparation*. Props and signs are essential when you pack a public event—for example, people wearing the same visible piece of clothing, such as a hat or T-shirt, or holding signs that state the organization's name boldly.

> **Packing a Public Event**
>
> CVH turns out more than four hundred transitional jobs workers to a city council hearing about the future and effectiveness of the transitional jobs program. CVH members fill every seat in the chamber, and people are overflowing into the hallways. Because of their extensive preparation, they chant on cue and stand on cue. CVH controls the room. It has the power to either end the hearing by frustrating the council or to keep it going by stopping the chanting. When members do stop chanting, they hold up signs and put on their CVH hats to make it clear that they still control the space.

Alter the Dynamics of Hearing or Meeting Rooms

- *What it is*. You throw targets off in their space by altering the dynamics of a room they usually control. For example, members enter the hearing room and sit in the seats of legislators or commissioners. They rearrange audience chairs in a circle as opposed to theatre style. Members stand right next to officials as they conduct the hearing.

- *When to use it.* To many public officials, one hearing can be the same as another, particularly on issues they do not really care about. When you want to show a target and potential allies that there is dedicated support for your issue, you alter the dynamics of a meeting room. Just as when you pack a meeting room, you can also use this action when you can't get the target to meet with you or when you need to keep the issue in the target's face.

- *Time required.* As long as the hearing lasts, or at least until the target leaves the space.

- *Legal considerations.* None, unless you ratchet up the action and do more to disrupt the meeting.

- *How many people.* Although you can do some of this action with a small group of at least ten people, the more people you have in the room, the more you not only alter but control the space.

- *Preparation.* Altering power during a hearing or other scheduled event requires extremely trained leaders who can effectively deal with confrontation.

- *Action tip:* There is a difference between altering the dynamics of a space and controlling it. You can only control a space when you have enough people.

Street Theater

- *What it is.* A group of people develop and perform a theater piece or engage in a short skit that dramatizes an issue or demand. Street theater usually includes speaking roles, costumes, and props, as well as singing and playing instruments.

- *When to use it.* Street theater gets media attention. It is also public education. You can do it in the street or at the target's home or office. It is a great way for members to bring their cultural experiences and creative skills directly into an action. You can use a theater piece over and over again in different places. You can also tie it into holidays or other events.

- *Time required.* You need at least two hours, including time to set up and clean up. Members can perform the piece over and over again, but after an hour so, they usually need to rest.

- *Legal considerations.* You can do street theater with or without a permit. If you need a stage, equipment, or to amplify sound, or if you want to make sure the police will not move you to where the media cannot find you, a permit can be useful.

- *How many people.* You need a minimum of about ten people, but the more people you have, the more able they are to attract attention.

- *Preparation.* Theater skits require extensive prep. Members need at least two meetings to conceive an idea and start to write it out. They need another two meetings for practice. If they make props or costumes, they need to meet more often. If the piece is more visual than written or spoken, it can take less time to produce.

- *Action tips:* Preparing an effective script can be harder than it sounds. It may help to invite a person with some theater experience to help. The best approach is to keep it simple. Go for broad strokes and statements, not nuanced dialogue.

Street Theater: Two Examples

As part of the National Campaign for Jobs and Income Support, hundreds of leaders of low-income organizing groups from around the country descended on the corporate headquarters of Halliburton in Dallas, Texas, to hold a mock trial of U.S. President George W. Bush and Vice President Dick Cheney. Bush and Cheney had awarded substantial government contracts connected with the war in Iraq to Halliburton, where Cheney is a former trustee. Timed to coincide with a debate in the U.S. Congress about cutting funding for social services, the action dramatized the view that the administration's decisions are not based on sound public policy but are made to enrich their corporate friends and campaign supporters. Protesters dramatically read indictments of Bush and Cheney, charging them with putting profits over people. A judge sentenced each of them to participate in workfare and live the life of a poor person in the United States. The action drew a great deal of attention. In addition to shaking up a powerholder's space, it invited people passing by on the street and reading press coverage of the mock trial to think about the connections among domestic policy, foreign policy, and corporate profits.

In another example, leaders from the same organizations traveled to Washington, D.C., to the home of U.S. Senator Hillary Clinton when she was considering what her position on reauthorizing welfare legislation would be. It seemed to keep changing. Three buses arrived early one morning and dozens of welfare recipients and supporters gathered in front of Clinton's home. Some of the protesters waved a larger-than-life Hillary Clinton costume and others carried waffles. Several went up to the door, waffles in hand, and told the person who answered that they would like to ask the senator about why she is "waffling" on welfare. The action garnered extensive press coverage, including an article in the *New York Times*.

Additional Actions: From Town Hall Meetings to Boycotts. There are many other types of actions, too many to describe here. Some other internal actions include town hall meetings where community members discuss an issue without a target present, or petition drives, where members go out and get signatures on petitions.

Other external actions include press conferences and legislative lobby days that members and leaders plan and run and where they serve as spokespersons. In addition, many organizations use boycotts and mass walkouts to great effect. Powerful historic examples include the U.S. Civil Rights Movement's actions to expand voting rights and the United Farm Workers' grape boycott and campaigns to improve working conditions for farm workers. More recently, actions in 2006 by immigrant-rights groups to move the U.S. Congress to pass pro-immigrant legislation also offer highly instructive examples of using boycotts and walkouts to engage community members, train leaders, build power, and move targets.

These kinds of actions and others sometimes involve civil disobedience, when participants intentionally risk arrest as a tactic for reaching their goals. On the Internet or at the library you can find stories and how-to guides about these and other actions and about civil disobedience, in order to consider them in your own work. Inviting someone to speak with your organization who has participated in civil disobedience actions can be a great way to learn more about how to use these actions effectively. See Resource G for contact information for movement-building organizations that can help direct you to readings, tools, and possibly people in your area.

The following example describes an internal action, external action, and direct action for one campaign.

The Campaign for Clean Supermarkets

Internal action: membership canvass. Members of Westsiders Together gather at the office, then go out in teams to the local supermarkets. Each team has a clipboard with a survey form they fill in about the conditions in the markets in one neighborhood. The goal for this action is to develop a report card on the cleanliness of local supermarkets for the press and elected officials. The objectives are as follows:

- To build a list of at least fifty people interested in participating in the campaign.
- To train five members of the organization in outreach and survey skills.
- To get the organization's name and presence known in the community through at least two news reports.
- To identify a list of other problems in local supermarkets.

External action: press conference. Westsiders announces the results of its survey. Members invite the press and key stakeholders to a press conference outside the offices of the local food-safety inspection agency. Westsiders leaders talk about the key findings and make demands of the agency commissioner, who is the target of the campaign. The goal for this action is to deliver the demands and the survey directly to the agency commissioner and officials who monitor the quality of supermarkets. The objectives are as follows:

- To get five press reports of the findings and the issue of cleaning up dirty supermarkets.
- To develop the public speaking skills of three Westsiders leaders.
- To invite potential allies, including the local union that represents supermarket workers, to support the campaign.

Direct action: office takeover. The mayor is a secondary target of the clean supermarkets campaign. She is holding a meeting in her office. Ten members enter the office and try to disrupt the meeting while ten additional members chant in the hallway. The members seek to deliver their report on unsanitary conditions to the mayor and invite her to meet with them about the report. They know the mayor's press corps will come immediately. The goal of the action is to get a meeting with the mayor at which the organization will ask her to pressure the commissioner for results. The objectives are as follows:

- To get five articles on the supermarket report and the issue of cleanliness in the markets.

- To train and develop twenty-five members in direct actions and using confrontational tactics.

What Do We Need to Pull Off a Great Action?

You need to have a few things in place prior to the action, whether you have been planning it for three months or for three hours!

Prepped and trained leaders. You build in time before the action for leadership prep and take advantage of the multiple opportunities for leadership development during the action.

Tactical team. You agree on a tightly organized team of members and leaders to make moment-to-moment decisions at the action, as well as people designated to report back to the full group about decisions or negotiations with the target. More information about the tactical team follows later in this chapter.

A clear identity and message. In successful actions, organizations clearly communicate who they are and why they are there. Sometimes called "branding," this communication includes displaying the name of your organization, its insignia or logo, and a concise message about what you want. Branding is important in actions where the target is not in the room or where you are working with partners. There is nothing worse than mobilizing people for an action, having reporters there, then realizing no one knows who organized the action or what it is about.

Exhibit 12.1
Ways to Establish an Identity

- Everyone wears a shirt with the name of the organization on it.
- If people are in coats or at a formal event, they wear hats, buttons, or stickers.
- You display a huge, sturdy, well-made banner with the organization's name and insignia.
- You place the organization's name and a consistent message on every poster and on all materials you distribute at the action.

Agitation. Targets move when you make their public life uncomfortable. For example, a target is in a room with people who use her agency's services. They know what they want, articulate it clearly, and will not budge.

Negotiation. Actions that challenge the legal limits of protest and seek to gain access to targets require negotiation. Negotiations may occur with police officers, property managers, security guards, representatives of targets, and targets themselves. Negotiations take place when, for example, you want to move a growing march from the sidewalk to the street, or when you show up at an office building with fifty people to request a meeting with the target and the security guard won't let the whole group in. A member of the tactical team leads the negotiations, usually with staff support. You will have explored many of the issues for negotiation in pre-action planning, and the tactical team refers to these agreements in the on-site negotiations. Random or individual members do not negotiate. After the action, the full group evaluates the action and the negotiated decisions. (For more on negotiation, see Chapter Eleven.)

Discipline. You do pre-action role-playing. You clearly delineate roles and procedures. Participants in the action stick to what's been agreed upon in advance, including what they do and the tone and manner in which they do it. For example, if the organization has decided to hold a vigil-like action, participants do not start chanting unless the tactical team instructs them to do so. One participant in an action who does not follow directions can ruin months of work.

A clear beginning and a clear end. You start on time. You end on time. Everyone knows when the action is over—people don't just trickle away.

What Is a Tactic?

Tactics are the activities you do in an action that actually challenge, agitate, and engage people with power.

Through strategic use of tactics, you meet the goals of your action. The types of tactics and the types of actions are generally the same. For instance, if the action is a march to the target's home, it can include the tactic of delivering a letter to the target. Tactics may be linked with demands. For example, you deliver the letter and ask for a meeting with the target. Then, you use the additional tactic of sitting on his front lawn until he agrees to meet with your organization.

Organizations often use the terms *tactics* and *actions* interchangeably. The important distinction is that there is a whole event (an action) made up of distinct, strategic components (tactics).

How Do Actions and Tactics Work Together in a Campaign?

Actions, tactics, and demands go together.

Exhibit 12.2 gives an example of the types of actions and tactics a "Clean Supermarkets" campaign might employ.

Exhibit 12.2
Overview of Actions and Tactics in a Campaign

Campaign	**Clean supermarkets campaign.**
Goal	Ensure supermarkets in our community are up to health and safety code standards.
Demand	Increase funding to hire ten more food inspectors.
Objective	Get mayor's public support for increased funding.
Action 1	**Community inspection day.**
Tactic	Mass surveying of all supermarket customers in the neighborhood (internal action). Ask them to fill out a survey and sign a post card.
Action 2	**Deliver surveys to mayor.**
Tactic	Confront mayor at his weekly press conference and deliver surveys (external action).
Demand	Meet with us to discuss our proposal.
Action 3	**Target meeting.**
Tactic	Directly ask the mayor for support for more funding and to announce this support at a joint press conference with the organization.
Demand	Support our proposal and attend a press conference to announce your support.
Action 4	**Clean supermarkets campaign event with mayor to announce his support.**
Tactic	Press conference where mayor announces support for increased funding.
Demand	Call on city council speaker to match mayor's funding in this year's budget.

How Do We Choose the Best Type of Action?

You choose the action that will move the campaign forward.

In choosing a type of action, the organizing committee reviews the following questions:

What is our campaign objective right now? What concrete result do we need? For example, do we need to get a meeting with the target, to get the target to come out publicly in support of our demand, to get a secondary target to sign a letter to the primary target?

What are our organization-building goals? Do we want to develop new leaders, recruit new members, solidify our member base, train new members in direct action skills, get press, or move our allies to support us?

What is our leadership capacity? How many leaders do we have who can take on key roles in an action? Do we have the staff capacity to prepare people to take on roles, such as making public demands of a target?

What is our turnout capacity? How many people can we turn out for our issue right now? What are their skill levels and commitment to the campaign? Do we have five hundred people or thirty people? If it's thirty, then what can thirty people do to show their power?

What tenor does the campaign need? How well is the campaign going? Has the target been accessible? Does the campaign need energy, celebration, regrouping, some clear result? Although being confrontational or being militant can be an important way to get attention, it's the last approach to use. If the target responds to your calls, there's no need to march to her home.

How does our target respond to action? How does he act in a public setting? Does our target face rallies held outside of his office all the time? In meetings, does he listen or does he deflect questions? Does he come late and leave early, or will he give us the whole time? Even if you already know a great deal about the target, before you engage him in a public action, you learn more. This information helps you know what your best course of action is and enables you to assess your capacity to do effective leadership prep for the action. Knowing about the target also helps you to create an action that is outside of his experience.

The type of action depends a great deal on your relationship with the target. Do you have access and therefore the ability to get a meeting with the target? For instance, can you make a phone call or mail a letter and know it will reach the target, or do you need to march to the target's home to deliver it? If you do march, how much power does the organization have and is the target aware of the organization's power? Once the target knows your organization is outside his home, will he say yes to a meeting, or will he think he can afford to ignore you?

Tool 12.3, Choosing an Action, shows what an assessment of goals, results, actions, and power might look like when you are choosing an action.

What Are the Steps for Organizing a Successful Action?

The main steps for a successful action involve preparation, mobilization, and evaluation.

The following steps take place in every action, no matter how much lead time you have to organize the action or how large or small the action is:

Pre-action planning. Using the questions above as a guide, the organizing committee decides what the action is, when and where it will take place, and who will participate. It determines an overall goal for the action and the following kinds of objectives for the action:

- *Demands.* Example: We want the target to agree to meet with us.
- *Visibility.* Example: We want two news reports of the action, to get our name out.
- *Skill development.* Example: We want two new leaders to negotiate with powerholders under pressure, three new leaders to speak in public.
- *Recruitment.* Example: We want to collect one hundred pledge cards from new people who attend the action.

Action recruitment. The organizer uses the database to develop a list of people to mobilize for the action.

Pre-action prep. The organizer and organizing committee make sure everyone understands why the organization is planning the action, what it is, and who will communicate with them on the day of the action. Members help print materials to distribute while staff and leaders provide skills training or political education so people can effectively fulfill their roles. The organizer prepares members and leaders to make demands.

Action mobilization. The organizer makes sure people who commit to attending the action in fact do so. Along with leadership prep, this is the most critical part of ensuring you have an effective action. You make wake-up reminder calls, rent vans and buses to pick people up and take them to the action, assign captains to turn out their block or building, have members meet people at the train or bus station. Generally, you cannot do too much to ensure turnout. More on mobilizing for actions follows later in this chapter.

Final action prep. The members and leaders run through the roles they will play just before the action to make sure everyone is ready to go.

Action. Members show their power—the main event!

Action evaluation. The organizer, leaders, and members who played roles in the action review how it went and evaluate what worked, what did not work, and what they would improve.

Action follow-up. The organizer and organizing committee take steps to ensure that the action's achievements actually turn into results.

Who Makes Decisions About Actions and What Kinds of Decisions Do They Make?

Actions have three decision-making groups: an organizing committee, an action planning team, and a tactical team.

The following groups make decisions for the action:

Organizing committee. As described in Chapter Eleven, the organizing committee is the primary decision-making group of a campaign. The organizing committee's tasks for planning an action include the following:

- Referring to the campaign plan and making the initial assessment as to whether or not the campaign needs an action
- Deciding what the action is
- Determining when the action will occur
- Identifying the goals, demands, and objectives
- Determining the target of the action, who may or may not be the target of the campaign as well
- Planning for recruitment and mobilization

Here's an example of an organizing committee's work: The fifteen members of the organizing committee for a campaign seeking to improve health benefits for veterans sees that the campaign plan calls for mobilizing members. They assess that the campaign needs to energize members and be more public in its demands of a dismissive health commissioner. They decide to hold a Veteran's Day march to the commissioner's home to ask for a meeting.

Every action needs members and leaders who have the time, interest, and desire to organize and lead actions. A combination of people who have had experience in actions and people who are new makes for the best mix. Creative people and people who are comfortable challenging authority are the types of people you recruit into the organizing committee and the action planning team, which the organizing committee empowers to do action planning.

Action planning team. This group of members and leaders plans the action. It makes decisions within the goals and objectives set by the organizing committee. Its tasks include the following:

- Planning length of time, location, and other logistics
- Identifying roles and people to take on the roles
- Deciding on what tactics the action will include
- Potentially serving as the tactical team for the action

Continuing with the example above, the organizing committee empowers eight of its members to plan the march to the commissioner's home and make final decisions. This action planning team decides the march will gather at 8 A.M. at the gym where they know the commissioner often begins her morning and end at 8:30 A.M. at her home where she returns to get ready for work. They will do a legal march, staying on the sidewalk. They identify veterans of three different wars to bring the letter to her door, and get other members to lead chants, distribute literature, talk with the press, and carry signs. They agree that if the commissioner ignores the group, members will do a sit-in on the lawn, though they will leave before risking arrest. The action planning team assigns three of its members to serve as a tactical team at the action.

Tactical team. The action planning team empowers this group of members and leaders to make on-the-ground decisions in the course of the action. Its tasks include the following:

- Making decisions at the action when questions come up about what to do next
- Communicating what is happening during the action and what participants in the action should do
- Making decisions regarding what to demand of the target during the action

On the day of the action, the commissioner is at the gym when the group arrives. She stays inside past 8:30. The tactical team decides to continue the march to her home and wait for her there. When she does not show up, the team tells the group and the media that have gathered with them what will happen: three veterans will tape the letter to the commissioner's door and the group will then sit on the lawn and wait for her to arrive. If the police arrive first, a member of the tactical team will stand up, signaling everyone else to do so and immediately create a moving picket on the sidewalk.

When the police do arrive, a member of the tactical team steps forward and the picket begins. Ten minutes later, the tactical team tells the group and the press that it is ending the action and will call the commissioner to get her response to its demand for a meeting.

What Is a Pre-Action Prep Meeting?

In the pre-action prep meeting, members get an overview of the action and who is on the tactical team and clarify goals, messages, and tactics for the action.

In a pre-action prep meeting you review the what ifs: What if the target does not show, what if it rains, what if our members don't show up? This is the last time for the tactical team to get membership input before the day of the action. Tool 12.4 provides a sample agenda for a pre-action prep meeting.

How Do We Make Sure We Have Enough People at Our Action?

You mobilize members using effective and persistent contact.

You improve your chances for a strong turnout for an action when you have the following:

A clear message. You clearly communicate to members why it is important for them to come to the action. For example: "We need you because the governor will be responding to our demand that he pass legislation protecting our communities from hazardous waste. The more people he sees in the room, the more he will understand people are concerned about this issue."

A good list. You need a list of names that is large enough for you to meet turnout goals. A good list also includes people who have turned out before for actions. Organizations with a culture of action and turnout are more likely to get the numbers they need. If you are doing your first actions, you cultivate that culture as you develop your organization.

People to make calls. You have to make a lot of phone calls to turn people out for actions, so you need staff and members to work the phones.

Effective mobilization system. An effective system for mobilizing people includes having live, one-to-one personal contact with them. You make this contact by calling or visiting. In addition, you mail a notice that clearly states the date, time, location, and directions to the action. You make a confirmation call and a final reminder the day before the action. In live phone calls you engage people, assess their commitment, and talk through with them their questions about the action and the logistics they need in order to attend. Keep in mind that leaving a message on an answering machine informs a person about an action, but it does not replace a conversation. Unless the person calls back and says he or she is coming, you call again to get a commitment. Tool 12.5 provides a chart of how to use this kind of mobilization system and Exhibit 12.3 gives you a sense of the number of calls you need to make.

Exhibit 12.3
The Number of Calls You Need to Make

You need to get one hundred people at your action.

Depending on your organization, you start with a good list of one thousand people. You make commitment calls and reach and talk to about eight hundred people. Half of these say yes on the first contact. You now have four hundred "commits." These are soft. They have only said yes once and the action is still a few weeks away. In addition, you are making these calls quickly, so you are not able to make a foolproof assessment of how committed someone is to coming.

When you call a second time to confirm, about one-third to one-half will drop out or you cannot reach them again. Now you have two hundred commits.

When you do final reminder calls, you can expect to reach and confirm about three-fourths, meaning that around 150 people say they will come. Actual turnout will be between two-thirds and three-fourths of that final number—about one hundred.

This number is an estimate and not a firm calculation. Every organization is different and every organization has a different connection to members. The stronger your connection to your members the firmer the numbers will be. The important thing to remember is that you need to make many calls, including that final reminder call, and you need to have conversations, not just leave messages.

How Is Mobilizing People for an Action Different from Turning Them Out for a Meeting?

It is easier to get people excited about doing something energizing and fun than it is to get them excited about attending a meeting. Also, you set and meet goals for turning out specific numbers of people for an action.

You call many more people for an action than you do for a meeting, but you have a much larger pool to draw from. This larger number comes from the fact that most people prefer to come to actions rather than meetings, members bring their networks, and you can draw from the new people you meet during recruitment. Another difference between action mobilization and turning people out for meetings is that you spread the mobilization effort out over about four weeks. For meetings, the time frame is usually shorter.

How Do Mailings Help Mobilize People?

A piece of mail makes something real.

Although technologies such as e-mail or text messaging are changing the picture, for many people, having information in front of them spread out on their kitchen table makes it more real and increases the chance they will come to the action.

You send mail to tell people about the event before they get your call, to prepare them. Mail gives them more information than you could offer in a brief phone call. It also gives them the address, phone number, and directions they can grab when they leave for the action. Having something in writing helps people to invite their friends and neighbors to participate as well.

A final reminder postcard helps to firm up commitment. It expresses appreciation, which motivates people: "Thanks for coming and being part of this important community event!"

Can We Use E-Mail, the Internet, and Other Forms of Technology to Turn Out People for Actions?

Yes, but technology is a tool that supports mobilization, not a replacement for live personal contact and relationships.

To get the most out of using these technologies for turnout, you will increase your success if you ask for a confirmation back from an initial e-mail and follow up with two live contact calls: one in which you talk to people about the event and increase their buy-in and one reminder call the day before the action.

Remember, the more commits you have from an individual, both live and via the Internet or text messages, the more likely someone will come out. And keep in mind that not everyone has e-mail, a computer, or access to e-mail. Calls work.

LEADERSHIP DEVELOPMENT OPPORTUNITIES
FOR ACTIONS

- *Act as a tactical team leader.* Leaders prepare during planning meetings to be one of the two to four people who make decisions during an action, or to be the primary action leader.

- *Present demands to the target.* Gain skills in public speaking, negotiation, and facilitation by directly asking the target to respond to an action demand.

- *Be a media spokesperson.* Leaders speak to the press before, during, and after the action, on the basis of being trained in how to stay on message and how to handle questions about their personal story in relationship to the action, and on being fully prepped on the background of the issue.

- *Lead chants.* Working with two to three other members, leaders develop and practice chants, and lead people in chanting at the action.

- *Serve as a marshal.* Leaders are part of the team that includes one marshal for every twenty-five people expected, stationed throughout the site, and one lead marshal for every five marshals. Keep the group orderly and get trained and prepared for dealing with the police or potential conflicts.

- *Coordinate volunteers.* Leaders manage database lists of volunteers and participants who sign up in advance of the action.

- *Manage props.* Coordinate the preparation and use of props and visuals for the action.

CHALLENGES
IN RUNNING ACTIONS

"Members want to plan actions that require large numbers of people. We do not have the capacity to turn out these numbers." Review with members how large your last three actions were so they can see they are being unrealistic. If they persist, go around the room and ask each person to say specifically how they see the organization producing high numbers. Push people to be specific.

"Our members are afraid of being arrested or facing other repercussions." Fear is real. You talk with members about what they are afraid of and why and address it in ways that are appropriate for the action. For example, if they fear arrest, you can try talking about how many times people in your organization have been arrested for participating in an action. For example, in our experience of more than twelve years of doing hard-hitting actions on poverty issues in New York City, in our state capital, and in Washington, D.C., CVH has not had any arrests. If arrests or other repercussions are possible, you can try to develop a safe zone in the action for those who do not want to get arrested. If members want to engage in civil disobedience, you make sure legal advisors work with them before, during, and after the action. For all actions, everyone brings personal identification and agrees not to carry anything illegal.

"Members develop actions that don't directly confront the target." More experienced leaders can challenge people to consider how their actions will move the target without confronting him.

"We are just starting and we really don't know how many people we can turn out." Internal actions help you to determine your turnout capacity without jeopardizing your campaign by not being able to show your power to a target. In addition, small, external actions that don't require large numbers, such as pickets or legislative visits, are good ways to test your ability to turn out people. Always consider the possibility of low turnout as a "what if." If you are part of a coalition, you are honest about your turnout capacity. It is better to promise fewer people than it is not to deliver. And remember—every organization has had an action where turnout was low.

ESSENTIAL ELEMENTS
FOR EFFECTIVE ACTIONS

☑ *Only engage in actions your organization has the capacity to pull off.* If you do not think you can pull off an action, don't do it. If you want to try a more complicated action, plan for it, seek help, and take your time.

☑ *If the issue requires a quick response—move to action quickly.* Even if you are not 100 percent ready, if you are in a crisis, act. Build with smaller actions consistently over a few weeks rather than one large action. This approach gives you time to test and evaluate a crisis campaign.

☑ *Remember the Alinsky principle: The best action is within the experience of your members but outside the experience of your target.*

☑ *Keep it fun and keep it simple.* Actions are the most fun for organizers, leaders, and members. You don't get too complicated. Your actions are direct, simple, and to the point.

☑ *If all else fails, chant and picket.* Low turnout? The target isn't showing up? An energetic picket with people chanting usually helps salvage an action that is just not working.

Tool 12.1
Picket Rules!

The following is a handout you can use for preparing people to participate in a picket.

Keep It MOVING!
We cannot get arrested if we keep moving, out of the way of pedestrians.

Keep It LIVELY!
Chant, sing, play drums, and move to the beat.

Bring VISUALS!
Good props, signs, and costumes and clothes get attention. Our cause is serious, but we can still be creative, visually appealing, and upbeat!

FLYER While We Picket!
Our flyers make sure people know exactly why we are here.

Get Our SUPPORTERS to Take Action!
Use the cell phones, portable computers, fax machines, or postcards, letters, and petitions we bring to get people who support us to take action right away by contacting the target. We have enough clipboards and people designated to get the names and numbers of supporters so we can follow up with them.

Keep It SHORT and to the Point!
A short, fun picket of thirty minutes is much more effective than milling around for hours. Or move the picket from one site to another.

Tool 12.2
Sample Agenda for an Accountability Session

The following is a sample agenda for an effective accountability session. You can use this for planning your session or for training members and staff to plan and execute it.

An accountability session is tight and to the point. The target will probably be available for about an hour, and the whole session should last no more than two hours. Note that each timed period in the agenda is an opportunity for a leader of the organization to play a role. Everyone needs to be focused, prepared, and disciplined.

What	How Long	Who (Example)
Before target arrives:		
Gather, sign in, practice chants	30 minutes	All
After target arrives:		
Welcome	2 minutes	Board chair
Purpose of meeting	5 minutes	Leader #1
Introducing speakers and other key leader roles	5 minutes	Action chair
Testimonial from a member	2 minutes	Leader #2
Song or chants	5 minutes	Chant leader
Welcome of target	2 minutes	Action chair
Review of format and ground rules	5 minutes	Leader #3
Member testimonial	2 minutes	Leader #4
Target opening statement	4 minutes	Target
Demand	2 minutes	Leader #5
Response	2 minutes	Target
Demand	2 minutes	Leader #6
Response	2 minutes	Target
Closing remarks from target	5 minutes	Target
Thank you to target	2 minutes	Action chair
After target leaves:		
Evaluation with large group	10 minutes	All
Close	2 minutes	
After session ends:		
Evaluation with leadership team	20 minutes	Team
Total	1 hour and 49 minutes	

Note that the target speaks for only thirteen minutes. The program itself is only an hour. The rest of the time is devoted to gathering participants and engaging in evaluation.

Tool 12.3
Choosing an Action

The following chart shows what an assessment of goals, results, actions, and power might look like when you are choosing an action.

Goal for Action	Concrete Result	Example Action	Power Needed
Build membership, recruit members.	New active members.	Neighborhood canvass, town hall meeting, rally, lobby day.	Small leadership Small membership
Announce the beginning of a campaign.	Community or public know about the campaign.	Press conference, march, releasing of report.	Small leadership Small membership
Get media coverage of your issue.	News articles about your issue and campaign.	Editorial board meetings, report release, effective media actions.	Small leadership Small membership
Move a powerful stakeholder.	A new stakeholder to work on your campaign with you.	Mass action that your ally sees.	Small to large leadership Medium to large membership
Train a new group of leaders.	A core group of leaders who have experienced action and are ready to lead actions.	Small direct actions, town hall meetings.	Small to medium leadership Medium membership
Get a target to meet with you.	A meeting with the target.	Mass letter delivery, press conference, office takeover or disruption.	Small to large leadership Medium to large membership
Show power to your target.	Your target understands you have power and that she needs to respond.	March, rally, accountability session, card or letter signing.	Large leadership Large membership
Move a target to deliver on your demand.	Target gives you what you want.	Accountability session, target meeting.	Large leadership Large membership

Tool 12.4
Sample Agenda for Pre-Action Prep Meeting

Facilitator: Leader from the tactical team.

Introductions and go-arounds. Everyone says what role he or she will play at the action. **(5 minutes)**

Action background. Action planning team reviews why you are doing the action and where it fits into the overall campaign. **(10 minutes)**

Goals of action. Action planning team reviews what concrete things you want from the action. **(10 minutes)**

Overview of action. Tactical team describes what the action is going to be, how many people are coming, press, and other matters. **(10 minutes)**

Run-through of action. Tactical teams says specifically what is going to happen and when. They point out when people will need to do something or play a leadership role. Role play as needed. **(20 minutes)**

What ifs. Brainstorm as a group and discuss every possible circumstance. Agree on a plan to address each if it happens. **(30 minutes)**

Review action rules. Review who will be making on-the-spot decisions and giving direction at the action. Review the importance of discipline and cohesiveness. **(10 minutes)**

Questions and Clarifications. (10 minutes)

Close. (10 minutes)

Tool 12.5
Mobilizing Members for an Action

The following chart shows how to use an effective mobilization system.

Type of Contact	Who You Contact	Message	Who Makes the Contact	Goal
First mailing: Inform Send a mailing or e-mail. When: Four weeks before the action.	Everyone on your list who would potentially come to the action.	Why we are doing the action. What we hope to achieve. The date, time and location.	Volunteers at a mailing party.	To inform people about the action so they know about it when you call.
First contact call: Commit When: Three to four weeks before the action.	Everyone on your list who would potentially come to the action.	"We need you to attend our action that will achieve the following . . ." "Will you come on date, time, place . . .?"	Staff, members. (These calls do not have to be the strongest.)	The largest number of "soft" yeses possible. You need three to four times the number of people to say yes at this point than you need to attend the action.
Second contact call: Confirm When: Two weeks before the action.	Everyone who said yes on the first call and anyone you left a message for.	"I am calling to confirm that you are coming out on date, time, place . . ." "Are you still planning to join us?"	Staff and strong members. (These have to be strong calls.)	To get the list down to the people who have a real interest and who really commit to come. You need to confirm two to three times the number that you need for the action.

Action	Who	Script	Done by	Purpose
Second mailing: Confirm Mail out a confirmation postcard. When: One week before the action.	Everyone who has said he or she is coming after the second round of phone calls.	"Thanks for joining us and coming out. We look forward to seeing you on date, time, place."	Volunteers at a mailing party.	To strengthen the possibility people will come and to give them the information about the event in writing.
Third contact call: Remind Make a round of reminder phone calls. When: Two or three days before action, up until the day of the action.	Everyone who has said she or he is coming.	"We are calling to remind you that the action is happening. Are you still coming?"	Staff and members.	To remind and get everyone out to the action. Only one-third to one-half the number of people who at this point say they will come will actually attend the action.

Evaluating a Campaign from Beginning to End

WHAT'S WORKING, WHAT'S NOT— DETERMINING HOW TO MOVE FORWARD

Editorials in local papers are making the city council speaker nervous about advancing the transitional jobs program. The editorials suggest he is a government liberal. He wants to run for mayor and does not want voters to see him as undoing Mayor Giuliani's success in cutting the welfare rolls. He stops moving the Transitional Jobs Bill forward. Community Voices Heard (CVH) members, along with allies and partners, evaluate their campaign strategy. The legislative and alliance-building strategies that are under way are not enough. At organizing committee meetings, CVH members examine what is happening in the press. Gail, a former leader who is now on staff, holds conversations with members about how the media works. She leads discussions about how CVH can have an impact the next time one of the papers writes something negative about the jobs bill. The campaign organizing committee of CVH members and allies decides to incorporate an additional strategy—a media and public education strategy to help move the council speaker. Committee members develop a plan to write and solicit others to write op-ed pieces, letters to the editor, and articles that attack WEP and support the Transitional Jobs Bill. The new strategy helps cover the speaker politically and helps move him to advance the bill.

What Is Campaign Evaluation and Why Is It Important?

Campaign evaluation is the process of monitoring the impact of your campaign on moving your target. Through campaign evaluation you gain insight into what works and what does not work.

When you evaluate, you examine how well you are achieving your objectives and how effective your actions are. You monitor changes in power dynamics and conduct a final assessment of the effectiveness of the campaign. You engage in evaluation both as you implement the campaign and after it ends.

Evaluation gives you the information you need to adjust the campaign plan and keep things on track. It helps you clarify your organization's capacity, allies, other stakeholders, the target, and the issue. Campaign evaluation solidifies learning. It develops members and builds the expertise and political savvy of the organization. It ensures that the campaign fits with a changing political dynamic. You use the lessons learned from evaluation to repeat what you do well in your next campaign, strengthen organizational weaknesses, and improve your overall effectiveness.

What Do We Evaluate?

You evaluate four main areas of the campaign: progress in meeting objectives, the impact of your actions, other elements including changes in power dynamics, and the effectiveness of the entire campaign.

We introduce each type of evaluation here and describe them in detail in the sections that follow.

Progress in meeting objectives. As you implement the campaign, you monitor how the campaign is meeting the objectives laid out in the campaign plan. If the campaign is meeting objectives, what is working well and what is not working as well? If it is not meeting objectives, why not?

Impact of actions. You evaluate each action after it happened. Did the action move the target and achieve the goals you established? Did it move the campaign forward? If not, why?

Other elements, including changes in the power dynamics. Are there any new stakeholders, allies, or opponents since you started the campaign? Have you neutralized potential opponents or created new ones? What new things have you learned about the target? How do these developments affect your campaign? Has your strategy been effective? Has your membership grown?

Effectiveness of the entire campaign. After the campaign ends, members, leaders, and staff step back, reflect, and determine how effective the entire campaign was. Is the organization on track toward accomplishing its big-picture goal? What did you learn about the target, the landscape, and your organization that can affect your future work?

How Do We Evaluate Progress on Objectives During the Campaign?

You evaluate progress on objectives by asking whether the action to achieve an objective accomplished its goals.

You use the following process to evaluate progress on objectives.

1. Identify the objective in the campaign plan. What do you want to achieve?

2. Execute action to achieve the objective. Mobilize into action.

3. Evaluate the action. Did it work? Did it accomplish its goals?

4. Proceed on plan or adjust the plan to meet the objective. If it worked, go ahead with the plan. If not, do something different to achieve the objective.

5. Continue on to the next objective.

Here is an example of evaluating progress.

Evaluating Progress on Objectives During the Playground Safety Campaign

Our Children's Future is implementing its Playground Safety Campaign to improve safety conditions at public playgrounds. Members have identified garbage in the playgrounds, broken equipment, and poorly maintained surfaces (broken cement, cracked sidewalks) as hazards to local children. The campaign demand is to get the commissioner of the city's Department of Parks and Recreation to release funding for capital improvements to local playgrounds immediately so playgrounds can be fixed by the summer. The organization's research shows that the money is there, but the commissioner wants to save it for other capital projects. The campaign plan includes the objective of getting three to five articles in the press to pressure the commissioner to spend the funds on playgrounds. The campaign will get these articles by releasing a survey on playground safety and turning out press to cover it.

The organizing committee conducts the survey and decides to release the results at a press conference in the largest local park. On the day of the release, all the press is at the mayor's office waiting for an announcement of a new initiative by the mayor, which the organization did not know about. No reporters come to the event at the park.

At the next organizing committee meeting, members evaluate both the action (the survey release) and the impact on the campaign. Since they did not meet the objective of getting press coverage, they review some options. They decide to try to get the chair of the city budget process to tour the playgrounds and hold a press conference to highlight the survey and the conditions. To move him to agree to take the tour, they will ask a reporter to take the tour first and write about the survey, generating some initial press coverage.

The following chart outlines how this step—evaluating progress on objectives—worked:

Playground Safety Campaign Evaluation

Evaluation Process	Example
Identify objective	Get media attention—three to five stories in press—on playground safety issues to put pressure on the parks commissioner.
Organize and execute action	Press conference at largest playground to release the results of the organization's survey of local parks.
Expected outcome	Press stories. Commissioner feels pressure to address the recommendations in the survey.
Actual outcome	No press show up.
Evaluation	Reporters did not show up because they were covering the mayor's announcement of a new initiative.
Impact on campaign	No press means the survey and issue did not make it into the media. No pressure on the parks commissioner. The organization has to figure out how to get press before the next budget cycle.
Campaign implementation process	Organizing committee meets to evaluate and adjust plan.
Campaign adjustment: Organizing committee develops new campaign actions to achieve original objective	Get press coverage to move the chair of the budget process to take a tour of playgrounds and hold press conference about unsafe playgrounds.

Evaluation Process	Example
Organize and execute actions	Two leaders give the survey report to a reporter and take her to the worst playgrounds. She writes a story in a daily paper, which moves the budget process chair to agree to do the tour and hold a press conference about conditions. This happens three weeks after the original press conference.
Outcome	After the tour and press conference with the budget chair, there are three additional newspaper articles and two television reports on unsafe playgrounds. The press attention gets the target, the parks commissioner, to respond to the issue about unsafe playgrounds at an event to promote the state summer youth program. He makes a soft commitment to address the issue before the summer. The organization will now follow up.

How Do We Evaluate Actions During the Campaign?

You hold an evaluation meeting immediately after or within a week of each action to assess if you achieved your goals and examine how well you executed all aspects of the action.

After you execute an action, you look at all of its elements to determine how effective it was. You conduct an evaluation with leaders and members who participated in the action, especially the tactical team and action leaders (described in the previous chapter), either immediately following the action or within a week.

The following are the kinds of questions members consider when they evaluate an action. These vary depending on who is having the evaluation discussion, the nature of the action, and how much time you have.

Action Evaluation Questions for Members

- How was the action effective?
- How could it have been more effective?
- Did we achieve our goals?
- How well did the organization perform?
- What did we learn about ourselves?

- How was turn out?

- Which allies and supporters turned out or did not turn out and why?

- Did the target meet our demand?

- What did we learn about the target?

- What are our follow-up tasks?

Tool 13.1 provides a sample agenda for conducting an action evaluation, followed by tools for evaluating objectives (Tool 13.2) and actions (Tool 13.3) that members can use to begin their thinking on these topics. Exhibit 13.1, Action Evaluation Form: Sample, is a sample of how the Action Evaluation Form might be filled out.

Exhibit 13.1
Action Evaluation Form: Sample

Campaign Objective: Recruit 300 new members by August 1.

Action(s): Hold four Membership Canvass Saturdays. Doorknock in the Southside neighborhood to get contact information. Ask people to write letters on the spot to the school superintendent, to engage them. Each Saturday, 20 members will canvass.

Action Goals	Achieved?
1. Develop 30 leaders	No, only 10
2. Recruit 300 new members	No, only 100
3. Get 100 letters	No, we didn't get any

If we achieved our goals, what do we do next according to our campaign plan? We did not achieve our goals.

If we did not achieve our goals, why? Turnout of members to do canvasses fell way below goals, so we could not reach our weekly goals for getting new contacts. Letter-writing at the door is overwhelming people because we are asking them for too much.

What do we need to change to reach our goals? Increase the amount of time we will have to conduct membership recruitment. Increase the amount of staff time to do new membership recruitment. Identify new leaders to develop to do the recruitment canvasses. Drop the letter writing.

How does this affect or change our campaign plan? We will have to stop all other campaign activities until we conduct more membership recruitment. We need to consider if the letter-writing is important in and of itself, and if so, do it some other way.

Within a week or two of the action staff conduct their evaluation. In addition to the questions that members consider, staff also use the following questions:

- What did we learn about our staff capacity?

- How did our organizational systems work?

- Which leaders turned out?

- How well did we prep the leaders, based on how well they performed in the action?

- Which leaders did not turn out and why?

- Who is now going to do what, by when, in order to follow up on the action?

What Other Elements of the Campaign Do We Evaluate?

You evaluate key meetings and activities as well as changing power dynamics.

The case study that follows illustrates how to get to a shared understanding about what happened in a key meeting and why it happened in order to move forward as effectively as possible. It also shows how staff and leaders work together to involve everyone, especially a new member, in the evaluation. These types of evaluation sessions help organizers to assess how members can interact more deeply with one another and what their leadership potential might be.

United for Power Evaluates a Key Meeting

Four members of United for Power are evaluating their meeting with Pastor Stevens, a prominent clergyperson whose congregants are active in United for Power. The evaluation meeting includes Amanda, an organizer for United for Power; Pete, the team leader; Leeanne, a new member; and Mario, an experienced member. They had asked Pastor Stevens to participate in their delegation to the governor to present an alternative plan to a developer's proposal to build a new football stadium in their city. The clergyperson's presence would get the governor to attend the meeting and the press would cover it. United for Power would be able to present its alternative plan to the governor and achieve the objective of getting five articles in the local paper about alternatives to the stadium.

Pete (team leader): That meeting was terrible. I got so rattled.

Mario (experienced member): You did a good job keeping us focused on the meeting, even if Pastor Stevens did say no. (Engages new member.) Leeanne, what did you think?

Leeanne (new member): That was my first meeting and I was impressed.

Amanda (organizer): (Follows up.) Why were you impressed?

Leeanne: Peter was consistent. When Pastor Stevens talked about the last time the city built a stadium, Peter pointed out how the governor was involved. Then he brought it back to now. It's too bad the pastor said no.

Amanda: (Confirms understanding.) Does everyone agree he said no?

Pete: He seemed interested. But yeah, he said no to what we asked.

Leeanne: No question about it.

Amanda: (Probes for why.) Why did he say no? Was it the ask itself, the way we asked him? Does he really support the stadium even though he's said publicly he opposes it?

Pete: Everyone says he doesn't like that people try to use him all the time. He has to see his congregation's self-interest in using a chit with the governor on this.

Mario: He kept referring to his "folks" and giving us the chance to talk about his self-interest and we didn't do it.

Pete: (Reflects on own actions.) You're right. I felt like I had to make him feel important, but he already knows he's pretty important. That's not gonna move him.

Mario: I think it's worth seeing if he'll do a one-on-one to explore his self-interest. He met with us for a long time and said to call him if there was something else he could do.

Amanda: (Summarizes and moves to next steps.) So what's the next step? Here's where I think we are: We think he doesn't see his congregation's self-interest. He said no, but the door might be open for more of a relationship-building meeting.

Pete: It's worth asking if he'll meet again. We have to ask him directly what he needs to get out of this. And we have to have a "what if" plan to get the governor to the meeting if we just can't move Pastor Stevens.

How Do We Determine If the Campaign Is Over in Order to Evaluate the Campaign?

When your actions have moved the target to meet your demand, the campaign is over and you won. The campaign is also over if your actions are no longer moving a resistant target or achieving objectives and the organizing committee goes through the process of making the decision to formally end the campaign. This final step is important for members to go through. If you skip it, you can lose frustrated members and leaders who do not understand why the campaign is ending or have the chance to express their views about it.

Sometimes the campaign links with a budget process, a legislative calendar, or other process that determines when the campaign ends. For instance, if you demand funds be allocated in a capital budget, once the legislature passes the budget you know if you won or lost.

When the target is not directly meeting your demand, you assess if your actions are having an impact. If they are not, the organizing committee and leadership team address the following questions:

- Do we move to a new phase of the campaign?
- Do we develop a completely different campaign?
- Do we put the campaign on hold and go back to it at another time?

For example, at the end of the Transitional Jobs Campaign, the New York City Council met the demand and passed the transitional jobs bill. However, the mayor refused to implement the bill, rendering it ineffective. CVH faced a decision. It could move on to something else and wait for a council member or another organization to push for implementation of the bill, it could wait for a new mayor to come into office in the next year and try to move her or him to implement the bill, or it could develop a new phase of the campaign to demand implementation.

The organizing committee chose to demand implementation of the bill. It then developed, implemented, and evaluated a series of specific campaigns in order to continue to pursue its goal. Each distinct campaign had its own goals, objectives, demands, target, and plan.

How Do We Conduct Campaign Evaluation at the End of the Campaign?

After the campaign ends, you hold a series of group meetings in which you pose questions and push for honest, deep answers.

When you evaluate a campaign, you answer specific, probing questions that go beyond the "what" in order to get to the "why."

You keep evaluation questions specific and open-ended and push for well-developed answers. You follow up answers, especially yes or no answers, with the question "Why?" If you understand not only what happened but also all the dimensions of why it happened, you will have data to use in your ongoing work. You ask the following kinds of evaluation questions at the end of the campaign:

How did the campaign affect the organization? What was the positive impact on the organization? What was the negative impact? For instance, did the campaign bring in new members? Did it develop members into leaders? Did the campaign deplete the leadership or maintain it at a steady rate? Did it build your power and capacity by adding resources, such as funders, or did it drain the organization and turn off potential resources?

Did the research, landscape, and power analysis prove to be accurate? Did allies and stakeholders respond the way you thought they would? Did the stakeholders change? Did the message bring on more allies, supporters, or new constituencies? Did the media respond to the issue the way you expected? If not, why?

How well did the organization execute the campaign? Of the actions laid out in the campaign plan, what were you able to accomplish and not accomplish? What were the obstacles and opportunities, both inside and outside of the organization? What did you do well? What could you have done better?

How did the strategy move the target? How did the target respond to the strategy and tactics you used in the campaign? Did she or he respond the way you expected or differently? Why? If you shifted strategies, did that action help or hurt? Why?

Did the target deliver on the demands? Did the target deliver everything you asked? Some of what you asked? Nothing?

What was the concrete improvement in members' lives? When you look beyond the fact that you reached the objectives of the campaign or that the target delivered on the demands, is the problem resolved or have members' lives improved? You revisit this question again after some time has passed.

Two tools will help in this step of evaluating the entire campaign. Tool 13.4, Parts of a Campaign, is a reminder of the goals and activities for each step of a campaign as well as the roles of staff, leaders, and members. Tool 13.5, Campaign Evaluation Worksheet, provides a form you can use to help people prepare for a campaign evaluation session, in which they will address questions such as those we outlined earlier. There is a wide range of questions that you can use for evaluation. The following example shows how you can apply the kinds of evaluation questions presented here to a campaign, bearing in mind that you will determine and address the specific questions necessary for your own situation:

Evaluation of Southsiders Union Waste Incinerator Campaign

What changed? Because of our campaign, what has shifted or changed on the issue?

Southsiders Union demanded that Mayor Torre hold a public hearing on the plan to site a new waste incinerator near the elementary school in its community. After months of saying no, Mayor Torre's deputy mayor called and said the mayor would hold the hearing. Although Southsiders does not know what the final result will be, the hearing will slow the process considerably, allowing public opposition to grow.

If there was a change, what directly caused the change to occur?

The series of articles in the local papers about strong community opposition to the health effects of the incinerator influenced the mayor to change her mind, as well as the discomfort of donors who liked supporting a relatively popular mayor.

What other conditions influenced the outcome? In addition to the direct influences, what else was happening in the landscape of the issue that caused the change to occur?

Mayor Torre's name has been floated as a potential candidate for higher office. In her current reelection campaign for mayor, she became concerned that residents would see her as being unresponsive to local community needs. Also, Parents Alliance issued a report about how waste incinerators near schools increase illnesses in young children. This report generated meetings and panel discussions as well as a lot of press coverage.

Which of our actions specifically affected the outcome and how?

After the report came out, Southsiders Union sent members to Mayor Torre's campaign fundraisers to distribute flyers about the potential health effects of the incinerator. This action raised the visibility of the issue to her donors and kept the issue in the press.

How did we use opportunities to our advantage?

Southsiders Union met with the authors of the Parents Alliance report before they released it to talk about the findings and discuss what Southsiders Union could do to attract more attention to the findings after the release.

What were the challenges—expected and unexpected—and how effectively did we use them?

Mayor Torre was very effective in making the case publicly that she could not stop the incinerator. Southsiders Union was surprised by this statement, since the mayor rarely deals with opposition that directly. Southsiders handled this challenge by doing research and learning that the mayor could hold public hearings about the incinerator even if she could not stop it. The organization conducted teach-ins, held meetings with local editorial boards, and met with other organizations to raise understanding about what the mayor could and could not do about the incinerator.

How did our work on this campaign affect our organization in terms of capacity, members, leaders, allies, and overall power? What organizational assets or liabilities did we accrue?

As a result of the campaign, the capacity of Southsiders Union grew. It took on the new issue of environmental justice. Many community residents learned about the organization and fifty-five new members signed up. Southsiders Union trained four leaders in research skills. The organization also got a commitment from the mayor's office to hold a community meeting to talk about other issues in the neighborhood.

How did the target respond to our organization's actions, and which of them ultimately moved the target most effectively? Did the target respond in the way we expected?

When the press first presented the mayor as being unsympathetic to the community's concerns about the incinerator, she initially blamed things that were out of her control. When Southsiders Union directly confronted her with what she had the power to do, she became defensive. She is a former community activist and was not used to being put on the spot by Southside residents, who generally support her. It took consistent, high-profile pressure to move her. The mayor ultimately responded to Southside Union's public education and media strategy and to the strategy of disrupting her campaign when the facts of what she could do, combined with the information about the potential health effects of the incinerator and discomfort of her donors, became too much pressure for her.

What Is the Role of the Organizer in Campaign Evaluation?

The organizer guides members' evaluations and evaluates with other staff to learn more about what works and does not work.

The organizer suggests evaluation questions and provides worksheets and other tools as needed. In a community power-building organization, the organizer does not tell people what worked and did not, but probes and agitates to get members to go as deeply as possible in analyzing their experiences. In addition, organizers evaluate from their own perspective. They identify strengths and weaknesses on the staff and evaluate how to improve the capacity of the organization with stronger organizing systems.

Organizers also develop their own skills during the course of a campaign. When they reflect and evaluate on their decisions and actions with other staff and supervisors, they solidify their learning. They learn what they do well and where they need to develop further, and they can set goals for themselves in the next campaign.

LEADERSHIP DEVELOPMENT OPPORTUNITIES
DURING CAMPAIGN EVALUATION

- *Participate in organizing committee evaluation sessions.* Leaders prepare and facilitate organizing committee meetings to evaluate the campaign's progress and the impact of specific actions. This increases ownership, strengthens relationships, sharpens skills, and provides information to move on to future campaigns.

- *Push other leaders to evaluate deeply.* Since evaluation is the job of leaders, they push each other to examine all aspects of the organization's effectiveness.

- *Be on the Leadership Team.* Members of the Leadership Team may also hold distinct meetings for more in-depth evaluation and to make recommendations to the organizing committee about how to move forward.

- *Engage in board evaluations.* Board or steering committee members, depending on the structure of the organization, may evaluate during the campaign, but definitely do so at the end of the campaign. In this core role, leaders help determine the impact of the campaign on the organization's leadership, staffing, and financial resources. They identify the implications for future work and long-term planning, such as funding, staffing needs, or changes in the issue.

CHALLENGES
IN CAMPAIGN EVALUATION

"We're not sure when we should stop and evaluate what's going on." Generally, you evaluate after an action, when you meet a series of objectives, when a target changes his or her position, or when the power dynamics shift.

"It's hard for members to be completely honest in their evaluations, since they don't want to criticize each other." Evaluation is constructive, it is not personal criticism. When you use clear questions to guide an honest evaluation, the organizing committee can move the campaign forward as strongly and effectively as possible. Similarly, you use questions and evaluation sessions to go deep. You only advance your learning when you probe to examine a situation.

"When we do something great, members try to deflect the credit." It is important for members to give themselves and their organization any credit for what they have achieved with their hard work. You learn from what you do right as well as from what you can improve on.

"Members evaluate based on how they feel as opposed to what the organization accomplished." Push for a neutral assessment and probe. Ask questions such as, "What happened or what did the target say that makes you think it was a good meeting?"

ESSENTIAL ELEMENTS
FOR EFFECTIVE CAMPAIGN EVALUATION

☑ *Engage members in evaluation.* Evaluation offers the opportunity for members to develop their critical thinking and their investment in the campaign. You use "quick-and-dirty" evaluations as well as formal evaluation sessions as opportunities to see how members think, speak up, and interact with other members.

☑ *Campaign planning influences evaluation.* In order to conduct thorough campaign evaluation, the campaign must have clear and specific objectives.

☑ *Evaluation is an opportunity for political education.* During the campaign and right after it ends, evaluation allows members and leaders to deepen their knowledge and skills by taking into account the forces beyond their own community and beyond their own issue.

Tool 13.1
Sample 90-Minute Action Evaluation Session

Facilitator: one of the Tactical Team leaders. An organizer supports the facilitator during the meeting.

Introductions. Everyone says their name. **(10 minutes)**

Go arounds. Everyone says one good thing about the action and one thing that could have gone better. **(10 minutes)**

Worksheet completion. Members and leaders complete worksheets, either individually or in pairs, to get them thinking about the results of the action. (This step is more useful if some time has passed than if it is immediately following the action. Tool 13.2 provides a worksheet for evaluating how well objectives were met and Tool 13.3 provides a form for evaluating actions.) **(10 minutes)**

Review goals of action. Action Committee reminds the group what the goals were. (If you use the worksheets, the facilitator incorporates hearing what people wrote on them, here and through the rest of the discussion.) **(10 minutes)**

Turnout. Staff reports on how many people turned out. **(10 minutes)**

Analyze turnout. The group looks at the following categories for who turned out: members, leaders, allies, public, potential new members. Then it answers the question, How did our actual turnout compare to our commits? **(10 minutes)**

Action goals. The action committee goes through each goal of the action and the group evaluates how well the organization did. **(10 minutes)**

Action execution. The facilitator asks some prompting questions. For example: How effective was the action in getting what we wanted? Was the action good for members? Was it empowering? Was it easy to pull off or difficult? How did members take on roles? Was there enough training and support? **(10 minutes)**

Follow-up and next steps. The group creates a chart: What do we have to do and who is going to do it? **(10 minutes)**

Close.

Tool 13.2
Objective Evaluation Worksheet

You can use the following chart as a worksheet to prepare people to participate in a group evaluation.

What the Organization Is Doing	Example
Identify objective	
Organize and execute action	
Expected outcome	
Actual outcome	
Evaluation	
Impact on campaign	
Campaign implementation process	
Campaign adjustment: Organizing committee develops new campaign actions to achieve original objective	
Organize and execute actions	
Outcome	

Tool 13.3
Action Evaluation Worksheet

You can use the following worksheet to prepare people to participate in a group evaluation of an action. For a sample Action Evaluation Session see Exhibit 13.1.

Campaign Objective: _____

Action(s): _____

Action Goals   **Achieved?**

1.

2.

3.

If we achieved our goals, what do we do next according to our campaign plan?

If we did not achieve our goals, why?

What do we need to change to reach our goals?

How would this change affect or change our campaign plan?

Tool 13.4
Parts of a Campaign

You can use the following chart as a handout for training members or staff. It summarizes the parts of a campaign and the roles of staff and members at each stage of developing, implementing, and evaluating a campaign.

Campaign Part	Goal	Activities	Staff Role	Leader Role	Member Role
Issue identification	To find out what issue will move your membership and constituency to take action.	Survey members and affected communities through one-on-one meetings, phone calls, group meetings.	Collect information and cull data so leaders can review it.	Collect information, take a first cut at identifying issue and messaging.	Give input on the issues that affect them.
Goal development	To state your larger world vision and social change goal.	Framing with members and leaders.	Work with members to frame issue.	Facilitate meeting and discussions.	Make decisions about larger goal.
Demands development	To develop concrete demands to get what your members want.	Leadership meetings, conversations with members to get their input and to get research data, sometimes using a written survey.	Collect information, train leadership to conduct research and develop demands, organize meetings of leaders.	Facilitate leadership meetings, assist with and evaluate research. Help develop proposals for demands for the members to consider.	Decide the final demands.
Target research	To identify who has the power to give you what you want.	Research the target—how much power he or she has and who potential secondary targets could be.	Develop political education as needed for members and leaders. Train leaders and members.	Lead meetings, assist in developing political education for members.	Attend training sessions.
Power analysis	To identify what the landscape for the issue is—who cares about this issue and where they stand on it.	Talk with people one-on-one, engage in landscape conversations, conduct media research.	Assist in research, landscape conversations, one-on-ones.	Participate in creating a power analysis grid.	Participate in creating a power analysis grid.
Organizational assessment	To figure out what your organization has in terms of power and resources—money, staff, leaders, and members.	Engage in an honest evaluation with staff, board, and leadership.	Conduct group evaluations.	Make decisions on whether the organization will move forward.	May participate in assessment.

	Purpose	Activity	Role	Role	Role
Strategy development	To identify the strategy or strategies that will be most effective in ensuring that you achieve your overall campaign demands.	Power and target analysis, including political discussions with allies, staff, leaders, and members of other organizations.	Assist in research, ally meetings, developing strategy scenarios.	Assist in research, ally meetings, developing strategy scenarios.	Decide on strategies.
Objectives development	To develop clear and measurable objectives that will enable you to achieve the demands.	Developed during campaign planning. "We are going to reach 100 new members, have five news stories."	Work with members to develop objectives.	Work with staff and members to develop objectives.	Work with staff and leaders to develop objectives.
Campaign planning	To develop a comprehensive written plan that outlines goals, demands, and activities.	Hold one or more meetings to develop a campaign plan with staff, members, and leaders.	Help to formulate campaign scenarios and options.	Help to develop plan for proposal to membership.	Decide on plan.
Campaign implementation	To make sure the campaign is happening according to plan.	Engage in actions, meetings, and activities as laid out in the plan.	Keep the rest of the staff engaged in the campaign and help the organizing committee to conduct evaluations of objectives and actions and manage the campaign plan.	Lead meetings and actions. Help to evaluate campaign and make key decisions.	Implement plan through going to meetings and participating in direct actions and evaluations.
Choose actions and tactics	To choose the actions and tactics that reflect the strategy and will reach the objectives.	Hold action planning meetings with tactical team and action team.	Facilitate discussion using examples of other actions or readings about actions to get members to think creatively.	Facilitate meetings and help to talk about the organization's actions in the past.	Help to brainstorm and choose actions.
Campaign evaluation	To understand what worked, what did not work, and what we will do differently in the future.	Hold evaluation sessions, make calls, and distribute questionnaires.	Develop evaluations, evaluate staff performance and leader performance.	Lead evaluation sessions, help in evaluation.	Participate in evaluation through surveys, questionnaires, and phone calls.

Tool 13.5
Campaign Evaluation Worksheet

You can use the following worksheet as a tool to prepare people to participate in a group evaluation of a campaign. When you present this worksheet, fill in the goals, demands, and primary strategy to give everyone the same point of reference.

1. Our campaign goal:

2. Our demands:

3. What did we win in our campaign?

4. On a scale of 1–10, with 1 being the lowest and 10 being the highest, rate how well we did in achieving our original campaign goal.

        1   2   3   4   5   6   7   8   9   10

5. Why did you rate it this way?

6. What did we do that was most effective in helping us to achieve our campaign goal during the campaign?

7. Did we build our organizational power in this campaign?

    ☐ Yes   ☐ No

8. Why do you think this?

9. Did we build our base—bring in more members and become a bigger organization?

10. If we did not achieve our demands, what could we have done differently in the campaign to achieve them?

11. Our campaign strategy was primarily:

12. Did this strategy work?

    ☐ Yes   ☐ No   ☐ Mixed results

13. Why do you think this?

14. Of the following strategies, which do you think we could have used or used more effectively during this campaign?

Tool 13.5
Campaign Evaluation Worksheet, Cont'd

☐ **Disruption**—Stopping the normal flow of business till people give us what we want

☐ **Legislative**—Meeting with elected officials to pass a bill or change a law

☐ **Alliance-building**—Getting two or three other groups with power working with us

☐ **Direct Action**—Large, powerful direct actions with the campaign target that would require mobilizing 300 to 400 people in each action

☐ **Legal**—Using the legal system, the courts and judicial law, to put additional pressure on the target

☐ **Advocacy**—Improving systems and administrative procedures or getting elected officials to create new public programs

☐ **Media and Public Education**—Getting the media to cover the issue and put pressure on the target

☐ **Other Strategy**

15. Why do you think we could have used this strategy?

16. During this campaign we chose to be *more* or *less* (circle one) confrontational than we usually are. Do you think that was the right choice?

   ☐ Yes   ☐ No

17. Why do you think this?

18. What was the biggest disappointment for you about the campaign?

19. What made you feel best about the campaign?

20. If we could do this campaign over again, what are the three things we should do differently?

   1.

   2.

   3.

part four

Building a Movement

O rganizations that have won campaigns sometimes expand their activities to include forging partnerships and engaging in movement-building in order to achieve longer-term, social change goals.

Through strategic partnerships and alliances with other organizations, you gain the power to move a more systemic agenda over the course of many years. As you engage in activities that build the movement for social justice beyond your community's issues, you increase the skills and strengthen the perspectives of community leaders, foster political education, and cultivate a vast network of relationships among organizations and individuals.

Once members of your organization experience some concrete campaign wins, they have more opportunities to participate in partnerships, to take on issues that require a more complex response, and to work outside of their issue area. They can engage in more explicitly political projects, such as mass mobilizations and electoral organizing (described in Resource C). When they get a taste of power, they have a greater desire to consider these kinds of activities.

You first go through an internal process to get the buy-in of a range of leaders and members for investing in deep, long-term work. You conduct an internal assessment of what the organization has accomplished, what it has not, and why. You do a power analysis of what the organization needs in order to achieve its broader organizational goals in addition to winning its single campaign demands. You consider your organizational capacity: Do you have the staff, members, leaders, and expertise to engage in partnerships and movement work? Can you commit resources to these efforts?

Alliances and movement activities emanate from base-building and from running effective campaigns—they do not replace this core work. In the following chapters we explore how to continue your base-building and leadership development as you forge partnerships for power and move from focusing on narrow, organizational self-interest to pursuing a vision for social change and political transformation.

Forging Partnerships for Power

REAL PARTNERSHIPS REQUIRE WORK

As the Work Experience Program (WEP) expands in New York City, Community Voices Heard (CVH) starts to organize WEP workers to win real jobs with paychecks. Other ally organizations are also organizing WEP workers to win jobs, living wages, or better working conditions. Everyone encounters the same problem: resistance from the city's largest municipal union to working with them to address the issues. CVH leaders and organizers start out trying to neutralize opposition from the union, but ultimately they realize they need the union to win. The union represents the workers being displaced by WEP, and it has a lot of influence with the city council speaker—who is the target of CVH's campaign. CVH works hard to forge an alliance with the union by approaching the issue from a number of fronts at once. Gail, a former leader now on staff, and a group of members build relationships with reporters. They frame the issue in the press as a workers' issue, a women's issue, and a poverty issue. Organizers pull off a series of small but dramatic actions, showing the union leadership that it can bring WEP workers into an organization—something the union has not been able to do. WEP workers speak at union gatherings, moving rank and file members to better understand that they are not a threat but instead are exploited workers. Paul, in his role as CVH executive director, uses his contacts from a community labor coalition board he sits on to build relationships with senior staff who can move union leadership.

CVH succeeds in framing the problem and its solution and establishing itself as a major player on WEP. The union needs to move to the position of supporting transitional jobs and of partnering with CVH, if it does not want to appear to be out of touch on the issue.

What Are Partnerships for Power and Why Is It Important to Build Them?

Partnerships for power are the strategic partnerships you form with other institutions and organizations in order to win on your issues and shift power. Partnerships bring the power of other organizations into your campaign when your organization does not have enough power to move a target.

Broad-based partnerships build enough power to withstand opposition forces and win campaigns. By building alliances, your organization can move its issues in ways that reach a broader audience than you can achieve alone. Community power-building organizations that work with each other help build a stronger movement for social justice.

What Do We Bring Together in Partnerships?

Partnerships bring together the power of institutions.

Partnerships may exist between two organizations or among several organizations. Partnerships for power go beyond relationships between individual staff members or leaders.

In some partnerships, organizations have many common interests and similar constituencies and approach their work in the same way. But sometimes the participating organizations work on different issues or take different approaches to their work. Sometimes the partnership's goals are for one distinct campaign. Other times the goals are to build and shift power over time rather than to win on a specific campaign.

How Do We Know Who to Bring into a Partnership?

You go out and talk to others who have a stake in the issue to figure out what their self-interest is and what they could bring to the campaign.

You often first form partnerships when your power analysis shows that you do not have enough power alone to move the target. You look at other stakeholders—organizations that want something specific connected with the issue. Once you identify who you believe has a stake, you talk with them and with others who know them to identify what their direct self-interest is. You look for organizations that want something enough to put their time, resources, reputation, and political capital into working with your organization. You also determine what they would be willing to bring to the partnership and how it would complement what your organization has. Once you know what they want and what they bring, you figure out how you will get their support. Because organizations protect their turf, you often need to hold several meetings and sometimes come together on joint projects before you can get an organization to really work with you.

You don't necessarily only go to organizations that have been with you in the past or that generally share your mission. For instance, if you have a strong base of community leaders but need political access, you partner with the organization that can provide that access. If you have a base of active members and leaders but they are not in all the legislative districts you need, you build with those who have a base of power in those districts. Sometimes the groups you need may be long-standing allies, but to build real power you often go beyond the familiar and cultivate a range of partners.

How Do We Know Stakeholders' Self-Interest?

You directly ask what they need to get out of your work together.

Self-interest is not obvious. In a partnership, it is important to know your shared interests as well as your different priorities. Once you've done your homework about an organization and are in dialogue with it, you directly ask what that organization needs to get out of working with your organization.

You educate members about why potential partners have the interests they express. For example, during the jobs campaign, CVH organizers educated members, not only about how labor unions are structured and how they make decisions, but also about the broader workers' rights movement. CVH members learned the underlying issues that affect workers, such as wage suppression, prevailing wage laws, and displacement. They learned how welfare reform hurt all workers, not just people on welfare. This political education helped members to make decisions about the campaign that reflected broader interests. For example, the demand that the transitional jobs program pay welfare recipients a wage needed to align with the self-interest of union members, some of whom were the very welfare case workers that CVH members felt did not treat them with respect in the welfare office. At the same time CVH workers needed to understand that caseworkers, who sometimes came from poverty themselves, felt that welfare recipients should be working to improve their lives, just as they were doing. All this information helped

CVH members to incorporate the perspectives and needs of labor in order to move the union to bring its power to the campaign.

What Are the Different Types of Partnerships for Power?

Partnerships are alliances, coalitions, coordinated campaigns, and sign-on campaigns.

Alliance. An alliance is a strategic partnership that seeks long-term power change, not short-term resolution of a problem. Organizations in an alliance each have the ability to mobilize some real power of their own. They generally share the same political analysis of power and have a similar ideology. The partners in an alliance may apply their power to a campaign or they may even come together initially in a campaign. But as the alliance develops it does not exist for the purpose of winning specific campaigns. It exists to shift political power and move broad issues forward in a deep way. You sometimes formalize an alliance through starting an organization, but an alliance may be more relational than organizational, where the partners meet as needed and solidify their relationships over time.

For example, the National Religious Partnership for the Environment, where Joan was the communications director, is an example of a formal alliance, bringing together Catholics, mainline Protestants, evangelical Christians, and Jews on an institutional level to promote environmental justice and sustainability. Each of the partners conducts its own campaigns on specific issues in ways that reflect their own values and constituencies. At the same time, the alliance members conduct both parallel and joint education of the public and targets about the fact that care for the earth is a value that motivates people of faith. Each of the partners has a stake in shifting power on environmental issues to the religious community. This stake motivates their alliance whether or not the partners choose to work on campaigns together.

Other stakeholders are your most critical partners in an alliance, but you also seek out organizations and constituencies who do not have direct self-interest. A broad base of support shows that a range of institutions and constituencies are concerned about an issue and are willing to put their resources into it. These other organizations may mobilize their members for action or offer expertise on issues, even if they do not play leadership roles in the campaign.

Coalition. A coalition is the most common type of partnership. It differs from an alliance in that it seeks to win specific demands rather than to create a long-term shift in power. It usually presents itself publicly as an organization of organizations with a policy or program it wants to gain or prevent. Partners in a coalition may operate with shared funding and staff, or each group may use its own resources to do the work of the coalition. Similar to an alliance, a coalition usually has a core of active participating organizations that make decisions and set the agenda as well as organizations in supportive roles. A coalition can come together on an ad hoc basis, focused on achieving one goal and then disbanding, or it may operate over time and take on consecutive issues. In the fight for transitional jobs, CVH and another community organization, the Fifth Avenue Committee, formed a coalition in order to align their power formally. After the city council passed the jobs bill, the coalition disbanded.

Coordinated campaign. In a coordinated campaign, the partners have a specific demand they seek to win, but they do not pursue it in a joint campaign. Instead, the organizations develop their own campaign plans and coordinate their activities for maximum impact. They may or may not engage in joint actions. They sometimes have a formal or informal agreement about how to negotiate with the target. In coordinated campaigns, the partners may agree that the various organizations will stake out different positions as a way to force the target to meet the demand they all believe they can achieve. They also may understand, either directly or by implication, that one will use strategies, actions, and tactics that the other may not use. For example, in a campaign on the state level to win jobs for workfare workers, CVH participated in a coordinated campaign with statewide advocacy organizations, including the Hunger Action Network, Fiscal Policy Institute, and the New York State AFL-CIO. Although the organizations at times acted collectively, they often did their own campaigns and coordinated their activities.

Sign-on campaign. A sign-on campaign is also known as a "paper coalition." Usually one organization runs a campaign and gets formal support for its demands through a pledge, a letter of support, or a sign-on form. The signers may include individuals as well as organizations. Participation can range from just signing a pledge to agreeing to mobilize for an action or actively working within one's own organization to achieve the demands.

How Do We Get Other Organizations to Partner with Us?

Know exactly what you want from the partnership. Invest time and resources into understanding a potential partner organization and building a relationship.

Building partnerships, especially with new, powerful allies, can often take on the elements of a campaign. You research a potential partner similarly to the ways you research targets. Where are the organization's pressure points? What kind of partnerships has the organization made in the past? After the organizing committee conducts some research about a potential ally, it figures out how to move the organization's decision makers to agree to work in partnership. Tool 14.1 describes the elements of a letter requesting a meeting with an organization to initiate a partnership and provides a sample of such a letter.

The following are guidelines for building partnerships:

Know what you want. What is the most important thing you need from a potential partner? Do you want a letter of support or funds for an action? Do you want the organization to make the issue one of its top priorities for the legislative year? Do you want a long-term strategic alliance or a sign-on? Don't ask for a laundry list. Be selective and strategic.

Understand who makes the decisions. Who has the power to decide whether or not the organization will support your campaign? A small grassroots membership organization may simply need someone from your staff or leadership to make a presentation to its members, who will vote yes or no. With a larger institution such as a union, you may need to spend a significant amount of time figuring out who in its structure may support your campaign or who needs to be convinced to do so.

Understand an institution's political landscape. An organization, especially an institution such as a labor union or religious group, often bases its support on how the partnership would affect its members, reputation, and credibility. You learn about the institution's political landscape by looking at what it responds to: press, peers, organized pressure, its own members, its core leaders, or strong public policy arguments. For instance, some religious institutions respond to what local clergy want. Rather than going to the institutional leadership, you get local religious leaders to communicate to their leadership that it needs to work on the issue.

Invest time and resources into building institutional relationships. If you are seeking a long-term alliance or deep campaign commitment, prioritize relationship-building conversations. Ask questions about the organization's perspective on an issue and how it affects the organization's constituents. Many organizations will readily sign on to a campaign, but that only shows their support, it does not change or increase your organization's power. To build power, you need their institutional investment.

Manage individual relationships. Ultimately, it is people who get things done and who move their institutions. You keep individual relationships in perspective, but know that they matter. You understand where individuals are in the power structure of their organizations and where they stand on your issue. You are clear about your own role. You understand when a person is speaking for herself and when she is speaking for her institution. These are often staff relationships, but leaders have them as well.

Maintain a good reputation. You care about your reputation as a partner. Your organization's staff, members, leaders, or others associated with your organization can get a bad reputation, for instance, by not following through on things, by talking trash, or by saying one thing and doing another. If your organization gets a bad reputation, you have to intentionally work to overcome it. Having a bad reputation is more of an impediment to working in partnership than a having political viewpoint that is outside of the mainstream.

Show your power. Like targets, organizations and institutions respect and respond to power. Showing your power by mobilizing for collective actions, moving legislation, and similar activities shows allies that your organization deserves their respect.

Remember quid pro quo. If you ask an institution to work in partnership on a campaign, it will likely ask something of your organization, either during the campaign or after it is completed. You need to consider these requests seriously.

Should We Accept a Foundation's Offer of Money to Partner with Some of Its Other Grantees?

Possibly, but proceed with caution. The strongest partnerships come together when the partners themselves decide that collaboration is important.

Be clear about why a funder is asking you to collaborate with others. Donors and foundations foster partnerships for a number of reasons. They may believe that investing in an issue or geographic location is strategic, or they want organizations to work together in order to expand the impact of their money. Sometimes they don't have a lot of money to give or they don't want to get into the fray of turf and organizational politics, so they fund a collaboration. Although resources help you do more effective work, if the collaboration does not support your core work or expand it in ways the members initiate and want, you can get off track. You can wind up having to cut out issue areas when the funder's priorities change. You can build an infrastructure of staff around a project that is not core to your mission. You can confuse people about your message and focus. Being clear on the self-interest and goals of the funder helps you make a better decision about whether or not collaboration makes sense.

What Kinds of Meetings Do We Have with Stakeholders and Potential Allies?

The following are different types of stakeholder and ally meetings. In a community power-building organization, members and leaders participate in these meetings wherever possible.

Relational meetings. These are one-on-one meetings that build relationships with individuals who play pivotal roles in their organizations. For instance, the lead staff person for your campaign or the chair of your board may use relational meetings to foster a relationship with the political director of a labor union. In relational meetings, you listen most of the time. You do not try to sell something or make a request. You learn what is important to a person in his or her role and explore what motivates the organization. You build trust.

Campaign research meetings. These meetings are conversational, but they have more of an agenda than a relational meeting. You use these meetings to go through the completed campaign plan and to determine if the other organization is working on your issue or may want to support it. These meetings can include more than one person from your organization.

Ask meetings. These meetings have a clear agenda. You directly ask someone for something. For example, you ask for a meeting with a decision maker, a signature on a sign-on letter, or to have the person appear at a press conference. If the person with whom you are meeting cannot give a definitive answer before you leave, you find out the internal process for getting an answer. You sometimes follow up these meetings with a written request. These meetings are often one-on-one, but they may include more people.

Presentations. Sometimes an ask meeting is actually a presentation to a group of people. Usually it is part of an agenda of some other type of group meeting, such as a board or membership meeting.

With Whom Do We Meet in Different Institutions?

You meet with the person who can make the decision to give you what you want.

If you don't know anyone in the organization, you may have to meet with several people before you get to the person who can give you what you need. The following is an introduction to the key players and decision makers at the local level at three important institutions: labor groups, nonprofit community groups, and religious congregations. For these types of institutions, a local organization may be connected to a national, state, or regional body whose support you may also need to get. For instance, if you want the state Catholic Conference to support your issue, you may need to get decision makers in local Catholic congregations and the area-wide diocese to support it. If you need this kind of broader institutional support, your research includes finding out how to gain access to those decision makers.

Unions and Labor Groups

- *Leader: president.* This is the elected leader and the most significant person who represents the organization. When the president shows up at public actions, press events, and meetings, it means the union takes the issue seriously. Sometimes this person has the title of executive director.

- *Executive committee: president, vice president, secretary.* These are elected, high-level leadership positions. People in these positions are accountable to the union members who vote them in. They make monetary appropriations and policy decisions. With support and input from members, they develop political priorities for the union in legislative sessions and other arenas.

- *Primary staff: political director.* The union president or executive director appoints the political director. This position manages the political operations of the union, including electoral, lobbying, and legislative efforts as well as work with allies. The political director is key for getting real support behind a program or proposal.

- *Secondary staff: policy staff, researcher, community liaison.* It can be difficult to get a meeting with the political director of a large union. These secondary staff might meet with you more readily and help you figure out how to get to the decision maker. To find out who they are, check out your local labor community coalition. For example, Jobs with Justice has local chapters throughout the country. Find out who represents the unions you need in these coalitions.

- *Constituents: shop stewards, rank-and-file union members, retirees.* Union members have better access to union leaders and staff than an outsider has. The more members raise up an issue, the more it has a chance of being addressed by the union. Be careful and strategic with members. If there is any hint that your organization is trying to organize a union's members, the union will perceive that as a hostile act.

Nonprofit Community Groups

- *Leader: board president or executive director.* Depending on the organization, the board president or chair or the executive director are the leaders and decision makers of the organization. The executive director usually reports to the board chair. Their exact roles vary depending on the organization, and you may not understand who the real decision maker on your issue is until you learn more about how the organization operates.

- *Executive committee: president, vice president, secretary, and treasurer.* The executive committee, comprised of the board's officers, often makes decisions about policies and resources in an organization. In more process-oriented organizations or where you are requesting more than a sign-on, decisions may require full board approval.

- *Primary staff: executive director, lead organizer, program director.* Depending on the organization and what you are asking, people who supervise other staff or who are part of a management team may be able to give you what you need or give you access to the decision maker. The primary decision maker on staff is usually the executive director.

- *Secondary staff: program staff, community organizer, outreach worker.* It can be difficult to get a meeting with the executive director or program director of a large organization. These secondary staff people may meet with you more readily and help you figure out how to get to the decision maker.

- *Constituents: organization members or clients.* Similar to unions, members of an organization have more access to organizational leadership than a cold contact does. In membership organizations, members sometimes make decisions about the campaigns and issues the organization will support. You may need to make a presentation at a membership meeting to get their support.

Religious Congregations

- *Leader: pastor, rabbi, imam.* Depending on the religion, the congregation leader is the clergyperson who manages the congregation's resources and conducts its primary worship services. This person may be accountable only to the congregation or may report to an institutional leadership body as well. The person in this role must support the congregation's involvement or it will not be solid.

- *Executive committee: primary clergyperson, lay leaders, other clergy and religious.* A congregation usually has a body that makes decisions about resource distribution and programs. This body usually includes laypeople who are members of the congregation. It also usually includes the primary clergyperson and in the Catholic Church, other clergy or "religious," such as nuns or brothers who take religious vows but do not conduct worship services.

- *Primary staff and volunteers: school principal, clergy, congregation council chair, social concern chair.* If there are other clergy who work for the congregation, they may oversee primary programs. Most congregations employ lay staff to manage the place of worship and its programs and rely on lay volunteers to build the congregation. Their titles and roles vary based on the religion and on the congregation. If the congregation operates a school, the principal is often a decision maker. In addition, the chair of the lay leadership body or its social concerns committee can have influence with the clergy and the congregants.

- *Secondary staff and volunteers: religious educator, youth leaders.* Most congregations put resources into educating people about the faith and engaging young people in the congregation. The people running these programs can be important people to meet with, depending on the issue.

- *Constituents: congregants, lay people.* As in the other institutions, the lay congregants may have greater ability to move their leadership than an outsider. Try to identify the congregation leaders and keep in mind that sometimes congregants may need your help to show their primary clergyperson that an issue has broader community support.

Tool 14.2 outlines the goals and participants in meetings with stakeholders and potential allies.

How Do We Maintain Accountability and Trust in Partnerships?

You use clear and direct communication. You are honest and do what you say you are going to do.

The following are problems of trust and accountability that can come up among partners who are in a campaign together, along with suggestions for handling them:

Deal-cutting and negotiating on the side. One of the biggest challenges of working with other organizations is when one partner tries to cut out the others to negotiate a deal on its own. The organization trying this tactic may have side meetings with a target while the rest of the partners are out of the room, or it may cut the others out of final negotiations. You may experience this problem if you partner with an organization that has more power than yours or if another organization in the partnership has a prior relationship with the target. At times the target just reaches out to one of the partner organizations to be the one she or he wants to deal with.

What you can do. Making demands and holding negotiations in public meetings, such as accountability sessions or meetings the press attends, are the best ways to prevent deal-cutting. The more private the demand process is, the greater the chance that your organization can be left out of the loop. If you cannot get negotiations to occur in a public meeting, then develop a Memo of Understanding, which we describe later in this chapter, or other document stating that any decisions the partners make about what they will demand of the target need to be in writing and signed off by all the partners.

Turnout numbers. Many organizations do not deliver on the turnout they promise in planning meetings. Organizations may give vague numbers, such as saying they will turn out their members or that they will turn out a couple of hundred people. When you need to show your target that you have power, such as in accountability sessions and target meetings, weak turnout can kill your campaign and damage your organization's reputation.

What you can do. In initial planning meetings, assume that organizations are likely to bring half the numbers of people they say they are going to bring. Develop a plan of action based on that reality. As the action gets closer, make sure that you institute daily check-ins about numbers, using as many systems and with as much accountability as possible, such as seeing names and phone numbers on a list. An organization's reputation will help you determine if turnout is a potential problem. Understanding an organization's history of turnout capacity helps the partners hold them more accountable. For example, if an organization says it will turn out one hundred people but everyone knows they never bring more than thirty-five, you can plan around the lower number. In the end, there is no control you can have over what another organization does or does not do. Especially if you are working with organizations that do not do base-building, your numbers may be the only ones that really matter. Always try to increase your turnout over what you promise.

Follow-through. Many aspects of a campaign are connected, and if one group does not do what it says it will do, it can stall the campaign or set it back.

What you can do. You can schedule meetings and check-ins to help deal with this potential problem before it happens. These meetings do not have to be long. They can occur by conference call or in person. With e-mail and the Internet, you can also monitor task lists more easily. If a partner organization fails to do its work, address it directly, before a crisis occurs.

Lone wolf behavior. Some groups have a reputation for doing things that are not connected to the campaign the partners are implementing. This behavior is not helpful when it conflicts with the partners' plan. Lone wolf behavior is not so much related to side negotiations as to engaging in different actions on the same issue during a partnership campaign.

What you can do. Establish clearly at the start what kind of partnership you are entering into. If the partnership is undefined, it is harder to hold an organization accountable for going off on its own. Develop and write a campaign plan. When the partners agree on a strategy and objectives, you can hold each other accountable for straying from the plan. If one of the partners wants to do its own action on the issue, it lets the others know.

Different organizational cultures or priorities. Organizations have different internal priorities. Some put a lot of effort into member decision making and leadership development and others are more staff-driven. Some have clear distinctions between staff and leaders, others do not. Some use permits for actions all the time, others never use permits. As you work with other organizations, you begin to see that there can be huge differences in how organizations operate on a day-to-day basis. A partnership takes negotiation and give and take. You cannot operate in a partnership the same way you operate as an independent organization.

What you can do. Your organization determines what is most important to it in how the partnership operates. What elements do you want to be sure reflect your organizational culture and which do not need to reflect it? You cannot have everything. If your bottom line is that you bring a leader to every meeting or that you need to have daily number counts for an action, with names and numbers, you may not be able to have something else. You determine your bottom line and then you negotiate.

Sharing and distributing resources. Sharing resources can be a major source of tension. This tension can occur when there is money available for the campaign or when a donor or funder wants to fund a collaboration. One big debate that always comes up is how much should go to the groups to do the work they are already doing and how much should go to a central campaign operation or managing the partnership. Generally, membership organizations believe money should go to their base-building, and advocacy organizations believe in funding coordination and other strategies. Partnerships generally recognize that both efforts are needed. The debate is usually about priorities and how much to invest in one over another.

What you can do. Having a clear campaign plan can help the partners to identify where to put limited resources. When you lay out the tasks and responsibilities, it is easier to figure out who will do them and then to direct resources accordingly. For example, if none of the partner organizations can take on the very important work of central planning, it is easier to make a case for putting resources into hiring a coordinator to do this task. If base-building and turnout are critical and the partner organizations can do a better job on these goals with more resources, then you direct resources accordingly. A Memo of Understanding can be very helpful.

What Is a Memo of Understanding and How Do We Use It?

A Memo of Understanding (MOU) clearly delineates how the partnership will function and what the goals and objectives of the partnership are. It also specifies what activities, responsibilities, and tasks each group and any central body will do and how partners will share resources.

A Memo of Understanding is a written, agreed-upon, and signed tool to address the issues that may arise in a partnership. It outlines what will happen if an organization operates outside the parameters of what the partners agree upon. You usually have an MOU when there is money connected to a partnership or when partners are sharing staff on a campaign. However, an MOU can help overcome confusion even when there is no funding. If you do not use an MOU, you can write joint operating principles and agree upon them.

As a Member-Led Organization How Do We Effectively Manage Our Partnerships?

From the beginning, be clear with partners that the members of your organization make the final decisions.

The following actions will help keep your participation in a partnership clean:

Be clear about how your organization operates. Organizations in which staff have a lot of power or that operate in a top-down manner often want things to move quickly. They can find it challenging to work with member-led organizations that need to allow time for members to make decisions. Be clear from the beginning about how you operate as an organization and what your organization expects in the partnership. For example, you don't wait until the day before a decision-making meeting to ask that a member of your organization participate.

Negotiate, but know your bottom line. Not everything about the partnership can operate the way it does in your organization. The leadership of your organization clarifies with its partners from the beginning what is negotiable and what is not.

Maintain consistent member representation. If a member of your organization agrees to participate in partnership meetings, make sure she or he remains committed. Consistency with your potential partners is important.

Establish a structure for staffing and decision making. The more partnership-focused your campaign, the more it depends on one constant person, usually a staff person, to make sure all the partners are working well together. The partnership may hire a staff person or have a staff member from a lead partner organization play that role. In either case, the partners are clear to whom the staff person is accountable. The partnership also needs to be structured to help to ensure that a broad, representative group shares power and decision making. One way is to establish a meeting schedule and determine what the purpose of different meetings will be and who will participate. Another is to have a leadership team for decision making or explicitly agree on who needs to be included in various decisions.

Speak up. Stay flexible. When another partner does something your organization disagrees with, communicate it clearly, quickly, and professionally. Sometimes things happen that are outside of anyone's control. Honest, nondefensive communication helps keep the partnership flexible.

Maintain constant and regular contact with all key partners. Having regular contact with your partners also helps avoid or address problems. Make sure contact is equal with all partners. You can help maintain communication with a regularly scheduled conference call between meetings.

Do what you will say you will do. When you say you are going to do something, make sure you can do it and always follow through. For mobilizations, make sure you turn out the number of people you promise. If a leader from your organization is leading a partnership meeting or event, make sure she or he is prepared.

What Is the Role of the Organizer in Maintaining Partnerships for Power?

The more formal the partnership and the more time and organizational resources it takes, the more likely a paid staff person will be the main point person with the partnership.

The person who has a relationship with an institution, whether that is the organizer, director, or leader, is the person the partner will trust and want to deal with. Most often a staff person has the relationship with another staff person in a large organization like a union or a religious organization. In smaller organizations, such as churches or union locals, the relationship may be through a member.

Although the relationship may involve two staff people, it does not mean the organizer is the decision maker. As usual, the organizer implements the decisions and strategies members make. The organizer may attend partnership meetings, but goes back and checks in with members before giving the organization's decision to the partners.

Depending on the organization, the campaign, and the way the partners agree to operate, staff may need to make decisions quickly. Sometimes the partners agree that each representative has to make a decision at a meeting. In these cases, the only power members and leaders in your organization have is the accountability of the organizer.

LEADERSHIP DEVELOPMENT OPPORTUNITIES
IN PARTNERSHIPS FOR POWER

- *Build relationships.* Leaders participate in meetings with stakeholders to build and manage organizational relationships.
- *Negotiate on behalf of the organization.* Negotiate details about the campaign with allies on everything from messages to demands to tactics.
- *Do public speaking.* Make presentations to the membership or boards of partner organizations, ranging from outlining what the organization does

to sharing experiences and inviting people into the campaign. Opportunities include member meetings of local unions and religious institutions' social justice committees.

- *Bring in own network.* Leaders ask other organizations they are part of to participate in an alliance or coalition. For example, if a group of mothers working on a public school issue all belong to the same church, they can go to the social justice committee or the pastor and ask the church to get involved.

CHALLENGES
IN PARTNERSHIPS

"Our coalition work is taking up a lot of our time." Partnerships can be time-intensive, particularly at the beginning when you are building relationships and developing trust. You address this situation by staying focused and factoring the time it will take into the campaign plan and individual work plans. You balance meetings and conference calls with allies along with your essential recruitment and leadership development. The fact that partnerships take time is one of the important reasons you enter into them carefully and for clear reasons.

"Our members can't really participate in our partnerships as they do in our organization." Depending on the type of partnership, members who usually make decisions about campaigns may not be able to play leading roles at actions or even participate in campaign planning or action planning. Leadership development falls to a few individuals rather than a broad base of members. Because relationships with partners are based on trust, consistency is key. You focus on developing leaders who can commit a significant amount of time to go to trainings, participate in partner meetings, and report back to the larger membership. Use opportunities such as speaking at congregation or union meetings and attending solidarity actions such as union-sponsored marches to engage as many members as possible in alliance building.

ESSENTIAL ELEMENTS
FOR EFFECTIVE PARTNERSHIPS

☑ *Ask about self-interest.* You don't assume you understand what your potential partners need to get out of working together. Once you are in relationship and dialogue, you ask.

☑ *Build relationships.* Ultimately, partnerships involve people. You build individual relationships in order to maintain trust and work together effectively.

☑ *Do your research.* You understand the power structure of the partner organization, who makes decisions, and the power of the organization's representatives in the alliance.

☑ *Establish checks and balances.* You make sure that agreements about how the partners will operate are clear and in writing and that there are procedures to keep everyone in check.

☑ *Build your base.* As a community power-building organization, you bring an all-important base of members and constituents to your partnerships. You make sure you are recruiting, involving, and developing people who will turn out to show the power of your organization to your partners and to the targets of your campaigns. You train and educate members so that they make good decisions about how to enter into and cultivate effective partnerships for power.

Tool 14.1
Sample Meeting Request Letter

You can use the following as a sample format for initiating a partnership in writing. A sample letter follows the description of the elements of such a letter.

Paragraph one: The purpose of the letter. What you want, who you are, and why the person addressed in the letter should meet with you. The letter initiates a relationship between organizations, but it is addressed to specific people from specific people.

Paragraph two: Your organization's credentials. Information about your organization: how old it is, how many members it has, what it has accomplished.

Paragraph three: Your common self-interest. Information about your campaign, where there is potential to work together, and why their organization should do so.

Paragraph four: Summary and conclusion. The next steps to make the meeting happen, including when and how you will follow up.

When writing a letter, keep it to a maximum of a page and a half. Avoid rhetoric, buzzwords, and jargon. State the power of your organization and its accomplishments. Be clear about what you are asking and why the response should be yes.

Sample Letter

President Roberta Jones
Local 600 Municipal Workers Union

Dear President Jones:

We are writing to request a meeting with you and your community outreach director to introduce you to our organization, Citizens for a Revitalized Downtown (CRD). We would like to meet with you to find out more about your union's work with community groups, to introduce you to our organization, and to talk about our current campaign to increase funding for capital improvements in the central business district.

CRD is a two-year-old organization of residents who live in the central business district. We have three hundred dues-paying members. Our mission is to improve the downtown for residents, businesses, and for everyone who uses the area for recreational, business, or professional reasons. During the last five years, more people have been moving into the area, converting old factories into living lofts and opening galleries. New businesses have been increasing. We believe that this development is good for our city—bringing in new tax revenue, creating new jobs, providing new services to residents, and improving the downtown area's ambience.

We are involved in a campaign to get the mayor to put $3 million of the city budget into capital improvements in the downtown area, including renovating sidewalks, expanding and rebuilding portions of City Hall Park, and adding street fixtures such as lights, flower boxes, and public seating. We understand that there has been a history of these kinds of projects going to non-union companies. Our organization believes that publicly funded projects must go to union contractors that provide living wages and benefits.

We would like to meet with you sometime in the next few weeks to discuss our campaign and gain your support. We would like to learn how to make sure that all funds go to union contractors and see how we can work together on other issues affecting our city. We will follow up with you next week to schedule a time to meet. We are enclosing some informational materials about our organization and our campaign. Thank you.

Sincerely,

Robert Walker, Director   Susanne Beete, Board Chair

Tool 14.2
Stakeholder and Ally Meetings: Goals and Participants

The following chart outlines the goals and participants in meetings with stakeholders and potential allies.

Type of Meeting	Goal	Who from Your Organization Should Do It	Union or Labor Group	Religious Congregation	Community Group
Relational meetings	Relationship-building.	Organizer or person who has a contact.	Organizer. Highest level person you know.	Congregant, clergy-person, or who you know.	Organizer, member, staffperson, who you know.
Informational meetings	Get to know the organization.	Organizer and member or leader.	Political or community liaison department.	Social concerns committee, clergy-person, lay staff.	Staff.
Campaign research meetings	Find out what their interest is in an issue or campaign.	Organizer and members of orga-nizing committee.	Legislative, campaign, or political staff.	Clergyperson or social concerns committee.	Campaign staff people, legislative office, organizing department.
Ask meetings	Get them to do something to support your campaign.	Organizational lead-ership, executive director, board member, president.	Leadership and decision maker.	Primary clergy-person or lay leader.	Leadership and decision maker.
Presentations	Talk about what you are doing in the campaign.	Organizing com-mittee members and organizer.	Membership com-mittees or appropri-ate internal groups.	Congregation, social concerns committee.	Staff, membership, board.

Moving from Self-Interest to Social Change: Movement-Building

FROM THE GRASSROOTS TO THE GLOBAL— WORKING TO CHANGE THE WORLD!

A friend of Emma's recruits her to join Community Voices Heard (CVH) because Emma is connected to her community and her church. She is concerned about the lack of jobs in her South Bronx neighborhood and decides to join CVH to organize for job creation. When CVH starts working with economic justice organizations around the United States to plan a national march on President George W. Bush's ranch in the small town of Crawford, Texas, Emma signs on.

Because CVH is a participating organization in the National Campaign for Jobs and Income Support, CVH staff and leaders help organize this march and related demonstrations at corporate headquarters in Texas where Bush and Vice President Dick Cheney have ties. At small-group meetings at the CVH office and in individual one-on-one meetings with organizers, members think about the connections between the lack of jobs and services in their community and the priorities of the Bush administration. These conversations educate members about the real cost of the war in Iraq and how the Bush administration's support of corporate power directly affects them. The discussions spark side conversations. Emma talks with other members and together they form a deep understanding about why CVH is going to Texas.

On the day of the march, the president's security personnel stop the busloads of protesters on a road approaching the ranch. Hundreds of low-income people get out and march through fields and ranchland. Emma is invigorated. She recounts to the others how she has not felt so powerful since she marched for civil rights in the 1960s. "We need to get the president to know that poor people and people of color are angry about the choices he is making and the priorities that he has for the country," she says. Later, on the bus ride back from the ranch, Emma captivates the others as she reflects on the day and its impact on her. "They made it up," she insists about the war in Iraq. "There's no need to be at war and no one wants it!"

She knows that CVH is spending resources on something that is not directly part of the campaigns she is working on. "But it is all connected" she tells the protesters. Because of her grounding in the community, her passion, and her experiences as a leader, Emma commands the group's attention. "When the president starts a war to give contracts to the companies his friends run, well that affects the community where I live. That means there's no money for jobs programs, housing, and services. We—poor and working people—we pay for it. So we have to do something. Even if it means getting on a plane, busing a hundred miles, and putting our other work to the side for a few days."

Emma is feeling it—she is part of a movement.

What Is Movement-Building and Why Is It Important?

In movement-building you use the resources of your organization to engage in activities that are not solely connected to winnable campaigns or organizational self-interest but that pursue the goals of the larger movement for justice.

Activities that go beyond the day-to-day functions of campaigns and organization-building provide members, staff, boards, or steering committees with the chance to connect with people and issues beyond their own.

Sometimes people agree that a distinct movement is under way. For example, the Civil Rights Movement in the United States stands out as a moment in time during the 1950s and 1960s when people engaged in sustained organizing that tapped into a shifting national consciousness. When we talk about "the movement" in this chapter, we refer more broadly to the actions, organizations, and campaigns for social and political justice in which people engage, on the fullest possible range of issues, worldwide. These can be one-time actions, such as demonstrations or projects to move an issue you don't address in your core campaigns. Sometimes your actions in movement-building are as targeted as they are in your local campaigns. Other times they make more of a political statement.

Movement-building addresses the root causes of community problems. For example, although globalization and free-trade policies may affect your local economy by exporting good union jobs to other countries, it can be hard for a single organization in a local community to organize a winnable campaign to address this issue. Working with other organizations in a limited, targeted way can help to address the problem over time. It also provides members with political education about free-trade policies and their impact on communities. Seeing the bigger picture helps reenergize and sustain everyone in your organization. Exercise 15.1 provides a way to get people thinking about how globalization affects their lives.

How Does Movement-Building Support Our Organization?

Movement-building is reciprocal. You use the intersection with the larger movement to accomplish organizational goals, such as developing leaders and staff and building relationships with other organizations. At the same time, you move a broader agenda forward.

A steady line of campaigns disconnected from larger social movements and other people in the social justice community can wear down and isolate your organization—even if you win.

While movement-building moves an agenda forward, it also helps to sustain your organization. Working on campaigns for months or even years leaves people with little energy and personal resources to work on other issues they care about. Social movement-building helps to feed the people involved in the organization. Leaders feel connected to other issues and to like-minded people. They see their own situation in a broader context. Staff stretch their skills and gain experiences. They are more energized and less likely to burn out. The following are ways that movement-building supports your organization:

Expands your limited power. Statewide, regional, national, or even international policies may have a substantial impact on your community. You partner with other institutions to have enough power to move targets on these levels.

Relieves isolation. When leaders, members, and staff are in tough campaigns or between campaigns, they can start to feel disconnected and alone. Movement-building connects them with the exciting aspects of organizing. Mass actions that target vast powerholders deepen their sense of their own power and build their solidarity with one another and the movement.

Leaders have opportunities to strategize at different levels than they do on local campaigns and to take on leadership roles with a larger and different audience. They think about issues and their work in new ways. Staff have the chance to work on larger actions that require different skills and provide new learning opportunities.

Avoids burnout. Similarly, when leaders, members, and staff are burning out, movement-building can help to bring back their energy. They spend time learning about other struggles—current or past. Learning about the personal sacrifices, obstacles, and challenges others face or have overcome puts their work and their own individual concerns in context. It can be invigorating and freeing just to go to another city or town and move to action, not getting involved in administrative aspects that can be frustrating.

Builds the infrastructure of the movement. When there are more trained and effective organizers and leaders as well as stronger organizations, you have more partners to work with, a wider range of potential staff, and more experienced leaders for actions and campaigns. Stronger organizations and leaders mean a stronger movement, and a stronger movement means more capacity and power to win on your core issues and demands.

Provides a space for intensive political education. Your work is rooted in the history of social change. Your day-to-day organizing may give you some opportunities to educate members, leaders, and staff about this history, but in movement activities, this political education can occur at a deeper level. Members learn about the history of struggle in a place they are visiting and about other people they need to work with but may not understand. When they go outside of the United States, they can examine root causes of social problems from a variety of perspectives, from liberal to Marxist, and consider all kinds of critical analyses.

Creates opportunities for political debate and connection. Movement-building promotes broader political conversations—through discussion groups, movie nights, and chat or open mic nights where people can discuss a range of issues they are concerned about.

Although organizations work on different issues, many have the same political analysis and concerns. They share a desire for a world that is more just, equitable, and community-oriented. However, in the United States, the prominent political debate takes place in parties that are not based in the grassroots. Instead, political consultants and media strategists dominate. In addition, with fewer union members, most people cannot address issues through the labor movement. Religious organizations and congregations provide some opportunity for people to participate in the movement for justice, but community power-building organizations offer one of the few places where people can be a part of a larger movement.

How Do We Engage in Movement-Building in a Strategic and Focused Organization?

Have goals for your movement-building; use it as a way to support your organizing and campaign work.

Community power-building organizations are effective because they are focused, strategic, and make clear, winnable demands of targets they can confront directly. Movement-building activities are different, particularly when the demands are not winnable or when you can't bring the target into the room. For example, the President of the United States is unlikely to meet with your organization or even with you and partner organizations. The following are ways that you stay focused and engage in movement-building:

Clarify your goals and objectives. Understand why you are doing it. Are you engaging in the movement-building activity to develop leaders or do deeper political education, or because you want to build relationships with new constituencies? Are you doing it because members, leaders, and staff need to do something fun, big, and connected to others in order to get revitalized? When you are clear about your goals, you develop the appropriate project or activity. You are also able to evaluate after the activity whether it built your organization, resolved a problem, or was useful in the way you sought.

For example, Community Voices Heard sent members to participate in a march at a Free Trade in the Americas Agreement (FTAA) meeting in Miami in order to build a relationship with the national labor movement and strengthen CVH's working relationship with a local community-labor coalition. In addition, it set an objective of using this experience to help develop ten leaders to be more active in CVH's global justice committee.

Calculate the resources required. Every activity or project has an organizational impact and requires resources. The more you put into the project, the more resources it will take. If your organization plays a leading role in a movement-building project, that activity will take leaders, staff time, and other resources. Even turning out some members to show basic solidarity will mean making phone calls, having members spend time attending the action, and having organizers or leaders spend time prepping and explaining what the action is. You assess these costs and understand the impact on your core work of campaigns and building your organization.

For example, the cost to CVH of sending people to Miami was not only the cost of airline tickets and hotel rooms. It had to devote three meetings to prepping leaders and debriefing with them. A senior staff person took on fundraising for the trip, which affected her other work. In addition, four leaders who were active on other campaigns instead focused their time on the project.

Identify point people. Because organizers, leaders, and members are usually focused on their core campaign work, you don't assume someone will just pick up a movement-building project. Use a membership meeting, a portion of an organizing committee meeting or board meeting, and discussions with staff to identify the point person and what that job requires. Who can others in the organization hold accountable for making sure follow-through occurs? If you can't identify someone or no one has the time or capacity, don't do the activity.

If an issue is large or controversial, get organization-wide buy-in and approval. The larger the project, the more impact on the organization and the greater the need for an organization-wide decision to do the project. Depending on your structure, the board or steering committee, a leadership team, or an organizing committee evaluates the impact, the resources needed, and where they will come from and makes a recommendation to the membership about whether or not to go forward.

Engaging Members in a Movement-Building Decision: Should CVH Take an Anti-War Position?

As the United States engages in war in Iraq, a range of organizations ask CVH to participate in antiwar activities. CVH has not taken formal positions on issues of this scale before. The first question leaders face is whether or not to take a position, the second is what the position should be. Since these are mission questions, they are the board's decisions. But given the level of national concern and range of strong opinions and feelings about the war, the board believes it cannot decide alone.

Leaders meet to consider how waging an expensive, deadly war is a statement of national priorities that will affect communities for years to come. Many express

---

the opinion that because the war is unjust, CVH needs to take a position against it. The group decides to take a vote at the next membership meeting. In a written ballot, a majority of people say they want CVH to take a position and a majority also wants that to be a position against the war. The number of people involved in the decision give the board members confidence that when they ratify an anti-war position at the next board meeting, they are truly reflecting the will of the membership.

Communicate the goals to members and provide some background education. Members need to understand both why the organization is choosing to engage in the activity and what the goals are. They then understand why a campaign might be on hold and why the organization is spending resources doing something that does not seem to be in the members' personal self-interest. Also, one purpose of engaging in social justice movement-building is to develop leaders and provide political education opportunities. Effective preparation helps to ensure that people are not just bodies at an event.

For example, CVH's global justice committee educates members about globalization and its impact on communities. The committee connects with a network of groups around the United States and sometimes sends CVH members to attend meetings and other activities in other cities or countries. If members want to engage in these activities, they must attend global justice committee meetings to learn about the goals. For activities that can only accommodate a few leaders, CVH requires people to fill out a questionnaire and go through an application process. The questionnaire asks what they want to get out of the activity and how they will integrate what they learn back into CVH.

Be willing to say no. Sometimes you are not able to do effective movement-building. For example, during a critical campaign when the organization lacks extra resources, or when an organizational development issue requires significant time and energy, such as strategic planning, staff transitions, or fundraising, there may be no leaders, staff, or financial resources available to support a movement-building activity. Although movement-building should be strategic and connected to your work, it is not critical to the core work of the organization—building a base, engaging in campaigns, and winning. You can lower the priority for movement-building at times, then pick it up again when your capacity allows.

What Kinds of Movement-Building Activities Can We Engage In?

The following are some examples of movement-building activities:

Power shifting. Power shifting can include developing a shared information and training network that builds new organizations or the capacity of existing organizations, or participating in a national collaborative with a variety of different demands or in order to build power on an issue that is not core for your organization. This type of activity can also have the aim of shifting political power through voter mobilization or electoral organizing. (For more on electoral organizing, see Resource C.) Power shifting is closely linked to alliance-building.

For example, organizations from across the United States gather to discuss how to work together more effectively to address a range of environmental issues. Instead of focusing on one environmental issue, which would be forming a coalition, they develop a strategy that seeks to raise the issue of the environment in the upcoming congressional elections. They engage in shared strategizing, fundraising, and training to develop a unified message that resonates locally and nationally. They also work to develop an infrastructure for shared work after the election.

A specific campaign with a clear demand. An organization may decide to work on a campaign in a limited capacity. The organization may want to show solidarity on an important ally's campaign, or the issue may affect many of its members but they have not yet identified it as a priority. Sometimes the issue connects to the organization's core work although it is not central. The organization may participate in a single action, engage in a series of campaign activities, or agree to take on a time-limited piece of work.

For example, Work for Justice addresses workers' rights and economic justice issues. Its current campaigns include stopping privatization of a local hospital and getting the city to create more affordable housing. New corporate development has driven out union jobs and increased housing costs so that many members of Work for Justice can no longer afford housing. When a union group, Local 550, asks the organization to join it in a campaign to stop a free-trade bill that will increase the ability to move jobs overseas, Work for Justice leaders decide to support Local 550 in the campaign. They approve the use of an organizer to work on a four-week project to get the local congressperson to oppose the legislation.

Relationship-building. Sometimes members engage in movement-building with the goal of deepening relationships with other constituencies. These activities are usually not strategic or campaign-oriented but have the aim of creating goodwill and trust and deepening relationships for the future. This type of relationship-building can include study tours, exchanges, and conferences.

For example, Northwest United, an established organization in the northwestern United States, works on land preservation issues. Northwest members know members of Save Our Lands, a new organization in the southeast, from going to conferences together. Staff members in the two organizations also have good relationships with one another. Northwest United offers to send an organizer and two leaders to Save Our Lands for a few days to help train its staff and members to develop a message based on the message that has been effective in the Northwest.

Political education. Although all movement-building activities have political education as a goal, here the primary goal is political education. You want to educate or move members on an issue or a set of issues. You have movie and discussion nights in the office, hold a study tour, or send people to an international convening that addresses issues that are different from those of your organization. For instance, you hold a town hall meeting to bring together immigrant workers with unemployed local residents so that people learn about each others' lives and break down differences.

For example, one of your funders invites your organization to participate in an international convening about community organizing around the world. People from each country will talk about how they do this work in their country. A large component of the meeting will be discussing the views that leaders from other countries have about the role of the United States in the world. You send one staff person and three board members with the goal of learning about how other countries view the United States and assessing what opportunities exist for international organizing.

What Are Some Examples of Movement-Building Organizations?

Movement-building organizations represent all aspects of the larger social justice movement.

Some movement-building organizations are national in scope. They may bring groups together on an issue or to build power, they may provide training and political education, or they may build alliances between organized labor and community groups. Still others are small, local organizations that develop political consciousness in their members.

The following examples describe two movement-building alliances in which CVH has engaged, each for a different purpose.

Movement-Building to Win Policy Demands:
The National Campaign for Jobs and Income Support

In 2002, the welfare program that went into effect in 1996 would be coming up for reauthorization in the U.S. Congress. Organizations would have an opportunity to try to change key components of this program and to address other anti-poverty issues. In 2000, the Center for Community Change, a national advocacy organization based in Washington, D.C., initiated a series of meetings among independent community power-building organizations as well as community organizing networks to discuss the possibility of coordinating to take advantage of this opportunity both to change policy and build their power.

After several meetings, the organizations formed the National Campaign for Jobs and Income Support. Scores of local and statewide organizations, including Community Voices Heard, developed and pursued a common policy agenda. Over the next three years, the organizations conducted joint strategizing in conference calls and national meetings and engaged in joint leadership training and actions. CVH had expanded opportunities for leader and staff development and political education as well as to move policy demands. In addition to the mass action at President Bush's ranch described earlier in this chapter, CVH leaders took on leadership roles in an accountability session with more than two thousand people present on the Mall in Washington, D.C., testified at federal hearings about welfare reform, spoke at national press conferences, and met leaders and members of organizations from throughout the United States.

Movement-Building for Long-Term Social Change:
Grassroots Global Justice

Grassroots Global Justice is an alliance of grassroots organizations that gives participating organizations based in the United States a way to engage in the international movement for global justice. Founded in 2002, the alliance helps facilitate popular education and addresses issues such as immigration law. CVH members participate for these reasons and also because their participation makes a statement to the labor movement, allies, other community groups, and social movements throughout the world that CVH members care deeply about issues beyond their own neighborhoods and city.

LEADERSHIP DEVELOPMENT OPPORTUNITIES
IN MOVEMENT-BUILDING

- *Participate in decision making about organizational resources.* In an organizing committee or membership meeting where people are deciding whether or not to support actions that require limited resources, leaders play the role of offering political education, background, and context for the decision. As board or leadership team members, they directly decide about more resource-intense work. Leaders can also help form or participate in a movement-building committee of leaders and members to decide what kind of movement work the organization engages in and to develop specific programs associated with movement-building.

- *Raise funds.* Because movement-building involves travel, it provides opportunities to build leadership skills by engaging in grassroots fundraising. Members have something concrete and exciting to ask friends and family members to help support.

- *Engage in systemic and large-scale strategizing.* Leaders in an independent local organization rarely, if ever, have the opportunity to develop strategies and think about shifting power beyond their city, state, or region. Participating in movement-building work provides leaders as well as staff with opportunities to strategize about national power with other organizers and leaders from around the country. They learn about national trends, different political analyses, and how national strategies, actions, and tactics differ from local ones.

- *Deepen political understanding.* Gain opportunities for political education, both formally through campaigns and actions and informally through travel and relationships with leaders in other places, confronting other issues.

CHALLENGES
IN MOVEMENT-BUILDING

"We barely have enough money for our core work. How can we afford to send people to other countries and national meetings?" Although you can develop leaders by having them raise money for travel, it can be hard to find funding to pay for staff to devote time to activities that do not move your work forward in ways that are

as measurable as your campaigns. You can address this challenge by assessing when the organization will have some down time, either during or between campaigns. Staff who are funded for their work on campaigns can use this down time for movement-building. In addition, during your yearly budget planning you can assess where you might have untapped funds that you can use for movement work. In some cases, you are able to access the funds that movement-building organizations raise to help offset the travel costs of local leaders. If someone from your organization wants to attend a conference, you may be able to cover the costs by offering to conduct a workshop at the event and having the conference planners foot the bill.

"Some of our members, especially the newer ones, have more conservative positions on issues other than the ones we work on." Even when members have solidarity on the problems and issues that bring them together in a campaign, on other issues—from immigration to war and the military or gay, lesbian, and transgender rights—members and leaders of grassroots organizations can foster a full range of opinions. Members may not always agree on whether or how the organization should expend resources on addressing broader concerns, which can cause division.

Giving people facts and talking about the impact of social policy helps them to think more openly. Bring in speakers, show documentaries, travel to other places, and encourage dialogue. If something becomes too divisive, you can use your organization's mission statement and operating principles to help guide a discussion of how the organization should address it. Sometimes you need to consider if the only leaders who are bringing larger issues to the organization are the more experienced ones who have gained political savvy. Is there enough room for newer people to get involved and develop during the course of their participation in the organization? Do you need to incorporate more political education into your daily campaigns?

ESSENTIAL ELEMENTS
FOR EFFECTIVE MOVEMENT-BUILDING

☑ *Complement the core campaigns.* You don't prioritize movement-building over your core campaign work. Participating in movement activities only builds your power if you continue to develop a base of constituents around their direct concerns.

☑ *Establish goals and objectives.* You get involved in movement-building activities for specific reasons that move your work forward, such as political education, leadership development, or relationship building. These reasons may be different from the ones determining campaigns, but they are still necessary to clarify so that you can evaluate your movement building.

☑ *Take advantage of political education opportunities.* Movement-building offers a range of creative, exciting ways to do hands-on education with members about the politics that affect their communities and beyond.

☑ *Develop a broad base of members and leaders.* Engage the entire base in movement-building, not just a few select leaders.

☑ *Watch your resources.* Make sure you calculate the real costs of overhead and staff time, not just travel to meetings. Use any opportunities to develop leaders by getting them to do grassroots fundraising that helps build the movement.

Exercise 15.1
Globalization Limbo

(Used by permission of Community Voices Heard)

You can use the following exercise to get people thinking about how globalization directly affects their lives. It makes a good warm-up or transitional exercise or an entrée into deeper conversation about global issues. This exercise also pairs well with a reading, film, and discussion. For example, you can use a profile of a worker in another country, the story of a labor organizing campaign, or something similar to guide participants in deeper discussion and analysis.

Time: 15 to 30 minutes.

Materials: Wages Around the World Handout (see below). Limbo stick.

Roles: Facilitator. Limbo stick holders.

Room set-up: Enough room for participants to stand around limbo stick and do the limbo.

- Facilitator asks people to find a partner and look at one another's clothing labels to see where the clothing was made. They are likely to see that their clothing was made all over the globe.

- Facilitator distributes "Wages Around the World" handout listing wage levels around the globe or writes the wage levels on a chart.

- Two participants loosely hold the ends of a "limbo stick," a long, narrow stick such as a broomstick. As each participant reports back where his or her clothing was made, the stick holders hold it parallel to the floor, at a height that represents the wage level of that country, with all of the levels being relatively low. For example, Malaysia, at one dollar, might be at waist level, and Bangladesh at nine to twenty cents might be at knee level. The participant then tries to limbo under the stick and come out on the other side without hitting the stick or falling on the floor. The point is to create a visual image of how precarious it is for workers trying to survive on these wages.

- Facilitator guides a discussion asking open, pointed questions, depending on the goals of the workshop. For example: What does it mean when the things we wear are made in other countries? What does it mean when we pay $20 for a shirt that someone earned a few cents to produce? Who profits from this situation? What policies perpetuate this situation? What effect does this kind of trade have on jobs and wages in our community?

Exercise 15.1
Globalization Limbo, Cont'd

Wages Around the World

The following are approximate hourly wages, as reported to the National Labor Committee (www.nlcnet.org) by workers in these countries. Keep in mind that wage levels change frequently, and those presented here are approximate. You can contact the National Labor Committee for up-to-date information.

United States: $8.42

Bangladesh: $.09 to $.20

Burma: $.04

China: $.23

Colombia: $.70 to $.80

Dominican Republic: $.69

El Salvador: $.59

Guatemala: $.37 to $.50

Haiti: $.30

Honduras: $.43

India: $.20 to $.30

Indonesia: $.10

Malaysia: $1.00

Mexico: $.50 to $.54

Nicaragua: $.23

Pakistan: $.20 to $.26

Peru: $.90

Philippines: $.58 to $.76

Romania: $.24

Sri Lanka: $.40

Thailand: $.78

CONCLUSION: PUTTING YOUR PRINCIPLES INTO PRACTICE

Across the United States, community power-building organizations are making a difference. Their accomplishments include getting developers to provide housing and jobs in communities they develop, forcing the clean-up of environmentally denigrated communities, creating green belts and open space preservation laws, and winning improvements in the way the government meets the needs of constituents—from public school students to seniors. Many of these organizations move beyond issue campaigns to include political education of their members and participation in the electoral arena—turning targeted, often disenfranchised voters out to the polls. They are also forming state, regional, and national alliances. Moreover, many organizations are collaborating with others to address problems that manifest locally but have global justice connections.

Throughout this book, we describe the process for running campaigns and building organizations that are part of this exciting, transformative, and successful work. In this chapter we review ways to sustain your organization and we provide suggestions for people who want to engage in social justice work for a lifetime.

RUNNING A WINNING CAMPAIGN, BUILDING A POWERFUL ORGANIZATION

In this book, we have laid out the following key principles for running successful community power-building organizations:

- Build a base of members: more people means more power.
- Get members to understand what organizing is: action fosters commitment.

- Develop members to be leaders: leaders learn by doing.

- Implement strategic campaigns: campaigns deliver wins.

- Engage members in the social justice movement: neutrality is not an option.

Here we summarize some of the main points related to these principles and make suggestions for being effective and troubleshooting problems in various areas.

Setting recruitment goals and evaluating numbers to build a large base for power. Setting realistic goals for the number of people you want to recruit, and then evaluating the numbers of people you actually recruit, ensures that you bring more people into the organization. Generally, you check new organizers daily or weekly and more experienced organizers weekly or monthly. If you are not reaching recruitment goals, evaluate and adjust the rap you are using, the points of entry, the number of hours, and the times when you are doing new contact work. If things do not improve, have a more experienced organizer go out and assess if you have identified the right issue or see if the organizer needs some development.

Tracking active members to target for development. You track member activity using sign-in sheets and your database. You track total numbers for group activities as well as participation, including all meetings, leadership prep, and volunteer activities and actions. Once a month, you review the numbers overall as well as who specifically has been active. If tracking is not happening, evaluate sign-in practices and data-entry systems.

Developing leaders to run their own organization and help lead the movement. You constantly evaluate who leaders are, who is emerging, and what they need in order to develop. You do a monthly or bimonthly assessment of whether or not you have reached your goals. If you are not developing new leaders, look deeper than systems and consider the following:

- *Opportunities.* Do leaders have enough opportunities to actively build the organization: recruiting and mobilizing members, representing the organization to powerholders, and making core organizational decisions? Are the same leaders always dominating meetings and doing all the desirable tasks?

- *Training.* Are you providing enough training? Is the training participatory in nature and are you using a variety of formats to engage and reach everyone?

- *Priorities.* Are organizers letting other priorities take over? Leadership development can tax organizers' time, especially if they are focusing on other campaign tasks such as recruitment or mobilization. They may start relying on one or two strong leaders instead of developing new ones.

- *Leadership clique.* Has a clique formed, either intentionally or by chance? This can be very disempowering or daunting for new members.

Sometimes, to understand the problem, it helps to talk to people who were part of the organization and left or are not as active as they once were. Once you understand the problem, you develop a plan to address it with clear benchmarks and goals. It could include doing more one-on-ones to identify new leaders, investing in a leadership retreat so that old and new leaders can build relationships and get training, developing organizers to manage their time, or adjusting the campaign plan to include more actions in which people can take on leadership roles.

Conducting an annual evaluation to assess your progress on base building and campaigns. At the end of the year, you use the database to look at the numbers of who has been involved in the organization. Key things to look at include how many people you got contact information from, how many people came out to actions, how many people participated in organizational activities, and how many new leaders you developed. You also review how well you did on achieving your campaign goals and objectives.

Maximizing opportunities for member involvement and decision making. You engage as many constituents as possible in issue ID, using broad informational conversations, one-on-ones, small focus groups, and phone surveys. You can use these same approaches for involving members when the organization is engaging in strategic planning or organizational development. Campaign strategy development is also an excellent opportunity for participatory decision making. In addition, campaign structures such as organizing committee meetings, leadership, and tactical teams all ensure that decisions are rooted in the community. If people are not getting involved or fully participating, evaluate if you are providing enough real opportunities like these or if staff are taking too strong a role in actions and the organization.

Maintaining a board to ensure community control. One of the surest ways to guarantee an organization is member-led is to build a board or steering committee that has a vast majority of its members from the constituency. Organization members may elect the board or the board can identify and elect its own board members. A board meets regularly and has procedures and systems to ensure it functions properly and does its oversight job well.

Checking the organizational culture. Look at what the organizational culture communicates to members. Build a culture of transparency, openness, discussion, and debate. All the structures in the organization will not foster participatory decision making if its culture—the unsaid things, the environment, the way things are perceived to really happen—communicates a closed circle of decision makers.

Making sure action happens to build your base and power. You use your written campaign plan as an outline for moving your campaign forward and keeping actions on track, monitoring it at organizing committee meetings and campaign evaluations. Twice a year you directly assess how much action has been occurring and evaluate its impact with members, leaders, and staff.

Campaigns may develop without mass action, but this can affect your mobilization potential and limit your leadership development. To address this, sometimes you develop actions in order to build the organization, not to move the campaign forward. For example, you participate in a national march to keep your mobilization machine well-oiled and current. You work your lists, check in with your larger base, and ensure that organizers and leaders don't lose their ability to mobilize. You keep the base engaged in the campaign and invested in the organization, and show the larger community—allies, supporters, targets, and donors— that you are active and powerful.

Communicating your power. Understand your power and communicate it effectively. Winning campaigns and having strong leaders interact with allies, targets, and stakeholders communicates that you have a large base of people behind those wins and those leaders. Powerholders respond as much to the power they think you have as they do to your actual power. You can develop a public relations strategy to raise your organization's profile. Newsletters, Web pages, media coverage, special events, and briefings all make your work known. You conduct mobilizations with an eye not only to your target but also to any stakeholders or allies to whom you need to show your organization's power. Who aligns with you shows your power, so you invite key players to your events. You stage and organize actions at places where influential people will see them, such as a large march through the central business district or holding your accountability session in the hall of a church or union whose leaders you wish to experience your power in full swing.

Working in partnerships to expand your power. Follow-through and honesty matter. Meeting your numbers matters much more than saying you will produce a number that is beyond you. Don't become known as an organization that does things poorly. Powerful organizations are clear on their priorities, their objectives for the year ahead, what they will do, and what they won't do, and respect organizations that operate in these ways.

Engaging in the social justice movement to connect your community to bigger issues. The question of when to introduce the ideology of your organization to new members and recruits is complicated. We do not believe in litmus tests for membership, but rather that people understand early in their interaction with the organization that there is a set of principles and values you believe in. The following are some tools for helping your organization introduce ideology and values-based work into the organization and helping people understand that they are part of a movement for justice:

- *Operating principles.* Through a process that involves members, you develop a set of operating principles, a sense of your social change model, and a vision statement, along with your mission statement. The development of these documents based on clear, agreed-upon principles institutionalizes your ideology and values. You share these one-on-one with members, distribute them at meetings, and engage in discussions about them.
- *Political education.* You introduce clear analyses and critiques of the social infrastructure that creates problems in your community. You provide a space for members to state their views of why things are the way they are and then provide opportunity for dialogue and analysis.
- *A political community space.* By creating a political center, spatially or socially, that engages people formally within meetings and informally through side conversations, you build the ideological component of your organization. Everything from the set-up of the office to the way meetings are configured and how members use the space and for what factors into conveying your ideology.

BUILDING AN ORGANIZING PROJECT IN AN EXISTING ORGANIZATION

Building an organizing project in an existing organization is a possibility, but there are several factors to consider.

By involving people, getting constituents to meet with powerholders, and mobilizing people into action, any organization has the potential to mount a campaign. Developing an organizing project can be an effective way to win on a specific piece of legislation or to defeat a proposal, if that is the goal. However, if you want to shift power in a community, develop leaders, and have community members and constituents leading and running their own organizing campaigns, you will likely need to build a free-standing organizing project or organization. You might start out within an existing organization if there is clear understanding that power to make decisions lies with constituents. Eventually, however, this project, if successful, will need to spin off and become an independent organization.

If you decide to start an organizing project in an existing organization, make sure you get approval from the necessary people in the organization to engage in organizing. Approval includes a clear understanding, possibly in the form of a Memo of Understanding, of the parameters of the work, specifically, how much control members and leaders have over the project. (For more on Memos of Understanding, see Chapter Fourteen.) Then, be clear with leaders and members about what power they have and what power they do not have. (For more on organizing within existing organizations, see Resource E.)

APPLYING FOR LEGAL RECOGNITION OF YOUR ORGANIZATION

Whether you decide to incorporate as a nonprofit organization depends on your goals and fundraising strategy.

In the United States, organizations incorporated under Section 501(c)(3) of the Internal Revenue Code are tax-exempt. If you start a volunteer organization with no paid staff and no significant budget and fundraising, there is no reason for you to need tax-exempt status. If your project is part of an existing organization or if you will use a fiscal sponsor, you minimize the impact of having to deal with issues of nonprofit status. But if you are looking for some significant resources to hire staff and pay for other expenses, eventually you will have to deal with registering your organization with your state and the IRS.

You can apply for 501(c)(3) tax-exempt status if you are doing limited advocacy and lobbying (a rule of thumb is that less than 20 percent of your budget should be spent in indirect lobbying and less than 5 percent in direct lobbying; for definitions of these terms, see the Alliance for Justice Web site listed in Resource G). If you are incorporated as a 501(c)(3) organization people can donate to your organization and receive a tax deduction for their contribution, making it more likely they will give. Tax-exempt status also qualifies you for foundation and institutional support.

The other common type of nonprofit designation is as a 501(c)(4), which allows for more lobbying and advocacy. Although there are less strict rules governing political activity in this legal entity, it is more difficult to fund. Individual donations are not tax-deductible and foundations cannot fund this work. It relies mainly on membership dues, individual contributions, and funds from institutions like unions.

There are pros and cons about institutionalizing your work in either of these ways. There are even debates within the social justice movement as to whether institutional status for nonprofits has killed social change by making it part of the mainstream infrastructure. Although we support and actively seek out new forms of organizations, currently the 501(c)(3) structure is what is available to people who want to build organizations that raise tax-deductible dollars.

For additional information on how to apply for legal recognition, contact local nonprofit technical assistance providers. Your local United Way may have information about local groups offering free or low-cost legal services for the not-for-profit community. We include more about legal recognition in Resource F.

JOINING A NETWORK

Organizing networks sometimes recruit established or start-up organizations whose involvement will move their agenda forward. "Network" organizations are different from "independent" community organizations. A network is a specific kind of affiliation of organizing groups. In the Introduction, we provided more information about organizing networks, such as the Industrial Areas Foundation (IAF) and the Association of Community Organizations for Reform Now (ACORN).

Whether you view some of the characteristics of networks as pros or cons depends on your community and the goals of your organization. For example, some networks operate in a decentralized manner, while others have powerful central decision making that applies to some of the actions of their affiliates. Network organizations also have a specific model they implement, usually with limited variance from the basics. Therefore, by joining a network, you may give up some authority. You may have to be willing to negotiate and compromise on your key principles or strategies. You may have to work on an issue that is not core to your work that will take financial resources as well as staff and leadership time. There may be no guarantee that the members of your organization will have a seat at the negotiating table with powerholders. Sometimes a network may engage your organization for a tactical reason, because you have a large base in a key legislative district for example, and not really want to work together over the long haul. In this case, you are clear on what you want to get out of some short-term partnership and make sure you do not expend resources and time without really gaining anything.

However, networks can provide access to powerholders that your independent organization cannot gain. They provide opportunities for large-scale actions and movement-building as well as the ability to act on larger issues at local, regional, and national levels. Networks can provide opportunities for your members, leaders, and staff to interact with others from around the United States. They sometimes provide funding or access to funding. Some networks put a lot of time and resources into developing organizers, which is something that can be hard for independent organizations to do, as much as they would like to. Networks often run training institutes and offer good pay, benefits, and sabbaticals for long-time organizers.

If you consider joining a network, make sure you get clear answers to any questions that members, leaders, and staff have about how this will affect the organization. Engage members directly in the discussions with network representatives as early as possible. Establish who in your organization will ultimately make the decision—the board, for example, or a special task force of board, members, and staff. As in any other negotiation or decision, do your homework, engage members and leaders, examine all the implications, do a power analysis of how much leverage your organization actually has, and operate from your strengths.

HOW TO KEEP STAFF STRONG

Staff development, training, supervision, and mentoring are just as important as leadership development.

Staff work hard, put in long hours, and receive typically modest pay. For most staff in community power-building organizations, their work is more than just a job. But it is still their job. They deserve the same respect and benefits as any other workers. One of the weaknesses of the movement is that, while many people might take a job in organizing right out of college, most don't stay in the field for long. This attrition means a big loss of knowledge and skills. Just as an organizer needs strong leaders, leaders need a good, strong organizer.

All organizations need to address the basic needs of the people who work there. These are the same things we fight for in campaigns: a living wage, health care, and benefits. If organizations wish to sustain staff over long periods, they show appreciation. They accommodate people's interests, address their concerns, and implement sabbatical time to take a break, reflect, and have fun. They add a day off to a long weekend, encourage people to take their vacations, and try to provide a range of creative personnel policies and benefits.

It is up to the board or steering committee and the director of the organization to lead the way. If the director does not take vacations or agree to a salary increase, and if the board doesn't encourage it, the staff is likely to do the same. However, while a director may stay on for the long term, especially a founding director, other staff will eventually leave.

Make sure your organization provides good staff supervision and support. Daily check-ins, weekly meetings, and some longer sessions help to keep staff working productively and feeling supported. Give staff members the opportunity to develop their own workplans with feedback and direction from a supervisor. Supervisors periodically go out in the field with staff and observe their organizing meetings. Organizations with several staff members devote time to staff retreats and full-day staff meetings to address issues that can't be dealt with during the course of a one- or two-hour meeting.

Provide opportunities to develop new skills through access to trainings, workshops, and college courses. Give staff opportunities to exercise leadership. Senior staff can participate in meetings with donors and strategic partners. Midlevel staff can represent the organization in alliances, projects, or coalitions.. Taking on such responsibility not only relieves the senior staff person, it also builds the investment, skills, and experience of other staff people. Be open and clear about the opportunities staff members have to progress in the organization.

HOW ORGANIZERS AND LEADERS CAN SUSTAIN THEMSELVES

For those who want to engage in social justice work for a lifetime, the following are some suggestions based on what we've experienced ourselves. Although much of this advice applies to staff who are spending most of their time organizing, it also applies to leaders who volunteer tremendous amounts of time.

Work when you have to, not when you don't. The nature of organizing does not fit a typical forty-hour work week. At times, the hours for a staff organizer go well beyond this structure. So when you do not need to be working, take some time off. The same is true for leaders.

Take vacations and breaks. Your work suffers if you do not take vacations. Sometimes this advice is easier said than done. We have found that it can be helpful to schedule time into your calendar at the beginning of the year or take the same time off every year so that you and the organization settle into a pattern. And although this solution cuts down on spontaneity, it helps to ensure that you take a break.

Don't sacrifice your family. Organizing often requires working long, sometimes unusual hours that can have an impact on family life. Develop family-friendly policies and a work environment where children of staff and leaders have space to do homework or play. Have roles for family members at celebrations and recognition events. If appropriate, allow staff to take children on weekend work trips and make sure that staff can attend to family members who need them. All this, however, does not change the long hours and days. When your work as an organizer or leader is having a negative effect on your family life, take a break or even a leave. When you want to come back, the movement will still be there.

Maintain a network of friends and activities outside of organizing. For an organizer, usually more than for a leader, when your network only involves other people in the movement and everyone you spend time with shares the same world view, your life can feel a little claustrophobic. You can find yourself talking about work when socializing. It can help you to get more out of your down time if you vary your networks of friends.

Read, write, and reflect. Take a break from the tasks of organizing to think about the process of organizing: What are you learning? What is working or not working? Organizers and leaders can try writing down thoughts and ideas in a notebook or journal. Also, reading about other campaigns, organizations, and history helps you to put your work into perspective and can give you ideas and inspiration.

Find a mentor and build a support team. Formal and informal mentoring relationships have been critical for the two of us in our development as organizers at all stages of our careers. Mentors can be, for example, more experienced staff (keeping in mind that mentoring is different than supervision), senior practitioners in the field, and those who have retired from full-time work. Find people who have a vested interest in you, not in the organization. Mentors can help you think about how to do your work better. Mentors and others can help you vent frustrations and talk things out. Schedule this support into your life, asking people to play this role.

Take care of yourself. Ultimately, all of the leadership development activities or personnel policies in the world will only sustain you if you take care of yourself and seek out the support and community you need to stay healthy—physically, emotionally, and, if you choose, spiritually.

Enjoy your work and have fun. Organizing is fun and rewarding. Our organizing experiences have included many incredible and energizing moments, from filling city hall with four hundred welfare mothers who could stop a public hearing in its tracks to seeing someone we developed as a leader hold a powerful politician accountable to the community.

Celebrate your work and accomplishments and mourn your losses collectively. While the issues you address are serious, sometimes even matters of life and death, remember that members of every social movement have celebrated, sung, danced, and laughed.

WHY WE NEED INDEPENDENT COMMUNITY POWER-BUILDING ORGANIZATIONS

Independent community power-building organizations often do the work that others avoid. They address the toughest issues, in the toughest neighborhoods, and with the constituencies that are toughest to organize. Immigrants, welfare recipients, homeless people, and youth are just some of those who make up the constituencies of community power-building groups. These constituencies are hard to organize. Immigrants may have language barriers, homeless people have few personal resources, and young people may be more transient.

Independents bring new voices and perspectives to the movement. Without large hierarchies and many-leveled structures, they can move more quickly on an issue. They help to bring strong voices from local communities into national movements and organizations.

We believe that independent organizations are strategically moving the political debate and the politics of the United States toward a more radical redistribution of power. With their investment in political education, leadership development, and democratic decision making, independents can take positions that are riskier, challenge the status quo, and are more controversial than those of groups that have staked out the center of the political sphere. Independent groups not only widen the debate but can strategically move other organizations to take on campaigns and issues they might first believe they have no chance of winning.

Now is the time to use the tools we lay out in this book. Go out, talk to people, and get them involved. Bring them together to strategize how they will address the issues they care about. Train them to be leaders. Take your work to the streets, city hall, Congress, and corporate boardrooms. Build the power of your community, your organization, and the larger social movement. We know that people will participate when they have the opportunity. You can make a difference. Take it on!

Supporting the Work of Organizing

RESOURCE A: ORGANIZING LINGO

The following terms and concepts are commonly used in organizing for community power:

Accountability session. A mass meeting in which constituents publicly ask yes or no questions of a person with power so that they can later hold her or him accountable to the answers.

Agitation. The skill of asking questions or suggesting ideas in order to get people to think deeply and critically about something.

Base. The members of an organization who are directly affected by the issues the organization addresses.

Base-building. The core strategy for building community power. Engaging people in a campaign or organization and developing their ability to collectively address their issues.

Call to action. A quick, concrete act someone can take while an organizer is recruiting him or her, such as writing a letter on the spot, calling a local legislator on a cell phone, completing a survey, or signing a petition to a landlord. A call to action helps meet the objectives of a campaign and serves as an engagement tool.

Campaign. A planned series of strategies and actions designed to achieve clear goals and objectives.

Campaign action. A public showing of an organization's power.

Campaign demand. The concrete, measurable request that a campaign makes of an individual person.

Campaign message. A two- to three-sentence statement that states the problem, its solution, and the way to implement the solution.

Campaign objectives. The steps an organization needs to take in order to get what it demands.

Collective action. The acts of constituents who are building an organization and taking public, political action together aimed at decision makers.

Commit calls. The series of calls, usually three, that an organizer makes to ensure someone comes out and does what he said he would do.

Community power-building organization. An organization in which constituents make decisions and take leadership to build their collective political power.

Constituents. People who are directly affected by the problems an organization addresses.

Cutting an issue. Changing the approach to an issue, talking about it differently with constituents.

Debriefing. A conversation in which organizers, leaders, or members evaluate an activity.

Direct action. Planned, collective activities in which you confront, challenge, and negotiate with a person who can give your community what it wants.

External action. An action, such as a march, that moves members to exercise their power publicly.

Ideology. A worldview, and how to realize it.

Internal action. An action, such as a survey project, that engages members in order to test commitment to an issue or to train them to conduct larger public actions.

Issue. A solution to a community problem; what an organization focuses on in a campaign.

Landscaping. The process of developing a full picture of an issue.

Leaders. Constituents who are core organizational decision makers.

Leadership team. The group of people at the core of the organization who make key decisions about campaigns and the development of the organization.

Members. Constituents who are in relationship with an organization, constituting its base. A member has taken a step defined by the organization that indicates he or she is part of the organization.

Mobilization. The process of moving people to action.

Move. What people do when they are uncomfortable to make the discomfort go away.

Movement-building. Ways in which organizations or campaigns use their resources to engage in activities that are not solely connected to winnable campaigns or the self-interest of community members, but support other communities or pursue a larger vision for social justice.

Negotiation. The process of determining a compromise between different positions.

One-on-one meeting. An "agenda-less" meeting that helps an organizer to understand a person's self-interest, motivations, and leadership potential.

Organizing committee. The group of members who oversee the development and implementation of a campaign plan.

Political education. A form of training about issues, social movements, and history that organizations use to develop and communicate an ideology or worldview.

Popular education. A form of interactive adult education that incorporates what people already know from their direct experiences, emphasizing reflection as an essential learning tool.

Power. The ability to act and to make things happen.

Power analysis. A systematic way of looking at who is with you, who is against you, and how important their support or opposition is to the campaign.

Powerholders. Decision makers, such as elected officials or CEOs, who are the targets of community power-building campaigns.

Public relationships. Goal-oriented, rather than personal, relationships among members and between members and staff of an organization.

Self-interest. What someone needs to get out of the time and energy she or he puts into being involved.

Stakeholders. Other individuals or organizations that want something specific connected with the issue an organization is fighting for.

Strategy. An overall approach to achieving objectives. In a campaign, strategy is the way or ways that a community power-building organization uses to exercise its power to win what it wants.

Target (primary). The person who can give an organization what it wants from a campaign.

Target (secondary). A person an organization has the power to move and who can get the primary target to do what the organization wants.

RESOURCE B:
RAISING MONEY
FOR ORGANIZING

You need money to sustain organizing. All of the organization's leaders and staff either directly raise funds or actively support the fundraising efforts of the campaign or organization. This resource provides a brief overview of how to engage in fundraising. We recommend you consult other texts that explore this critically important topic in much greater depth. Two very helpful books are *Fundraising for Social Change, Fifth Edition,* by Kim Klein, published in 2006, and *The Accidental Fundraiser,* by Stephanie Roth and Mimi Ho, published in 2005.

GETTING STARTED

To do fundraising for a community nonprofit, keep the following key principles in mind:

Integrate your plans. Effective organizations and movements integrate fundraising into their work. Like a campaign, fundraising is strategic. You include plans for fundraising in your overall organization and campaign planning goals. For example, a large action that moves one thousand people will require not only the time of staff and members but also cash to rent sound equipment, pay for printing, and hire buses.

Remember that everyone is a fundraiser. In a community power-building organization, everyone is a fundraiser. You train both organizers and leaders to prepare and understand budgets, pitch funding needs to donors, and in some cases, write basic fundraising materials.

Remind yourself that everyone is a donor. Everyone can potentially give money to support your work: members, staff people, and your full range of supporters, allies, and volunteers.

Cultivate relationships. A good database tracking system helps you to track and identify the relationships you have with foundation funders and major donors that you need to develop and nurture. You take the time to meet with donors and the staff of foundations. You inform them of upcoming actions and activities, invite them to events, and thank them for their contributions. You move individual people to become major donors and then move them from writing a check, for instance, to holding a house party to get others to support the organization or campaign.

Identify what you need money for. Are you raising money to hire a first paid staff member or funds to develop a new campaign within an organization that already has staff? Do you need to cover the cost of buses to get members to a specific action or support the operations of the organization over the coming year? People (and foundations) like to see where their money is going.

Figure out how much money you need to raise. Develop a budget that shows how much money you need to raise and how you will use it. The core staff and board members develop an organizational budget that includes rent, staff costs, and other operational expenses. In addition, in order to approach specific funding sources, you develop project budgets to cover, for example, buses for an action or printing of leaflets or flyers. You do some research about both your costs and potential sources of revenue so that members and leaders can make informed decisions about spending priorities and so you can present knowledgeable, accurate estimates to potential funders. See Tool B.1 at the end of this resource for a sample budget format.

Identify potential sources of funding. It is important to have a variety of funding sources so that you do not depend on any one type of funder for the bulk of your income. Your mission, programs, and campaigns drive your fundraising and determine who you go to and how, not the other way around.

The following describes some of the main types of funding sources:

- *Grassroots support.* These are the small donations, up to about $500 (or whatever you decide to define as a major gift), that you get from individuals in a variety of ways, including direct mail, special events, canvassing, and membership dues.

Through grassroots fundraising you build lists of people you can keep going back to and who you can develop into larger donors.

- *Major donors.* Major donors are people who give what's considered a major gift, however an organization defines that amount. It takes organizational commitment to build a broad base of donors who feel a connection to the organization or to someone in the organization. Similar to the membership development process, you identify potential donors and cultivate them, then move them to give more.

- *Foundation support.* Foundations are organizations set up by wealthy individuals or corporations to give money to a variety of causes. Foundations range from small organizations controlled by members of a family to larger, international institutions such as the Ford Foundation or the Rockefeller Foundation. One way to learn about foundations is by talking with others in your field or local area. You can also look at the Web sites or materials of organizations similar to yours to see who funds them. You can then go to the Web sites for those foundations and look at their guidelines, their sample grants, and how they say to approach them. You approach foundations that have expressed interest in the problem or issue you address, and you do so in the ways they require. Examples of foundations that support community organizing are the Jewish Fund for Justice and the national network of local foundations in the Funding Exchange.

- *Government contracts and grants.* Government funding includes contracts with local, state, and federal agencies as well as small grants programs and grants from elected representatives. In an example of a contract, an agency wants community groups to provide after-school programs for youth or information about community health. It issues a formal Request for Proposals (RFP) that provides details about what it needs, the kinds of organizations it wants to contract with, and how to apply for consideration. Groups that challenge traditional forms of power frequently do not fit the guidelines of these RFPs or they choose to not seek government funds to avoid having to moderate their activities for political reasons. The pros and cons of government funding are matters for every organization to consider for itself.

- *Institutional giving.* Religious groups and unions sometimes give money to organizations engaged in social justice work. The money comes from member dues or contributions. Some institutions have a formal process for making grants; others are more informal. For unions, the leadership of the union, specifically the executive committee or the president, must sign off on the request. Examples of institutional funders include the Campaign for Human Development, which is the fund of the Roman Catholic Bishops, and the Presbyterian Self-Development of People Fund.

• *Corporate giving.* Corporations sometimes directly distribute funds, usually within the communities where they do business or where their employees live. Banks often give some portion of their funds to their community. They tend to focus on economic development and housing, whereas corporations generally have broader interests.

• *In-kind donations.* Donations of services and materials, called *in-kind* donations, help sustain an organization, especially when it starts out or if it has no staff. Volunteers, for instance, directly give their time—everything from supporters who come in to do phone calls to pro bono consultants who assist with legal services, graphic design, technology, and other specialized skills. Other in-kind services include office space, printing, phones, or meeting space. For more established organizations, in-kind donations can help meet a substantial portion of a budget. Remember, if people give their time, they are committed to the organization. You ask them to donate money as well, as one more way to show their support and because giving time alone cannot meet the expenses of the organization.

Develop a fundraising plan. A fundraising plan helps you stay on track and helps you to evaluate your success. A basic fundraising plan includes your overall budget and a "pitch," which is a two- or three-sentence statement of what you will do with the money you raise. A fundraising plan also includes a breakdown of who you intend to ask for support. You list who the sources are, how much you are requesting from each of them, the likelihood of getting support, and what you need in order to approach each one. For example, for one potential funder you may need a two-page letter on your letterhead, for another you may need a ten-page proposal. For members and individual donors, you will need letters, newsletters, and other materials, such as brochures and reply cards. In addition to this overall plan, sometimes you create a simple plan to meet short-term goals, such as raising money for buses and lunch for a lobby day in two weeks.

Establish tracking systems. Similar to the way you track the deepening relationship of members in your organization, you track the money that supporters give to your organization. You use a good database or fundraising software to track when someone gives, how much, for what, and how. These records are important for tax-deduction purposes as well as for identifying when to ask someone for a larger financial gift.

Develop an effective pitch. A pitch is a two- to three-minute message that clearly states the problem, what you seek to do to resolve the problem, why your organization is the one to address it, and how much money you seek. Although the specific contents of a pitch vary depending on the funding source, you essentially deliver the same message whether you are at a door with an individual, speaking to a supporter at an event, or calling a foundation. There is a difference between pitching something in a particular way to connect it to someone's interests or an organization's guidelines and changing the focus of your work to fit into someone else's ideas about social change.

A pitch is clear, it communicates the problem, the solution, and how the person can help. A pitch is not conversational, like a rap. In a pitch you are selling. You are firm and confident.

WRITING A FUNDRAISING LETTER

You often make an initial approach to a potential major donor or a foundation with a two- or three-page fundraising letter. In writing a fundraising letter, you also lay out the components you will need to develop further for foundation proposals. The following are the components of a fundraising letter, with illustrations from a letter CVH developed to ask a union for support of an action:

Overview of funding request. This paragraph states your pitch:

> Community Voices Heard (CVH) is seeking funding to stop welfare cuts proposed by the governor in this year's budget. These cuts will hurt hundreds of thousands of low-income families by seriously diminishing their ability to purchase the basic supplies they need to live on, including food. CVH is organizing an emergency day of action to raise public awareness about these cuts. We are bringing five hundred low-income mothers to Albany to meet with their legislators to tell them to reject the governor's budget. CVH is raising a total of $15,000 to cover the cost of ten buses as well as breakfast and lunch for these five hundred people. We are seeking $5,000 in funding from the United Federation of Teachers to bring families connected with schools.

Organizational background and accomplishments. This short statement provides information about the organization's history, mission, and most significant recent accomplishments:

> CVH is an organization of more than ten thousand low-income members—mostly women on public assistance. We were founded in 1994 by a group of low-income mothers who wanted to increase the participation of low-income women in the policy-making decisions that affect their lives. Since that time we have won more than fifteen thousand jobs for people on welfare, improved local and state welfare-to-work programs, and educated more than 25,000 people about their rights to anti-poverty programs.

Problem statement. This paragraph states what the problem is, why it is important, and why the potential supporter should care about it. For instance, if a letter is going to a union, it describes how the problem affects labor and its members. If it is going to an individual donor, it focuses on how the problem affects the community. This part of the CVH letter to the union reads as follows:

> The governor's proposed budget cuts will harm more than one million individuals in New York state. Proposed cuts would mean that an average family of four would receive almost $40 dollars a month less in cash benefits. These benefits help to cover the costs of food and other essential household goods, such as detergent and Band-Aids. Studies have shown that low-income families on welfare already are cutting back on food significantly enough to affect children's performance in schools. A further cut in benefits will only exacerbate this problem. Children who are hungry end up being harder to teach and can cause disruption in classes, something that we know the United Federation of Teachers is concerned about.

Proposed activities. This section tells what the organization will do to address the problem:

> Our day of action on February 25 will include the following components: a march from a local church to the state capitol, a mass meeting with the chair of the state assembly committee on children and

families, and legislative meetings with more than fifty legislators from across the state. The goal of these actions is to educate the legislature and the general public about the impact of these cuts, to get media coverage of how the proposed cuts affect low-income families, and to get the chair of the committee to pledge to fight the proposals in a public forum.

Conclusion. This paragraph sums up the goals and impact of what you are planning, the amount of money you are seeking from the donor, the total budget, the contact person at your organization, and the timeline. Always include a thank you and a statement that you will follow up on the letter with a phone call:

> Support from the United Federation of Teachers will help us reach our goal of bringing five hundred low-income people to the capitol to stop these cuts. We have raised $6,000 from the city's municipal union and its affiliates, $2,500 from St. James Church, and $1,500 in bus seat sales. With $10,000 of the $15,000 needed already in hand, $5,000 in support from you will help us reach our goal. We are aware that your executive committee meets next week and would appreciate it if you would consider our request at that time. Please feel free to contact our office manager or myself if you have any questions about our request before the meeting. We will follow up with you in a few days to make sure you have everything you need.

In addition to a fundraising letter, you also prepare the following:

Budget. Have a budget you can print up or adapt for specific potential funders that clearly lays out what their funding will pay for, how in-kind contributions are helping with the project, how much money you have already raised, and pending sources.

Organizational papers. Depending on the funder, you may need to provide 501(c)(3) determination papers (or a letter from a fiscal sponsor), income and expense forms for the year, a formal audit or an annual report, and a list of board members.

Supporting materials. Other materials can be included that offer some background information or illustrations of your work, such as news clippings, a flyer about the upcoming event or action, or a current newsletter.

After you send a fundraising letter or proposal for funding, you take the following steps:

Follow up with a phone call. A few days after sending the letter, call to make sure they actually got the request. If you were instructed to e-mail or fax your request (although generally not a favored approach), call that day and mail a hard copy as well, unless you are instructed not to.

Provide updates. If something happens on the issue or in your organization that could have an effect on the funding decision, send a note or call. Provide only one or two significant updates.

Send a thank you. If the funder or donor gives you money, send a thank you note immediately. If you have a relationship with the person, call to thank her or him for the gift as well. Sending an e-mail alone to say thank you is not appropriate. The thank you letter should include the gift date and amount, that it is tax-deductible to the extent allowable by law, and that no goods or services were provided in exchange for the contribution.

If they turn you down, ask again. Just because someone says no to one request doesn't mean the donor will never give. Probe when people say no to find out why they have declined to fund you. Is it because of a lack of agreement with your mission, a lack of interest in the current need, or because of an inability to give right now, due to lack of available funds or the timing of your request?

Report back. If you did get funded for a specific activity, let the donor know how it went. With foundations or other institutional funders, you will most likely have to submit a formal report.

Communicate on a regular basis to all of your donors about how their contributions made a difference. Newsletters, e-mails, phone calls, or even personal visits to larger donors are all appropriate forms of communication. When you celebrate campaign wins, invite your donor base to the party. Don't assume people will just know their money made a difference. Tell them and thank them for their support.

Ask for more. As you develop relationships, especially with major donors, ask them to repeat their gift and, over time, to give more.

Tool B.1
Sample Budget Format

The following chart shows a sample budget format for presenting requests for funding.

Organizational or Campaign Goals:

Budget Period: (begin date–end date)

Organizational Resources Needed	Budget Amount	Committed	To Be Raised
Staffing expenses			
Position: (Salary)			
Position: (Salary)			
Total salaries			
Total benefits			
Office expenses			
Rent			
Phones			
Technology (computers, programs, consultants, other)			
Printing			
Supplies			
Mailing			
Other			
Campaign activities			
Meetings			
Training/leadership development			
Travel/mobilizations			
Actions			
Administration/overhead			
Total expenses			

RESOURCE C:
POWER IN THE VOTING BOOTH
Electoral Organizing

As more community organizations engage in electoral organizing, they are gaining influence in the political landscape. Conservatives have been building power in the voting booth over the course of many election cycles. They have done it by using basic community organizing principles. Progressive organizations have been doing so in more focused and strategic ways since the 2000 presidential election exposed deep flaws in the U.S. election system and raised the national consciousness that voting makes a difference.

In this section, we focus on how to decide whether or not to engage in electoral organizing. There are many other aspects of electoral organizing that are beyond the scope of this book. For example, although we review a sample voter contact plan, we do not provide information about how to do all of the tasks necessary for effective electoral organizing or introduce all of the possibilities in electoral organizing. We do not cover the historical reasons that different constituencies do or do not vote in large numbers or the ways in which voting policies disenfranchise particular groups. If you are interested in doing electoral organizing, we encourage you to explore these topics further.

If your organization is incorporated as a nonprofit, there are strict rules governing how you can operate in the electoral field. Before you engage in electoral organizing, it is absolutely necessary for you to contact a legal advisor in your state to understand what you legally can and cannot do. There is a lot that you can do that is legal and will have an impact. But failure to comply with the law could devastate your organization.

WHAT ELECTORAL ORGANIZING IS AND IS NOT

In electoral organizing you build a base of voters to increase voting in areas with historically low turnout and to raise the visibility of your issues. Electoral organizing in a nonprofit organization is a nonpartisan activity. It focuses on increasing turnout of everyone in an election district, such as a state senate district, or within a specific constituency, such as lesbian and gay voters. Organizations incorporated as 501(c)(3) cannot do partisan organizing, where you move people to vote on specific candidates.

Electoral organizing can include voter registration, but only if you connect it to strategically mobilizing voters in the ways we describe later in this resource. Voter registration as a stand-alone project, not connected to mobilization, is not electoral organizing.

In fact, you have the biggest impact by targeting people who are already registered to vote but do so infrequently. It is easier to identify these people, contact them, move them to the polls, and prove that you got them to vote. When you move a base with a historically low turnout, such as low-income people of color, you are likely to be the only organization out there doing so. Unions, political parties, and candidates are not trying to shift power—they concentrate on people who vote frequently.

ELECTORAL ORGANIZING ACTIVITIES

In electoral organizing, you focus on a number of interrelated activities. Like all of your organizing, you do effective electoral organizing through face-to-face live contact and leadership development. You train community people to build voter mobilization networks and their own voting institutions. The following are electoral organizing activities:

- *Voter contact.* Based on voter files from your local board of elections that will provide information such as name, address, and voting history, you contact people in a specific target area or constituency who are registered to vote. During the contact you get additional information, including phone number and what issues they care about. With this information you develop a voter database.

- *Voter registration.* You register people who are not registered to vote. You usually focus on people who have never voted before, particularly young people and new citizens.

- *Voter identification (Voter ID).* You identify the position people have on an issue or a candidate, record their positions in the database (for, against, don't know), and build a list of voters who support your organization's position so you can contact them again and mobilize them to vote.
- *Voter mobilization (Get out the vote: GOTV).* You get the voters who pledge to support your candidate or position out to the polls on election day (or during the voting period in states that hold multiday elections).
- *Voter education.* You educate people about the electoral system and the role that elected officials play in their lives.

WHY DO ELECTORAL ORGANIZING

One purpose of doing electoral organizing is to shift power, strategically and over the long term. You identify and move specific groups of people who have not participated in the past and who support your issues. You do so in ways that are strategic and focus on goals. You can develop a stand-alone electoral project—for example CVH built a voter base in East Harlem to build power with respect to a new city council person in that district. Electoral organizing also offers opportunities for collaboration. For example, CVH helped to form a national alliance called the PUSHBACK Network to increase the power of low-income, working-class people and people of color.

Another purpose of electoral organizing is to wield a base of voters who identify with an organization and its issues. Your organization increases its ability to pressure specific elected officials to deliver. For instance, CVH built a base of five thousand voters who identify themselves as "economic justice voters." They have agreed with CVH's policy agenda on job creation, wages, and training for workers and the unemployed.

A third purpose is to influence an election. Your organization, on its own or with partners, organizes to achieve a specific goal, such as defeating a ballot initiative. (In some states, only a group incorporated as 501(c)(4) can do this work.)

Finally, electoral organizing moves candidates to address issues. Your organization uses an election to get candidates to support the issues you are pursuing in your campaigns. Although if you are a 501(c)(3) organization you cannot come out for or against a specific candidate, you can educate voters on candidates' positions on issues through the media, candidate forums, and voter education. For example, CVH and NY ACORN held an accountability session with candidates for the Democratic nomination for mayor to move them to support the demands of the organization's issue campaigns: jobs for welfare recipients and workers' rights for people in workfare.

DECIDING WHETHER TO DO ELECTORAL ORGANIZING

In considering whether to undertake electoral organizing, you consider a number of key questions and subquestions:

- Will electoral organizing help us achieve our organizational and campaign goals?

  Are the targets of our campaigns elected or not (if you are considering partisan organizing)?

  Will changing who is in office improve our ability to win our campaigns (if you are considering partisan organizing)?

  Are conservative ballot initiatives undercutting our power? Will presenting a ballot initiative help us reach our goals?

  Will we reach our long-term goals only if we have more political power?

  Do we know exactly which voters we need to mobilize? Is it by geographic area or by issue? (By issue is harder to pin down.)

- Can we use our current organization or do we need to set up another structure?

  If we are 501(c)(3) nonprofit, do we need to establish a structure under which we can be partisan, or can we operate under our current organization and do nonpartisan activity?

- Do people in our organization want to do electoral organizing?

  Do our members and leaders see building electoral power as critical for our work?

  Are they willing to expend resources—time, money, and staff—to do electoral organizing?

Are they willing to deal with being more a part of the system and support candidates or ballot initiatives?

Are they willing to focus almost exclusively on electoral organizing in the eight to ten weeks before elections?

- Do we have the capacity to run an electoral project? Will it enhance our core campaign work or detract from it?

Does our organization have the staff and leaders with the skills and drive to engage in electoral organizing?

Can we work with numbers: numbers of people we need to contact to vote, the number of times we have to contact them, and proving the number of people we turned out? Can we get the volunteers and develop the systems to do these tasks effectively?

Will our current campaigns suffer or benefit from engaging in an electoral campaign in terms of staff, leaders, and funds?

What resources and assets do we need for electoral organizing? How will we get them?

Do we have the technology to develop internal systems for tracking voters, producing voter lists, and managing large quantities of data?

Do we have the research skills to work with registrars and the board of elections?

Can we assess our impact?

Are there other organizations with specific expertise that we should partner with?

- What is the political landscape in our community?

What are voter participation rates in our area? If more people vote, will it make a difference on our issues?

Who else is engaged in electoral organizing? How active are the political parties in contacting voters and engaging in door-to-door voter contact work? Will we get lost in the field because so many other people are talking to voters? Will people understand how we are different or will we be the only group out there?

What are the opportunities for collaborations, partnerships, and sharing resources?

What are our clear and realistic goals?

What is our three-year plan: objectives, goals, benchmarks that build off of one another?

What are some limited, short-term projects we can do to build our capacity and expertise?

HOW TO ENGAGE PEOPLE

Doorknocking and asking people to pledge to vote with your organization is your first and most effective approach. Going to the doors in an electoral project is different from going to the doors when organizing in an issue campaign. In electoral organizing, your rap asks people to participate in something that society sanctions and celebrates. Your job may be easier because people know what you are talking about. At the same time, you ask them to understand your role in an unfamiliar way. You are not just showing up a few weeks before the election with a flyer bearing a candidate's photo. You are talking to them early in the election cycle, asking them to make a pledge to your organization to vote, telling them they will hear from you again, and trying to identify if they will volunteer to speak with others in their community.

Here are some tips for access and acceptance at the doors:

• *Use a community survey.* Surveys are tools that open up conversations about what elected officials can and cannot do.

• *Provide a service.* You bring information that helps people to understand why they should vote, where candidates stand, what their powers are, how to register, where to go to vote, and when.

• *Talk up your organizational accomplishments.* Tell people about your track record in the community and what your organization plans to do in the future. Communicate that your organization is there throughout the year, not just during election season.

• *Empower people in a process they feel is disempowering.* You don't argue with people about whether or not voting matters. You talk with them about their chance to have an effect on candidates who are not addressing the issues in their community.

THE VOTER RAP: GETTING A VOTER PLEDGE

Here we describe the five components of a voter rap.

- Invitation to collective action

  Pledge to vote as part of a community organization.

  Exercise your political power!

- Political education

  What the race is.

  What this elected official does, what he or she can decide, and why the position is important. (What the ballot initiative will mean.) When you talk about the office, it is nonpartisan. When you talk about the elected official, it is partisan.

  Education about the electoral system, who can vote, primaries versus general elections.

  How the system works: how you actually vote and why you have to do it that way.

- Voting logistics

  When the election is.

  Where you vote. (The polling place.)

  What time you can vote.

  What you need to bring in order to vote.

- Ask

  Will you pledge to vote on (issue) with our organization on election day? (Nonpartisan ask: "Vote on this issue" not "Vote for this candidate.")

  Have a pledge card or tool to give people the chance to give their opinion on issues. They take a political act and you take the information back to your organization.

- Follow up

  If the person says yes, get him or her to sign the pledge card and give you contact information.

  Thank the person for his or her time and say that someone from the organization will be in touch again.

HOW AND WHEN TO CONTACT VOTERS

The main focus of electoral organizing is contacting and mobilizing voters. All voter contacts include political or civics education. The following is a suggested contact plan. Note the sheer volume of contacts. This is why you need to build a base of volunteers—so you can contact large numbers of people, in person or by phone, over and over again. You contact people face-to-face, by phone, and by mail, then repeat the cycle of contacts.

Contact #1. Go to the doors and get people to pledge to vote, as described. Depending on how many contacts you must make and the people doing the contacts, you start early enough that you can do your cycle of contacts two or three times but not so early that people are not yet thinking about the election. A safe bet is about three months before an election.

Contact #2. Although it is best to go back and talk with voters face-to-face, you can also use the phone for this contact. You start re-contacting voters a few weeks after the first contact, sometimes linked with a mobilization event such as a candidate forum.

Contact #3. Two weeks before the election, send out a mailing to voters that reminds them why they should vote and provides political education.

Contact #4. Ten days before the election you start getting out the vote, knocking again on the doors of all pledge voters. On the Friday, Saturday, Sunday, and Monday before Election Day, you try to reach all the people you have not contacted at the doors—either by trying the doors again or calling.

Contact #5. On Election Day, go out early and knock on all the doors of pledge voters or leave door hangers with the same message you've been using at the doors. If you find out people have not voted, you try to get them to the polls. In some places you can check the voter lists at polling sites to get this information.

Contact #6. Within a month, you re-contact pledge voters with a call or mailing and engage them in an event of some kind. Thank them for voting. Assess their interest in working with your organization on issue campaigns.

Mobilization contacts. When your organization is doing an action connected to the electoral campaign, such as a candidate forum or rally, you will need to make more contacts. Add the necessary contacts to this list.

ELECTORAL ORGANIZING AND ORGANIZATIONAL BASE

Electoral organizing may not increase the number of members and leaders in your organization. Because it is a list-building activity, electoral organizing increases the possibility of bringing new people into your organization, but there is not necessarily an immediate or easy payoff. Getting someone to pledge to vote is relatively easy. You get a lot of names and contact information in electoral organizing and it can be difficult for organizers and leaders to follow up and engage people after the election. You increase your chances of turning voter contacts into members if you do the following:

- Include issue ID in your contacts and analyze to see if a clear priority emerges.
- Keep good track of people who say they want to do more.
- Offer opportunities for action during the campaign cycle and immediately after the election. Candidate forums, mailing parties, and rallies all give people a taste of your organization and help you identify people for follow-up.

WHEN ALL OF THE CANDIDATES ARE BAD CHOICES

Having few good candidates is a big challenge. In an election system where it takes a lot of money to get on the ballot and get people's attention, not many candidates are attractive to the progressive social justice movement. Some 501(c)(4) groups run candidates from their own organizations, both staff and leaders. Even without a strong candidate, however, your work can still make a difference. Many groups and researchers have found that unregistered and infrequent voters are more likely to vote when someone from their community comes to their door or calls them and talks about issues and about how to make a difference. Candidates matter, but an organized community can hold its representatives accountable. Electoral organizing is one way to do so.

RESOURCE D: TRAINING TIPS

The following are some suggestions for designing and conducting group training sessions using popular education methods.

FOUNDATIONAL PRINCIPLES FOR POPULAR EDUCATION

The basic principles of popular education reflect the way adults learn.

Create personal meaning.

Training participants remember and use information if it means something to them personally. Popular educator Paulo Freire describes the difference between people being subjects of their own learning (*You decide what it means to you*) rather than objects (*I decide what it means to you*).[*] If you actively engage participants with the content of the training, not just tell them information, they can relate that content to their own life experiences and make it their own. They will use it more effectively.

Work toward goals and objectives.

You design a training to meet clear goals and objectives that you can measure or evaluate. Once you identify these components, you choose exercises and activities

---

[*]P. Freire, *Pedagogy of the Oppressed,* 30th Anniversary Edition. New York: Continuum International, 2000).

to effectively convey specific concepts and allow the participants to demonstrate what they learned, as in the following chart:

Goal	Objective	Demonstrate Learning
The purpose of the training	*What participants need to learn*	*What participants do to show that they learned*
Connect new people with the organization	Facts about the organization's history	Tell a partner what most surprised you about the history
Prepare members for an action	The roles in an accountability session	In small groups, write chants or role play asking questions of the target
Have leaders conduct recruitment	How to do a rap	"10 in 60" exercise (Exercise 3.2 in Chapter Three)

In most trainings, you try to influence participants' knowledge, skills, and attitudes. Knowledge is information, usually a combination of political education and background about the topic. Skills are the abilities people need to perform tasks. Attitudes are feelings and beliefs. Although it is harder to immediately evaluate the impact of training on someone's attitudes, training and action together can shift a person's attitudes over time.

Design the training in advance.

Keep in mind that it takes time to design a good training. Stay focused on the goals and objectives, pay attention to the flow of ideas and concepts, and figure out the time it will realistically take to do each of the exercises and activities.

Raise all voices.

People learn when they voice their thought processes, their questions, and their ideas and insights. You do not just give a presentation for people to listen to and discuss. You emphasize being able to hear both trainers and participants throughout the training. At the same time, you don't fill up every second of the training. Sometimes waiting silently for a few moments gives people time to think and invites those who have not spoken yet to do so.

Warm up and close out.

You begin with a go-around, hearing everyone's names and expectations for the training. You start with an exercise, even if it is very brief, to warm participants up to the topic. At the end, you clearly close the training, if possible with another go-around as well as a summary and clarification of next steps. The opening and closing exercises are relevant, not peripheral, as people tend to remember what comes first and last.

Set a positive, conducive learning environment.

Hold trainings in appropriate spaces, with adequate light, comfortable temperature, and good acoustics. In addition, agree on and abide by ground rules that encourage people to talk freely, exchange ideas, and listen.

Use a variety of methods.

People learn in different ways, so you include a variety of different methods with which participants can connect. In addition to trying to appeal to a range of learning styles, which we describe in more detail below, engaging people in some way with the content of the training is the best way to connect them. Overall, most people remember 20 percent of what they see, 40 percent of what they see and hear, and 80 percent of what they do. Therefore, include a variety of activities, such as having participants draw, write, sculpt, and work in pairs and small groups. Incorporate activities that are fun, make people laugh, and help people to get to know one another and to want to be there.

Periodically throughout the training, summarize what has happened so far to reinforce the learning, and remind participants what is coming up.

Some good ways to know if the participants grasp the content of the training are to watch them practice it through role-playing, have them tell someone what they learned, or have them make a list or draw a chart before they leave the training.

LEARNING STYLES

The following is an overview of the different ways in which people learn. It can be helpful in reviewing these learning styles to think about how you learn as well. Trainers often teach to the style in which they like to learn. For example, a verbal learner might design mostly discussion-oriented exercises and not enough charts or creative exercises to engage a fuller range of learners. Since any given training will have participants with a variety of learning styles, you have a better chance of reaching the fullest range of participants if you incorporate a variety of exercises and activities.

There are eight basic styles of teaching and learning:

Verbal: Comfortable with words. Needs to say it, hear it, or write it. Wants to talk about it in pairs or groups, read or write it.

Visual: Relies on sense of sight and ability to visualize, including creating mental images. Wants to draw it.

Mathematical: Understands through a linear flow of ideas. Likes numbers. Wants to quantify it, think critically about it, plot it on a chart.

Physical: Likes physical movement and listening to her or his body. (*Kinesthetic* is another term for this style of learning.) Wants to dance it, build a model of it, tear it apart.

Musical: Recognizes tonal patterns, sounds, rhythms, beats. Wants to sing it, chant it, rap it, learn it to background music.

Reflective: Aware of own internal states of being. Wants to relate it to a personal feeling.

Interpersonal: Able to "read the room" and learns from diving in with others. Wants to work on it actively in a pair or group.

Naturalistic: Inspired by the natural world. Uses nature as a point of reference. Wants to plant it, dig it up, compare it to a mountain, storm, or stream.

FOUR OPTIONS FOR PARTNERING

Getting participants working with one another helps to build relationships, keeps the training feeling energetic—it creates a buzz in the room because a lot of different people are talking, and gets everyone to talk to at least one other person.

Interviews.

Give participants specific questions to ask a partner or provide the framework for them to form their own questions. Write the questions or framework on a handout or chart. Always have partners reverse the interview so each person gets the chance to talk. Interviews can lead to more thorough dialogue later. For example, an interview question would be, "Ask your partner to list what she or he thinks of as three qualities of an effective leader." An interview framework would be, "Ask your partner two questions about effective leadership."

Sentence completion.

Write partial sentences and give them to the participants. They complete the sentences, then share their results with a partner. Examples: "An effective leader always . . . ," "An effective leader never . . ."

Think-talk-share.

Participants think about something, then talk about their thoughts with a partner. They then share some aspect of their talk with the group. For example, "Think about the most effective leader you ever met. Talk with your partner about what made this person stand out for you."

Teach and reverse.

Participants select a concept they believe they can explain to someone else. They explain, then reverse the process. For example, "Explain to your partner why it's important for leaders to understand self-interest."

KEEP UP THE ENERGY!

The following are some suggestions for keeping a training feeling energetic and engaging to a range of participants with different learning styles.

Time tasks.

Set a clear beginning and ending time for each activity or exercise. Announce when the time is up. Stick to the times you set or check in with participants if you are going to extend the time. Knowing how much time there is to work on something keeps people feeling grounded and clear about what's happening. Here are two sample trainer statements: "Talk in your small groups for five minutes, then we'll hear your responses." "How about one more minute to finish up this exercise?"

Quantify responses.

Open-ended sharing is useful at times, but it can lead to rambling and tangents. If you quantify the responses you are more likely to generate ideas the groups can really hear and work with. Some sample statements: "We'll hear one idea from each group." "Pick the best. Pick the worst."

Take timed breaks.

Offer frequent short breaks. Start again on time, no matter who is missing: "We'll get started again in exactly five minutes."

Use partner interactions to keep up the buzz.
"Tell your partner about the most difficult meeting you've experienced."

Keep moving.

Create a design that has people moving around the room periodically: "Post your responses on our group chart at the front of the room." "We'll do a Gallery Walk to look at what you made." "Group number one will meet in that corner, group number two in this corner."

Change locations.

Give the opportunity to complete tasks outside of the training room: "We'll go out to the park to ask people in this neighborhood what they think of the new regulations." "There are two break-out rooms down the hallway."

Summarize and move on.

Summarize what's been happening and move the process along: "So far, we've explored how leaders have a following. Let's move to another area, accountability."

MAKING EFFECTIVE CHARTS

For effective charts, you don't have to get fancy. If you follow a few guidelines, your charts work for you:

Print. Use large print—at least one or two inches high and across.
Write titles. Always write a title at the top of the chart.
Use colors. Use varied colored markers. For example, write the title in red and then underline it in black. Write one line of text in green, the next in blue.
Match the handouts. Ideally, prepared charts match the handouts so participants are not scrambling to write everything down.

When making charts during a session, you can try the following guidelines:

- If possible, have a cofacilitator (not a participant) write while you facilitate
- Both stand to the side of the chart, not directly in front of it
- Use lined chart paper to keep things straight
- Tell people that this information is going to get back to the group, so people can participate without worrying about detailed note taking
- Write things on charts only for a purpose, otherwise it is distracting and loses its impact

RESOURCE E:
APPROACHES TO ADDRESSING
COMMUNITY PROBLEMS

This resource considers how community organizing, which is the approach of community power-building organizations, is different from other approaches to addressing community problems. You can use the following as a handout for training members, leaders, and staff to understand these differences.

FOUR APPROACHES

There are generally four different ways to approach community problems, each with its own mission, strategies, and impact: social service, advocacy, community development, and organizing.

Social Service

Mission. To meet immediate, direct needs.

What they do. Provide goods such as food or clothing, or services such as job training, health care, or counseling, or both.

Sample strategies. Developing self-help skills among service recipients or community members, providing case management in order to meet needs holistically, guiding people through applications for benefits and other complex systems with one-to-one advocacy.

Impact. Primarily on individuals. Usually short term, although long-term effects are possible.

Effect on power structures. No real change in power structures.

How they refer to constituents. "Clients" or "consumers."

Advocacy

Mission. To protect or obtain rights, goods, or services, usually for specific interest groups.

What they do. Craft or react to legislation. Address elected officials and policymakers.

Sample strategies. Participating in issue-based coalitions, educating the public, giving public testimony, lobbying elected officials, collaborating with researchers and lawyers.

Impact. On interest groups. Usually medium- to long-term effects.

Effect on power structures. Power structures change moderately due to changes in laws and policies.

How they refer to constituents. "Constituents."

Community Development

Mission. To build physical infrastructure.

What they do. Finance or construct housing, businesses, parks, or other community resources.

Sample strategies. Engaging in community planning, analyzing economic impact, and training constituents to acquire skills for planning, business development, and property management.

Impact. On individuals and communities. Immediate to long-term effects. Sustaining impact is tied to financial resources.

Effect on power structures. Power structures change moderately, usually by building community participation.

How they refer to constituents. "The community."

Organizing

Mission. To build power to create change.

What they do. Recruit, train, and mobilize a large base of members directly affected by the organization's issues.

Sample strategies. Creating membership structures in which constituents are organizational decision makers, developing strategic campaigns, engaging in direct actions such as demonstrations, directly holding public and corporate officials accountable for their actions, and forming alliances to build power.

Impact. On individuals, their communities, and often others with similar concerns. Medium- to long-term effects.

Effect on power structures. Power structures change as power shifts to community members.

How they refer to constituents. "Leaders" or "members."

SERVICE, ADVOCACY, AND DEVELOPMENT GROUPS AND EFFECTIVE ORGANIZING

Service, advocacy, and development groups can engage in effective organizing, but some key components must be in place. It is often better for these kinds of organizations to seed organizing projects and help them become independent organizations.

In order for a service, advocacy, or development organization to organize for power, it must structure ways for constituents to lead the process. This change in structure can be difficult, as staff and nonconstituent boards often direct these organizations. In addition, organizing requires distinct skills and strategies. Some factors that make success more likely are as follows:

Support of the executive director and board. If the executive director supports member-led organizing strategies, organizing is much more sustainable. If the executive director is opposed or has no interest, the organizing project will inevitably conflict with the organization.

The board must be prepared to incorporate constituents as board members or to handle differences over political issues. In some cases, constituents may target the organization itself, such as when a tenant association formed by a community development organization develops a campaign to change the organization's housing management practices. Unless the board is prepared for these kinds of scenarios, oppression and bitterness are often the unfortunate outcome.

Distinct funding. Organizing projects with their own funding are much more likely to succeed. Constituents need to know what this funding is and be involved in its allocation.

Trained, supported organizing staff. It is very difficult to be a single organizer working among social workers, lawyers, or other professionals. The sponsoring organization must budget enough money to hire an organizer with some experience and allow her to develop a network of organizing colleagues and mentors. If an existing staff member is the force behind the project, she must be trained. If proper supervision is not available within the organization, a technical assistance organization or a trusted organizing group may provide this crucial support.

Self-determination of the constituents. A service, advocacy, or development group may start what it calls an organizing project to involve constituents in promoting its predetermined legislative agenda. Such a project may help educate constituents and win policy change, but if an organization wants to organize for power, it must allow for self-determination—constituents determine the issues and take the lead in winning the solutions they desire.

Given the missions, funding constraints, and organizational cultures of most groups, it is clearly not easy to incorporate community organizing. At the same time, many successful organizations, including Community Voices Heard, begin as seed projects of other organizations. They spend a couple of years with the fiscal support, office space, and other supports of a sponsoring organization. They raise funds, recruit members, establish a track record of accomplishments, and then spin off as independent, community power-building organizations. For service, advocacy, or development organizations, such sponsorship can be a very valuable role.

One variation is for organizations that do not have a primary mission of doing community organizing and do not want to incorporate that mission into their work to provide the support for community members to run a campaign to address a specific community issue. Even in that case, however, keep in mind the factors that make for the most success.

RESOURCE F:
CREATING A LEGAL COMMUNITY
POWER-BUILDING ORGANIZATION

Organizing often begins with committed volunteers and someone who is usually unpaid or on loan from another organization serving as an organizer. If and when group members decide to form a legal organization, they take the following steps:

- Incorporate with the state as a nonprofit organization, usually with a 501(c)(3) designation

- File for tax exemption with the Internal Revenue Service

- Possibly engage a fiscal sponsor—another organization that already has tax-exempt status and manages the finances until the new group is tax-exempt and able to manage its own bookkeeping

- Create bylaws (legally mandated in order to be tax-exempt)

- Establish a board of directors (legally mandated to be tax-exempt)

- State a mission, goals, and objectives

- Set a budget

- Raise money and implement fiscal accountability

- Hire staff, assign staff roles and lines of supervision, and establish personnel policies

- Clarify a membership structure

- Establish a decision-making structure

- Secure and set up an office

- Address technology needs for computers, database, and so on
- Identify campaigns and create organizing committees

You accomplish some of these tasks immediately and implement others over time. Some you periodically revisit over the life of the organization.

Technical assistance providers and private consultants help new groups accomplish many of these goals and enable established groups to evolve sensibly. Other nonprofits, local organizations, issue-based groups, and private foundations can provide information and contacts. Most organizations pay for help in some areas, but you can find free assistance as well. Foundation funding, if you can get it, sometimes includes technical assistance or additional funds to purchase these services. See Resource G for some information about technical assistance providers.

If you carefully establish an infrastructure and organizational policies, either inside of a legal structure or outside of one, you will be better able to sustain momentum, survive transitions, and negotiate internal disagreements. Poor administration can wipe out all your good work. It pays to attend to these matters with the same thoroughness with which you address political issues.

RESOURCE G:
FOR MORE INFORMATION

Many organizations provide assistance to nonprofits in a number of areas. Here are some that we have found to be helpful.

Legal Assistance
Alliance for Justice: http://www.afj.org/
Lawyers Alliance for New York: http://www.lany.org/

Technology
Progressive Technology Project: http://www.progressivetech.org/

Community Organizing and Organizational Development
Center for Community Change: http://www.communitychange.org/
Midwest Academy: http://www.midwestacademy.com/
Western States Center: http://www.westernstatescenter.org/
Center for Third World Organizing: http://www.ctwo.org/
Industrial Areas Foundation (IAF): http://www.industrialareasfoundation.org/
National Training and Information Center: http://www.ntic-us.org/

Movement Building
Highlander Center: http://www.highlandercenter.org/
Project South: http://www.projectsouth.org/
Grass Roots Global Justice: http://www.ggjalliance.org/
Jobs with Justice: http://www.jwj.org/

Media

SPIN Project: http://www.spinproject.org/

Research and Policy Advocacy

Applied Research Center: http://www.arc.org/

Fundraising

http://www.grassrootsfundraising.org

You can find out more about Joan and Paul and the work we do with community groups through www.toolsforradicaldemocracy.com.

RESOURCE H:
THE PHASES AND STEPS
OF A CAMPAIGN
An Annotated Case Example

You can use the following as a handout for training staff and leaders to understand the phases of a campaign and to see each of the steps for running an effective member-led campaign.

Every campaign has three phases: campaign development, campaign implementation, and campaign evaluation. Campaign development includes identifying an issue, conducting research to collect data, analyzing power, developing strategies, and writing a campaign plan. Campaign implementation is when the organization runs the campaign and engages in collective action. In the third phase, campaign evaluation, staff and leaders review the campaign and reflect on what they did and did not accomplish in order to learn from their mistakes and build on their strengths.

The following describes each step of a campaign, illustrated by a successful campaign.

Step One: Identify the Issue. An issue is the *solution* to a problem. First, form a leadership team of members that will move the campaign forward. This team has core members, but it is not a closed group. As other leaders develop, they can participate as well. The leadership team and staff identify the campaign issue by talking to as many members and constituents as possible about a problem they are experiencing and what they think would fix it. Clarity about the issue enables you to draft a clear goal for the campaign.

In 1997, to comply with the new federal welfare reform bill, New York City expands its workfare program for welfare recipients. As we describe in "The Story of Community Voices Heard," workfare requires people to work at jobs for no pay—they work in exchange for their welfare benefits. New York City's workfare program is the Work Experience Program (WEP). WEP workers often perform jobs right alongside union members and others who are doing exactly the same thing, but are getting paid a full salary.

CVH organizers begin talking to thousands of WEP workers in New York City about what they are experiencing and what they want in order to improve their situations. Organizers go to welfare centers and people's homes as well as parks and other sites. Organizers and leaders hold both one-on-one and group conversations with workers.

CVH learns that people want to work, but they want a paid job, not WEP. Most say they need education and training in order to obtain good jobs that will improve their lives and the lives of their families.

Step Two: Draft a Goal. The goal is what you ultimately want to achieve in the campaign. It is the big picture. You develop the goal by engaging in political education and analysis with members. You hold workshops and meetings, and talk with people individually. You get to the heart of the changes people ultimately want to see. A community power-building organization often sets a campaign goal that shifts the public debate on an issue in a more radical direction. The goal determines what policy or administrative demand you will make.

After identifying the issue, Community Voices Heard drafts the following campaign goal: to end WEP and replace it with paid jobs, education, and training. Other community-based organizations are focused on improving the WEP program or establishing nonprofit organizations as WEP placements. CVH's goal of definitively ending WEP shifts the debate on the issue. There is a strong group of welfare recipients calling for an end to WEP because they believe the program does not work and is unjust. This position helps to move the debate farther away from the position that WEP is a positive program.

Step Three: Develop Demands. The demands are the specific changes in procedures, programs, and policies that people actually want to see happen. To develop the demands, the leadership team works with staff members to conduct library or Internet research and to survey other members and constituents to learn what programs or policies would achieve the goal. Sometimes groups will work with other technical assistance groups to develop a program. This leadership team then checks in with the larger membership about these demands to make sure they resonate and to get as much organizational buy-in as possible. The demand determines who your target is. The target is the person who can meet the demand and give you what you want.

> The CVH leadership team, with help from the National Employment Law Project, drafts its own program, the New York City Transitional Jobs Program. It designs the program that members and constituents believe will alleviate their problem. The program will create paid twelve-month or "transitional" jobs with education and training. The jobs will be in city agencies and designated for welfare recipients as an alternative to WEP. The campaign demand is to create a transitional jobs program. After the leadership team develops the demand, it talks to thousands of workfare workers to make sure this demand is what people want to fight for.

Step Four: Research and Name a Target. The target is the lowest-level person who can give you what you want. It is always an individual, not an organization or group. You first conduct research to figure out who can meet your demand and who is most likely to do so. You examine factors including his or her position on issues like yours, his or her probable position on your proposal, what motivates him or her, and to whom he or she is accountable. To choose a target, you need to understand how much power you have to move specific individuals to meet your demands. Sometimes you identify secondary targets, who are people with power who you do have the ability to move. They can influence the target in ways you cannot. Once the target is clear, you create a landscape of the issue and assess the power dynamics surrounding the target.

The two people who could create a transitional jobs program in New York City are the mayor and the speaker of the City Council. The mayor can implement the transitional jobs program through his commissioner at the Human Resources Administration. The Council speaker can enact a city law requiring the city to implement the program. CVH researches each of the potential targets and determines it is unlikely the mayor will willingly support the program, and that the organization does not have enough power to force him to do so. The speaker of the Council does not necessarily support the program, but he is moveable. The organization has enough power, through its members and alliances, to influence him. CVH chooses the speaker as its best potential target.

Step Five: Create a Landscape of the Issue. The landscape is the fullest possible picture of the history and potential future of the issue. This picture gives you critical raw material for looking at the power dynamics that will play out in the campaign.

The CVH leadership team lists other organizations that are concerned about replacing WEP with paid jobs and training. It looks at their history of working on the issue. It sees that the labor movement is concerned about workfare but has no history of organizing WEP workers. The leadership team also looks at the opportunities that existed in federal and state programs. It sees that the federal government will be making more funding available for workforce issues.

Step Six: Conduct a Power Analysis. Power analysis is the process of laying out who else cares about the issue, who has a stake in it, and what their power is in relationship to it. Power analysis tells you what you need in your organization and through your alliances in order to move the target.

CVH knows that the Council speaker plans to run for mayor and needs the support of labor unions for his mayoral bid. When CVH looks at who else cares about the issue of replacing WEP with transitional jobs and training, it learns that several important labor unions are concerned. They see WEP as a threat to unionization and a way to cut wages. The unions could move the speaker. CVH has enough members and knowledge about workfare to get the unions' attention.

Step Seven: Choose a Strategy. With the information gained so far, you look at your strategic options. Your strategy is your plan for moving the target. Will a target move because he or she responds to media attention or because you mobilize a large enough number of people who can hold that person accountable?

Community Voices Heard's Transitional Jobs Campaign builds its supporting strategies around its core strategy of base-building.

CVH's base-building focuses on large-scale membership recruitment of workfare workers into the organization. By building a strong and powerful base, CVH can show others—unions, elected officials, and the media—that it has the ability to harness the power of WEP workers and that in fact, it represents WEP workers. With leaders, members, and the ability to mobilize, CVH can engage in supporting strategies such as:

- *Legislative.* Get city council members to pass a bill creating jobs for welfare recipients. CVH will train members to do this, not send professionals to lobby for its bill.

- *Alliance.* WEP specifically hurts the city's largest municipal union by displacing its members. CVH will use the union's self-interest on the issue to engage it in a strategic alliance to support the demand for jobs.

- *Media.* Because of the council speaker's mayoral aspirations, he wants good press. CVH uses a media strategy to publicize the problems with WEP and the solution—a jobs program—that CVH is fighting for.

Step Eight: Assess Organizational Power and Capacity. You explore if you have enough members and relationships with allies to move the target. Do you have money, staff, and other resources to conduct the campaign? Once you decide you have the capacity to use the strategies you want, you choose objectives.

The CVH power analysis shows that the speaker will move if he feels enough pressure from the constituents who vote him into office, from other members of the city council or from institutions that he will need to support him in his run for mayor. CVH's organizational assessment shows it cannot build pressure in the speaker's election district because it is a middle-class district with few welfare recipients. It does not have the staff or financial resources to build its membership in enough council districts to influence the full council.

CVH does have the staff and money to focus on forming alliances with the unions to move the speaker. Given what the organization learns through its research about the time and capacity it will take to introduce a bill into the city council and get it passed, it assesses that it has the resources and the fundraising potential to carry out the campaign. CVH also has the ability to draw attention to the issue in the media and to move the chair of the City Council Committee on General Welfare to champion the rights of workfare workers and fight for the bill.

Step Nine: Develop Objectives. The objectives are the steps you need to take in order to get your target to meet your demands, based on your strategies. If you decide to implement a media strategy, then you work to get stories in the press. If you decide to implement an alliance strategy, then you build partnerships or a coalition.

Members have been involved in each step of developing the campaign so far. But the fullest possible group of members now understands, finalizes, and accepts the proposed campaign. Members start to talk about their message and what the organization will communicate about its issue, both to constituents and to specific public audiences.

The objectives in the Transitional Jobs Campaign are as follows:

- To build a base of one thousand WEP workers who can be mobilized to actions

- To develop a leadership of fifteen to twenty WEP worker leaders who can speak to allies, press, and elected officials

- To develop reports and studies that show the problems with the WEP program

- To form partnerships with the unions to move them to support the jobs program

- To get media coverage of the WEP program that will support workers' demands for education, training, and paychecks

- To get a bill introduced into the city council to create a transitional jobs program.

Step Ten: State a Campaign Message. The message is the main point the organization will make about the issue throughout the course of the campaign.

> The message for the Transitional Jobs Campaign is "*WEP is a public sector sweatshop that forces mothers with children to work in no-wage, dead-end jobs that do not help them get off of welfare. It creates a permanent two-tier workforce in city agencies.*" This message appeals to union and labor activists, workfare workers, and antipoverty organizations.

Step Eleven: Engage Full Membership and Leadership. Staff and members of the leadership team talk one-on-one about the campaign with other organization members. This process culminates in a large campaign planning meeting. The membership walks through all aspects of the proposed campaign plan. You hold the meeting to do more than have the group sign off on the leadership team's recommendations. To continually train and empower members, incorporate real decision making into the process. You propose different scenarios, have places where people make decisions about actions and tactics, and have people analyze the pros and cons of the proposal.

> In the campaign planning meeting, WEP workers review how the objectives will advance the strategy. What will get the bill introduced into a city council committee? Will CVH need to get everyone on the committee to write a letter to the committee chair? Will CVH need to write a bill with its partners?

Step Twelve: Choose Actions and Tactics. Actions are the events and activities in which you engage members and leaders in order to achieve the objectives. The tactics are the components that you use in your actions. Actions and tactics reflect the strategy. They are also things that members are willing to do and are excited about. For instance, if getting media coverage is critical to the campaign, will holding your own press conference get coverage or do you need to disrupt the target's press conference? Do you need to conduct a research project and release the results? Have a militant march or a fun, creative protest? All of the above? In developing the campaign, you usually decide on general kinds of actions that you will plan in detail at specific points in the campaign.

Members identify what will move people on the issue of workfare and get press attention. They talk about how they cannot organize a WEP workers strike, but they can hold hearings and mobilize WEP workers to attend. They can do moving pickets and small-office takeovers. They discuss who needs to be at press conferences and how the organization will get them there.

Step Thirteen: Write a Plan. The campaign plan is a written map of the campaign, including a timeline. This helps make sure the organization keeps to its goals and objectives and doesn't go off course. The organizer usually writes this document and then reviews it with members and leaders. By the end of campaign development you have a decisive, written plan of action. Members and leaders are fully engaged and ready to win.

CVH develops a timeline based on three major factors: how long it will take to build a base of WEP workers, the city council legislative process, and moving important allies. The legislative process is out of CVH's control, so the plan is a living document that it will review and update. For example, when the local newspaper writes an op-ed piece critiquing the jobs bill and the speaker, CVH has to take actions it had not planned, namely, to respond to the op-ed and to shore up support for the bill and the speaker.

Step Fourteen: Conduct Actions, Organizing Meetings, and Other Events. Throughout campaign implementation, you engage in action. You hold regular organizing meetings to make sure the campaign is on track, to plan actions, and to assign tasks to specific staff and members. You prep and train leaders. The campaign provides countless opportunities to build your base, to engage and mobilize leaders and new members, and to show your power.

Community Voices Heard's first action in the Transitional Jobs Campaign is to get five hundred WEP workers to sign pledge cards supporting the campaign. To secure the pledge cards, organizers identify members who can go out and talk with WEP workers and ask them to sign the pledge. CVH develops a timeline and clear plan for getting the five hundred signatures, and trains the members in the skills they need to carry out their tasks effectively.

Step Fifteen: Stick to the Plan. The organizer uses the written campaign plan as a tool for managing the campaign. This includes updating the membership, facilitating evaluations of how the campaign is going, and enabling members to make informed decisions about how to move forward.

Step Sixteen: Conclude the Campaign. The campaign is over when you can determine that you have won, you have lost, or nothing else your organization does will make a difference. Sometimes you have a clear victory or defeat, but other times you assess that the campaign is just stuck. In such a case you need to develop a new campaign or move into a new phase of work on the current campaign.

Step Seventeen: Evaluate the Campaign. Campaign evaluation is the process of monitoring objectives, examining actions, and assessing the effectiveness of the campaign. You engage in evaluation as you implement the campaign and after it ends.

After the campaign ends, you determine whether or not the target met the organization's demands. You review how well your organization performed in the campaign and why. You assess if you met your campaign goal and your organizational power-building goals.

At the conclusion of the Transitional Jobs Campaign, the council voted CVH's bill into law, but the mayor vetoed the bill. The council overrode the veto, but the mayor still refused to implement it. Staff, member, and leaders evaluated that CVH successfully won a bill to employ welfare recipients. It built its own power by recruiting, mobilizing, and developing hundreds of new members and by building relationships with major local unions. CVH received a lot of press. Dozens of organizations and people with power now knew about the organization.

CVH won, but it did not meet the goal of creating paid jobs for people on welfare. At this point, the leaders declared victory and began a new campaign to force the city to fully implement a transitional jobs program.

Ultimately, the various transitional jobs campaigns were successful. In 2000, New York City created 7,500 transitional jobs for former welfare recipients.

INDEX

Anger quality, 16

Antiwar activities, 350–351

Arrest fears, 293

Ask meetings, 332

Aska, G.: as Community Voices Heard cofounder, 1, 6–7, 10; issue ID work by, 135; leadership abilities of, 88–89

Assessment: of campaign strategy, 190–192, 202; database record of recruit, 44; organizational, 165; of organizational power, 165–170; of possible recruits, 42–43; of potential leaders, 90; technology, 113–115; of where members fit in organization, 66–67

Assessment exercises: Visioning Exercise, 21; Where Are We At? 22

Assessment meetings: sample guide, 19; sample phone rap to schedule, 18; six Ss for successful, 20; tools for, 18–22; visioning exercise to use during, 21; Where Are We At? exercise for, 22

Assessment tools: Sample Community Organizing Assessment Tool, 19; Sample Phone Rap to Schedule Assessment Meetings, 18; Six Ss for a Successful Meeting, 20

Association of Community Organizations for Reform Now (ACORN), 367

Awareness of self-interest, 17

B

Base-building: campaign implementation related to, 240; campaign objectives in relation to, 215; components of, 35–36; as core strategy, 185; definition of, 35; information entered into database for, 116–117; recruiting constituents for, 38

Betsy, 10

Bloomberg, M., 142–143, 161, 164, 167, 193

Board (or steering) committee: benefits of maintaining, 363; described, 26

Boycotts, 280

Building takeovers, 270–271

Burnout: as challenge to member involvement, 71; movement-building to avoid, 348; protecting organizers and leaders from, 369–371

Bush, G.H.W., 3, 279

C

Call to action, 41

Campaign evaluation: of actions during campaign, 305–307; benefits of, 302; challenges in, 314; conducting the, 310–313; CVH example of, 301; definition and importance of, 301–302; determining campaign completion in order to start, 309–310; essential elements for effective, 314–315; leadership development opportunities during, 313–314; of meetings and activities, 307–309; organizer role during, 313; of progress on objectives, 303–305; Southsiders Union's, 311–313; tools for, 315–321

Campaign evaluation tools: Campaign Evaluation Worksheet, 320–321; Objective Evaluation Worksheet, 316–317; Parts of a Campaign, 318–319; Sample One-Hour Action Evaluation Session, 315

Campaign Evaluation Worksheet, 320–321

Campaign implementation: activities associated with, 240–241; challenges during, 254–255; CVH example of, 239; definition and importance of, 239–240; essential elements for effective, 255; exercises for, 256–259; inability of organization to complete, 195; kickoff event to begin, 240; knowing when to conclude the, 253; leadership opportunities during, 253–254; managing the flow of, 242; meetings related to, 243–244, 245, 250–253; member-controlled campaign and, 241–242; negotiation related to, 241

Campaign message: definition and importance of, 215–216; how to develop the, 216–217; mobilizing members through clear, 289; successful actions and role of, 282

using the, 291–292; using search engines of, 112, 122. *See also* Technology

Iraq War, 350–351

IRC Section 501(c)(3) status, 366–367

IRC Section 501(c)(4) status, 367

"Iron Rule" (Industrial Areas Foundation), 246

Issue ID: The Problem Tree exercise, 153–154

Issue ID: alignment with organization goals, 135–136; challenges of, 143–144; CVH example of, 133–134; definition and importance of, 129–130; essential elements for effective, 144; exercises for, 152–154; getting multiple perspectives on, 135; leadership development opportunities during, 143; organizers guiding process of, 130; strategies for, 134–135; time taken for, 136; tools for, 137, 145–151; written campaign plan on, 232. *See also* Campaign research

Issue ID exercises: Issue ID: The Problem Tree, 153–154; What's the Issue? 152

Issue ID tools: House Meetings, 148–150; Sample Issue Survey, 146–147; Sample Phone Survey, 145; Sample Target ID Questions, 151; who, when, and goal of using, 137

Issues: assessing active support for, 135; building an organization to address, 12–13; conducting research on, 42; connecting community to, 365; CVH organized to address, 3–11; differences between a problem and, 130, 131; getting organization-wide buy-in for, 350; how to identify the, 132–134; landscaping the, 159–162; researching the politics of an, 155–181; selecting the right, 130, 131. *See also* Campaigns; Demands; Social justice movement

J

Jackson, 82–86, 109

Jacqueline, 45–46

Janet, 10

K

Karen, 10

Keating, J., 95

Kickoff event, 240

L

Labor organizing, 28

Landscaping: definition of, 159–160; example of CVH, 161–162; strategies for, 160; understanding an institution's political, 330

Laura, 10

Leaders: able to challenge powerholders, 25; accountability of, 86; assessment of potential, 90; campaign strategy prep of, 194; description of member, 62–63; engaging in campaign research, 156; needed contacts to bring in, 94; organization recognition of, 86–87; organizers as, 94–95; pre-action and final action preps to, 286, 287, 289; qualities to look for in, 88–90; shared power among, 86; successful actions and role of, 282; tips on avoiding burnout, 369–371; tools for identifying, 90–91; written campaign plan on, 233. *See also* Members; Organizers

Leadership development: actions and opportunities for, 292; benefits of, 87–88; campaign evaluation opportunities for, 313–314; campaign implementation related to, 240; campaign planning opportunities for, 222; campaign research opportunities for, 170; campaign strategy opportunities for, 195–196; challenges to, 98–100; CVH's specific process of, 82–86; definition and importance of, 81–82; essential elements for effective, 100; exercises for, 106–107; issue ID opportunities for, 143; movement-building opportunities for, 355; ongoing process of, 86–87; partnerships for power opportunities for, 340–341; suggestions for process of, 362–363; targeting members for, 362; tools for, 101–105. *See also* Members

61–62, 64–66; exercises for, 76–79; identifying best fits for members, 66–67; maximizing opportunities for, 363; pros and cons of payment for, 69–70; strategies for facilitating, 63–64, 67–68; tools for, 72–75. *See also* Mobilization

Membership involvement exercises: Develop, Don't Destroy! Part Two, 79; Doorknocking Training, 76–78

Membership involvement tools: Phone Bank Evening, 72–73; Preparing Testimony, 73–75

Membership-controlled campaign: avoiding getting stuck in "meeting mode," 250–251; challenges during, 254–255; education of members related to, 242; effective meetings during, 251–253; essential elements for, 25; evaluating problems during, 250; exercises for, 256–259; knowing when to conclude the, 253; leadership development opportunities during, 253–254; negotiations related to, 247–248; organizer role in implementing, 248–250; running a successful, 244, 246–247

Memo of Understanding (MOU): on data security, 123; described, 26; on partnerships for power, 338

Memos of operating principles, 26

Michael, 132–133

"Mini" one-on-one meeting, 93–94

Mission check, 170

Mobilization: action, 286–287, 289–291; for action versus turning out for meeting, 291; campaign implementation related to, 240; database-produced lists for, 115; exercising power through, 25; mailings used for, 291; of other members, 63; phone calls made to facilitate, 290; power exercised through mass, 28. *See also* Actions; Membership involvement

Mobilizing Members for an Action, 298–299

Movement-building: activities for, 352–353; challenges in, 355–356; CVH example of, 345–346; definition and importance of,

346–347; essential elements for effective, 356–357; examples of, 353–354; Globalization Limbo exercise for, 358–359; Grassroots Global Justice, 354; inadequate resources for, 351; issues related to, 323–324; leadership development opportunities in, 355; National Campaign for Jobs and Income Support, 354; organizational benefits of, 347–349; power exercised through, 28–29; strategies for engaging in, 349–351

Multimedia productions, 112, 120–121

N

National Campaign for Jobs and Income Support, 279–280, 354

National Religious Partnership for the Environment, 328

Negotiation: campaign implementation and related, 241; choosing the main negotiator for, 248; deal-cutting and on the side, 336; developing demands for, 247; Negotiation Role Play exercise for, 256–259; from position of strength, 247; process of, 247–248; successful action and role of, 283; wins and loses in, 248

Network organizing, 367–368. *See also* Partnerships for power

Networked computer system: hacking into your, 124; security measures for, 124; using, 117, 121

Nonprofit community groups, 334

Northwest United, 353

O

Objective Evaluation Worksheet, 316–317

Objectives: Campaign Planning Worksheet on, 230–231; definition of campaign, 214–215; determining campaign goals and, 136–138, 215; evaluating progress on, 303–305; movement-building and clarifying your, 349. *See also* Goals

Ohio Valley Environmental Coalition, 95

Printed and bound by CPI Group (UK) Ltd, Croydon, CR0 4YY

13/04/2025

14656501-0002